First Things First

Keeping Your Classical Christian School on Track

Kathleen F. Kitchin

Dove Christian Publishers

Bladensburg, Maryland

Published by Dove Christian Publishers, a division of Kingdom Christian Enterprises
P.O. Box 611, Bladensburg, MD 20710-0611
www.dovechristianpublishers.com

Printed in the United States of America

Library of Congress Cataloguing-in-Publication Data
Names: Kitchin, Kathleen F., author.
Title: First things first : keeping your classical Christian school on track / Kathleen F. Kitchin.
Description: Bladensburg, MD : Dove Christian Publishers, 2020.
Identifiers: LCCN 2020906025 (print) | ISBN 978-1-7343032-8-5 (paperback)
Subjects: LCSH: Christian education. | Christian education--Aims and objectives. | Teaching--Religious aspects--Christianity. | Learning--Religious aspects--Christianity. | Schools. | BISAC: RELIGION / Christian Education / Children & Youth. | EDUCATION / Organizations & Institutions. | EDUCATION / Aims & Objectives.
Classification: LCC LC368 .K58 2020 (print) | LCC LC368 (ebook) | DDC 371.071--dc23.

Cover Design by Justin McAlister and Louis N. Jones.

For resources & additional information on *First Things First: Keeping Your Classical Christian School on Track*, please visit my blog at cceontrack.com.

This book is dedicated to classical Christian schools in their mission to serve God and parents & their children biblically.

 Cʒ   Cʒ   Cʒ

*"Let the favor of the Lord our God be upon us,
and establish* the work of our hands upon us;
yes, establish the work of our hands!"*

Psalm 90:17 (ESV)

"You are indeed the heirs of a remarkable legacy—a legacy that has passed into your hands after no little tumult and travail; a legacy that is the happy result of sacrificial human relations, no less than of stupendous human achievements; a legacy that demands of you a lifetime of vigilance and diligence so that you may in turn pass the fruits of Christian civilization on to succeeding generations. This is the essence of the biblical view, the covenantal view, and the classical view of education. This is the great legacy of truth which you are now the chief beneficiaries."

Arthur Quiller-Couch

*to establish - < *Latin* stabilire, *"make firm," from* stabilis *"stable"*

Acknowledgments

- The Lord for calling me & providing the path for this book
- My husband David Kitchin
- My children
- Elder Joe & Mrs. Shirley Clendenin for their encouragement
- Pastor & Elders at my church, Ladies' Bible study, & friends for praying
- Rob & Laura Tucker
- Board members
- Administrators
- Teachers & Staff
- Parents
- Students
- The entire Inscript Publishing staff for their professionalism & ministry
- What a blessing to hear you all & learn from the wisdom
with which God has gifted you.

"Now may the God of peace who brought again from the dead our Lord Jesus, the great shepherd of the sheep, by the blood of the eternal covenant, equip you with everything good that you may do his will, working in us that which is pleasing in his sight, through Jesus Christ, to whom be glory forever and ever. Amen."

Hebrews 13:20-21 (ESV)

Table of Contents

Preface

If everything runs smoothly at your school, then this book is probably not for you! But if you desire to be a school that reflects upon what, why, and how you are doing, then dive in!

Classical Christian Education is just at the *beginning* of its revival since 1992, and there are encouraging developments as it continues to be the fastest growing model of education in the United States. Nevertheless, as it matures, there are fundamentals that may be overlooked and red flags that may not be noticed. This book intends to propose "a Mere Christianity," so to speak, for Classical Christian Education (CCE) – a collection of "first things first" and tools to recognize, identify, & act upon red flags.

The concern is when "first things first" are missing or begin to recede or even vanish. Sometimes we go off the rails unintentionally due to inexperience or blind spots. Other times, it may be intentional. Either way, there is collateral damage. The following questions were guides for writing this book:

- When and how does a classical Christian school *begin* to go off the rails?
- Why are some classical Christian schools running off the tracks?
- What are the first things that we need to keep first, front & center?
- What red flags are classical Christian schools most prone towards?
- What are the red flags that must be recognized, identified, & acted upon?
- In the long run, how do we keep our classical Christian school on the tracks?

This book intends to start a conversation that promotes keeping our classical Christian schools on track. People from various sectors of CCE offer wisdom in their area – board members, administrators, faculty & staff, parents, students, and pastors. The hope is to read, reflect, and discuss as a community of colleagues; to listen, learn, and repent if necessary; and then go forward with the hope that Jesus Christ who "began a good work in you, will be faithful to complete it" (Philippians 1:6).

Soli Deo Gloria

Introduction

As Classical Christian Education (CCE) has spread in the United States (and beyond) over the past 25-plus years, most of it is strong, staying on the tracks, and functioning well, praise God, with children and their parents delighting in a beautiful, good, and true learning environment with Jesus Christ at the center. As with any organization or church or family or child, however, habits can emerge over time that can lead us to wander somewhat from our destination and, if unchecked, can begin to run us off the rails. No school desires to wander or run off track. But it happens. Much of this book explores how that wandering begins. What are the red flags that can warn us of danger ahead? How do we *recognize* red flags? How can we *identify* those red flags? How can we *act on* those red flags to avoid running off the rails? As we seek God's best, we will want to know.

After more than 20 years as an educator, I am more passionate than ever about Classical Christian Education. I have taught in public school, a national tutoring center, community college, homeschool, CCE private school, and CCE homeschool tutorials. In the present educational climate, I am more convinced than ever that CCE is one of the ancient ways that God entreats us to follow.

My journey through this topic of keeping *first things first* so that classical Christian schools can keep on track began when my former boss told me I should write this book. I declined, but four years later, the Lord made it clear: I was to write this book and I dared not refuse. This book has been prayed over every step of the way, and the Lord has introduced me to marvelous educators, board members, & pastors to whom I am indebted.

In the scope of this book, I have not sought to exhaustively interview hundreds of schools. The Lord led me first to professors at Grove City College (GCC) in Pennsylvania who founded and teach the classical Christian education minor. As far as I know, GCC is one of the few colleges that teach CCE. From there, I began to interview several classical Christian schools around the United States that are applying the model well, and I am sure there are hundreds more who are doing the same. These leaders shared generously with me what the Lord has shown them. I enjoyed learning from them, and I have shared in these pages their wisdom.

In the scope of this book, I did not exhaustively interview hundreds of educators. One does not need to siphon all a patient's blood to determine if there are problems. One takes a sample. I interviewed a sample. I interviewed teachers whom the Lord brought to me. These teachers are top-drawer, invested, hard-working educators. These interviews often brought us into the valley of pain and problems. I was blessed to hear their stories and to learn how the Lord redeemed their personal pain with His balm of Gilead. At some of their schools, the cure came; at others, the cure may be yet around the corner. I have recorded in these pages their wisdom.

As I have embarked on this book-writing journey, my consistent prayer to the Lord has been Your will, Your way, Your words. All errors are mine.

The following chapters include interviews with people who have worked at schools and have experienced red flags and interviews with heads of schools who proactively establish means to discern red flags to keep their classical Christian schools on track. Chapters range from your school's vision to your school's culture in the midst of culture, your board of directors, administrators, faculty & staff, curriculum, parents, students, feeder churches, community or area, volunteers, and finally your alumni & donors. My assertion is *To avoid running off the rails, classical Christian schools need to keep first things first and to recognize, identify, and act upon red flags.*

In what ways do schools typically run off the track? There are usually four kinds of deviating from the tracks:

1) Running off the track, but do not know it due to inexperience/blind spots,
2) Running off the track, but do not know it due to pride,
3) Running off the track, and know it but suppress the truth, or
4) Running off the track, know it, and humbly desire to change.

Firstly, some schools are running off the track but do not know it due to inexperience or legitimate blind spots. Many of us were not trained under the Trivium model and are learning in great gulps; others are now teaching who grew up under the model but may need to sip their teacher training in increments to understand more about the how's & why's of CCE teaching. Resources are available, including annual conferences offered on the Association of Classical Christian Schools (ACCS) website and the Society for Classical Learning (SCL) website, as well as articles, books, & websites, several of which are noted in the Resource section of this book.

Secondly, some schools are running off the track but do not know it due to pride. Are we feeling deep pleasure from being "king of the hill, top of the heap"? Did we begin our school in utter dependency upon God and upon daily prayers, and now that we are more independent, have we said, essentially, we can do this by ourselves? Are we remembering God? Are we praying for the Holy Spirit's help and guidance? Is God actively, daily acknowledged as the Author of any success we have?

Yet a third way to risk running off the tracks is for schools to know it – but suppress it. In nautical parlance, we intend justly to perform *damage control*. What often happens, though, is a problem may be denied and then covered up, and eventually gets worse. It pops up elsewhere increasingly until no "whack-a-mole" mallet can keep it down. Perhaps one fear is "wanting to keep a reputation to keep students." God says if we have sinned against others, we need to confess our sins and bring our deeds into the light at church, with the board of directors, with our administrators and faculty/staff, with parents, & students, as necessary. John 3:20-21 says, "For everyone who does wicked things hates the light and does not come to the light, lest his works should be exposed. But whoever does what is true comes to the light, so that it may be clearly seen that his works have been carried out in God." Christ died on the cross to pay for our sins and to cover them with His blood. God is in charge and He forgives. He redeems. He heals. He restores.

The fourth and final way of running off the tracks is knowing it – and humbly desiring to change.

God is a God of grace. As consultant Patrick Lencioni says in his book *The Advantage*, an organization can grow in "Smarts" over time, but what is more difficult is organizational health.[1] This book seeks biblical health. If we have not sinned, but made mistakes and poor choices, we need to own that. If we have sinned, we need to confess. First John 1:9 says, "If we confess our sins, He is faithful and just to forgive us our sins and to cleanse us from all unrighteousness." God restores the years that the locusts have eaten (Joel 2:25). We can trust in Him.

What exactly is the track we are trying to keep our schools on? The track is *God and the Bible*. The track is *classical Christian education*. There is debate and discussion on this very term at present, but essentially the track is *classical*, that is, it follows the Greek & Roman models of learning according to the Trivium (grammar, logic, & rhetoric) roughly corresponding in age to elementary school, middle school, & high school and focuses on the best that has been "thought and said," composed, created, & discovered – the classics. It is *Christian* in that all subjects have Christ at center, sovereignly integrating them all, Christ whose finished work has brought salvation and abundant life. It is *education* in that it seeks to "lead out" (from Latin, *educare*) as it teaches students made in the image of God to learn how to learn so they may become life-long learners to the glory of God, and provides them tools that have been lost since the seismic shift in educational goals and practices in the mid-1800s and thereafter.

This is not a how-to book on starting a classical Christian school; however, interviews with heads of healthy, on-the-tracks schools reinforced for me that the cornerstone truth is to keep *first things first*. What are those first things? In general, first things are the most important things. They are prime. The Latin word *primus* and Greek word *protos* mean "first" and *proto-* means "original or early stage." How you establish those first things in the early stages of your school is critical, so this book will identify strong, stable foundations, while not being a manual *per se*. We will also examine how strong, stable foundations help keep schools on track and explore strategies to keep those first things from slipping to third or fourth place, or even dropping off the radar.

---

[1] Patrick Lencioni, *The Advantage: Why Organizational Health Trumps Everything Else in Business* (San Francisco: Jossey-Bass, 2012), 6.

In addition, this is not a recipe book. Each classical Christian school has its own "soil" in which God has planted it. The beauty of how different all our schools can be, yet so alike in our desire to bring glory to God and to love our neighbor while pursuing education classically, can inspire us all. My focus is on *principles*. My prayer is that this book will help continue or start conversations that will help schools keep first things first and keep their schools on track as we fix our eyes on Jesus.

Each chapter of this book contains the following elements, modeled structurally on how Jesus spoke to the churches in Ephesus, Pergamum, and Thyatira (Revelation 2:1-7; 12-17; 18-29).

- Recognition/Root Words of Key Terms/Discussion of Topic
- Case Studies (in-depth interviews of individuals/schools)
- Common Red Flags
- Possible Trends (some chapters)
- Sober Reflection Questions (for the individual & for the group)
- Getting Back on Track
- Healthy School Distinctives
- Setting a Goal/Expressing a Desire
- Encouragement

May God lead us as we endeavor to keep first things first and stay on His track.

As the manuscript for this book was headed to the publisher, the Covid-19 pandemic broke out, changing our lives forever. Everyone homeschools now. Parents are stressed. Students are stressed. Administrators are stressed. Teachers and staff are stressed. Nothing appears stable as people are suffering, jobs are lost, parents are stretched, video lessons are created, students are struggling, eyes are worn from hours fixed on screens. Everyone is tired, exhausted, in fact. My eyes flood with tears about these struggles. My heart goes out to parents, to administrators, to teachers & staff, and to students who are wrestling with something we could never have imagined.

School after school is heroically salvaging a ragged school year. Is it perfect? No. Is God being honored? Yes. Parents, administrators, teachers & staff, supporting churches, and dear children are being reached out to as we all strive to keep first things first. Honor God. Honor man.

In CCE, we have always been rebuilding the ruins. Now we are all compelled to build with unfamiliar tools, but like Nehemiah rebuilding Jerusalem's walls with trowel & sword, we need to keep our focus on our mission. Our stability has come and will continue to come from God.

Sections entitled "Staying on Track during a Crisis" have been added to some chapters.

This book seeks to encourage all in our endeavors to keep our classical Christian schools on track.

Chapter 1
Your School's Vision

"Where there is no vision, the people perish..."
Proverbs 29:18

"Unless the Lord builds the house,
those who build it labor in vain."
Psalm 127:1a

Latin students at classical Christian schools recite, "*video, videre, vidi, visus*. To see." These young students have learned that to have *vision* means "to see." The word *school* itself derives from the Greek *skhole*, meaning "leisure, philosophy, a place where lectures are given." So, we find a place, hire some teachers, enroll a few students, gather textbooks, "stock up on pasta," and open our doors – right? But what is our purpose? What do we see?

Dr. Robert Godfrey, president emeritus of Westminster Theological Seminary in California, says that American education has changed in its mission over the centuries. In the 1600s & 1700s, the mission was to be "pious, moral, and utilitarian"; in the 1800s, it truncated to being "moral and utilitarian"; and finally in the 1900s & 2000s, it was reduced to being starkly "utilitarian."[1] We have indeed cut the moorings, yet classical Christian education (CCE) seeks to return the school to the Rock and not merely to be a place for lectures.

The founders of a school have a spark to start something that has not been done before, to bring the classical Christian model to their area, to create a school where they can send their *own* children and grandchildren. They desire to reestablish the pious and moral aspects of education because there often is no viable alternative. God paves the path for like-minded parents to gather to create a school, establish a board of directors, hire teachers, and perhaps even design a website and most definitely brochures that share the school's purpose and hopes.

But you may be saying, "Yes, yes, we have all that on our website and in our brochures and we're all set," but it is interesting to see that many schools may have the vision, mission, & values on the website, but – that's where it stays – or in the brochure, but – that is only for the new parents and new teachers. *The vision can often become a distant memory.* If we want integration, we need to be sure first, that the vision is from God; and second, that all roads at the school are leading back to it. How we treat a visitor in the front office or how we discipline a child – all need to trace back to "What are our vision/mission/values?" In our ever-more fragmented culture, we, too, can slip into saying X on our website, but doing Y in actual, everyday life. We need to be consistent. And that is the intention of this book. How do we make more conscious not only *what* we say we are doing, but actually *how* we are doing it? It will not be done perfectly, but if we write a vision and then place it far from our eyes, we run the risk of losing the very school we love.

Typically, organizations have vision, mission, & core values statements that guide their work. Oftentimes these three terms do not have consistent definitions in the business world. Using their Latin (L.) root words, these terms mean the following:

---

[1] Dr. Robert Godfrey (lecture, Rockbridge Academy, Millersville, Maryland, c. 2007).

- *Vision* – the broad picture (<L. *video, videre* to see)
- *Mission* – what God is sending you to do (<L. *mitto, mittere* to send)
- *Values* – principles or standards of behavior (<L. *valere* to be worth)

VISION STATEMENT

Keeping your classical Christian school on track is keeping first things first, and Step #1 of those first things is *vision.* Assuming they have counted the cost before building the tower, the founders need to have a *picture* of what they desire for these students. God says that where there is no vision, the people perish. If a school is formed and there is no vision, the people assembled to form this school will eventually disappear. Vision rivets people to persevere toward a goal that is unseen, yet worthwhile.

Regarding a school's vision, several questions arise:

- What is a vision-caster?
- Who is doing the seeing?
- What are they seeing? What exactly is in the vision?
- Who or What is the source of that vision?
- How far down the track are they seeing?
- Who is helping others to see this vision?
- How do you write a vision statement for your school?
- Do vision statements make for noble artifacts, doomed to darkness in file cabinets or, worse, just passed by as part of the furniture, nothing important?

First of all, what is a vision-caster? According to Dr. Nelson Granade, a vision-caster is "someone who can see beyond what is and paint a *picture* of it so others can see it and move toward it [italics mine]."[2] Secondly, who is doing the seeing? Just a man? Just a woman? The vision needs to be prayed for and the source of the vision must be God Himself, or the school will be built on sand. Founders can go on a retreat and devote much time to Scripture reading and prayer as they seek to establish the vision God will give them with the help of the Holy Spirit. As they pray, they can ask God to tell them what the desired goals are, and also what the mission and core values of this school should be. These children will not remain children. As Mr. Steven Sheets, veteran school administrator in North Carolina for 26 years, says, we need to "start with the end in mind."[3] We desire to educate the man, the woman; therefore, the vision must see far down the track and address what kind of men and women God desires to develop. Start to see the destination right at the very beginning. Write these golden nuggets of wisdom down in language that captivates parents' hopes for their children as they seek to raise them in the fear and admonition of the Lord. This will be your vision statement. *This is the first of six foundational documents.*

The *vision statement* should be neither too short nor too long. A single sentence will not do. A concise but nearly full page that includes goals for graduates, goals for faculty & staff, goals for parents, and goals for the community with which they interface should suffice. Define the terms used; at minimum, include a definition of *Christian, classical, Christ-centered,* and *Trivium.* Each aspect of the vision needs to be rooted in Scripture and needs to be explained in word pictures that captivate the heart & mind.

This vision is one of the most important undertakings parents do – raise the next generation for the Lord! A vision statement "looks forward and creates a mental *image* of the ideal state that the [school] wishes to achieve" through God's grace. "It is inspirational and aspirational and should challenge employees [italics mine]."[4] It is inspirational in that it urges its adherents to embrace it and do it. It is aspirational in that it can "never be fully achieved," and we must rely on God.

---

[2] Dr. Nelson Granade, *Wilkes Journal-Patriot*, September 23, 2015.

[3] Steven Sheets, interview by Kathleen F. Kitchin, Greenville, North Carolina, September 5, 2018.

[4] SHRM, "Mission & Vision Statements: What is the difference between mission, vision and values statements?" Society for Human Resource Management (SHRM), March 5, 2018, http://www.shrm.org/resourcesandtools/tools-and-samples/hr-qa/pages.

Questions to consider when drafting vision statements could include:

- Most importantly, what does God want our vision to be?
- What picture of a grown child are we oriented toward developing?[5]
- What situation are we seeking to solve?[6]
- Where are we headed?[7]
- If we achieved all strategic goals, what would our students look like 10 years from now? 30 years from now?" Sample vision statements may be found in the "Appendix" section of this book, but we will explore several, below. These vision statements vary in structure, but all provide word pictures to help their school *to see* the vision.

VISION STATEMENT EXAMPLES

Covenant Academy, Cypress, Texas

Character development at Covenant Academy in Cypress, Texas, covers six desired outcomes:

1) "*Virtue*: Students will demonstrate high moral standards. They will recognize obedience as an expression of love for God and His word. They will honor God and those made in His image, and rightly order their affections. Students will study the Bible as our moral compass, and the representations of virtue in classical literature.
2) *Wisdom*: Students will think deeply, reason soundly, recognize the consequences of ideas, and make wise choices. Students will learn to make all thoughts captive to Christ and love what God loves.
3) *Eloquence*: Students will demonstrate fluent and persuasive speech. They will listen discerningly and speak winsomely in articulate defense of truth, goodness, and beauty.
4) *Balance*: Students will demonstrate well-rounded foundations. They will gain mastery of the liberal arts. They will learn grammar (the rules and structure of each subject), logic (the ability to understand the implications and build on the foundations of those rules), and rhetoric (the ability to present and defend their conclusions). Students will appreciate the connections between literature, arts, athletics, and the sciences, enabling them to pursue lifelong learning in areas of special interest and the ability to be conversant and competent in other fields.
5) *Literacy*: Students will demonstrate knowledge in a range of fields. They will cultivate a love of learning, and a love of the true, good and beautiful through studying a broad selection of great works of theology, literature, history, science, mathematics, music, and the visual arts.
6) *Servant Leadership*: Students will demonstrate the ability to humbly lead others. They will seek to imitate Christ who came to serve, not to be served, as they practice leadership qualities honed through character training, mentoring, service and daily discipleship."

I traveled to Richmond, Virginia, where I met with Mr. Keith Nix, head of Veritas School. A former businessman and passionate proponent of classical Christian education, he says it can be easy to transmit the vision and to have agreement upon what comprises a good education. Then, hopefully and prayerfully, the school community does a "deep dive" and "there's a point when the vision grabs you and as you go deeper, it only gets more rich and more beautiful. It alters your life." This is a key phrase that Nix used more than once – a *thick, rich community* – something he treasures & protects.

Veritas School, Richmond, Virginia

The Portrait of a Veritas Graduate

"Veritas faculty, staff, and parents seek to cultivate graduates who:

---

[5] Ibid.

[6] Ibid.

[7] Ibid.

- Understand and believe the gospel, enjoying a growing faith in Jesus Christ
- Participate in the local body of Christ
- Study Scripture, pray, and serve faithfully
- Read deeply and charitably; reason truthfully and rigorously
- Speak and write with wisdom and eloquence
- Engage creation with wonder, pursuing beauty and working diligently
- Love and serve Christ the King, bringing *shalom* by sharing the gospel and acting for the good of others."

What can be tragic, however, is that so often the vision statement gets put out of sight and, therefore, out of mind. Include this vision statement in your school handbook, newsletter, yearbook, assemblies, and graduation ceremonies. Read this vision at the first board meeting, the first administrators' meeting, and the first faculty meeting – every year. Pray you will follow it. A new school will need to hear this vision statement often; an older school will need to hear it often enough so that they will not forget or wander. Remember, there are new teachers every year who have never heard the vision articulated before, so devote time in new teacher training to state this vision, as well as your mission & values, and to explain each component in an engaging fashion. We need to keep in mind, however, our wording in this document. Dr. Mark Graham, professor of history at Grove City College and creator of their classical Christian education minor, says that "Schooling is not done by slogan. It takes years and years of being faithful, consistent, humble. When it fails, it is repentant." This vision will be for the long haul.

MISSION STATEMENT

The second foundational document is a *mission statement* which "is a statement of why the [school] exists…the purpose states *why* the organization does the work it does, but does not define how that work is to be done [italics mine]."[8] Mission comes from the Latin *mittere* "to send." What has God sent you to do in your school in your community at this time in history? Questions to consider when drafting a mission statement could include:

- What is our school's purpose?
- Why does our school exist?

MISSION STATEMENT EXAMPLES

Below are several examples of mission statements from various schools throughout the country:

Covenant Academy – Cypress, Texas

- "*Mission*: Covenant Academy exists to serve Christ and His Kingdom by sharing the gospel and partnering with parents to train students by way of Scripture and the classical liberal arts:
- to be discerning, articulate followers of Jesus Christ;
- to be leaders who are equipped to honor and defend truth, goodness and beauty."

Grace Classical Christian Academy – Granbury, Texas

- "*Mission*: To provide an excellent classical education founded upon a biblical worldview which instills a love of learning, the ability for children to know how to think, not what to think, and in all things to honor and glorify Jesus Christ."

Veritas School – Richmond, Virginia

- "*Mission*: We exist to glorify God by cultivating students of wisdom and virtue through a Christ-centered, academically rigorous classical education. Our goal is to equip students with the knowledge, skills, and vision necessary to be effective leaders and servants for Christ in a wide variety of professions and vocations. We seek to raise up a generation of

---

[8] Sharon Richmond, "Mission, Vision & Values Facilitation," Graduate School of Stanford Business, accessed July 5, 2019, https://www.gsb.stanford.edu/alumni/volunteering/act/service-areas/mission-vision-values-facilitation.

young people who have a genuine love of learning, who love Jesus Christ with all their hearts and minds, and who can articulate the Christian message with clarity, creativity, and power."

The Geneva School – Orlando, Florida

- *"Mission:* The Geneva School seeks to provide students in grades K4-12 an extraordinary education, by means of an integrated curriculum, pedagogy and culture, both distinctly classical and distinctively Christian, that pursues goodness, truth and beauty in all spheres of life, while viewing these spheres as elements of a divinely ordered whole."

The Geneva School used Patrick Lencioni's *The Advantage,* a milestone that helped them explore the six questions of Lencioni's "playbook" that he believes every effective organization should have.[9]

Six Critical Questions:

1) Why do we exist?
2) How do we behave?
3) What will we do?
4) How will we succeed?
5) What is most important right now?
6) Who must do what?"

For the coming year, Geneva School is rewriting their playbook somewhat, but it essentially remains the same. [See "Appendix" for sample entitled "Playbook 2017-2018 – The Geneva School Leadership Team."]

CORE VALUES

The third foundational document is a *core values statement*. Core values are "The boundaries within which the school will operate in pursuit of its vision, values on which the school will never compromise and is willing to pay a price to uphold."[10] To be meaningful, values must be described in clear behavioral terms. The word *values* is from the Latin *valere*, meaning "be worth." As you pursue the mission and vision that the Lord has given you, how or in what worthy manner you will pursue them? Will you pursue them with love or with impatience, with kindness or brusqueness, with faith or self-reliance? In other words, will you pursue the mission and vision from God with the fruit of the Spirit or with the dregs of a drained dictator? Each person is of *worth* and our values as a school either are respecting the worth of each person made in the image of God or they are riding roughshod over them. How is our faith coming out our fingertips? We are human and will fail in this, and that is why prayer and coming humbly before God each day individually and corporately is of vital importance. It is only with the power and enablement of the Holy Spirit that we can pursue our vision & mission with godly virtues & values.

When drafting *core values statements*, pray first asking God's guidance and biblical direction. As you write, questions to consider might include:

- What values are unique to our school?[11]
- What values should guide the operations of our school?[12]

CORE VALUES EXAMPLE (with Mission & Vision)

Hope Academy – Minneapolis, Minnesota

---

[9] Patrick Lencioni, *The Advantage* (San Francisco: Jossey-Bass, 2012), 77.
[10] Richmond, "Mission, Vision & Values Facilitation."
[11] SHRM.
[12] Ibid.

- *Mission*
  - To foster hope in God within the inner-city neighborhoods of Minneapolis by providing youth with a remarkable, God-centered education.
- *Vision*
  - Believing that all children are created for God's glory and endowed by Him with an inalienable potential to acquire wisdom and knowledge, Hope Academy covenants with urban families to equip their children to become responsible, servant leaders of the 21st Century. Committed to the truth, discipline, and values of the gospel of Jesus Christ, Hope Academy pursues this aim by mobilizing educational, business, and community leaders towards the important goal of serving the children of Minneapolis with a remarkable education, permeated with a God-centered perspective. This inter-denominational school will seek to unleash kingdom citizens who work for justice, economic opportunity, racial harmony, hope for the family, and joy in the community.
- *Core Values*
  - The mission of Hope Academy is deeply rooted in the following core values:
    - *Redemption*: We are passionate about God's transformational work to redeem all things through the gospel of Christ.
    - *Relationships*: We believe in the necessity of building deep, authentic, loving relationships with one another.
    - *Radical Dependence*: We exercise a daily, moment by moment, radical dependence on God and His Word.
    - *Remarkable*: By God's power at work within us, we pursue excellence that goes above and beyond all that is expected or imagined."

Regarding core values, Hope Academy said they came up with a lengthy list, but knew that would not be most helpful, so they pared it down to 4, and suggest a number ranging from 3 to 7.

I smiled later as I transcribed this interview, for I observed their head of school returning consistently and naturally to Hope Academy's mission, vision, and values as he answered my questions. When I asked how their school manages so well in the inner city against such odds, he responded humbly, "Well, that would be our *radical dependence* on the Lord," their third core value. Throughout our interview, my questions invariably elicited replies that returned to Hope Academy's touchstone mission, vision, and values. [See more on Hope Academy in the Case Study at the end of this chapter.] Do we at our school know our mission so well that it is memorized and has indeed become a part of us? How about our vision? Our values? All roads in our schools must lead back to what God has provided as the vision, mission, & values for our school. As we stay on track with that *God-authored* calling, He will walk with us through the mountains & valleys of our journey.

In crafting (or redrafting) your vision, mission, and values, keep in mind the following:

1. Pray first, submitting all to Christ's authorship, not yours or what the school over in another town says or what sounds good and is convenient.
2. Consult excellent business manuals on these topics, but ensure that you are following Christ's path, not a man-made formula. (Man-made formulae often begin with "All you have to do is..." and a sense that the formula involves products rather than *people*.) Helpful books have been *Rocket Fuel* by Gino Wickman and Mark C. Winters, and Patrick Lencioni's *Five Dysfunctions of a Team* as well as his *The Advantage*.
3. "The words 'mission,' 'vision,' 'values,' 'purpose,' and even 'strategy' can hold very different meanings to different people. Each [school] must clarify what it means by each of these terms."[13]
4. Make certain the board of directors and head of school are in shared agreement for "a house divided cannot stand" (Matthew 12:25).
5. Bring the *best* of what your former career gave you whether it was the business world, military, etc., but be willing to excise that which is not helpful to the nurturing & admonishing of young souls. Again, we are working with people, not products.

---

[13] Richmond, "Mission, Vision & Values Facilitation."

EDUCATIONAL PHILOSOPHY
The fourth foundational document is your *educational philosophy*. Put in writing the educational philosophy of your school, including the Ephesians 6:4 charge, Christ's sovereign integration of all subjects, the commands of Matthew 22:37, 2 Corinthians 10:5, and Colossians 3:23, the focus of our work being done "heartily, as unto the Lord." What is the main goal of your school's education vision? Write that down, too.

STATEMENT OF FAITH
Since this is a Christian school, verbalize in writing, your *statement of faith – the fifth foundational document –* regarding the Bible, God, Jesus Christ, the Holy Spirit, the Trinity, man & sin, salvation, the church, the Great Commission, and eternity – just the essentials (primary doctrine). This is not a denomination or a church. A sample statement of faith is available in the "Appendix."

SCHOOL'S GENERAL RULES
Lastly, create a one-page document that encapsulates *your school's general rules, the sixth foundational document*. As Paul David Tripp says in his seminar "Creating a Culture of Grace,"[14] too many rules are not effective. A reasonable and memorable list of 6-12 rules or fewer should suffice. These rules should contain behavioral objectives, not rules about uniforms. Leave that for other pages in the parent-student handbook! Include rules for character qualities such as obedience, diligence, consideration, kindness, honesty, as well as rules limiting items brought to school and areas that are off-limits on the school property. All rules should be rooted in His Word.

ENROLLMENT MODEL
In addition to the six foundational documents of vision, mission, values, educational philosophy, statement of faith, and general rules, pray to determine whether your school should follow an *evangelical (missional) or covenantal* enrollment model. An *evangelical (missional)* school does not require the parents to be Christian, only to be willing to sign a document agreeing to read your school's handbook, to familiarize themselves with the Biblical philosophy & purpose of your school, and, in agreement, to have their child exposed to the teaching reflected in your statement of faith. A *covenantal* (or *nurturing*) school requires that one parent (or both) be a Christian by a statement of personal faith. Keep in mind that each type of school may have a different aroma. On the one hand, there is more uniformity; on the other, a sweet occasion for seeing parents and their families come to Christ. Both models have their merits. Dr. Jason Edwards who teaches classical Christian education at Grove City College in Pennsylvania says it is critically important for schools to be honest with their parents if this status should change, for example, the board of directors' changing a covenantal school to an evangelical/missional school.[15] One danger that sweeps up successful schools is an "over-commitment to growth," according to Dr. Edwards. Perhaps there is anxiety to fill seats to make budget and changing the requirements seems the best choice. On the other hand, a school's leaders can see the present growth as a "sign of God's blessing" and within this luster, have often proceeded to "forfeit their principles." First, pray for what the Lord wants. King David made a grave mistake when he succumbed to taking a census, instead of standing fast in his faith in *God's provision*. God has the exact answer that meets the need. As part of the enrollment process, a missional school has a document that is signed, saying, "The parents agree to have their child taught our school's statement of faith and they have read the handbook." For a model of a covenantal agreement between the school & parents, please see Veritas School's "Principles of Partnership" document, in the "Appendix."

ROLE OF ADMISSIONS COUNSELOR
Once a school's stance on evangelical or covenantal is established, it will be the role of the admissions counselor to be gatekeeper. That person conducts interviews with the parents and their child(ren) all together. Perhaps the head of school also interviews the prospective parents. Mr. Mark Cotterman, head of school at Mars Hill Academy, in Mason, Ohio, shares a general principle with prospective parents: "If what you are doing at home is the same as what we're doing here, and if what we're doing here is what you're doing at home, then this works

---

[14] Paul David Tripp, "Your Christian School: A Culture of Grace?" (conference, Tall Oaks Classical School, Newark, Delaware, December 9, 2009).

[15] Dr. Jason Edwards, interview by Kathleen F. Kitchin, Grove City, Pennsylvania, May 7, 2018.

well."[16] He says further that "We talk about the rhythm of the home" during the admissions interview. Are there times of Bible reading at home, or is this pattern foreign to their children? In a covenantal school, these habits would be expected; in an evangelical (missional) school, these habits would be encouraged and modeled.

The excitement in this venture toward an expressed, God-authored, God-anchored vision, mission, values, educational philosophy, statement of faith, general school rules, & evangelical/covenantal stance may lead us to feel as a school that we have all the tools we need in our holster, but we need to remember God is the leader. We need to *walk with* God like Enoch, not run ahead of Him. As Lisa Borgeson, former grammar school teacher and administrator, says, "Lord, give me the eyes, the ears, and the heart to know the Truth. The foundation is God. The foundation is the Bible."[17]

ACCREDITATION

The next natural progression is accreditation. Rev. Robert Ingram of Geneva School, founded in Orlando, Florida, in 1993, says an accrediting institution "wants to know if 'you're walking your talk'; to see if your vision expressed and actual practice are aligned. If they are not, it wants to talk about the gap."[18] Rev. Ingram uses the Florida Council of Independent Schools (FCIS), but does not participate in the parent body NAIS. He says the FCIS has "excellent standards, best practices, a rigorous 5-year cycle of re-accreditation, and are excellent resources. They are a recognizable, major entity immediately known by any college or university in the country. They support what we do, never insist or make us alter anything we do as a CCE, and are respectful of our historic evangelical faith position. They are a purely secular agency, but always very cheerful about populating the 10 accreditors who come in for three days with as many Christian administrators & faculty members as possible. It takes 8-9 months to prepare for accreditation; we produce a several hundred page self-study report in the process that documents the life of the school from policies to practices."

The Association of Classical Christian Schools also offers a truly fine, rigorous accreditation service, one that is specifically oriented toward classical Christian education and may be found in the "Resources" section of their website. They look closely to determine alignment with true classical, Christian philosophy of education. Whichever accrediting institution you choose, *it is essential to have outside evaluation in order to hear honest, impartial feedback on whether your school is keeping on track.*

Keep returning "home" to your vision, mission, & values document frequently to help you *see* and *reinforce* the overall vision of your school. Maintain your educational philosophy, your statement of faith, and your school rules. Remember, the Lord is the Master Builder, not you. There will be no perishing or laboring in vain. With the right vision, people will stay – and flourish.

CASE STUDY

Hope Academy – Minneapolis, Minnesota – 490 students

I traveled to Minnesota to meet with Mr. Russ Gregg, founder of Hope Academy in Minneapolis.[19] Years earlier while Mr. Gregg was an administrator in a wealthy school near Minneapolis, the Lord asked him, "What does it mean to love your neighbor?" Convicted, the Gregg family moved into the inner city, and later he established Hope Academy that today continues to help other start-up schools in inner cities throughout the United States.

I had read about Hope Academy in *World* magazine, marveling at the inroads the school is making with inner-city children. At the beginning of our interview, I shared with Mr. Gregg that when I read their website, tears had come to my eyes and as I read further, I was led to worship the Lord for the work He is doing in their school.

Hope Academy makes use of an entrepreneurial operating system that has been used effectively in the business world. Using Gino Wickman & Mark C. Winters' *Rocket Fuel*, the school seeks to gain "traction" by getting crystal

---

[16] Mark Cotterman, interview by Kathleen F. Kitchin, Mason, Ohio, May 3, 2018.

[17] Lisa Borgeson, phone interview by Kathleen F. Kitchin, May 11, 2018.

[18] Rev. Robert Ingram, interview by Kathleen F. Kitchin, Orlando, Florida, February 21, 2019.

[19] Russ Gregg, interview by Kathleen F. Kitchin, Minneapolis, Minnesota, May 20, 2019.

clear clarity on their school's vision, mission, & values. They then develop 1) a process for key goals & objectives and 2) a process for accountability around those key goals & objectives called a Vision Traction Organizer. If interested, please consult Wickman and Winters' book for further explanation.[20]

Following *Rocket Fuel*'s counsel, Hope Academy revisits their mission, vision, & values every *90 days* (quarterly). Their executive leadership team goes off-site "not working *in* school but working *on* school," a day away to refocus, and each time they review all of the following:[21]

1) mission, vision, & values;
2) 10-year vision;
3) 3-year picture (1x/year – update the 3-year picture);
4) 1-year plan (a focus on the 6-8 most important goals for the coming year). "Then we break down those into 90-day goals. We take 4-6 that we call '*rocks.*' *Rocks* are the 4-6 things that are the most important things to get done. Evaluate them every 90 days. Every one of the rocks is assigned to a member of the leadership team."[22]

Gregg continues, "The executive leadership team truly gets clarity off-site. They get clarity on the 4-6 most important things for the sake of the school that they are committed to as a leadership team by which we are going to judge the effectiveness of these 90 days. When you've got this kind of clarity of vision & accountability, you really develop what you call *traction* (on the most important things that you have determined together that need to be done over those 90 days)." Hope Academy is in this 90-day rhythm, like "taking the bone, and throwing it out another 90 days," says Gregg.

On the other hand, the leadership team also meets weekly. "As we meet on a weekly basis, we review each of these *rocks* to ask whether we are *on track* or *off track* related to those 4-6 most important things (*rocks*). Weekly meetings are a "very prescribed way of spending those *90 minutes* together." The leadership team starts a ½-hour prior to the 90-minute meeting, so this is a two-hour time block. "We begin with a devotional and praying together. We start with the Word of God and prayer." This focus reflects one of the school's core values: *radical dependence on God!* The agenda then proceeds as follows with a strict 90-minute protocol:

- Share personal/professional highlights (5 minutes).
- Review scorecard (5 minutes).
- Review 90-Day Priorities (5 minutes).
- Share school headlines (5 minutes).
- Check progress on to-do list from last week's meeting (5 minutes).
- Issues List (60 minutes). (Identify, prioritize, discuss, solve problems)
- Conclude (5 minutes). (Recap To-Dos, Staff Messages, Rate Meeting 1-10.)[23]

The *scorecard* lists the 8-12 most important things Hope Academy thinks they should be tracking on a weekly basis.[24] Some examples of these tracked items include the following "leading indicators":

1) Admission-based #'s
2) Director of development's fundraising #'s
3) Work going on in the classroom

Admission-based numbers were straightforward. The other "leading indicators" were challenging for the team to come up with, but for their development office's *fundraising numbers*, they track development of scholarships, the number of people committed to donating a scholarship, and the most important indicator is the number of

---

[20] Gino Wickman and Mark C. Winters, *Rocket Fuel: The One Essential Combination that will Get You More of What You Want from Your Business* (Dallas: BenBella Books, Inc., 2016).

[21] Ibid.

[22] Gregg, interview.

[23] Ibid.

[24] Ibid.

new visitors who are willing to spend an hour to visit the school. These visitors get excited about the school and want to support a student. Hope Academy had over 525 visitors in 2018.

Lastly, the leadership team tracks three *classroom work numbers* on a weekly basis:

1) # who have exhibited homework faithfulness
    - "If we can develop the habit of homework faithfulness, that will translate into a whole variety of good things that will set them up for a life time of success." It will be "a habit of the heart."
2) # of positive parent-contacts (to build relationships with parents):
    - 3 phone calls or positive contacts per week/child
    - Reaching out to parents with "good news." ☺
3) # of shepherding conversations with students
    - Paul David Tripp in his book *Age of Opportunity* says, "Instead of seeing these contacts as a negative thing that we should drive down, we believe that the power of the gospel is what we want to drive up. How many conversations about the gospel, about the state of their heart, about the good news can we have with our students?"[25]

Gregg says, "If we are seeing those numbers on a good track, those are giving us evidence that things we are aiming at are happening." I asked Mr. Gregg if arrogance might develop as students might gloat in the acquisition of knowledge gained through their homework and classwork, and he replied, "That, too, would need shepherding conversations. God 'opposes the proud but gives grace to the humble.'"

In the upper school in Hope Academy, they focus on Hope Values.

1) Honor for God & others
2) Optimism for the future
3) Perseverance in adversity
4) Excellence in all things

Parent-teacher conferences include the child at Hope Academy. At the beginning of every report card assessment and at the beginning of parent/teacher conferences, the student talks with both his teacher & his parent about the progress he is making in these Hope Values.

Hope Academy is a missional school. The #1 consideration in hiring staff is their devotion to the Lord. Hope is to bring that to their students & families. What surprised me is that eighth graders have to reapply for admission to high school. There is a special dinner in January with students & their parents where the school talks about high school. They explain that in grammar school it was the parents' decision, in middle school it was half the parent's & half the child's decision, but for high school it's 80% the student's decision & 20% the parents'. Gregg says, "Students have to have some buy-in. You really can't hold people accountable against their will." The speech at the special dinner explains that the main requirement for admission to Hope Academy high school is *desire*. At some level. That "I want to be here" determination. In January, it may be yes, no, maybe. Maybe you've got some time for repentance, fruit of evidence of wanting to be at Hope. Gregg says, "It is very helpful to give the students some voice. Why do you want to be here?"

At the end of our interview, Mr. Gregg gathered his books and after pleasantries, headed toward class, as twice per week he teaches 1st & 2nd graders the Bible. ☺

Red Flags

- The school's founders and leaders have no fear of the Lord (Ps. 36: 1-4). One set of founders began at the outset of their school as follows: "If this school is not faithful to God, close the doors." They were willing to have their vision & reality crumble if their commitment to God was forfeited.

---

[25] Paul David Tripp, *Age of Opportunity: A Biblical Guide to Parenting Teens* (Phillipsburg, New Jersey: P & R Publishing, 2001).

- There is no vision or vision statement.
- Abandonment of reading the vision aloud periodically in each group: board of directors, administrators, faculty/staff, and parents.
- Having a blasé or sarcastic attitude when reading the vision aloud. That person is not on board and is undermining the success of the vision.
- Schools can eventually "hit their stride," but leave the vision statement to gather dust and be forgotten. Review and careful adjustments may be necessary to hone the vision and/or how that vision is being implemented. 1 Samuel 12:9 "But they forgot the Lord their God." (Israelites who came out of Egypt)
- Loss of sight of what the school is all about. Are you inadvertently making "clever devils," instead of nurturing humble, winsome "little Christs"?
- A subtle but insidious shift in referencing the author of the vision: God's vision – or the headmaster's or the chairman of the board's?
- Institutions that compromise God's truth. "When you surrender at the core, it is only a matter of time until you cave." Tony Perkins, president of Family Research Council in Washington, DC, says it is essential to stand firm for "accommodation on foundational principles is a slippery slope that always leads to ruin and regret."[26]
- Thinking that a healthy school is achieved by formula or by slogan. (Dr. Jason Edwards (formula); Dr. Mark Graham (slogan))[27]
- A re-direction of vision without the unanimous concurrence of the board. Again, this often occurs when one person is remaking the school in his or her own image or imitating a particular model in a recipe, cookie-cutter fashion.
- Such intense focus is set on being or becoming a premier school that people get "trampled," especially teachers & staff. Being subservient to a "grand scheme" that becomes an idol. God pays attention to both ends and means. Beware of being gripped by ends only.
- Railroading out the founders of the school. Satan loves to remove authors of Kingdom work. Ideally, there would be continuity of the past into the future; conversely, it would *not* be an Orwellian disposing of the past.
- Loss of eternal focus. In Ecclesiastes, Solomon had wisdom, but his heart was not sold out to God.

Sober Reflection

For the Board & Head of School & Administrators

- What is our vision statement? Where is it located? Our mission? Our core values? Our educational philosophy? Our statement of faith? Our general school rules?
- Do we read aloud these foundational documents at the *beginning* of each school year to the entire board and to teachers & staff & periodically thereafter?
- Do we read these foundational documents at the *end* of each school year as a board and head of school and as faculty & staff?
- Do we assess progress in/divergence from the foundational documents?
- If we make changes, are those changes communicated ahead of time to the faculty? Are these changes then transparently communicated to the parents?
- Are teacher's lesson plans and teaching reflecting the vision? How so?
- Are parents familiar with these foundational documents?
- Do we make the foundational documents easily accessible through a parent portal on the website?
- How do we reinforce parents' knowledge of these foundational documents? Back-to-school night & conferences? Emails/handouts sent home?
- Is our vision blinded once the vision is documented?
- Is our vision/mission/values a work of the Spirit or a work of the flesh?

---

[26] Tony Perkins, *Washington Impact Report* 30, no. 1 (February 2019).
[27] Dr. Mark Graham, interview by Kathleen F. Kitchin, Grove City, Pennsylvania, May 7, 2018.

- Is there no vehicle or mechanism to report problems in a biblical and winsome fashion, bringing them to the attention of the right person or body? (Matthew 18:18)
- *Suggestion for a faculty meeting(s): Have a vision for the vision.* Have teachers provide practical examples of how aspects of your school's vision/mission/values are being carried out in a grammar classroom, a logic classroom, and a rhetoric classroom.

Getting Back on Track

- *Most critically important:* Each board member, each headmaster/principal, and each academic administrator needs to have a "Nathan," someone who knows and embraces the vision, and will, if and when necessary, lovingly and truthfully confront his fellow board member, his headmaster, or his academic dean with evidence of divergence from that vision. [More on this in Chapters 3 & 4.]
- Enter "Review of Vision/Mission/Values" onto administrators' calendar.
- The board needs to deliver a "State of the Vision" address to the faculty during summer teacher preparation week, assessing how the school has been fulfilling the vision – each year. They will create this address based on their own observations (one announced visit, one unannounced visit per year), and encompass feedback gathered from the headmaster & the faculty before the last month of school the previous year. Looking to the future, a few goals will be set, following the SMART guidelines (Specific, Measurable, Achievable, Relevant, & Time-bound).
- Professional workdays are a marvelous opportunity to assess progress against these SMART goals mid-year.
- "We cannot let frustration, fear, or discouragement choke what we have seen God do miraculously in the past. Ask God to soften your heart to learn from the loaves & fishes He has provided and will provide again in the future. Miracles teach us about who Jesus is."[28] Write down somewhere what God has done for your school, a list of Ebenezers, a list of "Thus far has the Lord helped us," and read various sections of this list when you need reminders of God's great providence. Have teachers & parents contribute to this list. Post it on your website. Share stories aloud to keep you humble. Your school is in the sovereign hands of the Lord.
  - Examples:
    - "God provided just the number of students we needed [in the year ---] so that we could continue to open our doors."
    - "God provided for our needs for space in the past. We refuse to worry or seek man-made answers for our need now. Let us pray for God's miraculous provision, for it shall be exactly what we need, when we need it."
    - "God provided my 'educational manna' this year when I was not sure exactly how to approach teaching my new class."
  - Note that in the examples, God is the Source, not we or I.
- Post your vision, mission, & values on your website, not buried in a menu sub-folder, but in some fashion on the home page so that all can see.
- *Discussion Suggestion*: Ask your board to memorize the vision, mission, & values. Discuss together how you see & do not see these being met.
- Read the vision, mission, & values aloud every meeting in some way.
- Administrators revisit the vision, mission, & values every 90 days.
- Rev. Robert Ingram says, there were "'bailout moments' especially during those 'precarious first years.'" But the Lord provided exactly the funds needed for the school to expand into the ninth grade through a generous gift given to us to hire the necessary faculty to develop grades 9-12.
- Create a vehicle or mechanism to report problems in a biblical and winsome fashion, for bringing it to the attention of the right person or body. (Mt 18:18) Is there an honest broker on your administrative staff (an impartial mediator)? [Chapter 4 further elaborates solutions.]

---

[28] Pastor Robert Wetmore, Christian & Missionary Alliance (sermon, Grace Alliance Fellowship Church, Statesville, North Carolina, June 23, 2019).

Healthy School

- The leadership team has assiduously brought sparkling clarity to the school's vision, mission, & values and communicates them with energy & joy.
- The administrators are actively ensuring the exact words of their vision, mission, & values are communicated frequently to the faculty, parents, & students.
- The faculty knows, understands, & supports the vision. They have bought into the vision. Everyone agrees to the train's destination (or, if not, they need to consider another mode of transportation).
- Over time, the parents know, understand, and support the vision. They have bought into the vision. Everyone agrees to the train's destination (or, if not, they need to consider another mode of transportation). Parents then become important promoters of the school.
- It is most often an individual or two who notices that a school is going off track. Leadership listens.
- Celebrates milestones and thanks God in all circumstances:
  - *First senior class* – "It's a significant moment for the senior class to build a pipeline all the way through to the end. It's a strong encouragement and inducement for everyone else then to stay" (Rev. Robert Ingram, Geneva School).
  - Becoming *accredited.*
  - Acquiring a *building.*
  - Financing a *new building.*
- Dr. George Grant says to "Constantly encourage teachers to take a discipleship mindset and to spend time with their students, walking & talking in the hallways onc-on-onc; it's outsidc thc classroom stuff. When a student says, 'I don't have anybody else to talk to but you. Could you spend a little bit of time with me? I'm wrestling with this.' *That* is a golden moment."
- Has both a direct and anonymous vehicle to report serious problems (hierarchy of communication (Mt. 18:18) and Survey Monkey feedback analysis). A school board and head of school have to distinguish whether a person is a chronic complainer or truly has identified a serious problem.
- "When we glorify God alone, we are keeping the first commandment (Exodus 20:1-3). Worship is telling God of His worth."[29]

Setting a Goal

- Pray for God's wisdom. Then set one or two goals *that depend on you* for getting your vision better centered or back on track. Enter goals in the binder or document that goes with you everywhere.
- Refer to this goal throughout the year at each type of meeting – board, administration, faculty, back to school night, parent-teacher conferences.
- Reflect on this goal at year's end. Rejoice in God's grace.

Expressing a Desire

- Pray for God's wisdom. Then write one or two desires *that depend on others' cooperation* for getting your vision better centered or back on track. Enter that desire in the binder or document that goes with you everywhere.
- Pray about this desire throughout the year.
- Reflect on this desire at the end of each year. Rejoice in God's grace.

Encouragement

- Steven Garber, professor of marketplace theology and leadership at Regent College, who had attended Francis Schaeffer's L'Abri [paraphrased by Veritas School headmaster Keith Nix]: "Schools ought to be places where you can ask honest questions and can get honest answers."

---

[29] Pastor Paul Hurst, "Soli Deo Gloria," (sermon, Grace Evangelical Church, Madison, Wisconsin, May 2019).

- Dr. George Grant:
  - "Ironically, the strongest, most vibrant manifestations of CCE are in the places where the least resources and the least expertise lies, where CC schooling is a passion & a revival, rather than an institution that is prospering. Our greatest danger is as Cotton Mather pointed out in *Magnalia Christi Americana* [published 1702, about the ecclesiastical history of America in the 17th century] our greatest danger comes, not when we face adversity and difficulty and obstacles, but when we really prosper. That's when we accommodate ourselves to either the dangers of the culture or the dangers of isolation from culture. So we either become Sadducees or we become Pharisees. But in the midst of renewal & revival, we're still so much in the process of discovering, learning, & growing that there is no appeal for either Sadduceeism or Phariseeism. Where I see the greatest strength is in our littlest schools, our struggling schools with headmasters who say, 'I don't know exactly what I am doing, but, oh, how I love this.' I think that any movement faces dangers as it matures because we begin to think that we have all the answers, because we begin to think that our way is the right way & there is no other way, and we become ossified. So, for me, the joy of discovery is what keeps the movement alive and it's recognizing our role primarily as *counter* to the culture and that holds us in a position of engagement and it simultaneously requires of us the sort of facility & flexibility that comes with fresh works of the Spirit."[30]
- "... [B]eing confident of this, that He who began a good work in you will perfect it until the day of Jesus Christ." (Philippians 1:6, ASV)

---

[30] Dr. George Grant, interview by Kathleen F. Kitchin, ACCS Conference, Atlanta, Georgia, June 13, 2019.

Chapter 2

Your School's Culture in the Midst of Culture

*"But thanks be to God, who in Christ
always leads us in triumphal procession,
and through us spreads the fragrance
of the knowledge of Him everywhere."*

2 Corinthians 2:14

Your School's Culture

"You have a special school here," said the Jostens yearbook representative. "The minute we walk in, we can tell it is different. Love is here." Is love in your school? Does grace abound? Is there humility? Or is there an elevation of superior intellect like an Ivy League prep school? Or a list of rigid and numerous rules?

The word *culture* derives from the Latin *cultura*, meaning "growing, cultivation." The French word *culturer* came from the Latin, *colere* meaning " to tend, cultivate." The Middle English word *culture* denoted a cultivated piece of land, and Noah Webster's 1828 *American Dictionary of the English Language* says *culture* is "the application of labor or other means to improve good qualities in or growth; as the culture of the mind; the culture of virtue." Webster also says *culture* is "any labor or means employed for improvement, correction, or growth." This preparing the soil for crops or gardening involves breaking up the soil in preparation for sowing or planting crops and, by extension, cultivating the mind, faculties, or manners. Webster's definition of *cultivate* adds further the notion of cherishing & laboring to promote & increase, as "to cultivate the love of excellence; to cultivate gracious affections." The notion of *growing* pervades all these terms, so how do we foster that growth? How does one cultivate a sweet aroma? Plug in the room fresheners or light a candle?

TRUE AROMA
Jesus Christ is the true aroma at a sweet school. One does not "plug Him in" or light a match to bring in the Light of the world. Christ is either there preeminently, or worldliness and sin is permitted to crowd Him out. Is Christ invited into your school from the dawn of its beginnings? As your school ages, is He still worshipped and invited in – *every* day? Do we truly take to heart that every day "Without [Him, we] can do nothing" John 15:5c (NKJV)? Is Christ leading your school in triumphal procession and through you spreading the fragrance of the knowledge of Him everywhere? If so, your school's culture will exude Christ. Head of Covenant Academy near Houston, Leslie Collins says, "Culture is what happens when what you desire and how you think become a part of how you live."[1] How we are living reflects what we desire. Is how we are living reflecting our desire for God?

RELIANCE ON GOD FOR THIS AROMA
How do we cultivate this sweetest of aromas? Both personally and interpersonally. Personally, the first assumption is that you have received Jesus Christ as your Lord & Savior. From there, rely on God daily and lean

---

[1] Leslie Collins, "Cultivating a Christ-centered Culture in Our Homes" (lecture, Pasadena EP Church, Pasadena, Maryland, April 11, 2009).

hard into Him for this sweet aroma in your school. The minute *you* start taking the reins back from Him is the minute your school goes from smelling divine to smelling of flesh. Interpersonally, the second assumption is that as an administration & faculty, you have each received Jesus Christ as your Lord & Savior. As brothers & sisters in the Lord, confront pride, favoritism, inner circles, gossip, & unkind speech swiftly and biblically, both amongst students and amongst teachers & administrators. Teach the Golden Rule and, equally important, model it. "So whatever you wish that others would do to you, do also to them..." (Matthew 7:12). In addition, "Take every thought captive unto Christ" and teach your students to do the same (2 Cor. 10:5). Hold a high standard. Students will emulate that, maybe not this year, but prayerfully, they will in time.

RELATIONSHIPS

We know that Christ exudes the sweetest aroma & the sweetest culture at a school and that we cannot produce that aroma ourselves, but Christ Himself does as we submit to Him. But what often happens is we get off track. In fact, we will always be "prone to wander." How do we as an organization help preserve that sweetest aroma? In the introduction, we looked at four kinds of schools:

1) Running off the track, but do not know it due to inexperience/blind spots,
2) Running off the track, but do not know it due to pride,
3) Running off the track, and know it but suppress the truth, or
4) Running off the track, know it, and humbly desire to change.

Head of Covenant Academy in Cypress, Texas, Mrs. Leslie Collins observes that these four ways of running off the track are also the spectrum of how people engage with truth and are the same ways an organization interrelates. Collins says, "The way you develop a healthy relationship with any human being is also how you develop a healthy relationship within an organization and the constituencies. It's about creating a climate where people have a true relationship; they're not just buying a service."[2] A significant part of maintaining that sweet aroma & culture is about *relationship* – laboring to cultivate relationships between administrators & the faculty/staff, between faculty & students, administrators/faculty/staff & parents, administrators & feeder churches to the school. Relationships involve being connected. Collins urges that schools give their parents and students a voice. Ask them, "How are we doing? What are the areas that you think we can improve on?" She says, "Schools that stay on track are schools that have that relationship; they survey their parents, they ask for their feedback." [More on feedback in Chapter 4.]

HUMILITY THAT GIVES GOD THE PRAISE

What does a healthy classical Christian school's culture look like? An educator who has had exposure to CCE students for the past two decades says what they look at regarding CCE is the *results* or product of classical Christian education. When asked what is the ideal model of CCE, they replied, "When I see teachers and administrators with humility. I see everything except that [with rare exception]." Young schools often have that humility because resources are scarce and prayers are plentiful. As former second-grade teacher and administrator Lisa Borgeson says, "There is a humility in having nothing" and sometimes third-generation teachers "Don't know from whence we came." Schools need to guard humility's presence. One way to do that is to document your school's history through yearbook and a one-page journal at year's end. Include what you are thankful for and record *God's glory and faithfulness*. Read it; share it every few years amongst faculty, as well as at annual school association meetings and celebration dinners. We are humble and thankful for what we have. A spirit of thanksgiving, not pride, reigns.

ARROGANCE

But classical Christian schools can be prone to arrogance. As Scripture says, "...knowledge puffs up, but love builds up" or in the Amplified Version, "Knowledge [alone] makes [people self-righteously] arrogant, but love [that unselfishly seeks the best for others] builds up *and* encourages others to grow [in wisdom] (1 Cor. 8:1)." How does a school train its students toward a culture of humility and love? Again, Leslie Collins says,

---

[2] Leslie Collins, interview by Kathleen F. Kitchin, Cypress, Texas, November 27, 2018.

One of the very intentional acts in our liturgy of our graduation, in fact the very first thing the students do is to humble themselves and bow low under the standard of the school, our standards being love and courage and perseverance and strength, the virtues of our houses [a grouping of pupils, based on the British house system] because we tell them that "Knowledge puffs up" and they will be given many opportunities to become prideful in their education, but they need to remember that to lead is to serve and to humble themselves because God will then lift them up. We also sing to our students "Humble Thyself in the Sight of the Lord." We know from Scripture that knowledge puffs up and so when you give children a lot of knowledge, you know that they are going to be puffed up and if you dispute that fact, then you are disputing Scripture. That is why *servant-leadership* being taught is so critical and that no one is above helping someone else, no one is above doing hard work, and that the way up is down in the Christian paradox of life. We want them to see that every single day, whether they are serving or being served.

The very posture of bowing low under the school's standard is a palpable reminder to be humble, from the Latin root *humus* or "earth." Major milestones like graduation need formal reminders of this humbleness, and daily, we need to stay low, kneeling in humility to Christ.

In his book *The Vanishing American Adult: Our Coming-of-Age Crisis – and How to Rebuild a Culture of Self-Reliance*, Nebraska Senator Ben Sasse asserts, "We all stand on the shoulders of giants [Aristotle, Augustine, Rousseau, Luther, & Calvin]."[3] This recognition of our place in the midst of history inspires humility. It reminds me of one of the miniscule human figures standing in the midst of the towering landscape in one of Frederic Edward Church's Hudson River School of Art paintings. In 1988 at Georgetown University's bicentennial, President Ronald Reagan urged men and women to make their work "a testament to the wisdom and mercy of God"; so too should we educators. Much as advanced degrees add to our knowledge, we should not pass on to our children homage to the number of Ph.D.'s on our school staff. Children are highly attuned to what we praise and what we value. If they hear accolades for advanced degrees, they will assume that a Ph.D. degree is better than a simple B.A. or B.S. degree. To do so is a work of the flesh. *A good teacher is a good teacher by the grace of God, not their degree.* Regardless of what degrees your faculty has, in order to produce a culture of humility & grace, that knowledge and those degrees need to be taken captive unto Christ, both by the recipients and by the administrators & parents of the school. God is on the pedestal, not man. Scottish minister Thomas Chalmers said, "The wider a man's knowledge becomes, the deeper should be his humility; for the more he knows the more he sees of what remains unknown. The wider the diameter of light, the larger the circumference of darkness." How do we extract from the mire of pride? From C.S. Lewis's chapter "The Perfect Penitent" in *Mere Christianity*:

> Now what was the sort of "hole" man had got himself into? He had tried to set up on his own, to behave as if he belonged to himself. In other words, fallen man is not simply an imperfect creature who needs improvement: he is a rebel who must lay down his arms. Laying down your arms, surrendering, saying you are sorry, realizing that you have been on the wrong track and getting ready to start life over again from the ground floor – that is the only way out of a "hole." This process of surrender – this movement full speed astern – is what Christians call repentance. Now repentance is no fun at all. It is something much harder than merely eating humble pie. It means unlearning all the self-conceit and self-will that we have been training ourselves into for thousands of years. It means killing part of yourself, undergoing a kind of death....[4]

In fact, when David Kern asked Dr. George Grant in a Circe Institute interview what his great concern is, he replied, "Humility. Gnostic "secret knowledge" vs. "the more we know, the more we need to know."[5] Dr. Grant's

---

[3] Ben Sasse, *The Vanishing American Adult: Our Coming-of-Age Crisis – and How to Rebuild a Culture of Self-Reliance* (New York: St. Martin's Press, 2017), 278.

[4] C.S. Lewis, *Mere Christianity* (New York: Macmillan Publishing Company, 1979 [Orig. 1943]).

[5] Dr. George Grant, interview by David Kern, Quiddity #68, Circe Institute, October 26, 2016.

biggest concern for CCE was pride. We must decrease, and Christ must increase. But how does pride & its antidote work?

SCHOOL AS STATUS SYMBOL

Over the years, a school can become a status symbol. It has more elite sports teams or it has top academics or a better college acceptance rate. The aroma & culture becomes pride, not humility. As Patrick Lencioni, CEO of a management consulting firm and author of *The Five Dysfunctions of a Team*, says,

> ...plenty of [leadership] teams fall prey to the lure of status. These often include altruistic nonprofit organizations that come to believe that the nobility of their mission is enough to justify their satisfaction. Political groups, academic departments, and prestigious companies are also susceptible to this dysfunction, as they often see success in merely being associated with their *special* organizations.[6]

Some schools can develop a "not invented here" hubris where they are the epitome of excellence, and they have little to learn from younger, newer schools. So, you know a lot. That is a blessing. Who was the author of that knowledge? God.

OUR NEED OF DIVINE GRACE

Mark A. Noll, Christian historian at Regents College and evangelical scholar, delves into the heart of academic culture; but his words apply to pre-college education and the danger of pride. He says in *Jesus Christ and the Life of the Mind*,

> Because for a Christian the tasks of scholarship are tied so closely to the unearned gift of salvation, there can be no genuine Christian learning that is arrogant, self-justifying, imperious, or callous to the human needs of colleagues, students, and the broader public. The tight conjunction of assertions in Colossians underscores the fact that all humans, including academics, are needy sinners who require God. All humans, including academics, remain in need of divine grace even as they explore the depths of "wisdom and knowledge" hidden in Jesus Christ.[7]

This should be our vision for our students: for them to delight in learning for it is "God who gives us richly all things to enjoy" (1 Timothy 6:17); to remain humble, literally "close to the ground"; to help them foster the love that builds up *and* encourages others to grow in wisdom; to always stand in the need of divine grace.

RESISTING ARROGANCE

How do we resist this delicious enticement to boast and brag? It is critical to focus on God's glory and faithfulness, for the word *culture* also shares a Latin root with the word *cult, colere* meaning "inhabited, cultivated, worshiped." After I interviewed Hope Academy in Minneapolis and thanked them for their time, the attitude expressed to me was truly an antidote to pride: "We are happy to share what God has shown us." The emphasis is on *Him*, not *we*. Over the next 10 years, their goal is to help come alongside 10 new Hope Academy-like inner-city schools. Not clones, but independent schools. Not lingering control, but a three-year mentoring. Another preventative to pride.

THE SIREN CALL OF GROWTH & ITS ANTIDOTE

A school can begin with godliness, prayer, and vision, but as noted in the previous chapter, Dr. Jason Edwards, history professor at Grove City College, says that when a school starts with a small group of families and the results are good & word spreads & growth occurs, the school can view this as a "sign of God's blessing" and too often, he has seen a number of schools that have "forfeited their principles" in the name of seeking further growth. In a different interview, I heard that it can be tempting at that point to start watering down their admission

---

[6] Patrick Lencioni, *The Five Dysfunctions of a Team: A Leadership Fable* (San Francisco: Jossey-Bass, 2002), 217.

[7] Mark A. Noll, *Jesus Christ and the Life of the Mind* (Grand Rapids, Michigan: William B. Eerdmans Publishing Company, 2011), 30.

requirements, but students still need to be trained up to honor the Lord, not have their elders compromise and hence create a culture of compromise. What does the board of directors do when those pressures are on? What is their first recourse? They know certain financial goals have to be met, so how do they handle that and where do they go? Pertinent to this discussion, as mentioned in the previous chapter, there are two types of schools – *covenantal* (or nurturing) and *evangelistic* (or missional). A covenantal school requires the parents to be Christians; an evangelistic one does not, but does require agreement to primary documents. Either type of school is honorable. What is not honorable is school boards' deciding to switch from the original type of school to the other model, most often a covenantal school to an evangelistic one to increase numbers but doing this *without informing the parents*. We should not worship numbers. Reverend Robert Ingram, head of the Geneva School in Orlando, Florida, is about to shift temporarily from one to two campuses with the accompanying staffing & transportation challenges since the campuses are 15 minutes apart and inconvenient for some parents to easily drive between them for a daily commute. As head of a school of over 545 students, he stipulates that growth can occur within the parameters of "maintaining expectations of students that align with mission, vision, and foundational values." Culture and vision are connected. As Christian learned in John Bunyan's *Pilgrim's Progress*, he needed to resist venturing off the straight & narrow path.

RATIONALISM

While some schools may be tempted to elevate growth while sacrificing culture, other schools may succumb unintentionally to worshipping rationalism. Rationalism is "the theory that *reason* rather than experience is the foundation of certainty in knowledge." Over years & years of memorizing facts, debating issues, & declaiming speeches, unless Christ is repeatedly placed central – so that "'all my springs are in You'" (Psalm 87:7) – the notion that "man is the measure of all things" can creep in. Students can rightly revel in Greek techniques of argumentation or the Pythagorean theorem. We most certainly need to worship, but with the correct object of our focus. Are we forgetting the Author? Are we remembering to pray before our class begins its heady plunges into philosophy & logic? Are we remembering the *ad fontes* (L. "[back] to the sources") but forgetting the true Fountain? Dr. Mark Graham, history professor at Grove City College, refers to the German idealist tradition and Wilhem Dielthey's *weltanschauung*, or view of the world, that *renders one standing in awe*. As the Stanford Encyclopedia reminds us, "A worldview attempts to provide not only a cognitive picture of the world, but also an estimation of *what in life is valuable and worth striving for* [italics mine]." Professor Graham said he would "like to see humility in the face of that awe and wonder," rather than analysis of the "riddle of life" and the essentialism of "being able to categorize and dismiss a piece very quickly by identifying its '-ism' (humanism, naturalism, etc.). That does not make one a scholar." He said, "If one is trained to dismiss and tear down, he also needs to be taught to rebuild, replace, and fill in. The fact that he can critique Plato's 'worldview' does not make him learned." The professor also referred to C.S. Lewis's reference in *The Abolition of Man* where the poet Samuel Taylor Coleridge "agreed with the tourist who called the cataract [spectacular waterfall] sublime and disagreed with the one who called it pretty" for he believed that "the object was one which merited those emotions."[8] As we learn, we cannot lose sight of rightly esteeming the value of all that God has created, standing in awe together as we gaze in wonder.

FAVORITISM

Yet another red flag in culture is favoritism. One of the quickest ways to demoralize a school and poison its soil is to play favorites. Favorites can range from favored children to favored teachers to a favorite sector of the Trivium. Are all children valued as precious creations of God to be loved and trained in righteousness? Does the school value each and every teacher and the God-given contributions they have to offer? Is each part of the Trivium – the Grammar, the Logic, *and* the Rhetoric – valued equally, just as the name Trivium implies it should, as "the place where three roads meet"? Christ did not play favorites. Neither should we.

THE INNER RING

Peeling back further behind favoritism, in his chapter "Binding, Blinding, and the Inner Ring," Alan Jacobs of Baylor University in his *How to Think: A Survival Guide for a World at Odds* says, "[C.S.] Lewis called his audience's attention to the presence, in schools and businesses and governments and armies and indeed in every

---

[8] C.S. Lewis, *The Abolition of Man, or Reflections on education with special reference to the teaching of English in the upper forms of schools* (San Francisco: HarperCollins, 1974 [Orig. 1943]), 15.

other human institution, of a 'second or unwritten system' that stands parallel to the formal organization – an Inner Ring...[that determines] how the organization works."[9] Inner rings, an allusion to one of the essays in C.S. Lewis's *The Weight of Glory,* are not an evil in and of themselves as there are needs for confidential conversations and closeness in friendship, but Lewis asserts that it is the desire to be in the Inner Ring that can be dangerous: "'I believe that in all men's lives at certain periods, and in many men's lives at all periods between infancy and extreme old age, one of the most dominant elements is the desire to be inside the local Ring and the terror of being left outside.' And it is important for young people to know of the force of this desire because 'of all passions the passion for the Inner Ring is most skillful in making a man who is not yet a very bad man do very bad things.'"[10]

The Inner Ring in a school can be the headmaster's or teacher's favorites or those who have never countered him or her, or the athletes, or the brains. Sounds like high school cliques, doesn't it? Inner Rings can be "Yes-men" or birds of a feather. Inner Rings organically develop habits of thinking & regarding and their own special language to maintain their walls of exclusivity.

STAND FIRM
What is insidious is that "The draw of the Inner Ring has such profound corrupting power because it never announces itself as evil – indeed, it never announces itself at all." Lewis says the step over into evil occurs over a commonplace event: "Over a drink or a cup of coffee, disguised as a triviality and sandwiched between two jokes . . . the hint will come."[11] And the fear strikes and "you cannot bear to be thrust back again into the cold outer world."[12] A biblically healthy school composes itself of individuals who will stand firm in Christ. And when pressed, will stand firm. And when the coffee cup nearly touches their lips, will say "No." And in that faculty meeting that has degraded into unhealthy discussion of a student or family, will speak up to get back on track.

FROM INDIVIDUAL HUMILITY TO CORPORATE PRIDE
A red flag that is a close cousin to favoritism comes from C.S. Lewis's *The Four Loves,* where he warns of a possible danger even in good friendships: "...[I]n a good Friendship each member often feels humility towards the rest. He sees that they are splendid and counts himself lucky to be among them. But unfortunately the *they* and *them* are also, from another point of view *we* and *us*. Thus the transition from individual humility to corporate pride is very easy."[13] Is our focus turned outward toward others?

GOSSIP
Another insidious sin is gossip. Do not join. Do not tolerate. Ask the person with the delicious tidbit if they have first spoken directly with the party involved. Walk away. Be willing NOT to be in the gossip club. It is amazing how the gossip fire snuffs out when there is no oxygen fueling it.

Your School's Culture in the Midst of Culture

CULTURE IN CRISIS
Over 20 years ago, historian Gertrude Himmelfarb asserted in her *One Nation, Two Cultures* that "America is confronting at least six challenges: 'the collapse of ethical principles and habits, the loss of respect for authorities and institutions, the breakdown of the family, the decline of civility, the vulgarization of high culture, and the degradation of popular culture.'"[14] These challenges were not new as they were set in motion many years ago.

---

[9] Alan Jacobs, *How to Think: A Survival Guide for a World at Odds* (New York: Currency, 2017), 55-56.

[10] Jacobs, 56.

[11] Ibid., 56.

[12] Ibid., 57.

[13] C.S. Lewis Institute, *Reflections*, June 2019.

[14] Michael Cromartie quoting Irving Kristol quoting his wife Gertrude Himmelfarb, "What Now? Faithful Living in Challenging Times" (lecture, C.S. Lewis Institute *Broadcast Talks*, Capitol Hill, October 23, 2015), 5.

BETWEEN THE CITY OF MAN & THE CITY OF GOD

In contrast to a Benedictine option, author and former vice president of the Ethics & Public Policy Center Michael Cromartie in his 2015 lecture on Capitol Hill entitled "What Now? Faithful Living in Challenging Times" offered an alternative – the "Augustinian Option." He said that we

> live at the intersection of the ages, between the City of Man and the City of God that is to come [which] means that we develop what one great sociologist, John Murray Cuddihy, called "*an esthetic for the interim.*" This is a way of looking at life with an awareness that we are living "between the times." Therefore we are encouraged to exercise patience and put a ban on all ostentation and triumphalism. As Christians in this sometimes awkward duality of our earthly citizenship, we are called to be faithful in these times not of our own choosing. But this is our time, this is our place, and this is our time of testing and challenge. ... And so there is comfort in the midst of all this transition: the central doctrines of the sovereignty of God and the providence of God over all of life, and over all of history and where it is going, should give us confidence that the principalities and powers of this age will not have the final word. ...This is our place of pilgrimage at this time until the future City of God comes [italics mine].[15]

We pray, looking up toward the City of God as we live in our culture and shine like stars by His grace.

MAINTAINING GOD'S FENCES

As Ravi Zacharias shared in his April 2017 lecture at a C.S. Lewis Institute banquet in Washington, DC, "The fences are being moved everywhere." He quoted G. K. Chesterton: "Whenever you remove any fence, always pause long enough to ask yourself, 'Why was it put there in the first place?'"[16] Jeremiah 6:16 tells us to "Stand by the roads, and look, and ask for the ancient paths, where the good way is; and walk in it, and find rest for your souls," and our CCE schools are doing this so well. An aspect of culture that can derail a CCE school is to assert that we can move the fences ourselves and make things better, not standing on the Bible, but essentially starting from scratch without the wisdom of God. In a time of shift & drift, we need to keep in place the boundaries & paths God Himself put in place.

TRUE TRANSFORMATION

Back on May 24, 2015, in a *Baltimore Post-Examiner* interview, Ravi Zacharias said, "As I see our world right now, I have never seen greater confusion, greater loss of meaning, greater uncertainty, and greater fear of what looms in front of us. Politics has gotten out of control everywhere. Nobody sees a mascot or a leader, and everyone wants to know what really lies ahead here. But instead of thinking on the outside of all that's wrong, the Gospel of Christ brings me inside. My life has to change, my life has to be transformed. Before asking the question of evil around me, I have to ask of the evil in me – my proclivities, my drives, my temptations, my struggles. And I believe only Christ is enough to transform my heart."[17] Amen. Let revival begin within me.

CHRISTIAN *PAIDEIA*, NOT GREEK *PAIDEIA*

In the midst of this cultural change, a commitment to a Christian *paideia* is essential. Commitment on both the school's and parents' parts is commitment to a way of life, a *paideia* or "full instruction and upbringing of a child" (Veritas School website). According to Pastor Douglas Wilson, prominent pioneer and advocate for classical Christian education and author of *Recovering the Lost Tools of Learning: An Approach to Distinctively Christian Education* (1991), a *paideia* in ancient Greek society was "nothing less than the enculturation of the future citizen. He was encultured when he was instructed in the classroom, but the process was also occurring when he walked along the streets of his city to and from school"[18] (back cover, *The Paideia of God and Other Essays on Education*, 1999). Indeed, in the New Testament, Paul "[requires] Christian fathers to provide their

---

[15] Cromartie, 13, 14, & 15.

[16] Ravi Zacharias @RaviZacharias.

[17] Ravi Zacharias, Ravi Zacharias International Ministries (RZIM) website, accessed July 24, 2019.

[18] Douglas Wilson, *The Paideia of God and Other Essays on Education* (Moscow, Idaho: Canon Press, 1999), back cover.

children with a *paideia* of the Lord"[19] when he says, "And, you fathers, provoke not your children to wrath: but *bring them up in the nurture and admonition of the Lord*" (Ephesians 6:4). The notion of *paideia* was "central to the classical mind"[20] and involves far more than formal education. It involved the "shaping of the ideal man who would be able to take his place in the ideal culture."[21] "The establishment of Christian schooling necessarily entails the establishment of a Christian culture."[22] We can argue till the cows come home about Christendom, but the fact remains, are we moving toward a Christian culture in our school or away from it?

CONSUMER MENTALITY

In *committing*, literally sending with or joining ourselves, to *paideia*, we need to resist aspects of our culture. Dr. Jason Edwards, history professor at Grove City College, says that we have a *consumer mentality* in the United States. CCE sounds good and a mentality of "it'll help get my kid into Harvard" can arise or, by the same token, public school grade inflation can cause a recoiling from CCE to "get the better grade point average." The focus here is grades and academic success. Again, this academic success can blind us to the ultimate purpose of education: to bring glory to God and delight in Him forever. Articulating why we do what we do in CCE is important so that parents can fully embrace the school's biblical vision for their own family and encourage other committed families to consider CCE schools. When the school clearly communicates & demonstrates the Christian Trivium model & vision, parents can engage. They will wish they had had this type of education. In Pastor George Grant's words, many parents "feel robbed" not having had this type of education. As a result, parents feel committed, that is, they can *join* wholeheartedly entrusting their children in this God-focused enterprise.

A Different Culture in Our CCE School with Each Soil Being Unique

SET APART

God is Edenizing. He sets us apart, as a kingdom of priests, a priesthood of all believers. Holy. Distinctive. Set apart. In contrast to the culture we find in the world. Reiterate this focus periodically. The classical Christian school is about making something different. Not infiltrated or bulldozed over by culture. Satan wants to claim everything and every square inch for himself, but we are not to allow that to happen. As Mars Hill Academy in Cincinnati, Ohio, says, "The culture is moving, and we don't want to move with it. We want to stay true to who we are." Seek to Edenize your school. We are to establish a different culture in our CCE school as we stand apart – in the world, but not of it.

TIMES HAVE CHANGED

The culture of today is vastly different from the culture of the early 1990s when classical Christian education was revived. Dr. George Grant says,

> People who have been with us since the early days – there are not very many – I have to constantly remind them that we actually live in a different culture than we did when we started our schools. CCE began before the cultural earthquakes that we are now experiencing were even tremors. As a result, we're not dealing with the same kind of families that we bring into our schools, we're not dealing with children that face the same kinds of temptations. For my kids growing up, the biggest temptation was too much TV. Now, we have computers in our pockets that can take us anywhere in the world and usually to the worst places in the world. That's a totally different cultural landscape and so I think one of the great dangers for a very successful institution in CCE is to think that we've got it nailed, that we've got it figured out, that we know what a student actually needs, that we know what spiritual disciplines will actually move them on in maturity. We're in a very different place. We've got to think constantly in terms – to use the business language – in an "entrepreneurial sort of way." We've got to think about the cultural challenges in a whole fresh

---

[19] Ibid., 10.

[20] Ibid., 10.

[21] Ibid., 11.

[22] Ibid., 12.

perspective. I don't think that we face grave dangers of slipping into an unbiblical perspective of life & culture from sort of a normative basis. The norms are pretty established at most of our schools. There are always temptations to accommodate ourselves to the world. *I think that the greatest danger is for us to not realize that the world we're ministering to is not the same world that we started out with.* When I was a young pastor, Evangelism Explosion by D. James Kennedy was a very effective means of evangelism. I ... remember taking groups of my most mature folks through this educational process and at the end of it, we'd go out, hit the neighborhood, and go knock on doors and we'd share the gospel. It was marvelous. If we tried to do that today, we'd be shot. It's not an effective means of reaching people. We live in a *very* different world. I think our schools are in the same place. I don't think the same arguments work any longer. I don't think the same methodologies work any longer. We've got to be a *lot* more intentional than ever before. *I think the personal discipleship aspects of CCE are more important than ever.* ... We're having to build these relationships oftentimes virtually with the advent of online CCE. That requires so much more intentionality. It requires much more personal-ness. ... We've got to think like that in our brick-&-mortar schools as well as in these pioneering online schools because it is a different world.[23]

We need to be like the Apostle Paul and be flexible with the changing times, but still biblical.

SPHERE SOVEREIGNTY

What guidelines can help us stay true to what we are? One is *sphere sovereignty*. Abraham Kuyper, Dutch former prime minister, theologian, and the man most feared by Adolf Hitler (despite having died 19 years before WWII) founded this notion of sphere sovereignty, based on the Bible. Kuyper of the famed quote, "...there is not a square inch in the whole domain of our human existence over which Christ, who is Sovereign over *all*, does not cry: 'Mine!'" In sphere sovereignty, each sphere has differentiated responsibility and authority, designed and directed by God. A sphere for church, a sphere for home, a sphere for government, a sphere for school. Boundaries are essential and need to be respected.

RESPECTING THE SPHERES

Schools need to respect the spheres of home, church, & school. Administrators and teachers, do what is *in* your sphere to do. Stay within the boundaries of the school sphere. Although we study the Bible and honor God, our school is not a church. Although there can be and often are warm ties, your school is not a family. Although more is unintentionally falling to the school, our school is not the state. Do hear different approaches in Logic-level Bible classes to baptism and predestination – but let that student's church and parents tell the student how they interpret the answer. Teachers, do email parents with a "cc" to administrators when there is a discipline problem – but let Dad and Mom do their job in the follow-through. Do enrich the curriculum with field trips – but do not do Dad and Mom's job of college visits or faraway weekend trips to dazzle and lure new students. Step away from what belongs in another's sphere. Peace and order follow when we follow God's ways, and our school culture will be the sweeter.

SEEKING THE APPROVAL OF GOD

We often think it will be worldliness that invades the school. It will. Or sin. It will. But as Oswald Chambers says in *My Utmost for His Highest* in the entry for April 24: "The trap we fall into is extravagantly desiring spiritual success; that is, success measured by, and patterned after, the form set by this religious age in which we now live. *Never seek after anything other than the approval of God,* and always be willing to go '"outside the camp, bearing His reproach' (Hebrews 13:13). ... Our work is not to save souls, but to disciple them" [italics mine]."[24] Know our sphere; know our space.

CCE AS A PROCESS

Leslie Collins, head of Covenant Academy, says, "The larger the school, the more like the schools with amenities that you become and that becomes the selling point; so then some people want the product, but not the process,

---

[23] Dr. George Grant, interview.

[24] Oswald Chambers, ed. James Reimann. *My Utmost for His Highest* (Grand Rapids, Michigan: Discovery House Publishers, 1992 [Orig. 1935]), April 24 entry.

and classical education does have a product, it is true, but if that is all you see is that product and you don't understand that that product is actually part of a process you are not going to fully gain all the benefit from it." Classical Christian Education is not a product on a shelf; it is a way of life that becomes ever more sweet as we place Christ and not ourselves at center.

SWEETENING YOUR SCHOOL'S CULTURE

If you would seek to sweeten your school's culture, first ask God how you can do that and what your priorities should be for overall & for this year as you are incrementing change. One way to sweeten your school's culture is to reflect on the tone that is set in the front office & lobby. Is it frantic, frazzled, and fried? Have your school administrators established systems and trained each of the office support personnel as needed for a smoothly flowing operation to serve parents, students, and teachers well? Is there an atmosphere of peace & order, bathed in prayer to the Lord? Are there plants and perhaps gentle music for refreshment of soul? Are you treated as an object or an appointment, or as a person made in the image of God? Furthermore, as a school grows from its roots with tiny classes and that "small-town" feel of knowing everyone, how does the school ensure it is not moving toward the very model it was seeking to avoid – the German industrial model? Roy Griffith, now headmaster at Rockbridge Academy in Millersville, Maryland, reflected that once the curriculum is solidified, focusing more on delighting in God's grace at work with and among the students helps keep the freshness each year.[25] Another sweetener is to consider what we are telling our students about the school itself and about they themselves. Are we telling them "how superior their education is that they come to believe that *they* are superior"? Or are we marveling at & expressing the joy at what God, not us, has done & is doing? Yet another way to sweeten your school's culture is to limit technology to after-school contact with parents. One administrator set the boundary saying, "iThings are my things." Technology is just after school and by permission, yielding a quieter, more focused atmosphere. Finally, every school needs a celebration gala or dinner or gathering of some type each year to celebrate what God has done in faithfulness to your school. Simple to elegant. Potluck to catered. Fundraiser added or not. Have a speaker to uplift and cast vision for everyone. A sweet evening for all!

A CULTURE OF INTEGRITY

Integrity means "wholeness." In math class, we learn that integers are whole numbers, not fractions. Applying integrity to the CCE school culture means valuing the whole student, the whole school, the whole faculty. Valuing students not just for their mind, not just for their athleticism, not just for whatever is their outstanding feature, but valuing them as a whole person. The way Christ would. One of my favorite stories about integrity and grace was after the grammar school spelling bee, a little girl in first grade sat at her desk, over lunch perhaps, cutting out little construction paper badges and writing on them. She herself had not won, but she worked diligently to honor those who had. The blessing of humility. A true servant heart. Success. The sweet aroma of Christ for your school culture.

CASE STUDY

Covenant Academy – Cypress, Texas – 150 students

At Covenant Academy, a *House System* has been established. At the moment of enrollment, pupils are placed in house groups to help build community and promote leadership, competition, & service to God together.

"Four houses united to love, learn, and serve Him" from *Our House Song*

"At Covenant, everyone belongs to someone. Our four houses organize our school community around the ideals that define our school: wisdom and virtue. House systems are a by-product of traditional British boarding schools, where students of varying ages lived together in a physical house, overseen by invested faculty members who would actively disciple and lead their students in school-wide activities and competitions.

British houses were named after the faculty member but ours are named after American founding fathers, Patriots deemed worthy of imitation. In keeping with the ethos of classical education, and with the purpose of

---

[25] Roy Griffith, in-house teacher training, Rockbridge Academy, Millersville, Maryland, c. 2011.

maintaining a rich culture of community, all students and faculty are placed into one of four houses: Washington, Madison, Hamilton, and Henry.

These houses (or teams) provide students with abundant leadership options and encourage excellence through friendly competition. Each of our houses has chosen a virtue and a motto that they will actively seek to define them. These virtues, wisdom, courage, perseverance, and love are worthy pursuits for all as we seek to be lifelong learners in community with one another.

House System and School Culture

- Each day one house of upper school students serves for 10 minutes during Grammar School lunch. This opportunity to serve younger students and connect with them builds confidence in both upper and lower school students that will last a lifetime. This strengthens relationships across grade levels building an inter-generational school culture; a school that feels like a family.

- Students participate in healthy competitions (athletics, fundraising, service to the community, and games). Our annual Patriot Day is a school-wide celebration of House Spirit that provides an opportunity for students of all grades to fellowship together and forge strong relationships.

- Student leadership is cultivated through daily service and mentoring but is most evident in our weekly school-wide chapel. Announcements, awards and discussions take place in House Huddles so that younger students are given an opportunity to learn from older students. This fosters an expectation that older students will be role models for younger students as they teach them to apply what they are learning in their everyday life. House Huddles provide a new relational dimension in student-teacher relationships as adults "lead from behind" giving older students the opportunity to take on more and more responsibility.

- Parents and siblings feel welcome during school-wide events. They know people outside of their grade level and are able to build strong relationships over many years since families remain in the same house during their tenure at Covenant.

Though our four houses compete with each other, we are also committed to serving God together as a community." From the Covenant Academy website:

> *Our House Song (*to the tune of "Let All Things Now Living")
>
> May we grow to love You with all of our being,
> With each breath we draw our praises we bring.
> May we grow to love one another completely.
> May we love as You love, Oh Lord fearlessly.
>
> To love what You love, Lord,
> Hold every thought captive,
> Our lives the reflection of Your Holy Word.
>
> Four houses united to learn, love and serve Him.
> One school following after our Master and King."

Red Flags

- *Being uncommitted* – "You know you're not there unless you are really serious about the Christian formation of your children." (Headmaster Keith Nix)
- *Being too distant* – A too cerebral community does not fully manifest the nurture of the Lord. Our training in this school culture is more than training of the *mind*. We cannot treat our students as "Minds" only. We need to prepare the soil to yield a good crop not only for their minds, but also for their entire being – heart, soul, strength, & mind (Luke 10:27). We are seeking to reach the heart, not always the

head. Since we are *in loco parentis*, or "in the place of the parents" during the school day, administrators, teachers, & all those in the school's employ are to nurture, or nourish, and train up these young men & women in the way they should go and do so with love, the greatest gift.

- *Being too close* – A community that considers itself a family or even seeks to replace the family is not honoring the spheres of authority. The family is the primary institution that God has ordained. Our schools need to give preeminence to Christ and to the child's family. Although a school is not the family of this child, we are its *alma mater*, its "nourishing mother," coming alongside the child's family and co-partnering to raise him or her in the nurture and admonition of the Lord. It is analogous to the relationship between a faith-based organization that works outside & across denominations and the Church itself. Warm ties should be the norm, reflecting the love and sweet aroma of Jesus.

- *Being too youth oriented* – We are raising young men and women. We are not raising children around whose whims we order our lives and our days. We are not a youth group. That belongs to the home and church spheres. We seek to nurture warm, Christ-centered community. Some students graduate saying that warm community aspect was the best part of their school experience.

- *Being classical only* – Having not enough emphasis on Christian culture. Emphasis only on classical. If we emphasize classical only, we inadvertently take on the complexion & nature of the world, the mind, the power of mankind, while neglecting the true Source of it all – Jesus Christ.

- *Being neglectful of appropriately expressing love to older students* – In 1 Corinthians 13:13, Paul says that of faith, hope, & love, the greatest is love. In the Logic & Rhetoric levels, we need to remember that these students are not minds only. They, too, need to know we have *agape* love for them, appropriately expressed, for example, through smiles, humor, & kind words.

- *Being worldly* – The aroma of worldliness prevails regarding success. Once you have proven you are a viable school that colleges and universities respect and offer admission to your students, temper the press to prove that respectability. Have the test scores available for parents, but do not covet or idolize these achievements that focus solely on the mind. If the aroma of love and Christ's Truth and compassion are lacking, we are merely clanging gongs who may turn off people with our puffed up knowledge & erudition.

- *Being limited in fellowship* – We urge our students to include others. Faculty members need to model that as well. If faculty members are consistently talking & sitting with the same people, that subtly communicates that the students may do likewise. We discourage cliques amongst students; we need to do the same amongst faculty.

- *Being exclusive* – The upper school's having an "inner ring," or cliquish inner circles, that exclude teachers and hamstrings collegiality. As one administrator says, "We are a team." (Mrs. Laura Tucker)

- *Being too large & too working oriented* – Schools suffer if their administration is too large or factory-like. Another element that sours culture is if leadership operates only as a "working group" instead of as a leadership team who "are collectively responsible for achieving a common objective"[26] for the school. [More on this topic in Chapter 4.]

- *Being arrogant* – The upper school's looking down on the Grammar and Logic levels, and considering itself "the big boys." Again, upper schoolteachers model Christ-likeness when they honor & respect their colleagues and all levels of the Trivium. We are not a one-man or one-woman show. Build each other up; don't tear each other down. Grammar is important, Logic is important, and Rhetoric is important. Rhetoric is the crown, but there is no crown where there is no foundation beneath it.

- *Being remiss in admissions* – Admitting older, worldly students who can potentially change culture detrimentally from the inside. The admissions office is the key gatekeeper.

- *Being preferential* – Teachers' kids consistently being given the jobs of honor. Make certain to include additional children who have earned this honor. Favoritism spoils the sweet aroma in a school and stands up walls.

- *Being disloyal* – The school culture changing drastically, turning from godliness to worldliness.

- *Being sinful without full repentance* – When sin is covered up or denied or euphemized, discerning people recoil & cultivation of growth is thwarted.

---

[26] Lencioni, *The Advantage*, 21.

- *Being forgetful & unthankful* – The school stops having a school-wide celebration gala or dinner that has always sought to honor and thank God.

Sober Reflection

Individual (Administrator, Teacher, & Staff)

- Am I making time to read my Bible & pray?
- Am I walking in the Holy Spirit?
- How is my demeanor contributing to the joy and grace of this school?
    - What do I talk about most? Is it too much of this world, or more so of heaven & Christ?
    - How do I walk and talk? Is it cynical? Is it sarcastic? Does it puff up, tear down, or build up? Is it pleasing me only or my God? "Keep your heart with all vigilance, for from it flow the springs of life" (NRSV).
- Am I willing to be in a circle of just two – God and me? Is being accepted more enticing than being a person of principle? (*God is forgiving*.) Am I willing not to rationalize the serious problems I see around me?
- Am I including a variety of my fellow faculty members in fellowship?
- Do I speak professionally about all people around me (even the ones who annoy me)?

The Group (Administrators, Teachers, & Staff)

- Do we show love & compassion to all our students?
- Do we have firm boundaries regarding obedience, speech, and body language, or do we allow the students to disobey?
- Do I confront my students and even my coworkers with the truth in private in a prayerful, loving manner?
- Do I always complain whenever I am around another colleague?
- *Discussion Suggestion*: What are our idols (e.g., school growth, academic accomplishment, high testing scores, athletic achievement, eliteness)? Is Jesus at center, or are humanist markers of pride?
- Can we say that our school is "A Place to Flourish"? (Veritas School, Richmond, Virginia, website)

Getting Back on Track/Staying on Track

- Confess your sins daily to God.
- Repent of sins to God.
- Repent of sins to others you have hurt & apologize to them, naming your sin.
- With God's ever-present love and help, be a man or woman of integrity.
- Ask a trusted friend to point out your blind spots confidentially.
- Talk with & sit with faculty, parents, and students who are on the fringe. Treat them as you would like to be treated. Just like Jesus.
- As more people expressed interest in Veritas School, head of school Keith Nix said they felt that "We had to double down. A lot of nominal Christians are going to say 'Yeah, yeah' now [in agreement with our values about school culture during an interview]." The school's literature and website have been getting traction; the plan, however, is to have their new website help prospective parents self-select out when they see that the school's culture is not a matching fit for their family.
- Consider having a common lunchtime and seating your students in groups of varied ages. As the older ones help the younger ones, it promotes thinking of others and fosters relationships across the Trivium, often lasting beyond the school years. Perhaps employ a house system to encourage this heterogeneous culture.

- Model humility. Conversely, call out pomposity. Explain how it is not focusing on God nor giving Him the glory. The hardest part of this is having the courage to delicately point this out to each other as colleagues. Heads of school set the tone by asking forgiveness publicly of their faculty & staff and privately, as appropriate.
- Like head of school Keith Nix says, "build a thick, Christian community." Invite pastors, speakers, & authors to speak to your school, addressing issues to enrich or clarify your culture so that flourishing can occur.
- Similarly, try recommending a choice of three or so books to parents & then gather in discussion groups by each book to discuss them. Keep it simple. Make a start. Grow your school culture.
- *Documenting & Discussion Suggestion*: Have administrators & teachers submit 1 or 2 examples of *God's glory and faithfulness* they have witnessed this year. Assemble these examples into a one-page journal and read aloud, perhaps at mid-year and at year's end. Praise Him.

Healthy School

- The board of directors, administrators, faculty & staff are walking in the Holy Spirit. As Ravi Zacharias says, "I can love like Jesus loves only through a supernatural enablement of the Holy Spirit."[27]
- The aroma of Christ is met at the school door, in the parking lot, & in the sports fields.
- A formal prayer team of parents & grandparents meets to pray weekly for the school; informally, families are praying at home and perhaps during car rides for the administration, teachers, staff, & students.
- "Canaries in the coal mine" who detect legitimate problems & concerns are listened to. This feedback may also come in the form of surveys of the school anonymously or through individuals who approach the head of school and possibly also the board of directors.

Setting a Goal

- Pray for God's wisdom. Set one or two goals to enhance the way *you as an individual* can contribute to the culture of your school. Enter that goal in the binder or phone that goes with you everywhere.
- Pray for God's wisdom. Set one or two goals to enhance the way *you as an administration or as a faculty* can contribute to the culture of your school. Enter that goal in the binder/document that goes with you everywhere.
- Refer to this goal throughout the year.
- Reflect on this goal at year's end. Rejoice in God's grace.

Expressing a Desire

- Pray for God's wisdom. Write one or two desires for getting your school's culture better on track *that depend on others' cooperation*. Enter that desire in the binder or phone that goes with you everywhere.
- Pray about this desire throughout the year.
- Reflect on this desire at the end of each year. Rejoice in God's grace.

Encouragement

- "Trust in the Lord with all your heart and lean not on your own understanding" (Proverbs 3:5). As we lean into God and pray about the culture of our school, we can trust that He will provide.
- Pray for Christ's sweet aroma to pervade your school.
- "...[W]here the Spirit of the Lord is, there is freedom" (2 Cor. 3:17).
- "For what we proclaim is not ourselves..." (2 Cor. 3:5).

---

[27] Ravi Zacharias, "Learn How to Do Apologetics in the Twenty-First Century with Ravi Zacharias," YouTube, accessed 9/16/19, https://youtu.be/W2zrHxbucOM.

Chapter 3
Your School's Board of Directors

"Without counsel plans fail,
but with many advisers they succeed."

Proverbs 15:21

Covenant Academy head of school Leslie Collins says, "Our board has the philosophy that they have no living constituency. So they don't view themselves as representing the kids that are here today; they view themselves as being responsible to make sure that there are kids 20 years from now still at this school." She further expands that saying, "Indeed, the board needs to be future oriented and present oriented. Both are necessary for the health of an organization." As my husband David Kitchin says, "If you don't do the *now* well, there may be no *future.*"

Consultant Dr. John Schimmer, Jr., says, "In chapter 15 of John's Gospel, Christ taught His disciples about vine life. The branch is completely dependent on the vine, and the vine must have an outlet, the branch, to produce fruit. This beautiful vine-life principle helps us understand the relationship that must exist between the board and the school. Understanding that Christ is our ultimate source of wisdom and knowledge, the branch (the school) submits to the board and depends on it for wisdom, direction, and resources. The vine (the board) enjoys the fruit of its labor as the school blossoms and increases its effectiveness."[1]

As I approached this chapter, several questions guided my interviews: How do you gain objectivity as a board of directors to help keep your school on track? What specific suggestions do you have for board members to maintain or refresh their objectivity? What actions can a board take to ensure it is not becoming a club? As a board, by what means did you detect red flag issues? What are the first things to keep first?

In this chapter, we will cover a range of topics from types of boards, board member qualities, a board's function & roles, authority, leadership, building relationships, meetings, communication, handling grievances, conflict, finances, hiring, self-evaluation & evaluation of the head of school, and thorny issues, to developing a future orientation toward board succession.

MULTIPLE KINDS OF BOARDS
Some schools choose to have multiple kinds of boards, such as the Geneva School in Orlando, Florida, that has three.

- The first is the *governing board* composed of 13 members (school population: 545), and they are accountable to the state of Florida.
- The second is an *advisory board* made up of local professionals and friends who embrace the school's vision who are called upon for advice.
- The third is a *reference board* constituting speakers who embrace the school's vision and come to give talks or to help be a keynote speaker at a fundraiser or donor retreats.

---

[1] Dr. John Schimmer, "How Does A Board Enable Effectiveness?" Association of Christian Schools International, (ACSI), accessed September 5, 2019.

Your School's Board of Directors

The rest of this chapter will be devoted to the governing board, also referred to as the board of directors.

DEFINITION & DUTIES OF THE BOARD OF DIRECTORS

In a school setting, a board of directors is a group of people who *govern* the school. *Govern* includes conducting the policy, actions, and affairs of an organization. The board of directors has the "ultimate decision-making authority" in a school and is empowered to the following duties:

- operates under the vision, mission, & values of the school
- sets the school's "policy, objectives, and overall direction"
- adopts the school's Articles of Incorporation as well as Bylaws
- ensures adequate financial resources
- approves annual budget
- sets salaries, compensation, & benefits for school employees
- names members of the advisory, executive, finance, and other committees; hires, monitors, evaluates, & fires the head of school and/or other administrators
- provides an accounting to the parents for the school's performance.[2]

The following should *not* be the duties of a board of directors: determining that secondary doctrine should be taught as primary (egs., infant/believer baptism, old earth/new earth, end times interpretation) or managing the school. *[handwritten: Yes]*

[handwritten margin: ?] *[handwritten: really? who should?]*

TWO TYPES OF BOARD MEMBERS

The Board may be composed of two types of members, plus an additional, optional associate:

[handwritten: Really?]
- *Permanent* member – selected by the board. Is not voted in by the school's parents. Maintains vision and does not change it unless overwhelming consensus and clear communication to parents accompanies it. Knows corporate history – for continuity of the original vision, for maintenance of corporate history, for wisdom.
- *Elected member* – nominated and, after biographies & personal statements are submitted, is elected by the school's parents. *[handwritten: ?, Perhaps - usually by board]*
- *Consultant* (non-member; optional)

These roles should be documented with *job descriptions* in the board's governing documents. These job descriptions safeguard and protect the vision, covenants, & corporate history of the school.

- *Idea for new board member(s)*: Begin as a non-voting member, walking alongside present veteran board members for one full year before coming on board.[3]

TWO TYPES OF BOARDS

There are two types of boards regarding how they are placed in office:

1) Majority-permanent member/minority-elected member boards, or
2) Totally elected boards.

Permanent board member of the Association of Classical Christian Schools, Rob Tucker says, "A lot of schools are going to totally elected boards."[4] The cost of this totally elected model is not having corporate history and, therefore, not having the principles & foundations of a school's vision. You have to have the vision. [See Chapter 1.] The benefits of a majority-permanent member/minority-elected member board would be 1) corporate history and vision would carry forward and inform decisions, *and* 2) elections would ensure both new blood and necessary removal of ineffective board members.

---

[2] http://www.businessdictionary.com/definition/board-of-directors.html

[3] Amy Shore, ""Intentionality and the Legacy of Truth: Succession Planning Among ACCS Schools," lecture, ACCS Conference, Atlanta, Georgia, June 14, 2019.

[4] Rob Tucker, interview by Kathleen F. Kitchin, Annapolis, Maryland, September 22, 2018.

The Association of Classical Christian Schools (ACCS) is a majority permanent board, also called *visionary members*. A visionary member serves a number of years and then sits out a year on sabbatical. He or she remains on the board, but has no vote that year. After the sabbatical year, the member rejoins. The remainder of the board is *representative members*.

QUALITIES OF BOARD MEMBERS

The board of directors is at the core of the school, and therefore the qualities of each board member are of paramount importance. Firstly, the role of the board is *to love & serve Jesus Christ*. As vital as each of the following roles is, the board is not merely an assemblage of business, legal, financial, & other experts. Secondly, as ACCS permanent board member Rob Tucker says, "*Character* is number one. Do they own it? Can they talk about Classical Christian Education?" A board member needs to "love the school and want to own CCE." Tucker says, "It is not a skill set issue." Mr. Keith Nix, also a permanent member of the ACCS board, supports that view as well, saying, "There can be a struggle with or amongst board members. They come on because of their expertise, but do not have an appetite for the vision."[5] As you consider nominating board members, consider the following first things first:

- Can they articulate the vision? [See Chapter 1.]
- Do they embrace the vision? There is a striking difference between owning a vision *versus* reading minutes from a meeting.

Other qualities and qualifications could include the following:

- Fruit of the Spirit
- Wisdom
- Leadership
- Record of volunteering at the school
- Willingness to serve without compensation.

THE BOARD'S FUNCTION

According to Rob Tucker, the board's function is two-fold:

1) to paint the vision &
2) to maintain the vision.

As Tucker says of the board of directors,

> We're the captain and heading to the North Star. There will be many challenges, and two in particular. There will be hurricanes (or crises) that the board will need to handle. But there is the more dangerous, insidious challenge of tropical storms when sailors will spot an island off in the distance that has alluring gold & tropical beverages (school vouchers, proposed changes to history class for the AP Test, & so forth). It is a red flag if a board is *not* having these challenges. Is the board of character & principle to maintain the journey to the North Star?

It is critically important to have a visionary on the board. In addition, in order for a board to effectively paint the vision & maintain the vision, they cannot be completely separate from the rest of the school in an ivory tower bubble.

DISTINCTION OF ROLES

It is important to make the distinction between the roles of the board and the head of school. The board of directors is pure policymakers. The head of school is the implementer of those policies. The board *governs* the school while the head of school *manages* the school. The chairman of the board & the head of school "must be a team, publicly and privately supporting and encouraging each other. The chair is not the

---

[5] Keith Nix, interview by Kathleen F. Kitchin, Richmond, Virginia, June 5, 2019.

CEO of the school or the administrator's boss. Only the collective, single voice of the board can give directions to the administrator."[6]

AUTHORITY

Authority of the Board

Mr. Russ Gregg, head of school of Hope Academy in Minneapolis, Minnesota, says in the early stages of a school, the board may possibly have more of a managerial role and that the governance role or function may be missing at this stage. Later, however, the school develops a leadership team, a true governance seat, and withdraws from managing. The board has one employee – the head of school – and the board's challenge is to stay out of the management role. The board both encourages and supports the headmaster. When necessary, hopefully rarely, it disciplines.

Authority of the Headmaster

How much authority should a board of directors give to a headmaster? Again, boards should have only one employee: the headmaster. Boards should try to minimize overlapping roles and responsibilities in authority. If the school is large, the headmaster will need to be a manager.

Keith Nix says the headmaster is the gatekeeper between the school & the board. He says, "It is incumbent on the head of school at communicating clearly and giving the board an accurate picture. You can't hide the ball, the bad news." Nix insists, "Lead with the bad news. Don't let them hear it from somewhere else first." Nix also asserts, "The board does not just trust me that things are going well at the school. I have empirical evidence that things are indeed going well. Years of survey."

Nix continues, "The ingredients for health for the headmaster aren't a secret. The ingredients are local church authority & involvement, personal spiritual growth, having a confidant, close friends, accountability." I asked him, "Who is asking the head of school about the ingredients for health?" Keith replied, "The board, or subset of the board (like the Head Support and Evaluation Committee) should be asking." I responded by saying that this is an opportunity for great encouragement & care. Keith said, "The board has to trust what I'm telling them is true, that I am not hiding the ball."

Nix says the board should "not just take a headmaster's word that everything's roses." I told him that my concern is that we can say all kinds of things, though, and give the appearance that the reality is actually *those very roses*. Nix was nonplussed, saying, "There's a lot of different ways I can...inform board members, communicate to board members where they're not just taking my word for it. I tell other heads of school, 'That's your job as head. You have to instill that confidence by how you give them an accurate picture.' The board does not talk to any of my staff about school matters without my permission, and no parent or faculty can go to any board member about school issues or concerns. That all has to come through me. Board members are taught to say, 'The Board isn't involved in school operations. You need to talk to the appropriate person at the school.'"

Authority of the Board & the Authority of the Director of Instruction/Curriculum Committee

I asked head of school Leslie Collins about the role of the board and the curriculum leaders. One of the purposes of the board is to garner expertise when an issue is beyond their purview. For instance, Collins says she "takes issue when a board who is not educators are trying to take responsibility for the curriculum. Board determines statement of faith and what is primary & secondary doctrine. Then that is done. Board determines what our six points of outcomes are .... Then the curriculum committee took those 6 points and then developed the curriculum map or the path to achieve those 6 points. [See Chapter 1, Vision Statement Examples.]

---

[6] Schimmer, "How Does A Board Enable Effectiveness?"

LEADERSHIP IN THE BOARD

Leadership on the board emanates from Christ first. The chairman of the board of directors should *follow Christ first and seek to please Him, not man*. The chairman should not be the head of school. Conversely, the head of school should not overly influence the chairman of the board. Furthermore, the head of school should not usurp the chairman of the board's position or role. The board makes policy; the head of school manages. They are different & separate domains. Each board member also should *follow Christ first and seek to please Him, not man*. The board should pray for a spirit of unity (not necessarily uniformity, however). Each member needs to be willing to speak up. Don't just "rubber stamp" without doing the reading, the homework, and, if necessary, the research. Be a critical thinker. Consider the implications. Ask the hard questions. Dare to speak out against oversimplification, untruth, misrepresentation, & ill treatment. Board members should not automatically approve & authorize everything the head of school champions. Again, as Ronald Reagan said, "Trust but verify." God has entrusted you to be a good shepherd of the school.

Rob Tucker says there are also leaders within leaders on a board. One leader of influence can tend to be an entrepreneur. This person can experience pushback against himself or herself as a new generation wants them pushed out. There is also "founder's syndrome" in CCE circles and beyond. [Founder's syndrome will be defined in more detail later in this chapter.] In general, the founder is used to getting his way. People submit to it. On the board's side, it can be perceived that this guy always gets his way; and there then is a push for a plurality of opinions.

VISIONARY & COMMITTEE ROLES

Determine who among you is a visionary. Their role would naturally spring from their passion to preserve the vision, mission, & core values of the school. Determine if you will have committees. Would each director on the board act as a committee head (audit, benefits, finance, legal, and so forth)? Some schools do not elect to follow a committee model while others do. Key question: *Is your model effective in governing your school?*

FIRST THINGS FIRST

Keep *prayer* first to keep first things first. The goal is God's wisdom, not man's. Seek prayer support from your spouse, church, & school prayer team. To help keep your school on track, go on a *board retreat* with all of the board members once per year. Make it a budget item. It is worth it. At that retreat:

- Pray together.
- Read Scripture together.
- Get to know each other as people, not just roles, especially new board members.
- Read aloud ALL foundational documents before each school year begins. [See Chapter 1.]
- Plan your part & contribute to the overall plan and wisdom of the school.
- Set goals for the next school year. A goal is a measurable objective or aim that is within an individual's/group's scope of responsibilities & abilities.
- Write down desires for the next school year. A desire is a wish or want that requires others' cooperation.

To keep first things first and to keep your school on track, board members need to educate themselves.

- Attend ACCS conferences or SCL conferences (Society of Classical Learning). It is a worthy line-item in your school's budget. If at all possible, *new board members should go the summer before they come on the board*. Make your voting timetable accommodate that.
- Before coming on the board – At absolute minimum, it should be required that new board members read the following:
  o "The Lost Tools of Learning" by Dorothy Sayers (1947)
  o *Recovering the Lost Tools of Learning* by Douglas Wilson (1991)
  o *Repairing the Ruins: The Classical & Christian Challenge to Modern Education* by Douglas Wilson (1996)

- o *Classical Education: The Movement Sweeping America* by Gene Edward Veith, Jr., & Andrew Kern (2015)
- o Additional books:
  - *Norms & Nobility: A Treatise on Education* by David V. Hicks (1999)
  - *The Abolition of Man* by C.S. Lewis (1943)

At least three of my interviewees said that boards can get to be "messes." The board continually needs to ask God to work through them. God needs to be at the helm, not man. Prayer first. Avoid allowing business to steal first place.

BUILDING RELATIONSHIPS

An extension of the annual retreat or off-site meeting in the summer is building relationships throughout the school year.

Relationship with Each Other (board member to board member)

- Truth & commitment to Christ trumps all.
- You are a team united by Christ, for Christ, through Christ to govern the school & maintain the vision He has given to your school.
- Don't be intimidated by each other's degrees or other professional titles.
- If you don't get the vote for a matter, let it go. Move on in Christian love.

Relationship with Headmaster

- Christ-honoring
- Friendly
- *Question for board & head of school*: How to balance professional distance & friendship?
- *Question for board*: How to detect dictatorship?

Rev. Robert Ingram of the Geneva School says he has

> outstanding relationships with every member of the board. The Board turns to me and they say, "We assume you have this." Trust is the currency. Through 27 years now we have found that the currency of trust is the gold standard. In addition to that, of course, there is a very healthy belief in the Providence of God. We have some strong notions about the character of God & His sovereign administration over things. We love what we do, & so we try to act boldly and trust that God is going to honor and bless. Our school song is the *Non nobis*. "Not unto us, Lord, but unto Thy name be glory." So we don't get in the way of that & rob Him of His glory. I love John Piper's ministry and books. He is famous for saying "God acts to gain glory for Himself." It is right and appropriate for Him to do that. So I want to say, "God, come here and gain much glory."[7]

Relationship with Faculty

- *A most valuable role of the board* is being vision-casters who help teachers see over the edge of the trenches, perhaps at the Christmas party & at the celebration dinner when you gather to praise God for all that He has done in & for your school. Come speak to the teachers at one faculty meeting, perhaps mid-year or toward the end of the year when a boost is most welcome & needed.
- Seek teacher input anonymously & confidentially through the head of school. [Developed in Chapter 4.]
- If a teacher declines to renew a contract, there can be an exit interview with just the headmaster, & another one with just the board.

---

[7] Rev. Robert Ingram, interview by Kathleen F. Kitchin, Orlando, Florida, February 21, 2019.

Relationship with Parents

- Be known. Oftentimes parents in a school do not know who their board members are.
  - *Suggestions for the school*:
    - In first school newsletter each year, post board members' names with a photo of each.
    - On your website, post board members' names & photos, and possibly include a taped introduction & interview with them.
    - Introduce board members at Back to School Night each year in person or by video clip.
  - *Suggestions for the board*:
    - Talk with parents in the parking lot, at academic events, at sports games.

Make a point to get to know the children. Greet them. *Ask how their day or year is going.*

BOARD MEETINGS
The following stipulations for board meetings should be in the school's Articles of Incorporation & Bylaws:

- Attendance requirement (with the number of missed meetings allowed before consideration of replacing a board member)
- Mandatory attendance at strategic planning meetings

Stay on track in the following fashion:

- Meet at least once per month for optimal effectiveness.
- Follow *Robert's Rules of Order*. Quick reference sheets are available online.
- Start on time.
- End meetings at a reasonable time. Most board members have work the next day. Be friendly, but avoid becoming a social club. One red flag might be – w*hich came first, the Board or the club?* Resist peer pressure. Don't become one of the "good ol' boys."
- Pray before each meeting, asking the Lord for His will, His way.
- Listen to each other. With godly counsel and many advisers, God says plans will succeed.
- *Advocacy*: State your case or your point.[8]
- *Inquiry*: Ask questions & seek clarity after others state their case or their point. Limit board size between 3 & 9 to allow for this inquiry.[9]
- When switching hats, identify which hat you are wearing (e.g., "I am speaking as a parent vs. I am speaking as a lawyer).
- Be prepared with homework from your specialty (theological, financial, legal, etc.)
- Note action items to follow up on for next month's meeting. Enter them into your phone/planner.
- Read the previous meeting's minutes prior to the next meeting.

Issues to consider: When warranted, should time be allotted for meetings of just the board, minus administrators, for example, regarding administrator salaries or job performance & evaluation? What are the parameters for recusal and for board-only meetings?

There are *three types of votes* at board meetings:

- A. Unanimous = 100%
- B. Supermajority = 67% or 75%
- C. Majority = 51%

---

[8] Patrick Lencioni, *The Advantage: Why Organizational Health Trumps Everything Else in Business* (San Francisco: Jossey-Bass, 2012), 22.
[9] Ibid., 22.

The higher the importance of the issue, the more likely a unanimous or supermajority vote will be the vote of choice. Rob Tucker says the critical question that rivets all these types of votes is "Do you trust God to work through A, B, and C types of votes?" Additionally, it is a red flag if there is majority rule only, not unanimity, for *all* issues, including issues of great import.

COMMUNICATION

Communication needs to flow both downwards AND upwards. Communication needs to flow from the board to the head of school & the head of school to the school AND from the school to the head of school & from the head of school to the board. If your school community does not see the board of directors, for example at a back-to-school night or on your website with a photograph of each, it can appear to parents that the board of directors works in isolation with little acquaintance or accessibility. Communicate the vision. Communicate major progress. Communicate major changes. Communicate how problems are being handled. One of the saddest phrases one may possibly hear regarding a board of directors is "Oh, don't go to them. They'll do nothing." As a board leans into Jesus and follows Him, they can know that He who has called them will equip them to do this great service to the school in His way, in His manner, in His love.

When I asked Rev. Robert Ingram, headmaster of The Geneva School in Orlando, Florida, when there are questions or concerns about the internal life of the school, what is the board's recourse? He responded, "The only place they can go is to me. They can't go directly to my faculty or staff. The board chair speaks to me in that *hourglass configuration*. The communication is between the board chair and me. I speak with them through the board chair & they speak to the school through me. There are excellent models of good non-profit governance for a board to follow, and it is imperative that the board and school honor each other's appropriate sphere of authority."

HANDLING GRIEVANCES

From time to time, grievances will arise that do reach the board level. To keep your school on track, keep a formal written record of grievances brought before the board. This could be the role of the secretary who could keep a log of the full date, name of who comes, the nature of their concern, & actionables with dates completed. If there is a chronic complainer, try to discern that from the truly concerned. Over time, you may see patterns. Most people are busy and tired. To go visit or write the board requires extra effort. If diligent, caring people are coming to you and there is a trend, it behooves you to take their concerns seriously. Every school has problems. Be a board that is attentive, not dismissive. Be a board that prays and operates from Holy Spirit power, not human-flesh solutions. Do not take only the head of school's word about an issue either. It could be that the permanent board members have a longer history with the head of school and more history and discernment if the head master is veering away from the vision, mission, & core values of your school; on the other hand, it may be that these longer-term board members have become inured to the headmaster's charisma. Again, do your own thinking for your vote on this issue. Do not relinquish your God-given decision-making to someone else out of convenience. Communications to the board should be sent to the headmaster. He or she is the neck of the hourglass. Sterling character is of utmost importance.

The grievance policy of a school should work up the chain of authority through proper channels that eventually percolates up to the headmaster. The primary principle is Matthew 18:15-17. In the spirit of this verse, we should handle sins/grievances in the following manner:

- Step One: Individual to individual
  - If they listen & you resolve the issue together, it is over.
  - If not, proceed to Step Two.
- Step Two: Bring one or two witnesses.
  - Talk the issue over again with the person but this time with the witnesses' additional corroborating stories.
  - If they listen & you resolve the matter together, it is over.
  - If not, proceed to Step Three.
- Step Three: Take it to the headmaster.
  - If the issue is resolved at this step, it is over.

- If not & you believe it is warranted (something that has legal or other ramifications), move to Step Four.
- Step Four: Take it to the board of directors.
  - If the issue is resolved at this level, it is over.
  - If not, you either live with the situation or leave the school in a peaceful manner, as far as it is up to you.

If there is a chronic issue, which tracking would reveal, a plurality of leaders needs to scrutinize these grievances. The decision the board makes may of necessity lead to new policy.

TRAFFIC MANAGEMENT OF GRIEVANCES

To keep first things first, the school itself must consistently model & adhere to the following pattern of traffic management of grievances:

- *Problem between parent & teacher?* Parent should approach the teacher, not the head of school.
- *Problem between parent & parent?* Head of school and the board should direct the conflict or concern to be handled between the parents without school interference.
- *Problem between teacher & teacher?* Teachers should handle this between themselves.
- *Problem between administrator & teacher, or teacher & administrator?* The two parties should handle this.
- *Problem about rules?* See the headmaster.
- *Problem about policy?* Contact the board through proper channels.

The challenge here is to ascertain who should be talking with whom, stating that, & then standing firm on that.

DEALING WITH CONFLICT WITHIN THE BOARD

In the course of interviewing headmasters and board members for this book, it became apparent that schools have encountered difficulties that were absolute turning points for the school. Sometimes it involves board members who have two different visions, a split results, with the board's becoming somewhat unsteady on its feet, but continues forward with the original vision intact. Other times, it involves feedback from an accrediting institution that says something needs to change.

In one instance, a school was told its board was micromanaging the school, yet the school was over a decade old, not a young school still needing such oversight. The board followed the accreditor's counsel and changed from being a managing board to being a policy, or governing, board. As a result, two board members resigned, yet did so in good grace with all involved. Yet other instances occur when original members of the board want matters to go only their way, but the parents actually want the course of the school to move in quite a different direction and move to hire another headmaster. These hurdles can be difficult, but can be peaceful, providing the parties involved handle it with godly virtue. These hurdles can also be fraught with great pain, sacrifice, and battle. They are not for the faint of heart.

INTERFACE BETWEEN BOARD & SCHOOL

Create a word picture of how your board maintains its independence and objectivity distinct from the headmaster, the faculty/staff, & parents? Is it an hourglass configuration, like at the Geneva School? Conversely, what policies need to be in place in order to hear, decide, and act upon legitimate inputs from headmaster, the faculty/staff, & parents?

FINANCES

Regarding the pressures of meeting the budget, Dr. Pamela McKee, head of school of Bayshore Christian School in Fairhope, Alabama, says, "Your budget should be based on what your teacher/student ratio is. How many students will pay a teacher? For her school she says, we can pay a teacher's salary, buy curriculum, buy the furniture for a classroom if we have 8 students. Eight students times the tuition will cover the cost of that."[10]

In determining whether to add a third 7th-grade classroom, Dr. McKee looked at their waiting list, had it confirmed by the admissions director's phone calls to those parents. Then Dr. McKee informed her board that the new group could pay the cost of a teacher's salary and the school building had one extra classroom, so it covered the cost. She asked her board, "Do you want me to go ahead and accept & open a third 7th grade? Will you approve that? They said 'Yes.' [Snap of the fingers.] Done. We had to know what would pay a teacher's salary and the overall cost. We have done a *cost analysis on every grade*. We know the cost of educating a child in our school. So if a head of school will spend time on that cost analysis to know exactly to the dollar how much it will cost to have students in this classroom, then you know what your threshold is. The same way with our budget."

Dr. McKee says their school budgets on tuition dollars. "We take what we are going to be bringing in and we work within those confines. That's our general operating expenses. Everything else is icing on the cake." As an example of that icing, every year Dr. McKee has given raises. Every year there is a 3-5% raise to cover cost of living. "If we get more students in after that, then that's icing." She has also started a teacher awards program.

> We have a teacher luncheon. I give out awards to teachers who have done outstanding jobs and it comes with a monetary bonus because we had some extra money come in. You look for ways to bless your teachers. I may not have the money next year, but I have it this year and so I want to bless them. After a couple of years of giving awards, I put my teacher awards in my budget so I am giving awards out every year. So, some of those things begin as programs that you're just kind of testing the waters on, and then you see the benefits that you're reaping from blessing your teachers and the improvement overall, you raise the bar like you recognize your top student on awards day, the valedictorian/salutatorian, you have all these other kids that are like "I want to be that, too." So they work harder. Our teachers are human. They are the same way. If you have teacher of the year, "Oh, maybe next year I can be 'Teacher of the Year.'" So everyone rises and improves. It's not competitive in any kind of snarky, jealous kind of way. It's acknowledging true achievement & professionalism. And the teachers want to be that. With extra money, try to find ways to bless your teachers.

[handwritten margin note: Wishful thinking?]

For the ACCS Conference, Dr. McKee's school pays for food (gives cash to each teacher to buy their meals) and transportation (either rent a bus/pay gas money). Bayshore Christian also hires speakers to come in-house.

In the teachers' contract, there are 3 paid professional development days at Bayshore Christian School. During those three days, a teacher could 1) visit another CCE school, or 2) attend a specialty conference. If a teacher chooses to study at a local university, the school works toward some level of tuition reimbursement.

Both headmasters Keith Nix and Pamela McKee insisted that schools "pay teachers a living wage." Dr. McKee has created a 20-year pay scale for her school and they try to match the public school pay scale. They are not there yet, but they "try every year to get it closer & closer to public school pay. They are now at 75% of public school pay. We pay their insurance. We give little bonuses. I used to take all my teachers to the beach for a weekend. She tries to have fellowship time once in the fall and another time in the spring. Maybe it's meeting at a Mexican restaurant on a Friday night. She says, "You look for those ways to create relationships. To get to know them personally. Ask the teacher whose son went off to college, 'How are you doing with that?'" Dr. McKee sums it up well: "Just getting to know & love on them."

---

[10] Dr. Pamela McKee, interview by Kathleen F. Kitchin, ACCS Conference, Atlanta, Georgia, June 13, 2019.

There should be transparency about your school's finances with the exception of salaries. Minutes of the meetings as well as the annual report of finances & loans (with salaries deleted) should be printed out & bound in a binder that is stored in the school office. The location of access to should be made clear to parents. Specific counsel on finances includes the following:

- *Again, to stay on track, at minimum, tuition fees have to cover the school's operating expenses.* The board should maintain the school on a balanced budget. Donations should never be used for operating expenses; instead, donations should go toward capital improvements, guest lecturers, & special events. Fight against being held captive financially by anyone.
- The board will also want to establish an emergency fund for a specified number of months' worth of the operating budget.
- Issue a monthly financial report as well as a quarterly balance sheet for each member of the board & head of school.
- Some schools pay teachers the same amount for the number of years' experience. Others pay in an unequal allocation. Some schools make their salary schedule public. Others do not.
- An independent organization should handle the school's audits.

CLASS SIZE & MEETING BUDGET
Class size can be a sticky wicket. On the one hand, the school needs enough students to keep its doors open. On the other hand, having classes that are too large can cause your school to go off track in a number of ways: diluting the fine nature of classical Christian education, overburdening teachers, reducing the time for character-building conversations. Dr. Pamela McKee, head of school at Bayshore Christian School in Fairhope, Alabama, says class size is a board decision. She says,

> The student maximum/class should be stated in your strategic plan for your school. Bayshore Christian School's max is 18. The board should put the cap on class size. The board should be informed by the head of school as to what the teacher/student ratio cap should be *for quality education to occur in a classical classroom*. The head of school can inform the board, but the board votes then and says, "This is what our school will be" and that just gives me a reason to cap a class, that gives me the authority to turn a family away or put them on a waiting list because we are full. Therefore, I give my admissions director that directive that we can only have 18 per class. They do the talking with the parents and say, "We're full for next year, but we would be happy to put you on the waiting list should anything open up." It's an organizational system then that you have clear directives and everyone is in agreement on. So a board member is not going to be surprised with an "Oh, we have 23 in a class? Well, that shouldn't happen." If everyone is clear from the beginning, this is our strategic plan: we are going to grow our school & this is how we are going to grow it. Once we get to 18 per class, that's it. Then everyone can do their jobs. Again, it's a *trickle-down effect*.

Dr. McKee suggests a maximum number, but the board makes the final decision.

HIRING
Hope Academy's Mr. Russ Gregg says their school's four core values "guide them in recruiting, hiring, & firing staff." Likewise, ascertain whether your potential candidates agree with your vision, mission, & core values by means of their words, résumé, application, character, countenance, & attitude. Look for consistency between their in-person vs. social media presence. Boards need to be careful to hire a Christian headmaster and teachers who have head & heart for God, who are not wolves in sheep's clothing, and therefore a team, not an individual, should hire to ensure discernment in this process. The board should hire the headmaster. The board, not the headmaster alone, should hire the teachers & staff. Many counselors are making these critically important decisions. God protects the school, and it may be one person's dissent that makes all the difference.

Hiring a Headmaster

The headmaster is the *nexus*, or central & most important point or place, deriving from the Latin *nex*, meaning "a binding together." Through him or her, all things connect or are bound; therefore, *interviewing carefully & hiring carefully are of the utmost importance as all roads lead to this person.* The following are steps in hiring a head of school:

1) Prayer – Ask the Lord for discernment when hiring the head of school.
2) Qualifications
   a. *Christian love*
      i. *Christ* – Love Christ & be a Christ-follower, infused with His truth, grace, & wisdom.
      ii. *Kids* – Love children.
      iii. *Content* – Love learning.
   b. *Competence* – Know both how to run a school *and* how to maintain vision.
   c. *Character* – Boards should follow up with the candidate's references, references' references, & prior employers & schools. If possible, meet the candidate's spouse/family as well. Choose the people yourself that you wish to interview and "trust but verify," to use President Ronald Reagan's motto. Phone calls to a wide variety of people associated with the candidate's former school(s) are critically important: chairman of the board, board members, fellow administrators, & faculty/staff. Again, call references and references' references.
   d. Former school board member Rob Tucker adds further qualifications:
      i. "The headmaster should not be a 'kid' – grey hairs and wisdom."
      ii. There will be maturity over time.
      iii. Skill set
         1. Young school?
         2. Large school – need an administrator.

Keith Nix says, "The board must be uncompromising on the head of school & classical Christian education." When considering a candidate for head of school, assess the following:

- How does one sense if a prospective administrator is godly & professional? Veteran administrator and school adjuster Mr. Steven Sheets says, "Ask the...interviewee why she left her former job."[11]
- What are red flags for hiring an administrator? Steve Sheets says, "You could tell the way they answer questions who had a heart for children, by their intonation, and detail." A high Emotional Quotient (EQ) is essential for board members.
- Does the candidate have prior experience managing a school of your size?
- Which of the two models of headmastership do you need?
  o A less-experienced head of school may require more of a hands-on approach by the board, or
  o A more-experienced head of school or executive may be given more latitude.
- I would suggest one step further: *If at all possible, visit the school the head worked at prior to their applying for the position at your school.* Interview board members, fellow administrators, teachers, staff, parents, bookkeeper, and janitors. Spend time in the cafeteria, in the parking lot afterschool, and, if possible, at a sports event. Such a visit is well worth the transportation costs: it gives a window into the "aroma" of their former school, it further corroborates their interview answers, and it may surface issues that did not arise in the interview. (Interviewees always put their best face forward.)

Hiring Faculty & Staff

The board also needs to be sharp about selecting faculty & staff. Have the entire board present when interviewing job candidates. Qualifications should include love of Christ, kids, & content (their subject matter). Competence. Character. Would you want this person to teach your own child? Follow up with references' references. Choose

---

[11] Steven Sheets, interview by Kathleen F. Kitchin, Greenville, North Carolina, September 5, 2018.

the people yourself that you wish to interview. Again, "Trust but verify." It is a red flag to hear that the school's board does not interview the teacher candidates. The board cannot trust just the interview, but again as the Bible instructs, "Without counsel plans fail, but with many advisers they succeed" (Proverbs 15:21). Interviews need a plurality of questioners/observers. There are also questions asked that are truly asking about other things. For more information on interview questions, see tablegroup.com[12] and ascd.org.[13]

Dr. Pamela McKee says, she looks for three things in teachers. Do they

1) Love the Lord – It is an overflow of their heart. They're talking about Jesus on a daily basis; they can't not talk about Him.
2) Love children.
3) Love learning – They themselves are lifelong learners. They love their subject more than anything in the world. How can I teach this the best or to the students' greatest advantage? They're wanting to transfer their love to the students. So, they are eager for processes; they're eager for that organizational way of doing it best."

Gino Wickman and Mark C. Winters' *Rocket Fuel* presents a masterful interviewer of a prospective candidate:[14]

1) How well do they fit with your Core Values? (They have to be a 100% cultural fit.)
2) How well do they align with your passion and purpose?
3) How well do they match with the roles and responsibilities you've identified for their seat in the accountability chart? Are you convinced that they *get* the role, truly *want* the role, and have the *capacity* to excel in the role?
   - "Ask behavioral questions along these lines to get them talking. Describe your Core Values with passion, paint a vivid picture of your culture.... Listen to their stories. Probe for details and other examples. Take enough time to get comfortable with your assessment. Understand what they really want – and where their passions lie."[15]

EVALUATION OF A HEAD OF SCHOOL

How is an evaluation executed for a head of school? At minimum, there should be the following:

- Anonymous, online surveys
- In-school observations
- Written evaluations
- Archived evaluations in personnel files

Some schools do anonymous, online surveys, often through Survey Monkey. For example, one school says, "The board does not have a boiler plate HOS [Head of School] annual evaluation (given the recommended best practice to create an annual HOS agenda with 4-6 strategic objectives for the year and 5-10 operational goals). Once this 'agenda' is created, a sub-committee of the board called the Head Support and Evaluation Committee (HSEC) meets with me quarterly to review progress – making the end of year evaluation and review process very straightforward. The committee also reviews results from the HOS 16 characteristics, as well as three other surveys we do annually (w/ student, faculty, parents)."[16]

---

[12] www.tablegroup.com – Interview questions > Products & tools > Organizational health > Scroll down to Free Tools & Resources > Discipline 4: Reinforce Clarity > Human Systems Tools: Overview, Establish a Core Values Hiring Process, & Sample Core Values Hiring Profile.

[13] http://www.ascd.org/publications/books/102047/chapters/The-Hiring-Interview.aspx.

[14] Gino Wickman and Mark C. Winters. *Rocket Fuel: The One Essential Combination that will Get You More of What You Want from Your Business* (Dallas: BenBella Books, Inc., 2016), 124.

[15] Ibid., 124.

[16] Keith Nix, interview.

Your School's Board of Directors

Some schools do interviews and then compose a written evaluation of the head of school. One school's HSEC met with each member of the head of school's leadership team for approximately 30 minutes. The HSEC's interviews with the leadership team encompassed an entire morning, and in each interview they asked the following "open-ended" questions:

1) What are the Head of School's strengths?
2) What are areas where Head of School can improve?
3) How do you view Head of School's administrative style and ability?
4) How do you view the Head of School's communication and leadership style and ability?
5) Anything else you'd like to share?

From there, the answers from the leadership team were added to other data points which all informed a 3½-page written narrative clustered around these questions, other areas, & summarized in topic areas. The scale was as follows:

- 4 – Excellent
- 3 – Above Average
- 2 – Average, but room for improvement
- 1 – Needs Improvement

The written narrative was outlined as follows:

- Overall evaluation
- School Culture evaluation: Is the Head of School helping create a school culture of God-centered instruction for both staff and students, with Christ at the center?
- Are students learning well from an academic perspective?
- Is the school recruiting, attracting, and retaining students from the target demographic?
- Are new students and families interested in the school?
- Is the Head of School wisely overseeing the use of the limited resources to create an environment for excellent God-centered learning?
- Is the Head of School supporting, encouraging, and holding accountable his leadership team?

Following the board's written answers to each question in the above outline, there was a section for ongoing improvement, by type of area.

After this ongoing improvement section, there was a "Presentation & Discussion" section with the plans to meet and go over this evaluation with the head of school and the month goal for that.

The final section was entitled "Areas for Possible Improvement/Discussion" that had a paragraph for each of those areas.

Still other schools may choose to do a "360-degree" evaluation that would include feedback from the following:

- the board of directors
- fellow administrators
- parents
- teachers
- staff
- students

The board should go over this evaluation, including results from anonymously processed surveys, in person, orally, with the head of school, just as the head of school or other administrator would go over a teacher or staff member's evaluation. Key elements to include would be the following:

- opening prayer
- oral review of the written evaluation
- oral review of the anonymous feedback surveys
- a time for questions & answers for both the head of school & for the board
- discussion of a 2-3 goals to set for the next year for growth
- closing prayer.

SAMPLES OF WRITTEN HEAD OF SCHOOL EVALUATION

- "Overall, our evaluation of your job performance as head of school is that you are doing an excellent job. We and your direct reports believe you are an exceptional head of school and are uniquely gifted to champion and lead the work of --- School. You have surrounded yourself with a gifted group of key leaders who trust you and enjoy working with and for you. They admire your spiritual maturity, your heart of a shepherd, your big picture vision, your gifts at dissecting issues, and your contagious joy in serving God in the work of the school. There are three items for discussion at the bottom of this evaluation, but overall, we continue to be so grateful to God for you and your leadership of this school."
- "It is very clear that your leadership team members feel spiritually and professional supported and cared for by you. They acknowledge you are a 'big picture guy,' and note your continued awareness of your gifts and areas of limitation. Each of your team members brings great leadership skills, and they seem to all have learned how to work well with you. They each admire your humble servant leadership in working together, they note you are 'open to criticism,' 'very gracious' and they appreciate your 'deep care for the heart and vision of the school.' They also appreciate your 'joyous and joyful' attitude toward the work, and how the...has created an effectiveness and efficiency in the leadership team that has helped you all create an environment of mutual accountability. In short, they report that your posture of support, joy, and passion helps make the challenging work of the school a joy for the rest of the leadership team. Statements like 'I know he's got my back' indicate this deep team approach."
- "This doesn't seem like a critical issue, and could simply be a product of a growing school, larger staff, but it was noted a couple of times that newer staff note a feeling that they don't know you, or don't know how to approach you. Obviously you can't be friends or a shepherd to all of the staff, but it might be good to get insight from your leadership team on creative and time-efficient ways that staff can feel like they get to know you better personally; even during new staff orientation."

My suggestion is that a combination of anonymous online surveys coupled with a formal written evaluation of the head of school is highly valuable in helping a school keep first things first with their headmaster & with keeping their school on track. Yearly, glance through these annual evaluations to ensure staying on course & to track trends.

THORNY ISSUES

There are several thorny issues that can de-rail your school. The first thorny issue is *growth*: to grow or not to grow? To build or not to build? Some schools are growing & building as money allows. Other schools are growing & going into significant debt to build and going beyond tuition dollars, relying on sizable donations. Still other schools are choosing to remain within their walls and reach capacity, but no more. The first-things-first question is "Will growth alter our vision, mission, & values?" The red flag is the reason behind the growth. We need to be clear about that. If we can grow in a truly God-honoring fashion, the growth will be blessed. We must caution, however, against gaining the world and losing our soul.

The second thorny issue is *promoting* your school. In promoting your school, emphasize Christ more, and "what a great school your child can attend" less. The question with marketing is to ask, "How does God want our school to market itself?" By word of mouth only? By posters at students' churches? By the web or social media? What will radio & television advertising yield in the final analysis? Headmaster Keith Nix says, "You fill the school with families one time. They will populate the school, and then parents will tell their friends."

The third thorny issue is *Founder's Syndrome*. I hesitate to quote Wikipedia, but they defined founder's syndrome well:

> A founder is the person who establishes an institution or settlement. In many cases, a board member(s) and/or administrator(s) may also be founders. This situation often produces exciting charisma, vision, creativity, and leadership in the beginning, but may present challenges in the future including thwarting productive growth & success, and occasionally complete derailment of an organization, depending on how they handle it. Founder's syndrome is a "popular term for a difficulty faced by organizations where one or more founders maintain disproportionate power and influence." There can be the sense that the founder "always gets her [his] own way." Characteristics may include the following:

- The founder may make decisions without significant input from others, and often in crisis mode with minimal forward planning.
- Staff meetings exist to reinforce the founder, not necessarily to lead the mission, develop strategies, or produce staff development.
- Infrastructure can be lacking and what little is there is not utilized effectively or correctly.
- Staff & board members are often selected by the founder and are friends who are chosen for their personally loyalty rather than their "skills, organizational fit, or experience."
- New administrators may be recruited to "resolve difficulties," but discover that they are not able to "contribute in an effective and professional" way.
- The founder begins to believe [his]/her own press/[public relations].
- The founder begins to become "increasingly paranoid as delegation is required or business management needs are greater than their training or experience."
- Anyone who "challenges this cycle will be treated as a disruptive influence and will be ignored, ridiculed, or removed."
- The work environment grows increasingly oppressive as trust decreases.
- The organization becomes increasingly reactive, rather than proactive.
- Alternatively, the founder or the board may recognize the issue and take effective action to move beyond it.
- Effective action includes
  - Discussion of the problem,
  - A plan of action, and
  - Interventions by the founder, the board, and/or by others involved in the organization.
  - "The objective of the goal would be to allow the organization to make a successful transition to a mature organizational model without damage to either the organization itself or the individuals concerned."

The person exhibiting founder's syndrome may also be someone who actually is not the founder, but thinks he or she is. These are behaviors to be aware of in your school so that you can take the effective action suggested and keep your school on track. It is important to recognize these thorny issues, identify them, & handle these red flags.

Regarding the final thorny issue, I asked Mr. Russ Gregg of Hope Academy if there were also a teacher feed-in to the board or if there were a member of the board who has an *education background*? He responded that a head of school needs to "be faithful to represent the concerns of people when necessary. We've found that people need to be clear about what their role is and to stay in their lane. Inevitably we will get out of our lane, and we will need to discipline ourselves, & repent of getting out of that role. If a board member has some concerns about something, they need to raise that with the head of school and not end-run that and the same the other way around. My sense is that in almost every case where people feel that their voice matters, then they don't fight over the vote." As Patrick Lencioni says in *The Five Dysfunctions of a Team*, the key fundamental is *trust*.[17]

Regarding board member composition, there are differing views. All agree that there need to be different areas of expertise on the board that could include financial, business, legal, theological, and other experts. This is essential.

When asked how valuable it might be to have at least one educator, who is independent of the school on the board, reactions varied. Most interviewees said an educator was not necessary on a board. Two interviewees said there should be at least one and, in fact, one person said they were presently bringing another educator on board. That same person also pointed out that they could not have a board of all educators as it is necessary for their board to have community leaders who are networked into the community via legal, financial, and business backgrounds. As one person implied, if an educator were to be on a board, he or she would need to be a person who would "not get in the weeds" of the school; in other words, one who could truly govern and clearly step away from managing. If no board members have ever taught, I believe it could enhance their understanding to add one member who was a former teacher, a window to the reality of the day-to-day, on-the-ground experience. Someone in addition to the head of school. All teachers I interviewed wished there would be an educator on their school's board.

SUCCESSION PLANNING

We now turn to our last topic, one of utmost concern but easily postponed – *succession planning*. What might passing the baton look like for your school? As your head of school reaches the autumn stages of life, who will be your next head of school? A non-existent succession plan can breed disaster. Sometimes whatever change comes next can involve what Dr. George Grant says is "a total flip in policy. This is where our schools blow up. There's a coup d'état, or we lose that central dynamic figure and now all of the parties are vying for the throne. So we've got to have real clear planning, not because we want our institutions to be eternal, but because we want our institutions to be eternally minded."[18] I asked Dr. Grant, "So who should be doing succession planning? The board?" and he responded, "I think that invariably it's the strongest visionary in the institution that has to do the catalyzing for succession planning. That person can't do the succession planning. The board has to do the succession planning. The faculty, everybody has to be on board with the succession planning. But if the chief visionary doesn't lead the way, it won't happen." Who is your Joshua or Elisha? Pray for God's wisdom. Should you be training that person to be your successor? [See "Appendix" for further study.]

With many advisors, God says our plans will succeed. Pray for God's wisdom, choose godly counselors, & then help them keep first things first so that they can help keep your school on track.

CASE STUDY

Geneva School – Orlando, Florida – 545 students

During re-accreditation in year #11 of their school, Florida Council of Independent Schools (FCIS) told head of school Rev. Robert Ingram: "Your board is not following proper protocol. They are intrusive. They are not just heads in, but hands on." Rev. Ingram knew he was guilty of having been a part of that because he had led that board for most of its first 10 years before stepping down to become headmaster. He said, "Boards at young schools almost always violate non-profit good governance because you don't have the administrative structure or financial wherewithal to build out the team and so the board is all hands on deck." As headmaster, he was now on the receiving end of it and did not care for it. "These people were all my friends. I had been their pastor a year or so before." FCIS told him: "You are no longer a young, developing school. You're in your eleventh year. This has to come to a screeching halt." Rev. Ingram admitted to me that he had been "Starting to bump heads with the board and they were very dear friends of mine."

---

[17] Patrick Lencioni, *The Five Dysfunctions of a Team: A Leadership Fable* (San Francisco: Jossey-Bass, 2002), 195.

[18] Dr. George Grant, interview by Kathleen F. Kitchin, ACCS Conference, Atlanta, Georgia, June 13, 2019.

FCIS called in the board chair. There was a conversation. The board chair understood. FCIS firmly stated that the "School won't be re-accredited until we see in your minutes this, this, and this change. Then we'll re-interview the headmaster to make sure the changes have taken place. We will hold up your re-accreditation because everything else looks good until such time as we see the fundamental change that the board becomes a policy board and safeguarding vision/mission/values and get their hands out of the administrative duties."

At the next board meeting, the chairman brought it up, and a motion was entertained. The board voted. "That was 16 years ago. There's never been an intrusion problem since."

Rev. Ingram said the board listened. They made immediate changes. There was not even a discussion of the motion. Rev. Ingram said, "I didn't know if I was going to have a job at the end of that board meeting because there were several board members who were agitated beyond measure over it." Fundamentally, however, they understood *a board has to speak with one voice*. Rev. Ingram said, "They had the good grace not to make an issue of it. Two immediately resigned at the end of that meeting. It has been a peaceable kingdom ever since. To their credit they didn't slam the door. They didn't undermine the school with parking lot conversations and slanderous conversations. They had the Christian good grace to say, 'You know what? We maybe disagree significantly, but we're not going to make this an issue that threatens the life of the school.'" The headmaster is still friends with them today.

Red Flags

- The head of school as sole gatekeeper between the board and all others uses that for his or her own *personal* agenda.
- On the other hand, the board relies mostly or even solely on the head of school for status of school operations and health instead of doing their own research and observation.
- Hiring practices do not carefully search a prospective employee's social media presence or investigate references from their former place of employment via extensive phone calls & perhaps visits.
- Vision, mission, & core values are not read at minimum once per year before each school year begins. There is no integration of these foundational statements in curriculum & lesson plans & daily conversation.
- Spouses and/or family members are on the board. Avoid all appearances of nepotism.
- One head of school: "Nor do you want them to get most of their information through their kids if their kids are at the school. They have to get their information from the head of the school."
- The board does not seek anonymous surveys from teachers.
- The board seeks CONFIDENTIAL written feedback/surveys from teachers that in fact are not viewed by board eyes only. Use disinterested third-party survey platforms.
- There is no ombudsman. [See "Sober Reflection: The Board as a Whole," below.]
- Fixation on needing property/location for expanding school sacrifices maintaining the vision, mission, & values.
- The board does not make the school affordable.
- The board does not ensure teachers receive a living wage.
- Finances reveal attempts to curry favor with donors.
- Chronic, legitimate concerns from teachers and parents are heard, but not addressed.
- The board lacks an understanding of CCE.
- Board members or even heads of school are not moving toward being steeped in classical Christian education.
- The board is not reading CCE books.
- Board members do not seek to enrich their education in reading about classical Christian education and in reading the classics themselves.
- The board is not connected to the larger CCE community.
- Board members do not attend a classical Christian education conference periodically, especially before coming onto a board of directors.
- Not finding how you can send your staff to conferences, even if it is just a small number per year.

- Becoming a little club of power people.
- Competency red flag: The board at one school was perceived as being "people with a lot of money, not necessarily vision."
- *Yellow flag*: There is no written evaluation of the head of school by the board.
- *Yellow flag*: There is no member on the board who has been a teacher at this level.

Trends

- Are board members resigning in close succession over a number of years?
- Are board members in fact being run out?
- Are multiple teachers leaving each year?
- Are multiple parents leaving each year?
- Keep track of these numbers in each category year by year in a spreadsheet that is reviewed at least annually.

Sober Reflection

Individual Board Member

- Am I making time to read my Bible & pray?
- Am I speaking kindly of my fellow board members, administration, teachers, staff, parents, and students in our school community?
- Am I asking God for a guard on my mouth so that I share what should be shared and do not share what should not be shared? Is there a "need to know"?
- Am I operating as a board member in my own strength, or am I relying on the empowerment of the Holy Spirit?
- Do I have courage and persuasiveness with that courage to defend why I voted the way I did in any given instance?
- Do I have founder's syndrome?
- Am I asking God for the ability to build up & encourage the school and its people, as well as for the courage to confront in a loving manner what is unbiblical?

The Board as a Whole

- Is our school surrounded & bathed in prayer?
- Regarding the aroma of a board, there are tell tales signs of red flags:
  o Is there a superleader vs. a plurality of leaders?
  o Are we seeking the wisdom of many counselors?
  o Is there graciousness?
  o Is there order? Is *Robert's Rules of Order* utilized in meetings?
  o If a board member loses the vote, do they let it go or hold a grudge?
  o Are we talking with passion, but not over-personalizing the outcome?
- What are our deepest dreams? Double classrooms? A sports complex? A thick, rich Christian community?
- Since we are a Christian organization, who on our board or in our school has the following special roles & holds them in the utmost confidentiality and keeps our concerns out of the secular court system?
  o *Honest broker* – an impartial mediator in disputes
  o *Ombudsman* – a person with a sterling ethical reputation who investigates individuals' complaints against maladministration at any & all levels of the school and has latitude & authority to engage an honest broker

- *Discussion Suggestion*: Does the next generation of board members know the vision? Does the next generation of board members own & embrace the vision? How can we help them understand & own the vision?

Getting Back on Track

- *Advice to founders*: Invest in relationship with the next generation of board member leaders. Invest in them by meeting person to person. Have lunch together. Have a dialogue. Make a personal invitation to a younger member of the board to the ACCS conference or other CCE conference. Seek out, nurture, and cast vision for these folks. Bring them in to watch, observe, and learn.
- Read about classical Christian education.
- Read the classics.
- Attend a conference: ACCS, SCL (The Society for Classical Learning), and so forth.
- Listen to podcasts, online resources, and so forth, on classical Christian education. [See Resources in this book. See also ACCS & SCL websites.]
- Keith Nix: "Take the board deeper."
- If as a board member, you are receiving consistent feedback that you are not leading well, choose to graciously leave and leave on as good terms as far as it is up to you. "If possible, so far as it depends on you, live peaceably with all." (Romans 12:18)
- "….[T]eamwork ultimately comes down to practicing a small set of principles over a long period of time. Success is not a matter of mastering subtle, sophisticated theory, but rather of embracing common sense with uncommon levels of discipline and persistence. Ironically, teams succeed because they are exceedingly human. By acknowledging the imperfections of their humanity members of functional teams overcome the natural tendencies that make trust, conflict, commitment, accountability, and a focus on results so elusive."[19]

Healthy Board

- A healthy board makes every endeavor to budget, if needed, for board members to attend a CCE conference. Head of school Keith Nix says his "board's new board chair wants to put this into policy: that every board member would attend a conference every third year (ACCS or SCL). They would cover their own cost or the school will help you."
- Keith Nix: "Board enculturation is key."
- Keith Nix: "Being on board. Going deeper in their understanding of classical Christian education."
- Keith Nix: "Every year each family has to re-enroll and sign core beliefs again. The board does, too. Gatekeeping things. Every year. Church involvement needs to be evident."
- A healthy board strives to keep both lower & upper campuses together.
- A healthy school & board of directors are protected by appropriate liability insurance.
- A healthy board obtains outside expertise when necessary.
- Leslie Collins: "Every board is a mess in their own way, but there are principles of health in organizations that can be pursued." She recommends two books:
  - *Managing Transitions: Making the Most of Change* by William Bridges, PhD, with Susan Bridges[20] – Look at the graphic for Organizational Renewal:[21]
    1) *Dreaming the Dream*
    2) *Launching the Venture*
    3) *Getting Organized*
    4) *Succeeding, Making It*

---

[19] Lencioni, *The Five Dysfunctions of a Team*, 220.

[20] William Bridges with Susan Bridges. *Managing Transitions: Making the Most of Change* (Boston: Da Capo Press, 2016), 99.

[21] Parentheses' content from Lee Rusty Waller, YouTube, May 24, 2012.

5) *Becoming an Institution*: (moving from doing to being) Everyone has the same philosophy, everyone has the same values, everyone does it the "School's name" way – consistent way, you know what to expect. There's a way to do things, and that's your school's way. When starting a new place (e.g., Trader Joe's, Chick-Fil-A), businesses bring the old people in to help new business start. If you are an institution, then there is a way and everybody's got it." Then there is a fork in the road here: Either you start . . .

6) *Closing In* – (Institution begins to take it easy, experiences self-satisfaction, sees no need to examine themselves.) "What happens typically we get to that point of health, and like human beings, we start to close in, we start to speak our own language, we start to take care of ourselves, and then we start to die."

7) *Dying* OR
   - *The Path of Renewal & Beginning Anew* – An institution begins anew & dreams the dream or launches the venture or gets organized for organizational renewal.

o *The Five Dysfunctions of a Team* by Patrick Lencioni – The five cascade into each other. Some of organizations are healthier than others; some are more mature. In the immature ones, there is dysfunction. Lencioni's book is a fable of five dysfunctions:
   - *An absence of trust* – unwilling to be vulnerable within the group. "The most important action that a leader must take to encourage the building of trust on a team is to demonstrate vulnerability first...must [also] create an environment that does not punish vulnerability."[22]
   - *Fear of conflict* – seeking artificial harmony over constructive, passionate debate. "Teams that fear conflict create environments where back-channel politics and personal attacks thrive."[23]
   - *Lack of commitment* – feigning buy-in for group decisions creates ambiguity throughout the organization
   - *Avoidance of accountability* – ducking the responsibility to call peers on counterproductive behavior which sets *low standards*. "'If we do anything between now and the end of the year, what should that be?'";[24] "'Are there any comments, questions, or concerns people want to raise before we leave?'";[25] "'I have no greater priority as CEO than making...us...more effective as a group.'"[26] [The preceding is denial of self. *Administer* is the key.] "'Are you making this team better, or are you contributing to the dysfunction?'"[27] Are you "helping the team win or advancing your career [ego, agenda, etc.]?'"[28] The end of this chapter says these are not mutually exclusive; "'...it's just one has to be more important than the other.'"[29] "...[T]he departure of even the most difficult employees provoked some degree of mourning and self-doubt among their peers."[30] Tolerance of bad behavior.[31]
   - *Inattention to results* – focusing on personal success, *status* and *ego* before team success. "...[W]hen everyone is focused on results and using those to define success, it is difficult for ego to get out of hand. No matter how good an individual on the team might be feeling about his or her situation, if the team loses, everyone loses."[32] "'...[W]hen a

---

[22] Lencioni, *Five Dysfunctions*, 201.

[23] Ibid., 204.

[24] Ibid., 105.

[25] Ibid., 111.

[26] Ibid., 113.

[27] Ibid., 122.

[28] Ibid., 124.

[29] Ibid., 124.

[30] Ibid., 163.

[31] Ibid., 167.

[32] Ibid., 72.

company has a collection of good managers who don't act like a team, it can create a dilemma for them, and for the company. ... [I]t leads to confusion about who their first team is...putting team results ahead of individual issues. Your first team has to be this one ["'loyalty and commitment'" to the team of managers];[33] "'building a team is hard.'"[34]

Setting a Goal

- Pray for God's wisdom. Set one or two goals for positioning *your board of directors* better on track. Enter that goal in the binder/document that goes with you everywhere.
- Refer to this goal at each board meeting throughout the year.
- Reflect on this goal at year's end. Rejoice in God's grace.

Expressing a Desire

- Pray for God's wisdom. Write one or two desires for positioning your board of directors better on track *that depend on others' cooperation*. Enter that desire in the binder/document that goes with you everywhere.
- Pray about this desire throughout the year.
- Reflect on this desire at the end of each year. Rejoice in God's grace.

Encouragement

- There can be tumultuous times when schools encounter crises and may waver. Lord, please help us with "being confident of this very thing, that He who began a good work in you will continue to perfect it until the day of Christ Jesus." (Philippians 1:6, Berean Study Bible)

---

[33] Ibid., 137.
[34] Ibid., 138.

Chapter 4
Your School's Administrators

"When one rules justly over men, ruling in the fear of God, he dawns on them like the morning light, like the sun shining forth on a cloudless morning, like rain that makes grass to sprout from the earth."
2 Samuel 23:3c-4

"People who rely most on God rely least on themselves."
Lemuel K. Washburn

"An institution is the lengthened shadow of one man."
Ralph Waldo Emerson

In 1513, Niccolo Machiavelli's *The Prince* poses the question regarding leaders, "Is it better to be loved or feared?" Is it better for a school to be comfortable with the "natural easiness of [a leader's] disposition" or to quake in their bootstraps in obedience? Administrators can lean toward being feared – at the sacrifice of kindness – or toward being loved – at the sacrifice of standards – but how would Jesus reply to such a question?

As we look to the past, when did our formal theories about how to lead emerge and how have they affected the ways we lead today? Leadership studies encompass the past two centuries and began with the Industrial Revolution (1760-1840). The Industrial Revolution saw a shift from an agricultural economy to an industrial one and in turn, influenced how leaders treated their followers. Hierarchical bureaucracies were created, and processes of administration became routinized much as the machine routinized production. Increasingly, people became viewed as machines.

Classical management theory fine-tuned the ideal design of the entire organization while *scientific management* made individual jobs streamlined with technological time-and-motion studies, both with the goal of achieving maximum efficiency & productivity.[1] During this era, "the focus of a leader was on the needs of the organization and not on the individual worker" (p. 2). Both theories placed a heavy emphasis on the *machine* metaphor, eroding the human element and failing to see organizations as complex organisms.

---

[1] A. Gregory Stone, Ph.D., and Kathleen Patterson, Ph.D., "The History of Leadership Focus," Regent University for School of Leadership Studies at Regent University, 2005, accessed August 2, 2019, http://www.regent.edu/acad/sls/publications/conference_proceedings/servant_leadership_roundtable/2005/pdf/stone_history.pdf. This source informs this and the following five paragraphs with page number references.

By the mid-1940s, a post-bureaucratic shift acknowledged there were drawbacks to a top-down-only approach. The organization's design & structure were important, but the workers' involvement was also deemed important to the success of the organization. They saw that people have both extrinsic needs (work environment & policies) and intrinsic needs (motivators about the job itself). The next two decades focused on behavior, environment, & worker needs.

In the late 1970s, a *transactional leadership theory* developed & remains "the most prevalent method of leadership." The leader focuses on *performance*. "Transactional leadership is based on bureaucratic authority, focuses on task completion, and relies on rewards and punishments" (p. 7).

On the other hand, *transformational leaders* focus on the *organization*. "The job of the transformational leader is not to make every decision within the organization, but to ensure that collaborative decision-making occurs" (Badaracco & Ellsworth, 1989; Book, 1998; Dixon, 1998; Wheatley, 1994). Transformational leadership is an expansion of transactional leadership. The transformational leader is *"more likely to provide a role model with whom subordinates want to identify* [italics mine]." "...[T]ransformational leadership focuses on a leader's understanding of their affect on how followers feel trust, admiration, loyalty, and respect toward the leader and how followers are motivated to do more than expected (p. 7). Transformational leaders transform the personal values of followers to support the vision and goals of the organization by fostering an environment where *relationships are formed* and by establishing a climate of trust where visions are shared [italics mine]" (p. 9). "The transformational leader articulates the vision in a clear and appealing manner, explains how to attain the vision, acts confidently and optimistically, expresses confidence in his followers, emphasizes values with symbolic actions, leads by example, and empowers followers to achieve the vision" (Yukl, 2002) (p. 10). "Trust between a leader and his or her followers is a cornerstone of transformational leadership." "Stephen R. Covey (1989) writes, 'Trust is the highest form of human motivation because it brings out the very best in people' (p. 178). It creates a moral foundation and leading from a moral basis allows full organizational transformation to occur as all of the leader's skills emerge to positively influence followers (Ford, 1991; Bottum & Lenz, 1998; Clawson, 1999). This moral basis starts, and ends, with trust. Trust relies on the leader's character, which makes values-based leadership possible (Maxwell, 1998)" (p. 11).

The *servant-leader* focuses on the followers. "Block (1993) posits that there is a deep hunger within our society for organizations in which people are treated fairly and humanely and supported in their personal growth and where leaders can be trusted to serve the needs of the 'many' rather than the 'few.' Block called for a new model of leadership based on teamwork, community, values, service, and caring behavior." "Servant leaders develop people, helping them to strive and flourish (McMinn, 2001)" (p. 12). "The extent to which leaders are able to shift the primary focus of their leadership from the organization to the follower is the distinguishing factor in determining whether the leader may be a transformational or servant leader. In so doing, they allow extraordinary freedom for followers to exercise their own abilities. They also place a much higher degree of trust in their followers than would be the case in any leadership style that required the leader to be somewhat directive" (p.12).

"Patterson's (2005) research has led to a servant leadership model encompassing seven virtuous constructs exhibited as behaviors by a servant leader and their interaction. These seven behaviors are *agapao* love, humility, altruism, vision, trust, empowerment, and service. McKenna (1989) notes that servant-power is a category of influence outside the traditional kinds of power. Real servanthood is a leadership style that relies upon the influence of self-giving without self-glory" (p. 12).

ADMINISTRATOR AS SERVANT-LEADER

To answer the opening question "Is it better to be feared or loved?" we look to Jesus. Whenever the Pharisees tried to press Him into a forced choice, our Lord typically responded with a third alternative, as when he directed them to "render unto Caesar what is Caesar's and unto God what is God's." We can get a clue for a third way of answering this love or fear question from the verse "If anyone would be first, he must be the last of all and servant of all" (Mark 9:35).

But wouldn't being a "servant of all" sound demeaning to a leader of an entire school? Wouldn't he or she lose respect and credibility? Wouldn't some level of chaos ensue?

Our leader is Christ, not man, and our leadership should model His leadership. Servant-leaders are what classical Christian schools need. Not leaders who rule by fear or milquetoasts who strain for popularity, but God-pleasers. Our vision statements may, in fact, include the term *servant-leaders* regarding what we hope to build into our students, our sons and daughters. But if we are to desire our students to be servant leaders, we administrators must be servant-leaders; in other words, we need to be good shepherds and models.

THE NEED FOR SERVANT-LEADERS

In his plenary speech at the 2017 Association for Classical Christian Schools (ACCS) Convention, Dr. Gregory Thornbury, former president of The King's College in New York City, declared, "We need a new generation of shepherds."[2] Thornbury compared the role of classical Christian education to the work of St. Patrick who returned to his pagan culture in Ireland and spread Christianity. Just as teachers need to shepherd students, administrators need to shepherd teachers. This type of administrating is a caring model.

DEFINITION OF ADMINISTER

The word *administer* derives from the Latin *ad-* meaning "to" and *minister* meaning "servant," from *minus* meaning "less." How fitting! To shepherd effectively, we must become a servant who becomes less. What exactly is a head of school? Head of school Leslie Collins says the head of school is "responsible to create the institution and make sure that it stays." The word *institution* comes from the Latin *sto, stare, steti, status* meaning "to stand." The primary definition is "they are the 'chief reminding officer' – constantly reminding people "why we are here, constantly reminding people why we do it this way, we are constantly telling people what they need to hear, and an administrator needs to be willing to beat the drum over and over again, and it gets tiring. You do not want five disciplinary perspectives. You want it to be the one way, and everybody needs to be trained in that. The head is responsible for the school itself, the institution itself growing and moving forward and transitioning to becoming an institution that is going to last [to stand] for generations." Is the school my personal kingdom, my self-glorification, my baby, my idol? Or am I washing the feet of those in my care? Am I daily dying to self and becoming less?

LENGTHENED SHADOW

While not an admirer of Ralph Waldo Emerson's philosophy, I find his famous words about leaders riveting: "An institution is *the lengthened shadow of one man* [italics mine]" ("Self-Reliance" essay). Often, as the head administrator goes, so goes the school. If the administrator is full of truth & grace, the students bask and grow under that light. If the administrator leads with fear, the teachers and students begin to cower and muzzle themselves. If the administrator begins to lie and cover his or her tracks, a cult-like feeling can descend on a school. Who is the next "betrayer" to be sought out? The shadow an administrator casts will reflect his or her character at heart.

CHARACTER

Indeed, the character of the administrator is of utmost importance when establishing a school. Is he or she a Christian as evidenced by their fruit? Written in 1746, Jonathan Edwards' *Treatise Concerning the Religious Affections* says, only God can know a person's true state; however, Edwards also says, "…I know of no directions or counsels which Christ ever delivered more plainly than the rules He has given to guide us in our judgment of people's sincerity. He says we should judge the tree chiefly by the fruit."[3] Christ declared, "For every tree is known by its own fruit. … A good man out of the good treasure of his heart brings forth good; and an evil man out of the evil treasure of his heart brings forth evil. For out of the abundance of the heart his mouth speaks" (Luke 6:44-45, NKJV). Therefore, we can look at the fruit, humbly, knowing only God can know a person's true state.

---

[2] Dr. Gregory Thornbury, "Cain, Abel, and Kanye: The Gospel & Pop Culture" (lecture, ACCS Conference, Pittsburgh, Pennsylvania, June 23, 2017).

[3] Jonathan Edwards. *Religious Affections: A Christian's Character Before God*, abridged and ed. James M. Houston (Vancouver, British Columbia: Regent College Publishing, 1984 [Orig. 1746]), 69.

APPRAISING CHARACTER

How do we know the fruit if we are hiring a new administrator? Naturally, there is the résumé, the application, the interview, and references. But too often decisions for hire are based solely on a candidate's own words in the résumé, the application, the interview, and their own list of references. If an experienced administrator is under consideration for hiring, prayer is first, asking for the Lord's direction & discernment. Secondly, it would be prudent to make phone calls to a variety of individuals from the candidate's past places of employment and, if at all possible, to invest the funds to visit their former school(s) and inquire from a wide variety of people there what his or her tenure & reputation was like. Conversely, how does a candidate for head of school ascertain the culture of a candidate school? If he or she seeks honest answers, they could observe a board meeting, observe an administrators' meeting, visit classes in session, stay after school in the crowds as parents arrive to pick up their children, and even interview the janitor. Ask the Lord for direction in appraising the character of your candidate head of school, the character of the candidate school itself.

LEADERSHIP MODELS

Four types of leadership in the Hersey-Blanchard Situational Leadership Model can be helpful for situational leadership. The two behaviors paired are supportive behavior and directive behavior. High directive & high supportive is the COACHING or selling model of leadership; high directive & low supportive is the DIRECTING or telling model; low directive & high supportive is the SUPPORTING or participating/co-laboring model; and low direction & low support is the DELEGATING model. Each has its place in situational leadership; however, Coaching and Directing are used more for working with employees with high/some commitment or with low/some competence whereas Supporting and Delegating are for working with employees with more competence and higher commitment. Each of these leadership styles can be employed helpfully in various situations; however, much more than the four leadership styles is necessary for the school administrator.

INTERVIEWING THE CANDIDATE

In the course of rigorous interviewing of a candidate, three key elements must be determined: 1) Most importantly, does he or she love the Lord? 2) Does the head administrator know how to maintain a school's vision? AND 3) Does the head administrator know how to run a school? Often heads of school are either good at vision or good at management. For full effectiveness, they need to do both. If not, it is essential to combine the "rocket fuel" of *visionary* and *integrator* that Gino Wickman and Mark C. Winters promote in their book *Rocket Fuel*. The visionary always "sees the big picture, inspires people, creates the vision and protects it."[4] The integrator is good at "running the day-to-day operations, is a steady force...who is obsessed about organizational clarity and [is] great at making sure people are communicating within the [school] ... and helps to eliminate hurdles, stumbling blocks, and barriers for the leadership team " and the school in general."[5] "The Visionary is the WHY-type and the Integrator is the HOW-type."[6] Wickman and Winters go on to quote Simon Sinek, saying, "'Visionaries...tend to be optimists who believe that all the things they imagine can actually be accomplished. HOW-types live more in the here and now. They are the realists and have a clearer sense of all things practical. WHY-types are focused on the things most people can't see, like the future. HOW-types are focused on the things that most people can see, and tend to be better at building structures and processes and getting things done. One is not better than the other, they are just different ways people naturally see and experience the world.'"[7] The Visionary and the Integrator are true partners. One is the telescope; the other, a microscope. Both are essential for keeping your school on track.

---

[4] Gino Wickman and Mark C. Winters. *Rocket Fuel: The One Essential Combination that will Get You More of What You Want from Your Business* (Dallas: BenBella Books, Inc., 2016), 8.

[5] Ibid., 28, 30, 32.

[6] Ibid., 53.

[7] Simon Sinek in *Start With Why: How Great Leaders Inspire Everyone to Take Action* (2011), quoted in Wickman and Winters, *Rocket Fuel,* 53.

SCHOOL HIERARCHY

Another consideration is what does your school hierarchy look like – pyramid or inverted pyramid? Administrator at the pinnacle or administrator undergirding and enabling the teachers & staff to flourish? The school handbook typically has the organizational chart for administration and communication with the board and then below that the administrator with everyone else below them. But on the ground in daily operations, is the administrator serving the school, or is the administrator expecting everyone to serve him or her? They are the boss and accordingly they must be respected and obeyed. But tyrant they are not, according to Jesus' servant-leader model. The administrator must decrease so that Christ's aroma may increase.

ADMINISTRATOR AS SERVANT-LEADER

How does an administrator serve day to day with such pressures? After all, he or she is often the first one at school and many times the last one to leave. All honor and all shame fall on that person's doorstep. The secret comes from Oswald Chambers *My Utmost for His Highest* (April 24), "Unless the worker lives a life that 'is hidden with Christ in God' (Colossians 3:3), he is apt to become an irritating dictator to others, instead of an active, living disciple."[8] The maxim once inscribed at the Temple of Apollo at Delphi, Greece, read, "Know thyself." And if you do not know yourself, consider asking your Nathan, the person who has the courage and love enough to tell you that you are veering off track. Even your strength needs temperance. Again from Oswald Chambers' classic devotional (April 19): "Unguarded strength is actually a double weakness, because that is where the least likely temptations will be effective in sapping strength. The Bible characters stumbled over their strong points, never their weak ones."[9]

So I began my interviews, seeking God's help in finding administrators who ran healthy schools, schools where these administrators dawned on them like the morning light. Each interview breathed refreshment.

****

INTERVIEW #1: My first interview was with Steven Sheets, former Ohio and North Carolina teacher for 14 years and administrator for 26, who was often called upon to adjust schools that were in trouble.[10] I asked him how one leads well. That led him to write a short paper reflecting on "What are some of the ideal qualities and knowledge sets of a Christian administrator?" He says,

> The administrator would know and practice from the standpoint of "To teach as Jesus taught," and using the Fruit of the Spirit in how he works with his fellow teachers. (It is important to note that originally the principal was called "the principal teacher"....) They would understand their moral compass must be the 10 commandments (loving the Lord thy God in action) and loving their neighbor as themselves.

Sheets says, "You've got to listen to God if you're going to be a Christian administrator. You cannot just use the tools of the world. I've always spent time before the Lord every day. You've got to pray. God wants you." Regarding teaching and administering, it "is your calling. You work for God. The only way to self-regulate is to be in the Word and in prayer, applying the Word, memorizing the Word, for example, the fruit of the Spirit in Galatians 5." He continues, "As administrators, we have to be *as Christ-like as anyone else.*"

Sheets further adds,

> A good leader is a person who has taught for multiple years and understands the expectations, weight of responsibilities and time required to teach at a high level (the same qualities as found in Timothy and Titus for leadership responsibilities). The person also

---

[8] Oswald Chambers, *My Utmost for His Highest*, ed. James Reimann (Grand Rapids, Michigan: Discovery House Publishers, 1992 [Orig., 1935]), April 24 entry.

[9] Ibid., April 19 entry.

[10] Steven Sheets, interview by Kathleen F. Kitchin, Greenville, North Carolina, September 5, 2018.

must clearly delineate what are the expectations based on the evaluation tool. LEAVE NO DOUBT ON WHAT IS EXPECTED DAILY – how students are treated, what lesson plan expectations are, how you will evaluate. This leader understands expectations of meeting mandates from boards ...to reach certain standards for all children, challenging upper-level students.

Sheets says a leader of a school is a also team member, one "who facilitates learning – knowing how to leverage the gifts and talents of each member of the school team (teachers, instructional facilitators, custodians, office personnel)." He or she is a listener – spends time talking with individual members so they know needs of staff members (remembers that they are ambassadors of Christ and Christ cared about others – a lot!). Being interested but not taking their "monkeys on your back."

The head of school "understands their role as disciplinarian and counselor. If necessary, he or she removes troubled students so learning can take place. The head of school works to get to the root cause of student misbehavior and develops a relationship with a troubled student and their parent(s)/guardian. He or she collaborates with others to work on long-term solutions and follows up on behavior and work of troubled students (e.g., goes to class to see them at work, talks to them in hall or lunch room, checks with teacher on progress, provides positive feedback)."

As practical follow-up, Steve Sheets says he always expected 360-degree feedback with the goal of "always improve." He "provided a survey to staff at the mid and end of year for them to provide feedback on the learning environment that included their leadership skill set. He also provided a survey to staff to provide the board of education...feedback." As for teacher evaluations, he "evaluated teachers once a semester, providing feedback that is SMART – (Specific, Measureable, Aligned, Results-focused and Time-framed). In turn, he required teachers to write a plan of action to improve area(s) of weakness. In each evaluation, he said "something positive, something to adjust, and again something positive."

Sheets says, "You wear multiple hats as an administrator, and teachers wear multiple hats also (friend, parent, daughter,...). You have to set priorities. An administrator is a hub of a wheel – board, teachers, parents, students, general public, education as a whole. When making a statement, you have to consider all those audiences." He used James 1:19 as a guide: "Everyone should be quick to listen, slow to speak, and slow to become angry." Sheet said it is about relationships and communication. "You've got to talk to people. All people, not just the teachers, but also the teacher assistants, bus drivers, and custodians. They would report things...custodians, secretary. You have to see the bigger picture through each person's lens. If you want an organization to improve, you have to believe that each person in that organization wants to improve. Even the outliers will give you a nugget about what is going on in the organization." Sheets called the outliers "prophets" and took their feedback seriously.

As an administrator, Steve Sheets said, "You've got to listen. The goal is to teach students to learn how to learn. If you are looking at a problem, you need to look at it as a school community." I asked why problems are ignored. Sheets replied, "Not wanting to admit failure, quenching information going up the ladder, not wanting the hard discussions with parents." Sheets asserted that you "have to change your perspective: it is a problem, but we have an opportunity to change it." Administrators need to ask the difficult questions.

About being in the trenches: "You can't be the sage on the stage. You've got to be the guide on the side."

Sheets set out guidelines for his faculty. Faculty meeting discussions operated with these rules: "Respect, Listen, Don't dominate." Regarding evaluation forms, there were several types. The first type of evaluation form was teacher evaluation. It was "Feed forward" and Sheets would go over teacher evaluation forms proactively with his staff. He would also evaluate the evaluation form. The second type of evaluation form was the 360-degree evaluations where each group gets feedback from everyone else. He starts with the top – "We are going to be looked at every year." Suggested groups were board of education, administrators, faculty, staff, parents, and students.

Sheets believes there needs to be intentionality in evaluations & feedback. "Everyone wants to know they're doing a good job." After an evaluation, have a post-conference during *one entire class period*.

In improving teachers, Sheets says, "Beware, you ...can use proof texts to bludgeon." Secondly, he recommended using a "laser beam vs. a shotgun" approach. Laser is one-on-one *versus* shotgun is blasting the whole group. If one or two teachers is in the wrong, address them each privately. Avoid scolding an entire group when only one or two people actually need to be addressed.

Regarding teacher preparation days before school begins, Sheets recommends having separate pre-prep days earlier for new teachers and give them comp time off later during prep days.

Sheets's final word to administrators was "Know your calling."

****

INTERVIEW #2: While at the Association for Classical Christian Schools Conference in Atlanta, I interviewed Dr. Pamela McKee, head of Bayshore Christian School in Fairhope, Alabama, and representative member of the ACCS board of directors. I had attended her class at the conference entitled, "God's Garden: Cultivating and Growing Schools." During her lecture, I was enthralled as she shared that just as life began in a garden, a place of refuge and solace, so too must we cultivate and grow our schools as gardens. With beautiful photographs to accompany each of the steps, Dr. McKee outlined site selection, tilling the soil, plant selection, sowing seed, providing stakes and support systems, watering/weeding/feeding, pruning and thinning, and harvesting the rewards, all corresponding to how a head of school cultivates and grows their school like God's Garden. Eventually, it dawned on me – interview her! And so we did over coffee & tea at the hotel.[11]

As I spoke with Dr. McKee, it occurred to me that each head of school I interviewed seemed to have an image that both defined and drove their mission. As head of school, what is your metaphor? Dr. McKee's metaphor for school is a *garden* – a place of "beauty, discovery, and encounter with God" – and she continued along this same theme as we talked.

Dr. McKee's undergraduate degrees are in Christian education & sociology with a minor in psychology. Reflecting on them she noted, "I was looking at the human condition along with Christian education. Little did I know how much I would use both of those degrees in education. As I reflect on that now, the Lord was preparing me for that balance. There are practical, real needs. We can't be philosophical all the time. This grounded me in that there are real needs, and they need Jesus. The *need* is Jesus Christ. These needs are met through Him." Her heart is to be with people and to serve them.

McKee says, "I think it has been beneficial for me to have been in the classroom before I went into administration." She taught for 7 years in Christian schools, was an assistant principal for a couple years, and eventually was head of Evangel School in Alabama for many years, and has now been at Bayshore Christian School in Fairhope, Alabama, for several years. When she first heard of CCE, she said that "The more I read, I found the equivalency of the Trivium in Scripture – knowledge, understanding, & wisdom. I saw it so clearly in Scripture and the Holy Spirit was confirming it in my heart that this was something He was doing in our nation."

When her church began to think about starting a classical Christian school unbeknownst to her, she was "investigating this on her own" and started to pray, "If You want me to be a part of this steering committee, have them ask me. Have them invite me to the party. I laid out this fleece before the Lord. I didn't tell anyone. I just made that my prayer to the Lord." Two weeks later when she went to church, one of the committee members came over to her in the foyer & said the steering committee wanted to ask her to be their first principal. Her jaw dropped and she said, "I knew without a shadow of a doubt in my heart that that was the Lord answering my direct prayer. My direct fleece was so clear there could have been no mistaking." She was asked in May, began on June 2, and opened the school in August. She

---

[11] Dr. Pamela McKee, interview by Kathleen F. Kitchin, Atlanta, Georgia, June 13, 2019.

was reading Nehemiah at the time. It took exactly 52 days to rebuild the wall, and there were exactly 52 days to open the school!

She already was an administrator. As for tilling the soil, she knew the "logistics to open school: desks, faculty, rug for reading time, and that every classroom needs a broom & dustpan." Regarding relational issues, she was familiar with the steps to hire the right teachers, interview parents, and test students to "set them up for success." She insists these were "not just warm bodies. This is school, this is education, this is serious"; therefore, "everything that we do from the original first phone call of a parent to make an inquiry has to be done professionally & with great care for the *soul* of the child." She procured 5 volunteers initially to be secretary, one for each day of the week, so that someone was there to answer after the first or second ring. They welcomed folks, answered the phone, and gave Pam the messages. These volunteers freed Pam "to be with those teachers, to help the teachers, to do the care & feeding of the teachers so that they could give the care & feeding to the students. It's always *a trickle-down effect*. Always. If I am caring for that teacher, the teachers became my 'students' and then their students were their students."

In fact, Dr. McKee gives her teachers the Christian classic by W. Phillip Keller, *A Shepherd Looks at the 23rd Psalm*. "It is what our Father God does for us. He always has set the example for leadership. He was *the* servant-leader. And so, the leadership of Christ, starting with God the Father, the Garden of Eden – what a great example for teachers. We talk about that in teacher-training. Look at the Garden. Look at what the Father supplied. First of all, security, peacefulness, love, companionship. The Father walked and talked with Adam & Eve. Don't be the teacher that is just on your computer while the kids come into your classroom & then you stand up & be that 'sage on the stage.' This is relational. Greet them at the door. Say, 'Good morning.' You are training them to have relationship with one another & with their own families. The way you treat them – 'the student will become like his teacher.' So, what examples are those teachers setting? And then what example am I as head of school setting for the teachers? Am I greeting the teachers when they come in in the mornings?"

I asked her, "Are we applying those same principles to how we treat fellow administrators, how we treat our teachers, how we treat every single staff member? Everyone is important." Pam added, "How do you treat your janitor? If there is a hierarchy of authority, then the head of school has to touch all those people that work underneath – you hate to say underneath but that's really what it is. The people that you hired to work in the school – that's your flock. The students really aren't my flock. From the larger picture, yes. They are in our field. But I have to shepherd who is going to watch *that* flock." I said to Dr. McKee, "You are tending those shepherds so they can tend their sheep," and she responded: "The teachers are my sheep, to care for." Dr. McKee further added, "What's really important for a teacher to feel secure in is to have systems and for the systems to be consistent because there's nothing worse than chaotic – 'Oh, we're going to do this. No, we're not. We're going to do this.' Switching."

Dr. McKee noted that it is "much easier to found a school and grow your teachers to train them the way you want." She said it is a "different type of challenge to go in and already have an established school." No consistent systems were in place because every couple of years there would be a new headmaster, everything would be uprooted, and each leader would do what they wanted, so there was little corporate history. "You can't have or understand or enjoy real freedom if you don't have boundaries. And to me, having guidelines & systems are those boundaries. And then you have all this freedom inside to make it look & have the flavor of your school's culture. That you have this framework & the backbone for knowing that if I'm doing these things, I'll have a successful & good school; otherwise, you don't really know if you're doing the right things."

For example, Dr. McKee established an office system in place for handling a topic we wish we could all avoid – lice:

1) Teacher sends child to the office.
2) The office takes care of this situation, not the teacher, and has supplies to handle the situation (gloves for examination for lice, etc.)

3) The office, not the teacher, emails the "lice letter" to all the parents.
4) This system frees up the teacher because there is a system for office support.

The above "template" is an example of systems that administrators need to establish for typical problems to keep their schools on track in a daily, very practical fashion.

Dr. McKee kept working at the soil of this new garden. "You have to do the hard things sometimes so that things are established. Our job is to set the school up for success. Plant the trees that we know we won't sit in their shade. This will germinate & grow, but we may leave, retirement for example, but I don't want the school to crumble." In establishing new systems, she delegates over time. Regarding the larger picture she has a succession plan, not only for the *who* but also the *what*. She says, "If I am ill for two weeks, say in the hospital, is that school going to run like clockwork? Have I set up the systems and have I poured into the office manager, have I done the training to give them the confidence that they are competent to handle things whether I am there or not? That's my goal." The goal is to administrate.

So many administrators administrate well, thank the Lord. What image do we have for being an exemplary model? Dr. McKee says that in *A Shepherd Looks at the 23rd Psalm*, it tells of the sheep coming in at night through the door into the corral, and the shepherd would stand at the door and really rub them down & see how many burs and sticks were in their wool, or mites or pests. He would anoint them with oil – this is the job of caring for your teachers. What is the state of your flock? *An administrator is a good shepherd.*

Dr. McKee says the same applies to shepherding our students. There is the *physical*, the *soul*, and the *spirit*. For the physical, we ask what is the state of this child? Have they had enough sleep? We do not take the parent's role, but we talk with the parent. We are partnering with the parents. Dr. McKee says, "The 'physical' is important because it gives you outward signs of a need." For the soul, we ask, "Are they happy? Are they joyful? Are they engaged? Those things have to be looked at also." For the spiritual state, we ask, "Have they made a profession of faith? Are you still planting the Word of God in them on a regular basis, pouring that water on them?" Dr. McKee says, "I have to ask myself the same questions about my teachers."

The priority is vetting your candidates. Dr. McKee says find the best fit on the front end. Are they Christian? If they are on spiritually solid ground, then you can work on these other areas, such as better understanding CCE. Dr. McKee says, "Equip them with everything they will need. Train them. It means getting the best & most training. Don't overwhelm them. In doses, don't overfeed or overwater or you get root-rot. Being wise to give little bits of information. Have a training on one particular concept. Have the teachers think about it. Implant this particular concept in your classroom. We'll come back together. See how that went. What questions you have. What went well; what didn't go well. Once that's learned, you can go on to the next one. Teachers have to feel confident and competent when they walk into the classroom. So, if you have given them training, and you've given them prayer & assurance that you are there with them, you are there with a support system – like Christ – you are going to check on them & you're going to help them; they are never alone."

Dr. McKee sets up mentoring situations for teachers that she said is so easy. She said as a teacher she learned more from other teachers than from administrators. For example, put the lead 4th-grade teacher with the new 3rd-grade teacher. *Partner a new teacher with an established teacher.*

Dr. McKee says, "Once you have teachers who love the Lord, love children, & love learning and they really love their job, they're getting feedback, they're getting that scaffolding help that we provide for them whether it's training or a new curriculum or whatever they need, then you *look at their whole person*, asking, 'Are we overtasking them? Are we asking them to do too much? How often are they staying late at school & why?' You go hang out with them after school. 'Hey, whatcha working on?' Just kind of find out what areas they're really struggling with. If the answer is 'It's loud at home & I'm just here doing my lesson plans because it's easier,' that's one thing. But if it's 'I'm so far behind' that's another."

An additional way to help your school stay on track is to look for ways to give teachers breaks. Teachers lack time because they are always busy, so

1) Hire a separate P.E. teacher.
2) *Give each teacher a full planning per*iod – "That shows them that you respect them as humans and as physical beings."
3) Equip them with any supplies they need, with a great curriculum, with training for that curriculum.

When Dr. McKee started at her previous role at Evangel School, she had three guides: 1) "The Bible – I wanted to imitate the Lord, whatever He did. That's why I looked to the Garden of Eden, and I looked at what God provided for His children. 2) The ACCS Accreditation Book of Standards. Every program that I added, I wanted it to meet the standards of ACCS because I knew I wanted to be accredited and I knew it would take 10 years to get there. In those 10 years, I wanted to be ready when they came to visit and didn't want to have to change this & fix this. From the git-go. Begin with the end in mind. 3) *The Principal's Companion* which gave me practical steps on security in the school. It is more for administrators – how to have systems, how to run a school."

In addition to her theme of growing a school like growing a garden and tending her teachers as a shepherd, the following words summarize Dr. Pamela McKee's role as a head of school: "You are the servant of all."

****

Interview #3: I spent a lovely day with Leslie & Dave Collins at The Covenant Academy in Cypress, Texas, near Houston. Dave is director of school operations at and Leslie is head of school. Throughout the day, we talked about the trials & blessings of Hurricane Harvey in 2017 and its effects on the school itself and on their school culture. If anything could derail a school, you would think it would be a hurricane. But Dave and Leslie Collins say it was one of the best things that happened to their school as it "brought us together" & the school community worked as a team to rebuild. Today, you would not know there had been a hurricane. Generous anonymous donations helped them replace all the furniture, bookcases, desks, & chairs, and a feeling of peace & calm pervades the school.[12]

We talked about their experiences at two other CCE schools where they helped one grow from the ground up and another to transition from a Christian school to a CCE school. My main focus for them both was "How do you identify *red flags*?" and "How do you keep your classical Christian school on track?"

As the new head of school at this location, Leslie looked at inconsistencies. Leslie says, "For me, I was looking at contradictions between what was being said and what was being done in terms of the academic plan and the academic results. I saw red flags in that. I also saw red flags in agreed-upon definitions of classical methodology within the larger classical Christian world. For me, what I walked into was a misunderstanding and misuse of terminology." There is a scholarly debate that exists within the CCE world over whether the Dorothy Sayers' model is overly prescriptive. Leslie says,

> Was Sayers really trying to set up a K-12 program in her essay, "The Lost Tools of Learning" and are they stages or not? CCE has always been developmental, but there are some who say you can do grammar, logic, and rhetoric all at the same time all the time. So I walked into a school that was confused. In the midst of that scholarly debate, this school was confused about pedagogy and that was, in my opinion, affecting the results in the classroom, so pedagogy needed to be cleared up with the understood wider use of the definitions.

First things first. It is absolutely essential to align definitions of words & concepts of your school's working vocabulary.

---

[12] Dave and Leslie Collins, interview by Kathleen F. Kitchin, Cypress, Texas, November 27, 2018.

Next, I asked Leslie, "How did you prioritize handling the red flags? What did you start with?" She says, "My top priority was what was happening in the classroom because if that wasn't being addressed, we wouldn't have a school to market. Some of that was implementing best practices of classical methodology and helping the teachers understand how to teach in a way that is effective in a classical model." Secondly,

> Order & structure was not effective. We had 137 school days in the school calendar. We could not get all the math curriculum completed. We were off every Friday. I believe that this school misunderstood the idea of "restful learning"; they interpreted it in a way it was not intended to be. Learning can only be restful when you understand how to work hard and then how not to let work rule you. Restful learning, which is a classical ideal, cannot be in opposition to rigorous academics and hard work because it's a biblical ideal to be a hard worker.

This is a dichotomy that does not exist in Scripture. Leslie continued to add,

> Educators see all the "kid" problems. I started with the kids. The person most closely connected with the kids was the teacher, and the teachers needed to learn how to partner with parents and how to equip children. We next worked on parent education and got that in a good place, and then board education. That's our school story. I don't think there's any one way to do it. I think you have to go with *what God has called you to do*. I think you have to walk into every school that you go into and say what here is true and what here is good and what here is beautiful, and then what here isn't and what is doing the most harm and what is doing the most good.

We explored further about practicalities. I asked, "What were the sources that helped you most over the past 25 years in CCE? What helped you problem solve?" Leslie responded,

> So many things were misunderstood, I thought, about classical pedagogy that I really had to do a more thorough reading. I had come out of ACCS which almost exclusively communicates about Dorothy Sayers, John Milton Gregory, & Doug Wilson – three patriarchs of ACCS – there is nothing wrong with what they say, but when I came here, almost no one was quoting from those resources so I had to learn the language that was being spoken and find out what we agreed upon before I could start just spouting off these three patriarchs. I had to find commonalities so it forced me to read more broadly which was good.

Several of her recommended sources include *The Trivium* by Sister Miriam Joseph; *Education for Human Flourishing: A Christian* Perspective by Paul D. Spears and Steven R. Loomis; *Building a Christian Academy*, a broad history of Christian education from Plato to John Henry Newman; *Wisdom & Eloquence: A Christian Paradigm for Classical Learning* by Robert Littlejohn & Charles T. Evans; and *The Liberal Arts Tradition* by Kevin Clark & Ravi Scott Jain. Leslie strongly recommends Mortimer Adler and reading C.S. Lewis again. Reading more broadly helped Leslie find commonalities and learn, in the process, that "the classical movement is so much bigger & richer & deeper than only three authors, that those authors don't contradict and are not undermining the rest of the heritage because it's a huge legacy."

What helped her at the school that was getting onto the classical Christian rails was "Trying to hear them and listen to them. And then tell them back, trying to build our own thing...because they were not trained." So reading a book at a time in a school that is transitioning is *building a culture amongst the teachers*.

On Covenant Academy's website, Leslie provided Thinkific courses, online training courses to bring her teachers in "to avoid hearing the same old thing." They cover "the basics without boring your veterans." The veterans have permission to skim, but must get 100% on every quiz after each course. Leslie was trying to develop a common language. I remarked to Leslie, "You have had to educate the culture of teachers here."

This book does not strive to be a recipe book, but instead has been seeking godly wisdom and best practices from educators in healthy schools. Leslie Collins says, "There are a lot of ways to do administration in schools right; there are just as many ways if not more to do it wrong." I asked her how not to do administration.

> Do not create an abusive culture in your school. Alternatively, put on a gospel-saturated culture. ...Avoid unintentionally creating a performance-driven culture. Alternatively, create a gospel-soaked culture. Avoid a culture that unintentionally teaches salvation by works by chastising, shaming, incentivizing students rather than encouraging them by relationship through the gospel. I am all for correction. Scripture tells us, "No discipline is pleasant at the time...." I have seen Christian cultures where they hit kids over the head with a Bible verse and chastise them and embarrass them for their bad behavior, rather than love them unconditionally and help point them to the gospel. A great book that talks about this is *Teaching Redemptively: Bringing Grace and Truth into Your Classroom* by Donovan L. Graham. Let's be honest. We don't want the gospel. We don't want to hear the truth. We would like life to be about our good works. Then we get the glory. We would like to not to have a Savior. We would like to be our own savior. Let's just be honest with who we are. And so because all of those things exist, we are going to create a culture in which our good works are honored. Honor what is excellent and praiseworthy. 4.0 students are not necessarily virtuous. There are things we can do to get what we want. Create a culture of honor, instead of a culture of shame. You want to honor one another. Speak well of one another in the way that you relate, both in authoritarian relationships but also in horizontal relationships. By creating a culture of honor, you give space for equality.

One of my favorite gems from Leslie concerns how she wants to treat teachers and staff at Covenant Academy. She says, "You will be my sister longer than you will ever be my employee." She went on to say, "The reality is, the nature of humanity is that we want power. We long for power. At the same time, we are designed to have power to do good for the Kingdom and to have dominion. Create a culture of empowerment of fellow image-bearers so that you are constantly looking for ways to give your power away, for example, to the curriculum committee."

****

INTERVIEW #4: Next, I traveled to Orlando, Florida, where I interviewed Reverend Robert Ingram of The Geneva School.[13] Rev. Ingram was a pastor for 16 years, senior vice-president with Ligonier Ministries for 9, and now head of the Geneva School for the past 17. His entry into CCE was prompted by the questions, "How do people best learn?" and "Are they growing in wisdom?" With a split campus starting this year, there have been challenges in managing both a 45-acre campus with a complete athletic complex and a new 55,000 square foot upper school (7th-12th grade) facility, and a smaller campus with K4-6th grade. The plan is to build the rest of the school on the new campus in the next few years.

While fundraising efforts have been extremely successful, they now have a mortgage and will need to populate the building without raising overall tuition beyond normal cost-of-living increases. They also have the problem of growth and managing growth. Rev. Ingram says,

> They are trying to maintain proper expectations of incoming students. We are trying to guarantee that we don't have a rush of students who upset the balance of culture here, but rather who are on board with what we are doing and not just glad to have a neighborhood school where parents could drop students off in three minutes from their house. We don't want parents to attend simply because it's a brand new school with state-of-the-art athletic

---

[13] Rev. Robert Ingram, interview by Kathleen F. Kitchin, Orlando, Florida, February 21, 2019.

fields, at a tuition they can afford. Maybe they're not "all in" for mission/vision/values. As we go through this admissions season now, we're having to be even more scrupulous in the interviews and asking questions like "Why are you wanting to participate in our school? and "Do you understand our mission/vision/values?" We desire to have families who over time can become strong advocates of Geneva's liberal arts distinctives.

****

Interview #5: Later, I traveled to Veritas School in Richmond, Virginia, to chat with head of school, Mr. Keith Nix.[14] Our conversation was far-reaching. He thirsts for developing a "thick, rich classical Christian culture" in his school, & I wanted to know what measures he takes to help protect that. Prayer, of course, is first. I then asked him, "How do you love your school without 'falling in love' with your school?" and "What do you do to not 'fall in love' with what you *think* your school is doing & actually see what *is* happening?" His immediate answer was "We do heavy assessment." He continued, "We to try to be, we try to make sure we are being brutally honest about our assessing ourselves against our promises, our desires, and expectations."

Keith leads the school in 8-10 self-assessments/year from each of the following vantage points:

1) Student culture assessment
2) Faculty culture assessment
3) Workplace satisfaction assessment
4) Grade-level assessments with every family
5) Head of school assessment (every 2 or 3 years)
6) CTP-4 Test (schools claiming to be academically strong) and the CLT (Classic Learning Test) New college admissions test
7) Parent survey – easy, online 5-minute survey (annual) using Survey Monkey: 8 questions on academics, 7 questions on culture & community. Mr. Nix has collected 8+ years of data on that now. He says, "If we start to go off track academically, culturally, we are going to have ways we are going to see it." He also has a parent exit survey for withdrawals.
8) Board self-assessment (annual) – Nix also has years of accumulative data.
9) Student culture – 5 minutes on one sheet of paper (annual) – 12 questions, scale of 1-9 on their classroom, teacher, feeling supported by school, loving school, peers, feeling cared for, learning, & so forth). Veritas School has a 97.5% retention (2018 and 2019). Parents stay because their kids are going home saying, "I like school. This is a good experience. I'm learning." Parents like & stay. Keith can look at each class over the years and each grade over all the years. Independent School Management (ISM) developed this survey. Keith Nix convinced as many as 20 other classical Christian schools to do this assessment, so they have comparable data.

Other ways Keith Nix assesses his school is when other CCE schools visit Veritas School. "Maybe 10-15 schools visit per year and they give you feedback. Affirmation. A lot of cross-exposure. A lot of schools are insular. Only comparing themselves with themselves. We visit other schools."

As I reflected on these interviews, my observation is *healthy schools are not afraid to have assessments. They invite evaluation.*

Keith Nix also utilizes School Stability Markers (SSM) by Independent School Management (ISM).[15] These markers are 16 researched-based distinctives that are true of stable schools and correlated with private-independent schools' ability to sustain excellence over time. A school taking this SSM survey gets points for meeting each stability requirement on topics ranging from various financial assessments to executive leadership to faculty culture & the student experience to the board of directors to donors to marketing to faculty salaries & benefits & budgeted support for faculty professional development to quality of facilities and a master plan for property, facilities, & technology infrastructure.

_____

[14] Keith Nix, interview by Kathleen F. Kitchin, Richmond, Virginia, June 5, 2019.
[15] Isminc.com.

He says it is a red flag "when a school that really 'gets' CCE, gets a little nervous about advice or best practices from outside the classical Christian world (which is totally understandable)." In a parallel example, Veritas School loves their capital campaign consultants "because they're good at what they do, they're the best at what they do (even helped InterVarsity raise $51M for their campaign). They are not in CCE, but their president is a board member at the CCE school in his area, which is ideal." Keith Nix says, "We can dismiss being attentive to good advice or best practices and be overly suspicious of it. ISM has great resources on running a school well. If possible, CCE schools should identify as much advice & best practices as possible from people who really get an understanding of classical Christian education, but at the same time ISM is research-based and is very good." Keith Nix also says, "Look beyond yourself to other classical Christian schools and even other independent schools or outside organizations that might have wisdom to offer. That's a red flag when you're so insular."

Later on in our interview, I asked Keith, "What practices do you undertake for yourself to make sure you are staying in alignment with Christ and what His will is for you as headmaster?" He responded that there are three parts. The first part regards the head of school that is in charge of the institution. The key questions are:

1) How do you take care of yourself?
2) How do you help the board know that you are spiritually healthy?

Keith says, "It's not just enough that I'm healthy spiritually & otherwise; they need to know it, too. And vice-versa."

The second part is the board's being confident that the head of school is involved in a local body. Years ago, his board asked where things were regarding his church search when it stretched to a 2-year period.

For the third part, he says you 1) look at the School's Strategic Plan. Look at it every year. Look at past years'. 2) Look around. What are some needs not necessarily captured in the Strategic Plan? From there you 1) create the board annual agenda. Then 2) you create a head of school annual agenda – his priorities for the year. In conjunction with the Head Support & Evaluation Committee, he commits to a list of 5-7 strategic items that "always includes a personal growth/personal development element" and 8-10 operational goals. As head of school, Keith meets with a sub-committee of the board called Head Support & Evaluation Committee (HSEC). There are 3 members of this committee: 2 board members & 1 outside local, respected Christian leader in the community, a wise outsider. "The committee's job is to care for me and to hold me accountable to that agenda. They ask, 'How are you doing?' 'Do you need help?' 'Are you growing?' They tell me their concerns. They hold me accountable to my job." Nix continues to say, "It is also my job to tell them if I am not doing well. It should be a safe place where I can say I am struggling here or what have you." I said to him, "It's like Patrick Lencioni's book *The Five Dysfunctions of a Team* says, 'You've got to have trust.'"[16] Keith responded, "You do need people who will speak truth into your life. Not only are you speaking truth into the lives of parents and students and teachers and staff here, or else there is an open circuit."

Red Flags

There is a possible problem in following up on red flags: ownership of the problems within a school could be deemed as "failure," which can be a humbling admission, says one administrator. As you face these red flags, know that God is an ever-present help in time of trouble and will help you correct what needs correcting. I have divided red flags by topic with the administrator's relationship to God first, and the rest in alphabetical order.

Admin & God – Are you devoting time for yourself alone with God? Do you have a rich relationship with Him? Are you going to Him with your school's problems and your own personal problems? Are you carrying past hurts into your present handling of your school? Do you seek out a mentor(s) who has some battle scars & great godly wisdom? Do you have prayer support from your spouse, your church, & your closest friends? Are you faithful with little? ("One who is dishonest in a very little is also dishonest in much" Luke 16:10, ESV.)

---

[16] Patrick Lencioni, *The Five Dysfunctions of a Team: A Leadership Fable* (San Francisco: Jossey-Bass, 2002).

- Sabbath rest
  - Gordon MacDonald's *Ordering Your Private World* talks about "rest beyond leisure," how "on the seventh day, God ceased from labor and was refreshed. The literal translation suggests the phrase 'He refreshed Himself.'"[17] MacDonald encourages a "rhythm of work & rest," thereby ordering our private world. He states that Sabbath rest is a necessity, not a luxury as it "penetrates to the deepest levels of fatigue in the inner, private world."[18] Second, in Sabbath rest we return to the Eternal truths.[19] True rest is to "pause regularly amidst the daily routine to sort out the truths & commitments by which we are living."[20] MacDonald also quoted the Jewish theologian Abraham Joshua Heschel who wrote,

    > The meaning of the Sabbath is to celebrate time rather than space. Six days a week, we live under the tyranny of things of space; on the Sabbath we try to become attuned to holiness in time. It is a day on which we are called upon to share what is eternal in time, to turn from the results of creation to the mystery of creation; from the world of creation to the creation of the world.[21]

    Is this happening in my own private world? Third, Sabbath rest helps us define our mission. MacDonald says, "[W]ithout this kind of rest, our lives will always be strained and disordered."[22] He says Sabbath worship with our Christian family is "non-negotiable."[23] Sabbath rest is "a deliberate acceptance of rest & tranquility in the person's individual life" and "God commanded it and created us to have a need for it."[24]
    - *Summary*: Look upon your work, enjoy its completed appearance, & reflect on its meaning, submitting to praising & serving God in all things.
  - Priscilla Shirer's *Breathe: Making Room for Sabbath* says, "Over-work is a form of unbelief."[25] Are we really trusting God to do what He says he will do? All things are possible. Like Mark 9:24, we, too, can say, "I believe; help my unbelief!"[26] Shirer says, "God repeats this miracle of provision over and over in history and in the experience of his children even today. When we curtail our efforts and interests in obedience to the Spirit's conviction – resisting the gnawing sense of guilt or compulsion to keep pressing beyond the boundaries, beyond that which honors God – He will bless our obedience and sustain us. He will miraculously give twice the harvest, twice the fulfillment, twice the return, even though we haven't done anything more to garner it."[27]
    - *Boundaries*: "'No' represents one of life's most basic and necessary boundaries. It keeps things, hobbies, work, and relationships in their proper place, and serves as a constant reminder of their position in your life…. It – whatever your 'it' is – isn't your god. God is. Once something is allowed to creep past its appropriate place in your life – once you're unable to say 'no' to it – it has become an illegitimate god. It has become, according to Colossians 3:5, 'idolatry.'"[28] Am I worshipping my school, or do I have my loves ordered?

---

[17] Gordon MacDonald, *Ordering Your Private World* (Nashville: Thomas Nelson, 2003 [Orig., 1984]), 193.

[18] Ibid., 194.

[19] Ibid., 196.

[20] Ibid., 196.

[21] Ibid., 197.

[22] Ibid., 200.

[23] Ibid., 202.

[24] Ibid., 205.

[25] Priscilla Shirer, *Breathe: Making Room for Sabbath* (Nashville: LifeWay Press, 2018), DVD Bible Study, Session #2.

[26] Ibid.

[27] Shirer, *Breathe: Making Room for Sabbath* (Nashville: LifeWay Press, 2018), 66.

[28] Ibid., 46-47.

Love God, love others, love the calling He has placed on my life to serve my school, not worship at its altar.

- "You are also honoring God's purpose by setting aside space and time to foster holy intimacy. The break we take from the regular pattern of our lives in any area gives us occasion to see Yahweh clearly without the distraction and distortion of excess."[29]
- Am I losing sleep solving all the problems or resting in Jesus' arms?
- Am I a lord or a servant?
- Do I have at least one member of our school that will tell me the truth in love to my face without fear of me, or do I seek to quash all differences & perceived threats?
- Do I talk with my spouse and my pastor as I shoulder my leadership responsibilities?
- Do I have prayer support?

Head of school Dr. Pamela McKee says,

I take care of myself. I have a prayer partner that I meet with once a week. It's always on Thursday morning. It's away from the campus at a little coffee shop. She has nothing to do with the school except she loves it & prays for it. We meet, we have breakfast, we talk, we pray. That's a morning that I go in late to school, but there's no guilt of being late. It's not 'I'm late'; it's 'I had a meeting.' It is scheduled in. That would be like feeling guilty that you had chapel instead of class. No, that's a vital part of what makes me healthy & therefore makes the school healthy. I let my office staff know, I have my prayer time. I want them to have prayer partners. That teaches them that prayer is a priority in our school & remaining humble before the Lord and needy before the Lord in that I'm human. I need that as much as anybody and that they need it, too. You can set the tone of busy-ness. You set the tone. Just like a mother sets the tone in her home. Whatever you love, that is what you're going to plant. I like people to walk in to our school & hear classical musical playing & for it to smell good & to look good, and so I make that happen in the front office. That's just part of my job & that's my privilege & my obligation to do that. What you love is what you'll promote in your school.

Reading suggestion: W. Phillip Keller's *God is My Delight*

Administrator's Background – Dr. Pamela McKee remarks, "A general who had never been a soldier first, or a doctor who had never been sick a day in his life. How could you empathize? If you have a head of school who really has never been in the trenches, I'm sure it's more difficult to understand a teacher's needs, but all it takes is *talking to a teacher to find out their needs*."

- Do you yourself have an academic background?
- Have you taught for at least seven years before becoming an administrator in a variety of levels & courses?
- If you are not an educator, do you know how to seek out those who truly are and to hire administrator-educators who work with you? Part of relating effectively to your teachers in the trenches comes from your own time in the trenches.

If you are not an educator or a person who can hire the right people to do academics, perhaps you may need to seek a replacement for yourself.

Admin & Board – Is this a board-led school or a headmaster-led school? Is the board directing you, or are you directing the board? Are you seeking to rule the board of directors? Are you taking orders well from the board and discussing points of disagreement constructively? Is the school administrator firing staff without the board's knowledge? Are you representing your teachers & staff to the board? Your parents? Your students?

---

[29] Ibid., 97.

Admin & Communication in General

I asked head of school Mr. Russ Gregg at Hope Academy in Minneapolis what mechanism he had in place for two-way communication of legitimate problems between school & parents. He said, "It gets back to the importance of building relationships. We want to make sure that every student has a relationship with a staff member to whom they can communicate those concerns." The upper school students are all in a weekly mentoring group with a teacher or someone outside the school to have lunch together. They have a house system, too, which has been helpful with communication. Gregg says, "The key is when people express concerns do they have the *trust* that those in authority are going to take those concerns seriously and address those? Some of the most exciting things I've seen along those lines has involved peer counseling. For example, one student was not treating other students with honor and respect, one of the four values of the upper school, but it wasn't until a group of his peers met with him and called him out on that that it finally got through to him and brought a measure of real repentance & change. So we have a video about that experience for Partner Evening that dramatized that story. More often it's peers that can be most effective. A lot more trust & conviction."

Admin & Community – Are your interactions with the business community above reproach? Do you do all you can to be a "good neighbor"? Are you serving the community in some fashion?

Admin & Other CCE Schools – Do I seek to isolate myself and our school from rubbing shoulders with similarly minded institutions, thus depriving my teachers and myself of valuable opportunities of "iron sharpening iron"? Keith Nix says it is a red flag when schools say, "We're too poor to invest in professional development. I see heads of school that we never see at conferences and are languishing without accountability and fellowship."

Admin & Control/Power – Throughout history, there is almost always a struggle between rule by the one vs. rule by the many. Administrators are the boss – period – and should be respected as such. But how does the boss create an atmosphere of collegiality and communication? Is communication only top-down? Is discussion encouraged between the administrator & his or her teachers? Secondly, how does a boss encourage respectful, honest feedback (discussed earlier in this chapter)? Thirdly, is there only one leader and no significant delegation? What tasks must be centralized and what tasks can be de-centralized? Some tasks & projects & areas of expertise lend themselves to delegation, for example, giving reliable teachers charge of morning devotions in the upper school.

As we look back in history, in the Middle Ages, England had a strong central government, France had a weaker central government with more local government in each county, and Germany had no central government but all power resided with each prince in each principality. Rule by the one, rule by the few, & rule by the many. It is a beautiful phenomenon to witness administrators' sharing their power with others who have earned it. The athletic director leading morning devotions and bringing to our eyes tears of conviction. The literature teacher beautifully explaining the thesis process to parents at thesis night. The Bible teacher delivering the lesson in chapel. Discretion is absolutely necessary in selecting with whom to share power, but not rigidity in having only the head of school being the sole source of leadership. Every year, reevaluate de-centralized assignments to determine if the person in charge is becoming power-hungry.

How does over-controlling leadership occur when the school's beginning was so biblical, hopeful, and refreshing? In the management-labor paradigm, heads of school can err on the issue of authority. They often don't understand the nuances of authority. They'll do a big focus on biblical authority and why everyone has to submit. Depending on how that biblical authority is asserted, it can pave the road for an abusive culture. In Ezekiel 34:2, an unhealthy model of power is contrasted with a healthy model: "Thus says the Lord God: Ah, shepherds of Israel who have been feeding yourselves! Should not shepherds feed the sheep?"

Admin & Courage – In the BBC series *Endeavour*, the Police Chief Superintendent Reginald Bright debated only briefly during a dilemma, but questioned himself, "A moment's courage, or a lifetime of regret? That's always been the choice." He chose the honorable path of confronting corruption within the police force. If something is going wrong, pray & then act.

Admin & Curriculum – Dr. Pamela McKee says, "I am not going to jump on the next bandwagon. If this isn't from God, this is a fad."

Admin & Faculty/Staff

- Do you have prayer time together at least once/week?
- In your private devotions, are you praying for your teachers/staff?
- Are you treating them as being made in the image of God? It is our tendency to treat students as being made in the image of God, but Dr. Pamela McKee says we need to "apply this to teachers, too."
- Are you communicating that teachers are important, not just the parents and students you are seeking to keep in your school?
- Are you treating teachers as you would like to be treated?
  - *Red flag*: Seeing teachers as cogs in the educational machine, easily replaceable. Becoming the German industrial model: becoming exactly that which we seek to avoid.
  - *Red flag*: Are you overusing or abusing young teachers' energy?
- *Communication*
  - Do you have both daily & weekly announcements to ensure everyone is on the same page?
  - Oftentimes, a Christian private school teacher can feel that their voice is not heard. In public school, there are human resource and personnel avenues and perhaps the teacher's union, but in a Christian private school, there is an unspoken assumption of doing the right, biblical thing. Administrators would treat teachers as they themselves would like to be treated. Both administrators and teachers submit to God and behave in a godly manner toward one another. In the course of interviewing teachers for this book, however, they often feel there often is no "honest broker," no person who hears their point of view. Much effort is invested in protecting student enrollments, future building programs, and curriculum development, but the teacher is often lost in the middle of all the priorities. The lack of examining how administrators are interacting with teachers can lead to entrenched unhealthy patterns, discouragement, and ultimately departure. It grieves me to see young, capable teachers exit the door. Young teachers will be carrying the torch for classical Christian education into the future, and their voice matters.
  - *Red flag*: Christianity should never be used as a weapon to manipulate faculty or staff. "Think the best" truly *is* the best mode but can be manipulated to pressure employees to suppress discernment even if they sense something unbiblical is occurring. "Being a living sacrifice" truly *is* our reasonable act of service, but can be manipulated to pile increasing responsibilities upon faculty and staff that go beyond reasonableness.
  - Pray before and after a conversation or email. Ask Jesus to guide. Before clicking "Send," ask Jesus if there is anything He would want you to add or subtract. After the conversation, examine yourself. Did you cross any lines of respecting others? If so, confess to God and as appropriate, confess to the teacher. You are not perfect, nor are they.
  - Build up; do not tear down. Remember, no matter how you *feel*, you need to be a shepherd. A good one – with Christ's help.
  - Completely *avoid* comparing one teacher to another teacher. That tears down. Treat teachers as unique – the way God made them.
  - Do not assume the teacher is wrong. Make inquiries first. Perhaps email is not the best venue. Ask in an earnest effort to understand, not judge. Speak together in person for real communication.
  - Are you treating young teachers with gentleness? Are you giving them time to learn & grow? Or are you expecting immediate proficiency?
  - Treat others the way you would like to be treated. Even if they are not behaving in the manner you would expect or wish, take the high road. Be mature. Be Christ-like.
  - If a teacher is overwhelmed or ill, do not cursorily acknowledge, and then bulldoze through with your agenda. Find out why they are overwhelmed, but do not pry into their private life,

Endeavor to understand their pressures. Work as a team. Help them. Be humble. Become *less*, so that they may become stronger, better teachers. Die to self.

o Just as there was Sabbath rest for the land (every 7 years & every 50th year), we cannot expect to draw out endlessly from our teachers, our students). We need shepherds who check the state of their flocks, and provide reasonable rest & times of restoration. We have to set aside these times.

o *Boundaries in Communication*
  ▪ Establish limits on when & by what means to communicate.
    • Communicate when necessary.
    • Laser vs. shotgun approach: Use the pin-pointed laser if a teacher/staff person needs correction, not the shotgun approach where everyone feels scolded about one or two person's actions.
    • In person for the following reasons:
      o Encouragement
      o Evaluation
      o Lengthier topics
      o Sensitive subjects
    • Email
      o Good for *information*.
      o Limit the number of emails to teachers.
        ▪ Ask
          • Is there a need to know?
          • If there is, then email.
          • If there is not, do not email.
            o *Red flags*:
              ▪ Too many emails.
              ▪ Not enough emails.
              ▪ Emails that condemn and draw conclusions before a conversation has taken place in which to ask questions, not deliver ultimatums. Be interrogative, not declarative.
    • Phone Calls
      o Good for *communication*.
        ▪ A problem that cannot wait until the next day (e.g., need for a substitute).
        ▪ *Red flags* – Respect the sphere of the home.
          • Do not call teachers after 8PM.
          • Do not call teachers on the weekend.
          • Do not call teachers on their vacation.

o *Conflict*
  ▪ When there is an upset about a homework assignment, go first to the teacher, not to the students. Go to the horse's mouth for the facts.
  ▪ Assume the teacher is right until otherwise informed.
  ▪ Do not use the gossip mill to feed your facts.
  ▪ Be more concerned about truth than your school's image when working through a concern with a teacher.
  ▪ Be humble at the beginning of a talk or an email: acknowledge that you need facts. Just don't draw conclusions prematurely before speaking with the teacher first. (Email is for facts; if you need to communicate, go talk to that person *in person, face to face*.)
  ▪ When a teacher says they are overwhelmed, avoid piling on criticism and expectations. Treat others as you would like to be treated.

o *How Not to Write/Talk to Faculty*
  ▪ No praise. Just criticism.

- No inquiry about why someone did what they did, when they did, how they did. *To communicate, speak in person.* Assume there is more to the story before coming to conclusions. Assume the best until you have more information (1 Cor. 13:7).
  - Look at your email before clicking "Send." Pray, asking Jesus to edit your work. Have you repeatedly said, "You, you, you" or "You could have…you could have" in a shaming manner?
- *Contract*
  - One teacher said their administrator was "not always aware of everything that teachers were doing and asked more & more & more from teachers – unrealistic expectations and at what level of quality they could do them."
    - When a new or seasoned teacher says they cannot do more, administrators need to respect that and not denigrate them or deem them unsubmissive whereupon they are reduced to tears. People do have limits and administrators need to respect them.
  - One teacher said, "A lot of times the women are expected to serve on more committees, to be more nurturing and relational, yet they are paid less."
- *Discipline of students*
  - School or parents? Different schools handle this different ways. Be consistent.
  - Behavior vs. the heart – a heart issue?
    - Reward system – Trains outward behavior, not the heart.
    - Marks on the board system – What is being trained?
  - Leslie Collins: Hard things might be good for your child?
- *Discipline in general*
  - Just as headmasters discipline students who are out of line, so too should headmasters discipline faculty & other administrators beneath them if they are behaving in an ungodly manner or not adhering to school standards.
- *Early dismissals* – Again, guard teachers' class time. Avoid early dismissals for sports that become imbalanced and intrusive.
- *End of year*
  - *Red flag*: Staying two full weeks after school has ended. Teachers are tired, exhausted in fact. Please let them go home, be with their families, & rest. *Suggestion*: If teachers meet the deadline for year-end tasks (grades, book returns, files, binders for administrators, classroom cleaning), allow them to go home earlier.
- *Evaluations & Feedback*
  - Former administrator Laura Tucker says, "At the beginning of the year, meet with every teacher about their goals. Contrast last year's goals with this year's. Could be a personal goal, too."[30]
  - From *Rocket Fuel*: "According to an old business maxim, anything that is measured and watched is improved."[31]
  - Do you evaluate your teachers once per quarter for a new teacher or at least twice per year (once on a mutually agreed to date; another unannounced)? According to Bruce Tulgan, author of *It's Okay to be the Boss: The Step-by-Step Guide to Becoming the Manager Your Employees Need*, says, "All across the workplace, at all levels of organizations in every industry, there is a shocking and profound lack of daily guidance, direction, and support for employees. This is what I call 'under-management' – the opposite of micro-management."[32] Do you walk the halls? Do you step into a wide variety of classrooms to encourage and join in the activity? Do you provide both positive feedback as well as constructive correction? So often employees hear only the bad. And it is tremendously discouraging. Or they hear

---

[30] Laura Tucker, phone interview by Kathleen F. Kitchin, July 26, 2019.

[31] Wickman and Winters, 176.

[32] Bruce Tulgan, *It's Okay to be the Boss: The Step-by-Step Guide to Becoming the Manager Your Employees Need* (New York: HarperCollins, 2007), 2.

nothing at all. Which is disheartening. Former administrator Laura Tucker says, "You really need to know the person."

o Evaluations need to be modeled on Revelation 2 & 3: Church in Ephesus (Rev. 2: 1-7) and the Church in Philadelphia (Rev. 3:7-12). Some refer to this as the "love sandwich." There are three parts: 1) *Praise* (concrete, specific, not short or effusive) 2) *Concerns/Crucial Questions* (concrete examples of areas that need attention or improvement), & 3) *Encouragement & hope.* Do I praise my teachers & staff, orally & in writing, naturally & periodically? *General public praise alone is not sufficient.* Proverbs 3:27 says, "Do not withhold good from those to whom it is due, when it is in your power to do it" (ESV).

o Leslie Collins: Sometimes teachers need an advocate, someone to defend them. She says there are "also times when you need to push them." She says the ultimate point is "We *talk through evaluations*. They know what I am looking for, and I'll tell them what I see. Evaluations end up being my perspective, but there is an underlying expectation that I am on their side, and that I am trying to help them grow, so they are not afraid to hear hard things, they are not afraid to hear good things. There is a commitment on their end, too, to professionalism."

o Dr. Pamela McKee: Dr. McKee began her administrative career doing these evaluations herself. At the beginning of school, she gives teachers a *pre-observation evaluation form.* [See "Appendix."] At a teacher-training session, she goes over the form & explains each section's purpose. On the pre-observation form, she has the teacher answer the following:

1) "What is your topic/subject?"
2) "What are 3 objectives for the lesson?"
3) "How will you integrate Christian worldview?"

Secondly, Dr. McKee does formal observations once per quarter for new teachers, and once per semester for returning teachers, totaling four evaluations per year for new teachers and two evaluations per year for veterans. For the first evaluation for all teachers, she lets them choose the day/class/time; for the following evaluations, she makes the choices. Dr. McKee invests 1 hour (maybe 1-1/2 hrs.) observing. [See "Appendix," "Observation Sample."]

> I want to see a transition from one subject to another. I want it seamless. I want to see how they begin & how they end a class. How organized is the teacher to begin class on time? Are they wasting the students' time? Are they fumbling around & looking for their paperwork? Are they saying, "I can't get this computer or technology to work?" Those are time-wasters. So I want to help resolve those problems.

Her evaluation form includes John Milton Gregory's *The 7 Laws of Teaching* (Law #1, etc.). [See Chapter 6, "Your School's Curriculum."] She evaluates and then "I always have a follow-up visit with the teacher, one-on-one, sitting down in my office and we just go over the evaluation form. That may happen 2 days later; it may happen a week later. [See Appendix, "Post-Observation Conference Form."] She begins the conversation by *asking questions* (not handing down the results): "How did it go from your perspective? What would you do differently?" In one instance, the teacher shared that she never had been observed. "That is a shame that heads of schools, that principals are not doing their jobs." For teachers and administrators, "It really is an experiment in grace." Dr. McKee says, "For a teacher whose observation did not go well, I want to comfort her. It goes something like this: "Listen, that's behind you. If you had this to teach this over again, what would you do differently?" The teacher herself has already gone over the discomfort so many times in her mind. Dr. McKee says, "I wanted to know if *she actually understood* what she had done wrong. I didn't want to tell her. I wanted to find out if she could see it." I said to Dr. McKee, "You were educating her. *Educare* means to draw or lead out." The teacher was spot-on in her self-assessment of the problem, and Dr. McKee reflects,

She discovered it herself. She knew. She learned from experience. She would never do anything like that again. It was a great experience. Had I not been in the room, had I not talked it over with her, I don't think she would have learned that lesson; rather, the failure may have turned into anger at her class or her blaming them, instead of taking the responsibility for the fault, understanding, & next time teaching to the child's frame. I was letting her experience it, though, because I wanted her to feel that pain. I wasn't rescuing her or jumping up to help. I just wanted to observe. And God taught her all those lessons. But we had to talk it all through.

Dr. McKee modeled the Good Shepherd to this teacher, coming alongside, helping her to process that painful lesson. This administrator asked the teacher questions. In addition, "...On the evaluation form, I always try to find at least 3 positives because I want them to be *encouraged*. I don't want them to walk away discouraged or think 'I'm the worst teacher in the world' or 'I really blew it.' I want to find the things that they are doing well and tell them those things, what I did like. I didn't have to tell her her problems. She was in tears. Examples of positives could include, 'You're a great teacher. Your heart is there. You love these students.'" Dr. McKee seeks to be very affirming in the teacher's calling, in her position, in her love for the students. She says, "If I can't find 3 positives, then maybe I've hired the wrong person, but I can typically find things to say about them. Then I move to 3 areas of needed improvement. This is what I'll be looking for next time."

The beauty of evaluations is that they also inform administrators of areas in which they need to train their teachers, so there is actually accountability for both sides. Dr. McKee owns it: "A teacher's weakness is my job. It's my fault if I don't help her improve. If I am aware of that need, I need to meet that teacher's need. If a teacher is not good at classroom discipline, then I need to train her in what classroom discipline is, what classroom management skills are. I need to provide that training. As I look over my teachers' evaluations and their weaknesses/needs, that tells me exactly what to do at my next faculty meeting." When Dr. McKee sees patterns amongst her teacher evaluation results, *those patterns inform her teacher training*. She says, "It is human nature for someone to have needs and to want someone to come alongside them who will encourage them in Christ. It's the body of Christ. It's the body of Christ working together. You're helping a fellow laborer to improve their skills." She does, however, separate new teacher training from veterans' teacher training.

- *Expectations*
  - *Red flag*: Not being aware of the hours that teachers are investing and then on top of that, asking too much of employees.
- *Faculty reading assignments/enrichment*
  - All-staff reading assignments
    - Not during school year – have enough already!
    - Not at end of school year – they are exhausted!
    - *Suggestion*: Schedule all-faculty book reading during summer teacher workdays and only 1 book, not 2. For that second book, start an optional book club. What books do you want your entire faculty to have in their toolkits? People like choices. Occasionally propose two books and take a vote.
    - Keith Nix: "We are so intentionally taking our teachers deeper & deeper in their understanding of classical Christian education. Our recently developed Faculty Training, Evaluation, and Certification program is quite robust and included important readings together. They read & discussed C.S. Lewis's *Abolition of Man* this year."
- *Faculty meetings* – The assumption here is that the administrator is organized and well-suited to the job. He or she is a leader who is able & willing to initiate & go out ahead.
  - Make faculty meetings lean & meaty.
  - Keep them short. Administrators without children at home need to respect that faculty with children need to have time to parent, not just teach.

- o *Suggestion for large schools*: Have a white board at the meetings where teachers can place sticky notes with questions & issues. The administrator can quickly affinitize the notes & address them.[33] Writing concerns & questions helps younger & less vocal faculty to be heard.
- o Do I conduct meetings with professionalism & collegiality?
- o At the meeting's end, the administrator should devote a final section of the meeting to ask, "Is there anything else?" and wait a minute, not a few seconds for the answer. Deliberately solicit non-agenda items. Make eye contact with each person at the meeting as you wait for answers. You are a leader, not a dictator. Allowing this "breathing space" communicates openness, transparency, and true concern and care; avoid steam rolling.
  - ▪ For different administrative roles: keep in mind the *visionary* focuses *on* the business; the *integrator* focuses *in* the business.[34]
- o Leslie Collins has two teacher meetings per week:
  - ▪ Grammar school (Wednesday – 1 hour):
    - • The first question by Leslie every meeting: "What are your concerns? Tell me your concerns." Examples of what she hears can vary: the way lunch is being run (heavy-handed), car line, discipline, & playground aggressiveness. She looks for patterns.
  - ▪ Upper-school meeting (Tuesday – 1 hour)
    - • 1st agenda item: They "look at the failing grade report to see who is failing and make sure that everyone who is dealing with that is on top of that."
    - • 2nd agenda item: "What concerns do you have?"
  - ▪ "If we have a special speaker after school, we do that in lieu of a regular faculty meeting. Meetings are for collaboration, peer to peer training, not information."
  - ▪ If school is closed Monday, the entire faculty meets Tuesday
  - ▪ Daily email updates inform teachers/staff, & they are "expected to keep on top of info."
  - ▪ Weekly email updates inform parents.
- • *Fellowship* – Do we have three or four times per year when we gather as an entire team of board members, administrators, faculty, & staff (e.g., before-school-begins picnic, Christmas party, fall & spring informal gatherings). Inspires esprit de corps, reinforces the vision, & encourages the faculty & staff.
- • *Firing*
  - o Do I fire teachers who are unethical and immoral?
  - o If a teacher brings to my attention that a biblical principle is being violated, am I seeking to push them out of the school?
- • *Hiring & supplying*
  - o Do not ask teachers to teach a subject they are completely unfamiliar with and then provide no curriculum for them to use.
- • *New teachers*
  - o Several days prior to school opening, give the new teacher time to meet with teachers at their same grade level and/or teachers who taught that level the prior year.
  - o Don't give them too many duties their first year.
  - o As one teacher suggested, "Don't give them added responsibilities, so they can focus on and understand the curriculum and implement it well."
  - o As one teacher expressed it, "Be willing to listen and learn from others who don't have as much experience so that in your decisions you understand what you're asking and can sympathize with them."
  - o Do you train new staff, coming alongside them?
- • *Planning ahead*
  - o A former administrator says his church small group was to meet, but one member who is a schoolteacher could not make it "due to a last-minute requirement by administration to create a unit on a country for the entire school. This is just one of many last-minute ideas

---

[33] Steven Sheets, interview by Kathleen F. Kitchin, Greenville, North Carolina, September 5, 2018.
[34] Wickman and Winters, 146.

thrust on teachers. The motto of 'lack of planning is planning to fail' rears its head way too often causing lots of consternation in the lives of teacher families." Emergencies require last-minute tasks; the regular school day does not. Place less stress on teachers by planning ahead.

- *Teacher-training* (1 or 2 weeks in duration before school begins)
  - o Dr. Pamela McKee says teacher training trains us how to become a good teacher so that we can teach. Basics she covers are classroom discipline, classroom management, & the importance of having a file for each student, amongst other topics. She says, "What you can't teach is someone's spiritual life, someone's relationship with Christ; you speak into it, but it has to already be there."
  - o Good repetition versus bad repetition
    - Have the entire faculty/staff together, especially for the first day.
      - Separate out new teachers & train them before the first teacher-training day (1 or 2 days). Do not train new teachers with veteran staff each year as the veterans do not need or want this.
    - In addition to face-to-face teacher training, one school develops teacher-training units online with quizzes. New teachers & new substitute teachers do the entire program. Returning (veteran) teachers need only to re-take the quizzes & score 100%. An effective & efficient use of everyone's time.
- *Tone*
  - o Am I exploding at my staff? Am I doing too much & taking this stress out on my staff? Am I getting adequate sleep? Am I quick to listen & slow to become angry? Do I need to do less & rest more (even 15 minutes)? Am I charming but not genuinely fearing the Lord? Am I operating in my own strength or in the fullness of the Holy Spirit? Am I loving my faculty & staff with the love of the Lord? Can they tell I am for them, or do they feel I am against them?

Admin & Feeder Churches – Do you host an annual pastors' breakfast or lunch to reach out to the pastors of your student body? This is an optimal opportunity to cast vision, build community, & work together in partnership. [See Appendix, "Principles of Partnership."]

Admin & Fellow Administrators – Are you serving in your area of strength (head of school, director of instruction & curriculum, academic dean, athletic director, etc.)? Are you a team united? Are there too many administrators? If you are a visionary, are you in a visionary role? If you are an integrator, are you in an integrator role? Do the visionaries and the integrators hold high respect for each other, knowing both are vital to this school? Do I trust or tromp on my fellow administrators? Do I respect their role & expertise? Am I placing people in positions to stroke my ego? Together, insulate teachers/staff from unnecessary stresses, tasks, & troubles.

- *Job Descriptions* – Do you have a job description for each administrator? Are they each doing their job? Are they placing their work into teachers' laps? For example, teachers should not be creating admissions tests and administering them...the admissions director should. Guard teachers' time so they can do what they have been hired to do. Administrators are to lead, love, & serve. Be sure they are doing that. As I interviewed for this book, I often found some teachers are not getting the help they need because the administrators' roles are not being defined or if they are being defined, sometimes the administrators do not know what they are to do in that role. Define each administrator's job description with as much clarity as possible:

  - Head of School
  - Grammar School Principal
  - Upper School Principal
  - Director of Instruction/Curriculum Committee
  - Athletic Director
  - Admissions Director

A comment regarding titles: "Classical folks have romantic ideas about mini-universities and use the term academic dean. 'I've finally arrived.' No. The reality is you're dealing with little kids, kids who pick their noses. You're not a dean. If you have a Ph.D., we'll call you a dean," says head of school Leslie Collins. It is important to ask, "Why we are giving these titles?" A culture of pretension can have the unintentional side-effect of producing unhealthy pride in our students. In addition, school structure can be "fat on administration." Leslie notes, "But we *still have teachers who are starving.* 'Nobody is reading my lesson plans.' Nobody is getting feedback." Keep first things first. Pray & then prioritize.

- *Meetings with Fellow Administrators*
  - Always begin with prayer. *It is remarkable how over time, this most essential aspect of meetings is dropped.*
  - If this meeting is held on Monday morning, it may impede teachers' being able to access administrators; therefore, perhaps a Tuesday would work better.
  - Head of school Russ Gregg told me Hope Academy has found Gene Wickman & Mark C. Winters' *Rocket Fuel* vitally helpful and practical to meet their vision, mission, & values. The Five Tools, below, outlined in *Rocket Fuel* are broken down into two groups: Tools #1 & #2 which *lay the foundations* and Tools #3, #4, & #5 which help an organization to *gain traction.*[35]

The "Five Tools" found in *Rocket Fuel*:

1) *The Accountability Chart*
   a. "...[D]efines the best organizational structure for your company.
   b. "...[C]rystallizes roles, responsibilities, and reporting structure to help make your vision a reality." (p. 152)

2) *The Core Questions* – Answering these "will lay the foundation to simplify our decision making. You'll have the clarity, the direction, and a guiding mechanism to make efficient decisions" (p. 161).
   a. What are your Core Values? *Choose only 3 – 7 core values.*
      i. "...[D]efine your culture, your guiding principles, and the rites of passage into your organization" (p. 153). Great resource on p. 154.
      ii. They are "who you and your organization truly are (not what you want to be)."
   b. What is your Core Focus?
      i. "Where do you excel? What do you love doing? What are you great at doing? What are you passionate about? Why does your organization exist?" (p. 155)
   c. What is your 10-Year Target (or 5-Year)? *A one-sentence, long-range goal that is specific, measurable, and attainable"* (p. 157)
   d. "Who is your ideal customer, and what is the most appealing message to them? *"...[A] short, sweet, and simple message and decide who your ideal customer is for that product or service"* (p. 157)
   e. What is your Three-Year Picture? *One page, 2-4 measurables at the top, and 5-15 descriptive bullet points that clearly paint the picture* (p. 159)
   f. What is your One-Year Plan? "[L]ess is always more," *one page, 2-4 measurables at the top, 3-7 goals for the year* (hopefully, closer to 3)

3) *The 90-Day World (Quarterly Meeting)* Meet to set quarterly priorities (p. 162). *"Set 3-7 most important priorities that must be done in the next 90 days.* These priorities are also called 'Rocks,' made popular by Verne Harnish, who borrowed it from Stephen R. Covey's time management illustration in his book *First Things First"* (p. 163).
   a. "When everything is important, nothing is important."
   b. · Dan Wallace, a certified EOS Implementer: "Do less better." (p. 164)

---

[35] Wickman and Winters, *Rocket Fuel*, 151-177. The remainder of this section includes specific page references.

    c. "Work on the biggest priorities – the Rocks (90-Day Priorities) – first. Everything else will fall into place" (p. 163).

4) *The Weekly Level 10 Meeting (Weekly meeting, 90 minutes)*
    a. Criteria:
        i.   Meet on same day each week.
        ii. Same time
        iii. Same printed agenda
        iv. Start on time.
        v. End on time.
    b. Agenda – Below, all on one sheet. See www.rocketfuelnow.com See also *Rocket Fuel*, pp. 166-176 for outstanding guidance & purpose of each of the weekly meeting agenda items:
        i.   Segue (Good News) (5 minutes) (p. 169)
        ii. Scorecard (Tool #5, below) (5 minutes) 5-15 most important activity-based numbers in the organization; on track? If not, dropped down to the Issues portion of the meeting (p. 170). (See vi, below.)
        iii. 90-Day Priority review (5 minutes) On track or off track - no discussion. (Discuss later.) Off track is dropped to the IDS portion of the agenda. [See vi, below.] (p. 170)
        iv. Parents/Students/Faculty & Staff Headlines (5 minutes) Good or bad – any needing further discussion are dropped to the IDS (*Identify, Discuss,* and *Solve*) portion of the agenda to be solved. (p. 171)
        v. To-Do List (5 minutes) from last week's meeting – accountability – 7-day action items. Done or not done? 90% of To-Dos should be "done" every week. (p. 171)
        vi. IDS (Issues List) (60 minutes) Problem solving/Discussion where you *Identify, Discuss,* and *Solve* (IDS). Add last week's issues and this week's issues & prioritize which are the top 3 (5-15 issues). Use whiteboard for improved focus & participation. If top 3 are finished, prioritize the next 3 & work on them.
        vii. Conclude (5 minutes) – Recap new To-Do List & due date in 7 days, discuss new communications & who will deliver them & by what means, & rate the meeting 1-10, hence the label "Level 10 meeting." (In the future, perhaps eliminate the scoring & instead ask what could be done to make the meeting better.)

5) *The Scorecard*
    a. Brainstorm to come up with the best 5-15 activity-based numbers that you would like to review on a weekly basis. Choose numbers that will give you a pulse on what is going on. Add the weekly goal you expect for each and the person who's accountable (p. 180). See p. 179 for scorecard template.
    b. The 7 Scorecard Truths – You Must Believe That … (p. 177)
        i.   what gets measured gets done.
        ii. managing metrics saves time.
        iii. a Scorecard gives you a pulse and the ability to predict.
        iv. you must inspect what you expect.
        v. you *can* have accountability in a culture that is high-trust and healthy.
        vi. the effort, discipline, and consistency to manage a Scorecard require hard work – but it's worth it.
        vii. one person must own it.
    c. The 6 Scorecard Fundamentals – These must be in place for a Scorecard to be effective: (p. 177)
        i.   It will be reviewed with your Leadership Team in the Weekly Level 10 Meeting.
        ii. It will contain 5-15 numbers.
        iii. Someone will be accountable for each measurable (who drives it?).
        iv. Each measurable needs a weekly goal.
        v. If the weekly goal is not being hit, you "drop it down" as an issue in your Weekly Level 10 Meeting.
        vi. You can see 13 weeks of numbers at a glance (helps you see patterns and trends).

Admin & Helping Other Schools' Administrators

Keith Nix, head of Veritas School, has continued to be involved in the Arete Fellowship – a group that originally involved around 10 heads of school. They are a fellowship. For years, they would meet, have retreats, invite others, call and email one another, discussing things like:

    a. What does a flourishing school look like?
    b. What are the common denominators in thriving schools?
    c. What's not working?
    d. How are you staying true to mission as you grow?

There are different categories, or stages, of school development:

    i. Start-up school, just trying to survive
    ii. Surviving, stable school
    iii. Thriving school

We want to help all of them move toward thriving!

This involves looking at which tracks you are on – 1990s or more truly classical? Nix explains, "It's not like we had all the first principles correct in the 1990s & we're just trying to stay true to those. We are doubling down & going deeper in discovery of what classical education looks like and what it should look like today. In what ways is it (and are we) still very 'progressive'? Staying true to mission is going deeper and discovering your mission vs. saying we had this set of things we believed back then and let's just not lose those things. I believe a lot of schools are doing that and are getting stuck. We have a commitment not to stay where we were, but to go deeper & double down to strengthen one's commitment to a particular strategy or course of action, typically one that is potentially risky." There might be a tendency to "drift back to the popular, the progressive, the easy, to what parents think they want. This is OFF TRACK and probably growth oriented." At Veritas School there are "no gimmicky things we are doing to grow, and no giving into pragmatic programs like Advanced Placement." On the other hand, schools can "hunker down to a '90s conception of what CCE is. This is OFF TRACK, too. The middle track is resisting these things – barnacles are collected – and scraping...off what is leftover from our own background." Tracy Lee Simmons' *Climbing Parnassus* covers *Vision* (easy to do), *Will*, and *Mind* (the hard work, the "beyond sips," when you dig deep). You need champions in your community for this." In fact, the most common word Keith Nix used was *deeper*.

Admin & Home Life – If I am married, do my spouse *and* I have a date night? Does it need to be more frequent? In the BBC series *Endeavour*, the Police Chief Superintendent Reginald Bright replies to a question about his official service saying, "It depends on my home life...upon which depends so much." It is vital to have quality time with your spouse that is treated as a "permanent appointment" on your calendar. As one teacher said, "Don't sacrifice your family on your school's altar."

Admin & Integrity with Entire School

Luke 11:17 says, "A house divided falls," so it is essential to have integrity or wholeness in the school. The Five Rules in *Rocket Fuel* for absolute core alignment or "same pageness" are

    1) Stay on the Same Page
    2) No End Runs
    3) The Integrator is the Tie Breaker
    4) You are an Employee when Working "in" the Business
    5) Maintain Mutual Respect.[36]

Admin & Intellectual Property – Are you archiving articles & essays written by your faculty & staff? Do you give credit where credit is due as to those articles' sources? Do not publish staff articles and essays without proper

---

[36] Wickman and Winters, 97.

attribution on your website and hard copy versions. Just as we expect our students to give proper attribution, so must we.

Admin & Office Staff

- *Red flag*: Do you have teachers and office administrative assistants still coming to you after 6 months for straightforward issues? Have you set up robust systems?
- Are you thanking your office staff & being courteous to them?

Admin & Parents – One former administrator told me "I was available every day, consistent, approachable. I was building a relationship. Build on what you know. Change hats and verbally identify as such, administrator to parent, or mom to mom." Inform teachers & staff of potential situations in the home that might impede productive talks and, ultimately, progress for the child. Do not take over the job of the parents. Inform them immediately of problems and consequences from the school's perspective. Do not attempt to be the Dad. Dad (or Mom if Dad is not in the picture physically or spiritually) should handle the discipline from the home front. As Dr. Pamela McKee says, "A short conversation earlier is much better than a longer one later." Have an exit interview with parents if they choose to leave the school, & "If possible, so far as it depends on you, live peaceably with all" (Romans 12:18).

While at Geneva School in Orlando, Florida, I asked Rev. Robert Ingram how their board handles legitimate grievances and concerns. He again responded that

> Trust is the currency. Communities can only exist where there is trust. Our trust here at school is so strong, and it makes for a wonderfully cohesive community. It can be almost disruptive to some churches. Kids are here five days per week. Parents are enamored with the school, so they bleed their energy into the Geneva School. We have a wonderful community. We love each other well. The key to that is trust & communication.

In reflecting over the past several decades, Rev. Ingram said, "I don't believe that a parent or board member or student has ever been told 'No,' you cannot talk to so-&-so or so-& so.' If a parent wants to see me, we try to schedule that within the next day or two. I will carve out whatever time necessary. I might ask them, 'Have you talked to the teacher? If you weren't satisfied, did you go through student services? If you're still not satisfied, then absolutely I will meet with you.'"

I inquired further, "Is there 2-way communication?" Rev. Ingram assured me that there absolutely was reciprocal communication. "I have never ducked a conversation in 27 years of the school. They're not all easy conversations. My approach to this is that I have had some really tough conversations in my life, and I figure that I have maybe already had the toughest conversations I will ever have to have had. Therefore, any I have now will be easier." He tries to be gracious to folks and thinks he has credibility with them after all these years. "I think they trust me to do the backtracking and find out what really is going on and that I will do my homework and will come prepared to the meeting and that I know how to resolve things. My job is to solve problems, or to anticipate things & prevent problems from taking place. I'm happy doing that. There's a lot of folks who don't like to do that and they're not available and the secretary protects them for weeks until the person finally gives up and gets frustrated. I think I have a reputation where people say, 'I know I can talk to Bob and I know that he will do the right thing. I may not agree with it, but he will act.' I don't just listen, and it may be that I have to correct something on our side of the ledger and it may be that I'll say to them I think you need to correct your side of the ledger. Maybe your understanding of what the school is isn't quite right, and I'd like to be able to help you understand what it is that we actually are trying to do."

Admin & Prioritizing

- What do you say to the administrator who also has stacks & stacks of work to do?
  - Dr. Pam McKee: "What is your priority? Are you going to be a better school by going through that stack or by spending time in developing those personal relationships? Which is going to improve your school the most?"

- How do you respond to the reality that many environments have become so task-oriented?
  - Dr. McKee: "I absolutely can see how that happens; that happens to me. I am a very task-oriented person, and I suspect that most administrators are. That's why we have the job that we have. I am on task all the time. I used to get out of my car in the morning and see little clusters of moms in the school parking lot drop-off line fellowshipping. If I'd go over & talk with them, then I was feeling guilty that I'm not doing the things inside the building, but I did want to talk with them & say 'Good morning' & greet them. I said something about it, probably to a board member. 'I just spent 30 minutes outside, I feel so bad' and they said, 'Never feel bad because that *is* your job. That *is* your job. When you're talking to parents in the parking lot, that's your job. And don't think, 'I'm not on the job yet.' That *is* your job." And that was just great advice. And I don't feel guilty. Now, personally I'm thinking something's stacking up inside, but mentally I know – I am doing my job."

Admin & Relating to Others

- Leslie Collins, about being a principal: "You have to have a relationship with every single group you work with. I work with parents, I work with vendors, I work with my students, with my faculty, with my directors. All of those people need to have the same kind of give & take. I'm not saying I do it all well. My main concern is always the approachability and the sense of people knowing that I have their back."
- Dr. Pamela McKee says having systems gives freedom, for example, for talking with parents in the parking lot. Systems gave her freedom. They are life-giving. That's what we have to do for our teachers, our students, & for our schools.

Admin & Students – A school is an *alma mater*, "a nourishing mother." Do you have an appropriately affectionate relationship with the students at your school? Do they return as alumni with fondness in their hearts?

- Do you love your students with Christ's love?
- Are you disciplining some students and letting others get away with disobedience? Is there favoritism?
- Do you pray for your students, present & past?

Admin & Substitute Teachers – Often not done, but do train them. [See Chapter 11, "Your School's Volunteers."]

Administrator/Pastor

When I was speaking with Rev. Robert Ingram at the Geneva School in Orlando, Florida, I shared with him that ACCS board member Rob Tucker had told me he thought that the "Two hardest jobs are being pastor and headmaster." I said, you have been both. How do you seek to incorporate rest for yourself and for your teachers & staff?

We explored these two offices more deeply. Rev. Ingram said that being a headmaster is more difficult than pastor by far. He was a pastor for 9 years at an earlier time and then later for 8 years. Touchingly, he said, "I've cried more in this office than I did when I was a pastor because parents love their kids and when their kids are hurting because of learning difficulties or disobedience or their friends turned on them, that's tough. When that happens, parents are going to come to the headmaster more than they're going to go even to their pastor with those difficulties...I've had more counseling that I've done in this office than I did as a pastor."

He continued saying, "I make considerably more decisions as a headmaster than I did as a pastor. And decisions must be made in a more timely fashion. Many are made in the course of a meeting and cannot be referred to other committees that meet weeks into the future. I am very collegial in my leadership. I huddle with my team. I believe in broad-based ownership. ...There are so many more moving parts. Here we have contractual relationships – 105 staff and 545 student tuition contracts – versus at a church where the people can simply attend another church if they no longer prefer the one they had been attending. Here we have contractual relationships. We have tuition. We maintain relationships."

Rev. Ingram demonstrated how vital it is to have exceptional staff with a high emotional intelligence (EQ) and trusting parents. To illustrate, each child sees perhaps 10 Geneva adults each day at school. These include car greeters, a homeroom teacher, specialty teachers, lunch helpers, aftercare caregivers, and coaches – all of those relationships have to go well each day. Rev. Ingram demonstrates further with a number scenario by multiplying the number of students by the number of adult interactions with that child at the school: 545 students times 10 encounters a day times 5 days a week equals roughly 25,000 encounters. If only 1% of these go badly, it still equates to 250 per week! Just think how many parent phone calls or meetings might result! No school could survive if that percentage was only 0.1% a week. We really have to have things go well. He says, "People just walk from churches and a lot of things never get dealt with because they just walk. Here they can't walk. Problems have to be worked out. I like it that way." I rejoined: "It gets messy. But then there's the great opportunity for Christ to move in a redemptive way through that relationship."

Admin & Vision – Do you have a naturally positive tone when presenting the school's vision? Stand firm on the school's foundational principles. Unhealthiness is turning your back on the principles. Maintain respect for these high goals that were prayed for & God-given.

Trends:

- Is a natural mention of Jesus Christ gradually disappearing from your prayers, meetings, invitations to homecoming & celebration galas, newsletters to your school community, and daily conversations?
- Is there a pattern of high turnover?
  - Teachers & staff-turnover
    - People leave for various good reasons, but is there a trend in your school of long-established teachers exiting?
    - Are you losing faculty at a higher-than-normal rate?
    - Are young teachers exiting?
    - Are teachers trying to inform you of systemic problems and you are not listening to their legitimate concerns and are not addressing their concerns with prayed-for solutions?
  - Families-turnover
    - Are godly parents bringing concerns to the head of school & the board, then not being heard or responded to constructively, and finally leaving?
  - Collect & analyze this data.
    - If the trends reflect a pattern, find out why people are really leaving. Dr. Pamela McKee says to ask, "Why are families leaving? Always evaluate and have ongoing relationships with those who have left." She does exit interviews. She says, "It's your job to check the condition of your soil."
- Is there an "honest broker" in the schoolhouse?
- Is there a lack of humility? "I have planted, Apollos watered; but God gave the increase." (1 Corinthians 3:6)

Sober Reflection

The Individual Administrator

- Am I making time to read my Bible & pray?
  - Am I reading God's Word in sips or soaks?
- Do you have someone or some people who pray regularly for you?
- Do I have any Sabbath rest each week?
- Am I scheduling periodic rest throughout the year?
- Am I speaking kindly of the board, my teachers, staff, parents, & students?

- Am I asking God for a guard on my mouth so that I share what should be shared and do not share what should not be shared? Is there a "need to know"? (Am I talking about one faculty member to another when I should not be?)
- Am I treating others as I would like to be treated?
- Am I a person of integrity?
- Do I confess my sins to the Lord?
- Do I apologize to teachers when I have wronged them?
- Do faculty/staff feel comfortable in confronting me when I have unknowingly wronged them?
- Am I intimidating my co-administrators or serving them in truth & love?
- If I am an administrator who is also a founder of the school, am I exhibiting characteristics of founder's syndrome? [See Chapter 3, "Your School's Board."]
- Do I seek to build up young faculty & staff and not tear them down?
- Am I overburdening new teachers so they burn out & leave? (e.g., 90-100 students for a first-year teacher)
- If I am single, am I considerate of time constraints on teachers who are married & have children? Is my goal minimal last-minute and long-hours expectations?
- Am I taking out my painful past on an innocent present?
- Am I demanding too many activities of my staff and not respecting nighttime, weekend, & holiday privacy?
- Do I listen? To the Lord? To the board? To my fellow administrators? To the faculty/staff? To the parents? To the students?
- Do I know that God loves me?
- Do I remember that He will give me strength for the task He has called me to?

The Group of Administrators (Peers)

- Do we begin our administrative meetings with prayer & ask for the Holy Spirit's guidance?
- Are our eyes on heaven?
- Are we a team (a house united) following the same vision, or have we splintered (a house divided)?
- When there are big problems, are we running to human solutions or to God? (Ephesians 1:23 "… the fullness of Him [Christ] who fills everything in every way.")

Servant-Leader

- Am I working in my own strength, or am I praying for God's strength to serve as Jesus would?
- Am I seeking popularity (love only) or ruling with intimidation (fear only)?
- Am I blessing my teachers & staff or being harsh with them (demanding they produce bricks with no straw)?
- Am I helping my teachers to grow (building up) or only emphasizing what they are doing wrong (tearing down)?
- Am I getting full of myself (not *minus* but *super-size*)?
- Is this my school or God's school?

Getting Back on Track

- Pray, asking for God's searchlight on your soul and His help in honest assessment of your administrating. "For nothing is hidden that will not be made manifest, nor is anything secret that will not be known and come to light" (Luke 8:17).
- Privately, ask your "Nathan" if anything seems veering or, indeed, off the track.
- Pray again, asking God what one or two objectives He wants you to change with His help and grace, to get your school back on track.

- Establish anonymous feedback systems with faculty/staff, parents, & students.
- From *The Five Dysfunctions of a Team* by Patrick Lencioni: "[Administration should prepare their team for] the bad weather every team faces on the way to shedding their dysfunctions."[37]
- Former administrator Lisa Borgeson says, "We are called to survey ourselves. What do we do well? What needs to be improved?" If we want to know how things are really going in a school, she says is it often "the janitor who sees the 'real deal' and the 'depth of the character of the students.'"
- Patrick Lencioni, in *The Five Dysfunctions of a Team* says, "...[T]he larger the company, the smaller the team should be at the top."[38] What is the absolute minimum number of administrators you need to 1) manage the school effectively, and 2) to ascertain how the school is running? Are any roles redundant? Are any roles superfluous? Should some jobs be naturally combined for one administrator who has a skill set in both? Are you using people's skill sets optimally?
- *Project Suggestion*: I encourage schools over a summer or on a professional workday to write or to review *job descriptions* for each administrator's & teacher's role. Engage more than one writer and editor; peers should review peers' job description. Re-view the job description before & after each new hire. Are you being Henry Ford and hiring interchangeable parts, or are you hiring capable people who may bring more to your school than the position they are replacing?

Healthy School

- A healthy administrator is a Christ-follower.
- A healthy administrator honors God and honors man.
- A healthy administrator knows they can do what they do only through Christ.
- A healthy administrator prays for strength from the Lord each day & casts their burdens on Christ.
- A healthy administrator sets the tone of the school; their school reflects this administrator's lengthened shadow.
- A healthy administration avoids the easiness of adding events to the school calendar without careful regard for necessity & existing workloads.
- A healthy administration gives ample warning of calendar changes.
- The *Magna Carta* of 1215 marked a turning point in history: The king was not above the law! Healthy heads of school make a rule and keep it themselves. *Examples*: If a parent comes to complain about a teacher, the administrator immediately asks the parent to seek out that teacher directly. If there is to be no swearing by students, there should be no swearing by administrators.
- Healthy administrators know that adrenaline can press a school too far. Is everything a crisis? Does every situation require a "full-court press" of energy? Take a break. Have a cup of coffee. Keep calm – and then carry on.
- Healthy schools have glass on office & conference room doors to avoid any appearance of evil where men & women have meetings.
- Healthy administrators have balance. They appreciate that school is not EVERYTHING. People have other activities, especially their family.
- From one administrator: "Heads of school don't actually get to be good at what they are doing until they have administered in their 7th year."
- From another administrator: "I love cheering my students on at whatever they do – theater arts, musical arts, sports. I love my extended family."
- A healthy administrator honors the Sabbath & delights in Sabbath rest, encouraging their staff to do likewise & respecting that space.

---

[37] Lencioni, *The Five Dysfunctions of a Team*, 176.
[38] Ibid., 182.

Your School's Administrators

Staying on Track during a Crisis

From one head of school...

- *Keep everyone on the same page, united in purpose.* We used our school's podcast and online Chapel to bring families together through recorded audio and visual segments. We immediately sent short videos to encourage and empathize.
- *Lead on communication logistics.* Faculty/staff spent a week on Zoom focusing on our team mission and how we would proceed, reminded them of our crisis plan and how they were to communicate, what they were responsible for before we communicated to parents.
- *Focus on biblical vision and mission of our school.* Remind everyone of our mission and vision and that this situation is not keeping us from these critical focal points for our school. Chapel focused re-stating the biblical roots of our mission, and I outlined each of the 6 outcomes in our vision. More parents were listening than ever before so I took advantage of that. Chairman of the board sent a great email reminding everyone of our mission.
- *Control the narrative.* When a lack of information is present, imaginations can often go awry. It's our job to control the narrative about our school. We kept our Facebook and Instagram presence very positive and regular to engage. We surveyed our parents for feedback, beefed up our weekly letters, had homeroom teachers in upper school reach out to encourage all to remind folks of what is really true, not what is presumed true.
- *Focus on the whole child.* Within one week of missed class, we had Zoom sessions just to connect with every child emotionally. Our workload was flexible so that parents felt the value of what they were paying, but knew we would work with them if they couldn't manage task completion all the time.
- *Emphasize the value of what we are doing so that parents will not balk when we will not lower the tuition.* I emphasized that teachers were working more hours, not less, learning new software and processes, and essentially creating daily substitute's plans for parents (every teacher's nightmare). Chairman of the board explained that lowering tuition would hurt their hard-working teachers.

In addition...

- The next school year may look vastly different from prior years'. Longer review periods at year's start, more tutoring hires for struggling students, perhaps more students repeating a grade – all will be summer-time considerations in consultation with parents. A typical classroom may look more like the one-room schools of years past with students of varying levels of comprehension and emotional recovery & maturity.
- Actively thank the board, teachers/staff, parents, & students for going above-&-beyond during this crisis. One boss once said, "On Fridays, I try to shake my employees' hands as they leave, and I thank them." You get a much-deserved pat on the back, too! ☺

Setting a Goal

- Pray for God's wisdom. Set one or two goals for getting *your role* better on track. Enter that goal in the binder or phone that goes with you everywhere.
- Refer to this goal throughout the year.
- Reflect on this goal at year's end. Rejoice in God's grace.

Expressing a Desire

- Pray for God's wisdom. Write one or two desires for getting your role better on track *that depend on others' cooperation.* Enter that desire on your phone or wherever you will see it often.
- Pray about this desire throughout the year.

- Reflect on this desire at the end of each year. Rejoice in God's grace.

Encouragement

- Being an administrator can be a lonely calling, a tiring job. It can also be an incredibly invigorating one. Thank you for your faithful work for Him.
  - "Behold, God is my helper; the Lord is the upholder of my life" (Psalm 54: 4).
- Simone Weil (c. 1942), "Reflections on the Right Use of School Studies with a View to the Love of God":
  - "In the first legend of the Grail, it is said that the Grail (the miraculous stone vessel which satisfies all hunger by virtue of the consecrated host) belongs to the first comer who asks the guardian of the vessel, a king three-quarters paralysed by the most painful wound: 'What are you going through?'" May we board members and parents and students see our head of school as a person made in the image of God who bears his or her own burdens. May we be kind to him or her.
- Encouraging words from a fellow administrator:
  - From head of Covenant Academy, Leslie Collins: "God cares more about the state of your families and your students and the churches that are represented in your community than even you do and you can know that He is up to something good and that what you are doing is something that is difficult and hard and like the apostle Paul, you will work tirelessly for the gospel and completely exhaust yourself and know that you are doing a good thing. There have been people who have gone before you doing even harder things and you are walking the path of people who know what you've gone through and you have a Savior who has been faithful and who is in the trenches with you."
- With God's help, you can dawn on your faculty & staff like the morning light, like the sun & the rain, fostering their flourishing and nurturing your students' thriving.

Chapter 5
Your School's Faculty & Staff

"I [Jesus] am the vine; you are the branches.
If a man remains in me and I in Him, he will bear much fruit;
apart from Me you can do nothing."

John 15:5

"Behold, how good and pleasant it is when brothers dwell in unity!"

Psalm 133:1

In loco parentis:

from Latin, "in the place of a parent"

Teachers are tired. ....In a lovely scene from the 1953 movie *The Bandwagon* after a long day of rehearsal under a "Type-A-on-steroids" director, Fred Astaire and Cyd Charisse take a leisurely night-time carriage ride through Central Park. They had had too much of "the bandwagon," of endless hours of rehearsal and the pressure of performance, but in that park they got off the bandwagon. They noticed the trees and the flowers along the way. ... As a result of this break, the production crew turned around the ownership and began to work as a team. How do we intentionally take time off the bandwagon? When do we have time to notice the flowers and trees?

Apples & blackboards & rulers & bells. These iconic symbols come to mind when thinking of teaching. To *teach* comes from the Old English "to show, present, point out" and from Latin *dicere*, meaning "say." Each day teachers are showing, presenting, pointing out, & saying. What we are showing, presenting, pointing out, & saying is of critical importance in the shaping of young lives. God says our careless words can be like reckless swords (Proverbs 12:18) hurting and damaging without warning. On the other hand, God says pleasant words promote instruction (Proverbs 16:21). When I think of pleasant, I remember a substitute teacher in grammar school carefully explaining each word of the Pledge of Allegiance to us. I have never forgotten it.

Most teachers I have met in CCE are devoted educators. In this chapter, we will focus on teachers as professionals, teachers as models, and teachers as human beings. Teaching is an honorable profession, and teachers themselves should seek to be honorable. We can do all things through Christ who strengthens us (Philippians 4:13).

TEACHERS & STAFF AS PROFESSIONALS – LOVE'S LABORS FOUND

OUR LABORS & LOVE
First things first: Love God, love students, love your subject matter. First of all, as an outgrowth of our love for God, we need to remember as Christian professionals to "work heartily as unto God, not man" (Col 3:23). It is God who calls us to this vocation, not man. Before I began teaching in CCE, I prayed for two years to work at my

children's school & pored over the books the Lord led me to read. After the school interviewed & wanted to hire me, I needed confirmation and the Lord gave me the following verse that I underlined & dated in my Bible: "If the Lord delights in a man's way, He makes his steps firm; though he stumble, he will not fall, for the Lord upholds him with His hand" (Psalm 37:23-24, NIV, 1983). I returned frequently to this verse for encouragement & the reminder of His steadfast hand.

Secondly, as Christian professionals, love your students. Pray for them each week. Perhaps before or after school, walk around your classroom, praying at each student's desk. Get to know them as individuals. Go out of your way to ask new students how their adjustment is going. If you sense something is troubling a child, call their parents. Have courage to acknowledge the limits of your knowledge and have humility to share your humanity with your students. One humble Bible teacher I know confessed to his class one morning that he had not been kind or loving to his wife or children before coming to school that day. He said it was his fault, & he told the class that he called his wife upon arriving at school, apologizing for his sin & asking her forgiveness. He shared that her response was "I still love you." A powerful message of truth & grace.

Thirdly, as Christian professionals, love your subject matter. Are you invested in your subject, even if perhaps you have never taught it before? Are you passionate about it? Are you not able to stay away from it? Are you still "doing your subject" even on vacation because it is such a part of who God made you to be? In the process of loving our subject, our ultimate goal is to point students to Christ, not to ourselves. In his lecture "On Stranger Tides: Maintaining Balance in an Unbalanced Culture" at the 2019 ACCS Conference, Dr. George Grant summed it up best: "The best teachers love what they love in front of those they love."

Sometimes we grow weary and wonder if our teaching is making a difference. At the same ACCS conference, CCE founder Pastor Douglas Wilson, in his lecture "Arrogance and Humility: Worlds in Collision," encouraged us that "Teachers labor in the dawn of everlasting results." What we are doing has long-term consequences! Wilson continued by quoting C.S. Lewis: "You have never met a mere mortal," and Wilson extended that by saying, "And therefore it can be said, 'You have never taught a mere mortal.' All of your students are going to live forever." In each day's work, we plant seeds.

FACULTY & STAFF WELL-BEING

While interviewing Keith Nix, headmaster at Veritas School in Richmond, Virginia, I said that in CCE we are rightly focused on teaching and growing children. That is essential. I then asked what measures he takes to ensure faculty health & well-being? He replied,

> Many schools operate out of a scarcity/poverty mentality. We need to treat the profession like a profession. We pay our teachers a living wage. Asking your teachers to work at a discount year after year after year is difficult. So we have really worked hard at our compensation & benefits package. That removes a potential distraction, providing for their family. We value them by valuing their labor. "The laborer is worthy of his wages" (1 Timothy 5:18). If we're not paying them the wages that they are worthy of and if you can't figure out how to do that as a model, then I think you're not a long-standing school. You can get founders & pioneers to do it for a few years for little or no pay, but your school is not going to last. Our schools are schools. They are going to need to outlast the founders, outlast us, & you've got to be able to attract serious talent that's graduating from schools and we're saying we'd like you to come teach here and not do X [salary-driven]. If we're talking about Kingdom building, then we're going to have to have teachers who are choosing to teach and not be an engineer. You can't do that asking them to work as a missionary.

His school treats faculty & staff like professionals, providing them with adequate compensation & benefits.

CONTRACT

In addition to sufficient salary & benefits, another key element of faculty/staff well-being is the clarity of their contract and the follow-through on those promises made. Both sides need to follow the stipulations of the contract. Teachers & staff must do their jobs, such as being present in the school during the stated hours, courses, duties, and so forth. Administrators must follow the covenants included in that contract, such as written evaluations twice per year, salary & benefits, and so forth. Accountability is needed on both sides. When discussing their contract with the board & head of school, teachers need to ask about class size limits. There is no magic number although the biblical 12 is ideal. Dr. Pamela McKee, head of school of Bayshore Christian School in Fairhope, Alabama, says that their maximum is 18. Professional teachers with years of experience know when too much is too much. The administrators & board need to listen to teachers and negotiate accordingly. Teachers who are just beginning their careers should not be given a 90-student workload in classical Christian education. In addition, they need a teacher-mentor to encourage them & share ideas with; they need a director of instruction or lead teacher who will shepherd them through their first couple of years until they are established. In your interview, ask who would most likely be your mentor & who would be your shepherd. Teachers are not just born; they are made, too.

FACULTY ALIGNMENT & ENRICHMENT

First and foremost, it is essential to revisit the vision statement of the school. Do you know what your school's vision, mission, & values are? As a teacher candidate, ask to sit in on a faculty meeting if possible. Are you seeing the vision, mission, & values reflected in the people? Are immediate concerns as well as big picture needs addressed? Are older teachers sharing respectfully with younger teachers (Jeremiah 6:16's "...show me the ancient paths, ask where the good way is, and walk in it, and you will find rest for your souls")? Are younger teachers sharing respectfully with older teachers newer, better ways? Are there times of refreshment to recreate and renew? Are there opportunities for further education & enrichment at CCE conferences and subject-specific conferences? Are speakers brought in to share their wisdom with the faculty?

WORKPLACE MOTIVATION IN GENERAL

Headmaster Keith Nix also mentioned Daniel Pink's book *Drive: The Surprising Truth about What Motivates Us* (2011) that includes the following three areas:

1) Autonomy – the urge to direct our own lives
2) Mastery – the desire to get better & better at something that matters
3) Purpose – the yearning to do what we do in the service of something that is larger than ourselves.

Pink's book discovered that carrots & sticks (extrinsic motivators) were effective only with certain sales or production-line goals, but it was *intrinsic motivators*, the impetus to do things for their own sake because they matter to them, that truly drive people. Pink found that the "if-then rewards" often destroy creativity.

WORKPLACE MOTIVATION AT A CCE SCHOOL

What do Daniel Pink's autonomy, mastery, & purpose look like in a classical Christian environment? The board & administrators provide the vision, mission, & values as well as contracts, job expectations, and training for teachers. They do not micro-manage and tell teachers how to do every aspect of their job. They give enough *autonomy* that the teachers thrive in being all they can in Christ's service. They give principles of business & inspect that those principles are met, but do not give teachers rigid templates in which to operate. At the same time, they give training to new teachers so that they are launched & maintained well. Shepherds know who needs more direction with the rod & staff and who may need less. For the second of Daniel Pink's "drives," *mastery* means teachers are given the "meadows & seas" to explore and to get better & better at understanding the course & the people that they are teaching. Finally, the *purpose* or yearning to do what we do in the service of something beyond ourselves is classical Christian education itself – teaching the liberal arts in a Christ-following fashion that truly makes a man's mind & heart free. With autonomy, mastery, & purpose, teachers – & their students – can fly.

EVIDENCE OF WORKPLACE SATISFACTION

Heads of school care to discern evidence of workplace satisfaction. Keith Nix says, "The meaningfulness of work, knowing that their work has significance, that they are making a difference in the world" is key for teachers. Again, my question was, how do you know that is happening at your school? Nix entered Veritas School in their city's "Best Places to Work" survey, and the results said that of all the businesses in that capitol of Virginia, Veritas School won first place for workplace meaningfulness! Keith says it "tells me my faculty are driven and that *meaningfulness* is a huge indicator – that goes a long way to their health. Faculty are also recognized & thanked." On accreditation visits, even to good schools, Keith Nix, as a visionary member of the ACCS board of directors, says, he frequently hears on school visits,

- We are under resourced;
- I do not have what I need to get the job done;
- I am asked to do too much;
- My workload is too heavy.

Nix continues, "But they love their job. They like whom they work for. They are not being negative or complaining. Their school doesn't have money to go to ACCS conferences." Meaningfulness of their calling keeps teachers wed to their work.

INDICATORS OF WELL-BEING

I asked Keith Nix about indicators of well-being for his staff. Nix says, "What I say to so many things when asked, for example, about how do you do parent education? I say, 'It's about a thousand little things.'" He then elaborated how Veritas keeps a pulse on faculty well-being:

- Intent-to-return (in December) tells us something.
- Our lack of faculty attrition tells us something.
- Top Workplace survey through Survey Monkey
- Annual faculty culture surveys (from Independent School Management (ISM))
- Administrators that are truly in touch with the teachers
- Lead teacher at each grade level (3 teachers/grade) is trusted & works with the teachers day in and out. They should know if something's up, something's not right, or someone is not well.

Nix says this same principle is true in a variety of different categories. "When we interview teachers, we do a really good job of saying what we are committed to, what we are striving for, and what that means is they can hold us accountable. We say very clearly what we are doing. We make promises to them. We provide faculty development. We assign mentors when needed." Keith went on to say, "When you set a high bar and you say it and you say it repeatedly and then you don't do it, you put yourself in a good space to be held accountable. It ought to be easy for a teacher who didn't feel supported to say so because of the commitments you make." Nix keeps his eyes on these indicators of well-being, for he wants his school to thrive.

SURVEYS

Headmaster Nix discussed workplace satisfaction and the 8-10 different surveys he uses each year. He said all teachers need to be valued, to be growing (not stagnant), to be invested in, & to be recognized. All of the bulletized indicators above can be somewhat measurable, but to get *anonymous* assessment, Nix uses the Survey ISM from Independent School Management (ISM) that has 16 questions.[1] It identified heads of school with long tenure, schools that met many criteria, and had high retention & satisfaction – it was a small group of schools. It found that 16 characteristics were in common, the top 16. The overall survey includes a 5-minute survey about the head of school. Sample statements in this survey about the *head of school* included:

- Gives public, positive reinforcement to deserving employees in all categories – especially in regard to laudable professional growth and achievements – and to students at all levels
- Seeks to establish a faculty-wide conversation about professional development
- Is respectful of others, regardless of their position in the organization
- Is steeped in moral purpose, moral clarity, moral conviction, & integrity
- Tries to be supportive all the time and with everyone, regardless of their successes or failures (i.e., gives support even when it may not be merited)
- Shows respect for others in her or his formal interactions, such as presiding over meetings
- Exhibits the moral courage & integrity to represent the school
- Gives public & private recognition & affirmation to the team of employees
- Demonstrates concern about individual students & their academic performance....

---

[1] https://isminc.com.

Keith Nix received the results of the 50 anonymous surveys from his faculty. The rating is 1 (lowest) to 9 (highest). He says, "Generally, I look at the head of school survey & find an area or two that's the lowest & say I'm going to give some real attention to that. I look for the real answers. If they are all 9's – they're blowing smoke; all 1's – that's unhealthy. I like to be in the 5-8 range with an average of 6's & 7's. One year one teacher gave all 1's" and Keith said to himself, "We have an unhappy person here." Keith went to the appropriate administrator and asked, "Is someone this unhappy, & we don't know it?" Keith said, in "Hiring the head, a board has to have confidence that through his lead teachers & his own personality & EQ ("Emotional Quotient" or emotional intelligence), that he should know if someone is feeling unsupported." At the end of year at Veritas, each teacher has a review with their supervisor. Keith said that if a teacher is not being supported, the administration is asking for feedback. If a teacher does not give feedback, at Veritas, it's their fault.

PATTERNS

One indicator in particular should be tracked over the years: the pattern of teachers leaving your school. Rarely does a teacher desire to leave on a dime, unless there is a dramatic change in their circumstances. Are administrators keeping a finger on the pulse of their faculty & staff [part of shepherding discussed in Chapter 4, "Your School's Administrators."]? I remarked to Nix that not all people (deans, directors of instruction, team lead teachers) are suited to read people. He immediately responded, "Then they shouldn't be in those roles. They don't have the necessary EQ. If any head of school does not have an EQ...You don't lead a team of people and not know how to read situations if you have decent EQ." This school year, Veritas had a new principal who had a lot of face time with his teachers. At the *Abolition of Man* faculty discussion at year's end, Keith asked him how the morale & spirit was among the team. I told Keith these leaders who report to the head of school are the eyes & stethoscope for the health & heartbeat of these teachers.

TEACHERS & STAFF AS MODELS

MODELS

Teachers & staff are professionals. Teachers & staff are also models as individuals and as groups. As individuals, they are first of all ambassadors for Christ. They need to reflect His love, truth, & grace to their students. We will not do this perfectly. When we have hurt students, we need to apologize publicly if it was a public hurt, and privately if it was not. Lawrence G. Derthick, United States Commissioner of Education under President Eisenhower in the 1950s "is a joyous man. He believes that when people get together for good purposes there is bound to develop a contagious joy from the smallest accomplishments. In this vein he recalls what his grandfather, Frank A. Derthick, told the Ohio School Improvement Federation in 1913: 'The personality of the teacher will be carried to the very hearthstones of the family.'"[2] I remember my dear octogenarian grandfather who was taught in a one-room schoolhouse telling me that he would visit his teacher through the years. The impact we teachers have goes not only to students' minds, but also to their hearts. Students see us as individuals, but what do our students see us doing as a group? In her ACCS conference talk entitled "God's Garden: Cultivating and Growing Schools," Dr. Pamela McKee said, "Students see us as a faculty praying. There are morning devotionals. Students should see you as teachers setting the tone, setting the culture." To stay on track, teachers need to think of their colleagues before themselves, seeking unity and one accord in Christ.

HIGH REGARD FOR PARENTS

As we assume the role of teacher as model, we need to maintain a high regard for parents. Being *in loco parentis*, in the place of a parent, we respectfully realize we are not the parent. We do not re-place the parent. God assigns parents as the primary educators of their children. The parents of your students have essentially hired you to work *in loco parentis*, "in the place of a parent" for that grade level or that subject. On their website, Mars Hill Academy in Mason, Ohio, respectfully guides teachers as follows: "They will not assume to know their students better than the children's parents, but offer encouragement and helpful criticism as appropriate." We teachers come alongside and work as partners with parents in educating their children in step with the foundational documents. [See Chapter 1, "Your School's Vision."] Teachers should work *in loco parentis*, not taking the parents' job away from them. Administrators should discuss how *in loco parentis* works at each of the three

---

[2] *The New York Times*, November 29, 1956.

levels of the Trivium and how it changes progressively: grammar, logic, rhetoric. Teachers should respect the authority, experience, and wisdom of the parents. We are all in need of learning more and need to be teachable.

SPEECH

As a faculty & staff, another aspect of being models is guarding our speech. Young minds & hearts are so impressionable. I strongly suggest no sarcasm until maybe 12th grade. Sarcasm, and its companions cynicism & sharp criticism, sears and undercuts. The Bible says students become like their masters. Much older students may understand the nuances better; sarcasm, however, can be misdirected negativity and young minds do not need that shaping their development. Be careful of your words, knowing that "Pleasant words promote instruction" (Proverbs 16:21). As James noted, teachers will be "judged more strictly" (James 3:1). We need to ask God to help us control our tongue and show the wisdom that comes from heaven (James 3:17-18).

KIND REGARD FOR STUDENTS

As models, we teachers need to have a kind regard for our students & remember their frames. We need to gauge what are reasonable expectations of grammar students, logic students, & rhetoric students. Academically, that will be addressed in the next chapter, "Your School's Curriculum." We need to know our flock and have excellent standards, but not exasperate those in our care.

DISCIPLINE OF STUDENTS

An extension of our kind regard for students is disciplining them. Head of school Leslie Collins at Covenant Academy in Cypress, Texas, says heads of school need to "give clear guidelines for what the teacher should do regarding discipline. Give clear guidelines for how the teacher should communicate with parents regarding their child's performance in school. Give clear guidelines for what your domain is in discipline. Having no boundaries leads to confusion and ineffective discipline." Communicate the expectations clearly & consistently. If you expect it, correct it. Praise it. Don't expect what you don't inspect. Do not be the school that posts rules, but does not enforce them. The four kinds of schools going off track mentioned in the Introduction are also the "spectrum of how we engage with truth."

1) Running off the track, but do not know it due to inexperience/blind spots,
2) Running off the track, but do not know it due to pride,
3) Running off the track, and know it but suppress the truth, or
4) Running off the track, know it, and humbly desire to change.

As models of discipline, we correct the children in our care with truth & grace, not wanting to be "a willing party to their death" (Proverbs 19:18). *In loco parentis* (in the place of a parent), we join with parents in training up a child in the way he should go (Proverbs 22:6).

In prioritizing heart before behavior (the symptom of the heart), Paul David Tripp "recommends 5 very practical questions that have a very specific order. These questions are to be asked when a child misbehaves and disappoints. He stresses there is a proper sequence to the questions."[3]

Five Questions to Ask When a Child Misbehaves

1) *What was going on?* The point is to get some sort of telling of the situation. Establish a story that reveals the facts.

2) *What were you thinking and feeling as it was happening?* This question goes after the heart. What was the motivation of the heart (causal core)? This question helps us teach our children that our heart is always desiring something and it helps us and them to evaluate it.

3) *What did you do in response?* This question gets at the words and behavior that flow out of the heart (See Matt. 12:34b). It's important to see the flow of how things work. Behavior is the result of the heart.

---

[3] Brent Prentice, "A Means to an End" blog, bprentice.wordpress.com, July 12, 2012.

4) *Why did you do it?* What were you seeking to accomplish? Again, this gets at the heart because it shows the motivation for what was done.

5) *What was the result?* What did the heart produce in way of actions and outcome? It produced consequences and a harvest. We reap what we sow, and we sow what we reap.[4]

Oklahoma pastor Brent Prentice says, "Tripp argues that these questions teach us to slow down so as not to react only to behavior, and they help us to see what is causing the behavior. Additionally, it helps our children learn to examine themselves in a biblical way to see that life is not just about behavior. After all, the older we get the more clever we are at crafting our behavior in a way that doesn't look so bad on the outside, even if we are out of control on the inside. We are masters at camouflaging our deficiencies. So the questions teach the parent and the child to think biblically because the Bible tells us that the reason we sin is because we are heart-sick.

We need to learn to be heart surgeons and not just plastic surgeons because it will not matter how good we look on the outside if we have lethal heart disease. And every person on planet earth does (Read Romans 3).

We must quit treating symptoms and treat the disease. Try these questions in order and see if they help you examine your heart and the heart of your [student]."[5]

HIGH REGARD FOR COLLEAGUES & COLLEGIALITY

Being models as a faculty & staff means having a high regard for colleagues & collegiality. *Christian collegiality* is shared responsibility among workers in a partnership effort for Christ. In this undertaking, there needs to be a professional relationship between each administrator and faculty/staff member. Wise administrators realize people like choices. A top-down-only approach kills the collegial and personal spirit of a faculty. Ask their opinion. And mean it. And actually put into practice some of their helpful ideas. Younger teachers should show respect to older teachers and not view them as "out to pasture" and irrelevant. Older teachers should not demean younger teachers. They should open the circle and include the newcomer. How "good and pleasant it is when brothers dwell together in unity!" (Psalm 133:1). Teachers should not have unreasonable expectations of the staff who are already working in accordance with their job descriptions; both should serve each other in Christ's truth and love. Staff includes receptionist/office manager, administrative assistants, director of school operations, the secretary/nurse, bookkeeper, and so forth. Students are watching. How do the adults treat each other? *Never* embarrass, scold, or demean another teacher/staff member in front of their class or in the hallway. Treat your colleagues as you would like to be treated; confront problems and sins privately, one-to-one. May peace & honor reign.

TEACHERS & STAFF AS HUMAN BEINGS

SABBATH REST

Teachers & staff are professionals. Teachers & staff are models. Teachers & staff are also human beings. Make it your goal to keep the Sabbath. God rested. He is our model. We need to rest, also. Ask God to help you honor Sunday, and He will. There will be those times when your ox falls in a ditch, but God knows our frame and knows we need to worship Him and rest in Him and dwell in fellowship with our families and friends. Regarding "rest" during school hours, when signing a contract, for example at a school that has 7-class periods/day, assure that two periods are not teaching (planning/study hall). In his lecture at the 2019 ACCS conference "On Stranger Tides: Maintaining Balance in an Unbalanced Culture" in Atlanta, Dr. George Grant said, "We need equilibrium, balance, which according to Pastor Chuck Swindoll, this struggle with imbalance is a daily grind." Dr. Grant defined Biblical balance as "a life of grace & peace & maturity & holiness. We are called to be human." Dr. Grant referenced Charles Spurgeon who reflected that he "lost sight of the vision he was trying to help others to see." People need to have a life. That life comes in seasons, "... not everything can be done at the same time. That there is an overflow of joy here & now." Sabbath is intended to restore what is sapped.

---

[4] Paul David Tripp, "Getting to the Heart of Parenting" DVD conference, CDR Communications, 2010.
[5] Ibid.

PRAISE

Teachers & staff are human and need praise. I asked Keith Nix, just as students want to hear individual comments, how do you do that, especially in a large school (587 enrolled)? He responded, "You have to divide and conquer." He gives public recognition. For example, at a faculty meeting one year, he shared the 97.5% retention rate and explained to them, "That's because of the students' experience with you in the classroom. That's it." He told me, "As you get bigger, you have to build out your team and you have to know that somebody is saying that to everybody." I still wanted to know how do you really know. He responded, "There is a safe place for them to tell us." There are the aforementioned surveys via an independent vehicle (not the board of directors, not the head of school). There is a faculty culture survey. On the other hand, veteran administrator Laura Tucker would leave notes of praise & encouragement on our desks or through email. She gave a crockpot cookbook to new teachers who were mothers as she knew their days would grow busier. She gave a simple gift at Christmas & at end of year, perhaps a candle, a plant, a bar of lovely soap for the women, and books for the men, with written appreciation for the teachers' labors. Little things mean a lot.

MENTAL HEALTH

Mental health is an incredibly vital factor for teachers. Stress is normal, but increasingly hearing that professionals need anti-anxiety medication is alarming. That should not be so in Christian schools that are concerned for the health of their faculty and staff. If there is too much stress, something is wrong. Attend to it. God will honor that. Teachers need breaks. Set *boundaries*. Do not call them after the time limit they have set in the evening. They have homes and households, too. Some heads of school simply do not call teachers at home at all, unless there is an absolute necessity. Most importantly, Christianity should never be used as a weapon to ensure employee compliance. A teacher should never be arm-twisted into carrying duties above & beyond their frame to handle. A teacher should never be told "this is your Christian sacrifice." That is between them & God. Steer clear of manipulation & honor the mental health needs of your faculty & staff.

OVERSCHEDULING

It is common to slip into overscheduling. One of the most important lessons we learn as individuals growing up is how much is too much. Your school does not need to meet everyone's needs. It needs to teach. It does not need to have elaborate fieldtrips, college visits, mission trips, or service projects. Leave those to these children's parents and to their churches. Keep within the school sphere. Your teachers need that. Your families need that. Less is more. How do we achieve balance?

EVENT OVERLOAD

One school I worked for had a wonderful idea. The administrators surveyed the grammar school regarding the master schedule of school events for the entire school year. They asked the teachers which events needed to be removed to prevent overload. They kept what was essential: *first things first.* Some suggestions:

- Meet for parent-teacher conferences *once* per year. Meet more times only if needed; otherwise, avoid redundancy. (E.g., "I keep telling the parents the same points as the last meeting." These additional meetings are unnecessary for both the parent & the teacher.)
- Email mid-term reports with a link to your electronic grade books. Do not overburden teachers with work that is redundant. The grade books tell the story adequately for upper school. Use written progress reports for maybe half the year for the grammar-level. Always email/call parents if students are at risk of failing – early in the marking period.
- In terms of special school events, avoid monopolizing multiple sequential weekends. Teachers & staff need time for their family & churches.

PRAYER SUPPORT & VOLUNTEERS

Teachers need prayer support & volunteers! As a teacher, I could sense when I was being prayed for and was so thankful for that. Teachers need volunteers to help bear the burden, not the daily tasks. Does your school have some type of teacher support team? [See Chapter 11, "Your School's Volunteers."]

HELPING YOUNG/NEW TEACHERS

Assign every new teacher a mentor who has agreed to meet regularly. One teacher had had heavy years at another school, but her mentor, a fellow teacher at her new school, brought her a meal during the first week of teaching, & this mentee said her mentor "cared for me as a person." Faculty, even in the upper school, need to reach out to each other & inquire how things are going for their new colleagues. *First things first.* How do we treat each other?

Through a Young Teacher's Eyes…

I interviewed a young teacher who said she "knew CCE philosophy & policies but had not had a lot of training." There were "two weeks of teacher training (before school began) which were 'great on goals and philosophy but needed the practical. It was hard to know where to get started'" and so there was much trial & error. One way to help new teachers would be to create "A Day in the Life of Teacher" video where they could see how to set up a classroom, how to set up a grade book, what expectations to have for classroom/class rules.

There were two classes per grade & the administrator kindly gave her, as the new teacher, the smaller of the two classes. One of the administrators encouraged her saying, "There is nothing you will do this year that won't be okay, that we can't fix because they knew whom they had hired." This gave her confidence; she knew she had their support and support from the parents.

She felt she could have used more training specifically for new teachers within her own school. As CCE schools hire young teachers, it is good to remember that it is "hard to be on your own." She said it would be great to have some structure in place to invite young teachers, but "Everyone is so busy." She could have used more people "checking in" as she was new in town and "meals or outreaches would have been nice."

She did not have a mentor teacher given to her.

This year she is teaching a different Trivium level. She says she "needs samples [or models of student assignments]" as she questions, "What writing is acceptable for this age?" She has no idea what her goals are. She has no curriculum director. She has no curriculum guidebook. There is a person at her school who has a nebulous role/title, but was not introduced nor their role explained.

Expectations are that teachers return papers the next day. She has found that unrealistic at the logic and rhetoric levels.

There are not a whole lot of faculty meetings. Her first year there was one per week. A lot of teachers coach after school so it is difficult to have the entire faculty present. The faculty now meet at the end of each trimester or at urgent times of year.

There is a communication difficulty. A lot of last-minute urgencies like "permission slip needed tomorrow." I asked if there were a school newsletter? Rarely.

…This teacher needed a kind shepherd.

CASE STUDY

Hope Academy – Minneapolis, Minnesota – 490 students

While out in inner-city Minneapolis, Minnesota, I asked head of school Mr. Russ Gregg of Hope Academy, "How do you, your school, & your board each incorporate the concept of Sabbath, of rest, so that the cup that is running over gets refilled?" He replied with their weekly plan:[6]

- Daily gathering of the staff for prayer & the Word of God
- On Monday AM – The head of school brings a devotional.
- On other days lower-school staff meet, upper-school staff meet.
  - At the beginning of committee meetings, they seek the Lord together.
- On Fridays

---

[6] Russ Gregg, interview by Kathleen F. Kitchin, Minneapolis, Minnesota, May 20, 2019.

- o Women meet at a home nearby for a time of sharing & prayer.
- o Guys meet to read the Word & to pray.
- o "That's been a part of our rhythm that we have found really important to sustain this kind of thing."

We spoke further about how to rest as an administrator and as a faculty & staff. Mr. Gregg said, "And we're pretty good with making sure that the weekend is protected. I don't look at email on the weekends." *A first things first question*: How are our practices matching our vision, mission, & core values?

I then asked if a faculty member were to have his or her need level rise pretty high, nearing burn out, how would they communicate this? Gregg replied that "To some degree, that sense of dependency or weakness is the normal life of a follower of Christ and of a teacher. We cannot do this in our own strength." He said that after the Friday women's prayer meeting that his wife has at their house, when he comes home and sees lots of tissues, they know it's been a good session. Gregg says this work is not easy and feeling overwhelmed is not uncommon. In true form to his academy's name of hope, he says, "If we build those relationships with one another, then you can carry those things together. I think most teachers here talk about that kind of staff-to-staff strength & community." Gregg says, "The model might be a spa vs. a M*A*S*H unit so we know *we do need to care for one another so that we can get back out into the battle*. The spa is where the care is an end in itself. The M*A*S*H unit model is where we're in the middle of a battle. You really have to be intentional. For our lower-school principal that's probably her #1 gift area – the spiritual shepherding & care of her staff." I responded that that care is critical and that it is also needed at the logic & rhetoric levels. They also need encouragement & positive feedback.

Red Flags

- Allowing non-Christian teachers to teach in your school.
- Relying on the flesh and not God for your strength, your lessons, your teaching, & your communication.
- Taking over the parents' job in discipline. Not immediately contacting Dad (or Mom).
- Not resting. Constantly being "on."
- Not setting limits with parents regarding: emailing/calling faculty beyond a set time in the evening, on weekends, on vacation. Respect their personal and family time.
- Your supervisory chain not all being acquainted with the terms of your contract for faculty & staff. (In other words, heads of school need to provide the contract document to their administrators so that both employer & employee know the promises the administration is making to the teachers. If a head of school is delegating, the other administrator(s) needs to know what the contractual responsibilities are between administrators & faculty/staff and needs to be followed up on to ensure compliance.)
- Having inner circles of "in" teachers or elite teachers, and "others."
- Allowing knowledge to puff up, but not focusing on love's building each other up (1 Cor. 8:1).
- From one new teacher: "There is a big habit of overwork. Administration & parents are trying to express gratitude to teachers but can glorify people who overwork (e.g., young teachers who arrive an hour before school, but don't have time for friendships or activities) and this prevented other aspects of life. I get concerned about them hurting themselves. This overwork is not a sustainable life. We are praised & rewarded for overwork. What are healthy boundaries? It can be confusing. You are praised for not having healthy boundaries. Your life is a model to your students, too."
- Expecting teachers to have papers graded & returned the next day, instead of the reasonable expectation of *one week*. *Note*: For early grammar reading & math, it is important to have immediate feedback, particularly in kindergarten & 1st grade.

Getting Back on Track

- One person who had been hurt in the process of educating said, "I'm not going to hang on to the old stuff." It was a process, but this individual has forgiven and moved forward, now in a new position. As a result, God blessed this person with even deeper understanding & healing.
- If financially feasible, hire a director of school operations. This person is invaluable to all.

Sober Reflection

Individual

- Am I making time to read my Bible & pray? To be still before my Lord? To delight in Him?
- Am I speaking kindly of the board, administrators, my fellow teachers & staff, parents, and students?
- Am I showing respect for my superiors?
- Am I asking God for a guard on my mouth so that I share what should be shared and do not share what should not be shared? Is there a "need to know"?
- Is there a lack of gentleness in my voice or manner?
  - Deuteronomy 32:2 "May my teaching drop as the rain, my speech distill as the dew, like gentle rain upon the tender grass, and like showers upon the herb."
- Without moving into psychobabble, we all tend to bring into current circumstances our past successes, hurts, and troubles. Are you bringing past hurts into your present situation?
- Where are you needing help?

Healthy School

- A healthy school cares about its faculty & staff.
- Administrators treat faculty & staff the way they themselves want to be treated.
- Administrators value in word & action that all teachers are important, not only the exemplars or the most popular.
- A healthy school faces problems head on.
- Healthy schools actively seek healthy resolution.
- If a relationship is off-kilter, the administrator pursues & asks questions.
- If there has been unintentional offense, the administrator apologizes.
- If there has been sin, the administrator apologizes.
- If a teacher has offended another teacher, they meet to discuss, repent, apologize, & forgive. They follow Matthew 18:18.
- If a teacher has been insubordinate, they meet to confess & apologize to their boss.
- Healthy schools know a house divided cannot stand.
- Healthy schools know there are going to be in-house problems & through their dependence on God & His Word, they resolve those problems.
- Headmaster Keith Nix: "You need a good percentage of mature & younger faculty. You have to have a core group of teachers, of parents, who are promoters, that understand the principles & to some degree the practices. They are out there being 'the mouth.'"
- In a first-things-first, healthy school, teachers can express legitimate concerns without fear of retribution.
- Healthy schools create "breathing room" for teachers, providing structures for rest, healthy boundaries, & rejuvenation (perhaps 3 personal days/year); commensurately, one teacher learned to "Give myself more space from school."
- Healthy schools regard parents as partners. They rejoice in sharing the vision and never look down on parents who lack the same understanding of CCE. Faculty & staff are servants, not superiors, and know we are all continuing to learn.
- *Project Suggestions*: One healthy school has "continuity meetings" at the end of each school year while memories of the year are still fresh. By subject, teachers in one grade meet with 1) the teachers in the grade after them to pass on what was actually covered, lessons learned, & observations made – in engineering terms, "feed forward" – and 2) the teachers in the grade before theirs – for both "feed forward & "feed back." In other words, teachers meet with the grade before and after them for continuity to set up the next school year for success. Then all the teachers from the same grade compose class rosters for the next year to be submitted to,

perhaps altered, & approved by administrators. There is also a vehicle for teachers to propose curriculum changes/fine-tuning in writing to the appropriate administrator or curriculum team.

Staying on Track during a Crisis

From one teacher regarding distance learning...

- Top stressors:
  - *Too much screen time (6-7 hours/day; 71 students)*
    - Take frequent breaks.
    - Be aware of sitting posture & neck fatigue.
    - Consider getting special glasses/screen filter or app to filter out blue light from the computer screen.
    - Grading/Reading onscreen is difficult.
      - Hone & simplify feedback.
      - The drawback is less encouragement to the students.
      - Pass/Fail Criteria
        - Pass = completed every assignment
        - Fail = did not complete or follow directions
  - *Inefficiency of distance learning*
    - Communication breakdown with some parents.
      - No response to email nor to a phone call (voicemail box was full and/or call not returned).
- *Choosing not to stress* about making the online experience stellar.
  - It takes double the amount of time to do this work.
    - "I am in survival mode, so I try to keep it simple, straightforward, and doable so as not to overwhelm the students."
- *How can parents help in this process?*
  - "The more the parents are involved, the better things seem to be going for the student."
    - Struggling students are really falling behind; they do not seem to have much help.
- *Faculty meetings on Zoom*
  - Once per week
  - Weekly agenda
    - Make announcements/updates.
    - Address teachers' questions.
- *Encouragement*:
  - Distance learning is still hard, but a new routine developed in about 6 weeks.
  - "God's grace is definitely at work."

Setting a Goal

- Pray for God's wisdom. Set one or two goals *for yourself* as a teacher or staff member to get better on track that depends on your own efforts. Enter that goal in the binder/document that goes with you everywhere.
- Refer to this goal throughout the year.
- Reflect on this goal at year's end. Rejoice in God's grace.

Expressing a Desire

- Pray for God's wisdom. Write one or two desires for helping yourself get better on track *that depend on others' cooperation*. Enter that desire in the binder/document that goes with you everywhere.
- Pray about this desire throughout the year.
- Reflect on this desire at the end of each year. Rejoice in God's grace.

Encouragement from Other Teachers

- "It's a wonderful thing to give yourself to and it's a job that you always know is important & has lasting, eternal consequences. There are so many people who have been in your shoes before & have gotten through it. The first few years are an investment into the later years of teaching." (from one new teacher)
- "The really effective teachers in a CCS are those who themselves thirst for knowledge, modeling that love of beauty and wisdom to their students." (from a CCS founder)
- "I have taught over 1,000 students in my lifetime. Whenever the Lord brings one of them to my mind, I stop & pray for them. Perhaps they are hurt or in need. I do not know. But my Savior does." (from another teacher)

Encouragement from a Student

- "What was most impactful for me was discipleship & mentoring teachers who poured into me. It meant so much to me that a teacher would say, 'I know you are struggling in your life, but I see the Lord working in you.'" (from a CCE student)

Chapter 6
Your School's Curriculum

"The fear of the Lord is the beginning of wisdom."

Proverbs 1:7

"You shall therefore impress these words of mine on your heart and on your soul; and you shall bind them as a sign on your hand, and they shall be as frontals on your forehead."

Deuteronomy 11:18 (NASB)

"For if there are prophecies they will be fulfilled and done with, if there are 'tongues' the need for them will disappear, if there is knowledge it will be swallowed up in truth. For our knowledge is always incomplete and our prophecy is always incomplete, and when the complete comes, that is the end of the incomplete."

1 Corinthians 13:8b-10 J.B. Phillips NT

"'One way the Devil can get in is to get us too focused on something that is good but not best. If we focus on the good of curriculum and neglect Christian love, we'll destroy everything, because we'll have made the secondary thing primary.'"

Dr. Christopher Perrin, The Gospel Coalition article

GRAVITAS ABOUT WESTERN CIVILIZATION

When I interviewed Grove City College history professor Dr. Mark Graham, who is a classicist and reads classics in the original Greek and Latin languages, I asked if he agreed with the following statement: "Classical Christian Education is the best model of education to employ in order for Western civilization to survive." He asked me to read the statement again slowly as he contemplated each word and then replied after some silence, "I come pretty close to agreeing with that."[1] We need to "preserve and pass on the Great Conversation." Rob Tucker, ACCS board member, expands this scope saying, "Classical Christian Education can be used in a variety of models" beyond "brick & mortar," including the University Model, online schooling, and homeschooling.[2] In any of these variations, what should be the curriculum in order to place first things first and avoid going off the rails?

---

[1] Dr. Mark Graham, interview by Kathleen F. Kitchin, Grove City, Pennsylvania, May 7, 2018.
[2] Rob Tucker, interview by Kathleen F. Kitchin, Annapolis, Maryland, September 22, 2018.

A WAY OF LIFE

In his lecture "Lifetime Learning: The Nature and Vision of Classical Christian Education" at the 2019 Association of Classical Christian Schools (ACCS) conference, Dr. George Grant said, "Education is more about a culture than a curriculum; it is *a way of life*." This way of life is not mechanistic. It is about relationships and community. It's not about "if we do the right stuff in the right order." Grant said,

> CCE is not about a single course of curriculum structure; instead, we want to run on the tracks of the richness of God's provision so that the brightness of the glory of the Kingdom may dawn in the hearts of our students.... In *paideia* (nurture & discipline of the Lord), we till the soil of children's hearts & plant seeds that will sprout & bring to full harvest the hope of their calling. ... The chief end of education is to worship and glorify God. We seek to shape virtues, not an excellent portfolio to show off to their peers; instead, we seek to cultivate students' habits of thought & action to align with God's great ideal. Our aim is ruination – to so acclimate them to beauty, what is right & true & good, that alternatives are seen for what they are – nihilistic.

CCE seeks to place *first things first*. Our lives, our work, and our form of education seek above all else to worship and glorify Jesus Christ. Dr. Grant says, "What we are doing matters for all eternity" and "The gospel brings a flowering we can't imagine."

NON-INTEGRATION

Dr. Grant also referred to Francis Schaeffer who was speaking of disconnectedness back in the 1970s but has even more application in our time:

> Today we have a weakness in our education process in failing to understand the natural associations between the disciplines. We tend to study all our disciplines in unrelated parallel lines. This tends to be true in both Christian and secular education. This is one of the reasons why evangelical Christians have been taken by surprise at the tremendous shift that has come in our generation.[3]

Veritas School in Richmond, Virginia, verbalizes the Christ-centered alternative:

> Instruction at Veritas acknowledges that all life, knowledge, and meaning extend from our Creator. Our Christ-centered curriculum means we do more than simply provide a religion class among many other classes; rather, by integrating the Scriptures throughout the curriculum, we present the Lord as the One in whom all knowledge is united. This approach requires that all subjects, whether history, art, music, literature, mathematics, or science, be taught in the light of God's existence and His revelation to humanity through His Son, Jesus Christ. We lead students in a pursuit of truth knowing that all truth points to God, and we encourage every student to develop a deep, genuine relationship with God through Jesus Christ.

Most schools would say that their school is indeed Christ centered. But there can be unintentional, hidden red flags.

KNOWLEDGE AS IDOL

I asked Dr. George Grant, "How do we avoid making knowledge and the power of knowledge an idol?" Dr. Grant replied that it is about "finding proper balance. We say all the time that what we are striving for is to inculcate *truth, goodness, & beauty*. It's more poetic." Dr. Grant prefers the following order of these three proverbial words: beauty first, then goodness, and then truth. He says,

> One of the things we are doing in CCE is we're saying, "Look! Do you see it? Isn't it marvelous? Isn't it beautiful?" It's *beauty* that causes us to yearn for *goodness* that then grounds us in the

---

[3] Francis A. Schaeffer, *Escape from Reason*, 1968 (Downers Grove, Illinois: InterVarsity Press, 2006), 17.

truth. We are inescapably incarnate beings. This is what Jarom Barrs...called "Being human." Part of the great task of CCE is to take these humans with senses and feelings and bring them into the presence of an almighty, all-holy God. Part of the balancing of all of the rigor and rationalism and propositionalism of CCE is listening to Bach, it's beholding Dürer, it's the balancing. That balance is something that is very, very hard to arrive at. The only way that you do arrive at it is through the overflow of the joy of the teacher in the classroom. It is that notion that we're *inculcating a culture*, not just feeding our students a lot of data.[4]

Speaking also to this difficult balance, Craig Doerksen, head of the school of rhetoric at Regents School of Austin, says, "We have a threefold goal – cultivating affections and character, developing skills and capacity, and building a foundation of knowledge and understanding. At our school, this is embodied in our mission statement when we say we work that students will 'know, love, and practice that which is true, good, and beautiful.'"[5] Doerksen caveats their approach saying,

> ...we fight a constant tendency to focus too heavily on the *knowing* at the expense of *loving* and *practicing*. In no place is this clearest than in our curriculum, which we will tend to talk about in terms of content we "cover," by which we mean the things we will want them to know. But, we want to focus on all three, and in fact are convinced that they are ultimately inseparable – when I come to deeply *understand* any aspect of God and His world and order, it will happen also with a *love* of God and His work, and I will discover my unique capacity to *participate* in His work with skill and wisdom. If we are only developing knowledge and skills, we are developing clanging gongs, not human beings fully in God's image. This challenge – to ensure the curriculum works towards all three goals, not just knowledge – is actually a rewarding one for every teacher. It is not just their minds we want to develop – this is why we teach! [italics mine].[6]

Let us pray and lean into God for the wisdom to balance knowing, loving, & practicing. Tear down our idols, Lord, and replace them with You.

THE ANTIDOTE – HOW TO VIEW BEAUTY

To avoid making knowledge our idol, we can read classics and study our subject areas in the light of beauty, goodness, & truth. As Dr. George Grant said, it first is beauty that captures our sensibilities. In *Jesus Christ and the Life of the Mind*, Christopher Noll says, "The historian Richard Jenkyns has remarked on the potential exuberance of Christian engagement in the world by comparing that engagement with an ancient Greek way":

> Platonism imposes a paradox: the beauties of the perceptible world are merely imperfect imitations of the eternal beauty of the world of forms. In a way this devalues the world known to our senses, but in another way it exalts it, for the perceptible world is indeed beautiful – that is not denied – and it is also our means of access to a higher and unchanging beauty. Christianity presents a similar paradox: this world may be of less account than the one to come, but that does not make it unimportant; it is, indeed, the theater in which the great drama of salvation and damnation is to be played out.[7]

Noll continues to say, "The centrality of Christ for aesthetics was intimated powerfully in the writings of Jonathan Edwards.... [In his] *Two Dissertations: Concerning the End for Which God Created the World* [and] *The Nature of True Virtue*: Conceptions of beauty played a large part in Edwards's description of God as the supreme being: 'For as God is infinitely the greatest being, so he is allowed to be infinitely the most beautiful and excellent: and all the beauty to be found throughout the whole creation is but the reflection of the diffused beams of that Being who hath an infinite fullness of

---

[4] Dr. George Grant, interview by Kathleen F. Kitchin, Atlanta, Georgia, June 13, 2019.

[5] Craig Doerksen, "Deeper Understanding by Design," *CLASSIS* 25, no. 1 (March 2018): 26.

[6] Ibid., 26.

[7] Mark A. Noll, *Jesus Christ and the Life of the Mind* (Grand Rapids, Michigan: William B. Eerdmans Publishing Company, 2011), 36.

brightness and glory."[8] We may fall in love with our subject matter, but we cannot allow it to be an end in itself; in Augustinian terms, we cannot just enjoy it for its own sake, but use it for what it was "ordained to be used." Dr. Mark Graham quotes George MacDonald who had observed:

> There have been men before now who got so interested in proving the existence of God that they came to care nothing for God Himself...as if the good Lord had nothing to do but *exist*! There have been some who were so occupied in spreading Christianity that they never gave a thought to Christ. Man! Ye see it in smaller matters. Did ye ever know a lover of books that with all his first editions and signed copies had lost the power to read them? Or an organizer of charities that had lost all love for the poor? It is the subtlest of all the snares.[9]

To use Professor Graham's adopted terminology from Augustine, we cannot "sail out into the open sea and forget home. ...this often arises from good intentions. There is grave danger in enjoying "art for art's sake" alone or "history for history's sake" alone or "biology for biology's sake" alone. In Augustine's words, there must always be a higher end."[10] Let us not forget the *telos* or higher end. Let us use our studies for "properly loving the Triune God."[11]

THE ANTIDOTE – HOW TO VIEW GOODNESS

Regarding the second of the trio, reading J.R.R. Tolkien's *Lord of the Rings* trilogy leaves a grip on our mental landscape of goodness – and evil. When we encounter power in our everyday life, our minds reel back to the Ring. As we read classics such as these, we confront the striking difference between good and evil. As Joseph Loconte says in his book *A Hobbit, A Wardrobe, & A Great War*, "In the worlds of Middle-earth and Narnia, evil is a perversion of goodness, which is the ultimate reality."[12] "The war against evil is the moral landscape of *our* mortal lives: a journey of souls degraded or redeemed, dragged into the Darkness of self or led into the Light of grace."[13] "'But one must face the fact,' Tolkien wrote, 'the power of Evil in the world is not finally resistible by incarnate creatures, however 'good.' Here is where Tolkien and Lewis depart most radically from the spirit of the age. Our modern tales of heroism – the gallery of superheroes, super cops, and super spies – offer a protagonist who invariably saves the day by his (or her) natural intelligence and strength of will, usually with lots of firepower at hand. The idea that the hero would need outside help – from a supernatural deity, for example – strikes many as a cheat. [They feel] it robs human beings of their 'dignity' and diminishes 'the human spirit.'"[14] With Tolkien and Lewis, however: "The heroic ideal ... is qualified in a much more profound way. The hero cannot, by his own efforts, prevail in the struggle against evil. The forces arrayed against him, as well as the weakness within him, make victory impossible. ... Frodo's defeat – our defeat – is overturned by a Power stronger than our weakness. Tolkien identified this Power as 'that one ever-present Person who is never absent and never named.' ...The Ring is destroyed, not by Frodo or by the Fellowship, but by 'a sudden and miraculous grace.'"[15] We stand hushed before His great goodness.

THE ANTIDOTE – HOW TO VIEW TRUTH

As for the third part of the trio, at the 2019 ACCS conference in his lecture "Arrogance and Humility: Worlds in Collision," Douglas Wilson said, "We are in the middle of a Truth famine. Going farther, our generation is on a hunger strike. We've lost our appetite for truth and therefore, we have lost our minds. We need to honor God and exhibit gratitude to God." He also said, "We have to fight the battle for the Bible and for the dictionary. CCE

---

[8] Noll, 40.

[9] Dr. Mark Graham, "St. Augustine's 'Fundamental Charter of Christian Education' (or, Dead-Ends, Dangers, and Delights of Christian *Doctrina*," Lux Mea, Fugitive Talk, CVV Talk (April 19, 2018), 10.

[10] Ibid., 9.

[11] Ibid., 10.

[12] Joseph Loconte, *A Hobbit, A Wardrobe, & A Great War: How J.R.R. Tolkien and C.S. Lewis Rediscovered Faith, Friendship, and Heroism in the Cataclysm of 1914-1918* (Nashville: Nelson Books 2015), 148.

[13] Ibid., 164-165.

[14] Ibid., 188.

[15] Ibid., 188-189.

schools are built on Truth, love the Truth, and follow Jesus. 'Buy the Truth and sell it not....' (Proverbs 23:23)." As far back as 1985, Neil Postman's *Amusing Ourselves to Death: Public Discourse in the Age of Show Business* riveted attention on the "trivialization of American culture and the evaporation of shared ideals."[16] Indeed, Senator Ben Sasse, a strong advocate of CCE, said,

> ...by the middle of the twentieth century, two developments had swamped that earlier wedding of warmth to tough love. The nurturing perspective had spun out of control and made cultivating self-esteem paramount, marginalizing competing concerns about cultivating virtue. (Importantly, though "virtue" has come over the centuries to mean "moral living," it evolved from an older Latin term meaning "strength." The two are inextricably linked.)[17]

What is so critical is training our children to think. This culture is taking over the mind, and students are not necessarily thinking as they soak in the bad influences masquerading as truth.

PAIDEIA

A fundamental concept in Classical Christian Education is the Greek word *paideia* or the "full instruction and upbringing of a child" (Veritas School, "Core Beliefs"). Douglas Wilson's discussion of *paideia* from his essay, "The *Paideia* of God" begins with Ephesians 6:4b, when Paul says, "Fathers...bring [your children] up in the nurture and admonition of the Lord" which is "in fact requiring Christian fathers to provide their children with a '*paideia* of the Lord.'" *Paideia* is translated "nurture and admonition." Wilson says, "...what we call education is more strictly a mere subset of the word *paideia*. Formal education is essential to the process of *paideia*, of course, but the boundaries of *paideia* are much wider than the boundaries of what we understand as education."[18] In Dr. Mark Graham's "St. Augustine's 'Fundamental Charter of Christian Education' (or, Dead-Ends, Dangers, and Delights of Christian *Doctrina*," he writes that "In Latin, "[*d*]octrina functions in a similar way to the Greek term *paideia*, "a comprehensive intellectual and moral formation – the living activity of the teacher in the classroom; it can also mean the arts and sciences collectively as well as teaching, instruction, education, learning, knowledge, scholarship. Because the term is so rich and inclusive, yet has no real English equivalent, I will leave the title untranslated and simply refer to it throughout as *De Doctrina Christiana*."[19] Deuteronomy 6:7 reveals the time & space dimensions of this full instruction and upbringing of a child when it says, "You shall teach [God's commands] diligently to your children and shall talk of them when you sit in your house, and when you walk by the way, and when you lie down, and when you rise." While the Old Testament's focus was on understanding and following the Law, the New Testament's focus is having a relationship with God Himself and getting to know His heart by reading His Word & delighting in Him. *Christian paideia* is all-encompassing enculturation encompassed in His love.

DEFINITION OF CLASSICAL CHRISTIAN EDUCATION

When I met with Keith Nix, headmaster of Veritas School in Richmond, Virginia, he addressed a difficult task facing classical Christian education: defining the classical Christian project in a sustainable way.[20] "The current challenge is to reach a base agreement on what classical Christian education means," said Nix. "What are the dogmas of classical Christian education? What are the non-negotiables, the hallmarks, the first principles?" Like the building of a cathedral, the renewal of classical Christian education is not a project which can be completed in a single generation. Many generations will be needed to complete it, which means many generations need to agree on a final destination; otherwise, one generation will simply erase the progress of the generation which came before.

Nix suggested the classical renewal has — at present— undergone three distinct stages over the last several decades. The first stage, which began in the early 1990s, primarily meant a recovery of classical *content*. Latin,

---

[16] Ben Sasse, *The Vanishing American Adult: Our Coming-of-Age Crisis – and How to Rebuild a Culture of Self-Reliance* (New York: St. Martin's Press, 2017), 50.

[17] Sasse, 50-51.

[18] Douglas Wilson, *The Paideia of God and Other Essays on Education* (Moscow, Idaho: Canon Press, 1999), 10.

[19] Graham, "St. Augustine's 'Fundamental Charter of Christian Education,'" 3.

[20] Joshua Gibbs, teacher at the Veritas School, contributed valuably to this discussion.

logic, and rhetoric were taught alongside Homer, Virgil, and Aristotle. Classical teachers conceived of every subject having its own grammar, its own logic, and its own rhetoric (or poetry), and taught their subjects according to this schema, which is more commonly known as "the Trivium." While no classical teacher today would deny the Trivium as a helpful tool in teaching, the Trivium is now regarded as a valuable, albeit partial piece of the classical puzzle.

The second stage of the classical renewal began ten years later and was chiefly concerned with *pedagogy*, or the manner in which classical content was presented to students. "How do we provide instruction that is more humane than the progressive "factory" model of education?" Nix asked. "It's not enough to have classical content. We have to offer our students classical content in a classical way." Classical teachers began tinkering with open-ended discussions, dialogue, debate and argument with students. They modeled class time after Socratic conversations.

In the past few years, many classical Christian schools have begun reconsidering *paideia*, a Greek concept which refers to the complete spiritual formation and orientation of the student. Perhaps the simplest and best way of approaching *paideia* is through a question first posed by Calvin College professor James K. A. Smith: *What if education is more about what we love than what we know?* Smith's question is indebted to the theological legacy of St. Augustine and Dante, both of whom insisted that being fully human meant rightly ordering human sentiments. Put another way, it does a man little good to know the truth if he does not care for it. It is one thing to know what is right, it is another thing to love the truth enough that one is willing to suffer and die for it.

What is next for the renewal of classical education? At the moment, many classical educators are considering what the ancients have to offer us in the way of *assessment*. What does it mean to quiz, test, and grade in a classical manner? Currently, a great many assessments at classical schools are still conducted according to progressive standards. Nix believes we can do better. Vestiges of John Dewey's imprint on education need reexamining. Nix refers to progressive prejudices and habits which yet cling to classical education as "barnacles" that classical educators are slow to notice. As much as classical educators have tried to reimagine and recover older models of thinking, we must admit that we still have many bad habits, unhelpful practices, and faulty beliefs that we have unconsciously borrowed from secular models, including our own experiences in school. "We need to work hard to scrape off those barnacles," says Nix, "and be willing to make hard, unpopular, but necessary choices. We must be careful of drifting back to what is popular, or what is easy. In other words, we often have to work against what parents want. We have to educate students, but we have to educate parents, as well." Sometimes we parents need to recognize we have gotten caught up in the culture.

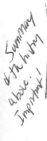

The challenge here is not to jettison the classics of *content* and the classics of *pedagogy* nor to make the ancients or the medieval an idol, but to cultivate a deeper, richer *paideia*. Classical Christian Education is the Trivium, is the pedagogy, is part of *paideia*, and loving, not just knowing, is about refining *assessment*; ultimately, it is about the Author of all of these – it is always about Whom we love and know, Whom we are learning to love and to know in a deeper, richer way. To achieve these high ends, where do we find our curriculum?

TEACHER AS CURRICULUM

As educators, we come alongside parents who do the major part of that *paideia*. Regarding curriculum, educators can be tempted to regard it as something to be purchased, which it may be, but Keith Nix asserts, "The *teacher* is the curriculum." He says, "You can pick a great book & not teach it. A teacher has to be 'undone' by a book and invite students into this love," quoting one of his teachers, Joshua Gibbs. The same is true for the transcendent beauty of math and so forth throughout the curriculum courses. Nix says you can read books "to know, to learn" OR you can fall in love with story. The driving question is "Why would I want to read that?" At the 2019 ACCS conference, Dr. George Grant, in his lecture "Lifetime Learning: The Nature and Vision of Classical Christian Education," exhorts us to "Stir in them an appetite that will never be completely sated." Who will oversee the culinary choices?

YOUR SCHOOL'S CURRICULUM COORDINATOR(S)

There is an absolute must in establishing classical Christian curriculum for your school – a gifted person who is the director of instruction or a curriculum team. Without a competent leader and a vision, teachers and students will be confused and that will impede teaching & learning. For continuity and integration, your school needs an overseer who can fluidly move amongst Grammar, Logic, and Rhetoric levels. The director of instruction should be both a global & local thinker, a person who sees the whole picture *and* the fine detail, who is a mastermind at bringing coherence and clarity in implementing the school's vision. Again, someone who is both a telescope & a microscope! I strongly advise that this should be one person who encompasses both the lower school and the upper school. It can be very tempting to have two people divide this role, but integration will be sacrificed. You ultimately need one person who will see the whole picture. Again, your school's curriculum guide is the focal point (more discussion of this later in this chapter). Each subject will have objectives that your school determines to meet.

Perhaps your school cannot afford a director of instruction. At one school, a curriculum committee was established. The head of school selected the curriculum committee members, based on experience, knowledge, & understanding of curriculum and classical methodology. If there were issues with the curriculum, they were brought to the curriculum committee. The committee was required to monitor it and implement changes & improvements. They were to determine if the issue was a curriculum issue or a user issue. The committee was then to report changes back to the community. A key question in this committee setting is "Is there reciprocity in your relationships?" The curriculum committee is not the teachers' boss, nor do they tell them how to implement the curriculum. The head of school or lead teacher teaches how to implement.

Suggested Reading: Since learning should be a delight, I encourage all curriculum coordinators to read *God is My Delight* by W. Phillip Keller.

ORIGIN OF CURRICULUM
The word *curriculum* derives from the Latin *curriculum*, meaning "course, racing chariot" from *currere*, "to run." The Logos School in Moscow, Idaho, says that *curriculum* is like a racecourse that "implies the necessary requirements for successfully completing a pre-set track."[21] Before launching into the *course* or "pre-set track," classical Christian schools know we live in a post-truth society. In his ACCS 2019 conference lecture "Saving Truth: Clarity in a Culture of Confusion," Abdu Murray of Ravi Zacharias International Ministries said feelings are elevated above facts, where "my preferences matter more, where truth claims are viewed as 'power moves,'" but he urged us to stand fast on the truth that there is absolute truth, true truth, God's Truth. Our culture has "sacrificed clarity & truth on the altar of human autonomy (<Gk. 'self-law'); therefore, [they see] no boundaries, [are] a law unto the self, and confusion results." Murray says, "The Bible is a freedom-giving book. The world views it as freedom-restricting." For true freedom to exist, there need to be restrictions. "Freedom requires some level of boundary…. Facts & truth equals freedom [which leads to] purpose. Just facts equals limitations." He cited John 8:31-32 that says, "If you abide in my word, you are truly my disciples, and you will know the truth, and the truth will set you free." Contrary to post-Enlightenment thinkers, we do not seek freedom through mere knowledge or data. We run on a course established in God's Truth.

CURRICULUM QUESTIONS
That leads to asking what *course* or "pre-set track" is to be run? What are the "necessary requirements"? What subject areas will be taught? How many subjects total should be taught? There is a medieval maxim *non multa, sed multum* – "not many but much." For the past 100 years, public schools have experienced an "ever-increasing burden" of topics to teach, ranging in its early years from lessons in basic hygiene to cooking & sewing to media literacy training.[22] There can be too many subjects and too much burden on the school, the teacher, the students, & the parents. Schools add more to the curriculum, but adding implies subtracting, too. What is left behind? CCE schools can be guilty of overload, too. The objective is to drink deeply in a subject for knowledge (grammar), understanding (logic), and wisdom (rhetoric), and to develop the ability to think and learn to help avoid what Chuck Evans in his December 2010 article "Doing less & learning more" in

---

[21] Logos School, *Spring & Summer 2000 Catalog* (Moscow, Idaho: Faith Ministries, Inc., 2000).
[22] Jamie Vollmer, Temple University's Center on Regional Politics, *Summer 2014 Bulletin*.

Paideia, Inc., says is "the burn-out inducing pace of their parents' lives...Do we help them to become thoughtful, balanced people by making them busier without making them much smarter?"[23]

To determine what subjects to teach, it is necessary to return to Abraham Kuyper's sphere authority, described in Chapter 1.

- What should be taught in the home?
- What should be taught in the church?
- What should be taught in the school?

Of course there will be overlap, but "Who is primarily responsible to teach what?" is the key question. Once those boundaries are established, the classical Christian school can focus on its God-given sphere and not drift, stray, or intrude into what is not theirs to teach.

THE BEGINNING OF WISDOM

Implicit in the word *course* is a sense of order, series, or method. Not something haphazard or undirected, but a deliberate, planned-with-forethought, linked-to-the-foundational-documents, driven-by-principles kind of order. But first things first: the beginning of wisdom is not the curriculum, not outstanding teachers, not a prestigious school, but *the fear of God* (Proverbs 1:7). Jesus Christ is center. Christ sovereignly integrates all Truth, all learning. The stained glass "Teaching Window" in the chapel at Grove City College in Pennsylvania places Jesus standing "foremost among all teachers and all knowledge is subject to His sovereignty."[24] Not Lady Wisdom, not the state, but Jesus. "*Nullus intellectus sine cruce.* 'There is no knowledge without the Cross.'" That doesn't mean nonbelievers cannot know things, but that we cannot get to the soul of education without going ultimately to its Author. When we recognize our duty and our privilege as children of God, we're on the right track.

John Milton, *Of Education* (1644), says, "I will point ye out the right path of a vertuous [sic] and noble Education... [that would] lead and draw them [students] in willing obedience, enflam'd with the study of Learning, and the admiration of Vertue [sic]; stirr'd up with high hopes of living to be brave men, and worthy Patriots, dear to God, and famous to all ages."[25] "Milton ran a small academy in his house and describes his curriculum in terms of results, not just content and methods: 'By this time, years and good general precepts will have furnished them more distinctly with that act of reason which in [Aristotle's] Ethics is call'd Proairesis: that they may with some judgement [sic] contemplate ... the knowledge of Vertue and the hatred of Vice ... but still to be reduc't in their nightward studies wherewith they close the dayes [sic] work, under the determinate sentence of David or Salomon, or the Evangels and Apostolic Scripture.'"[26]

Classical scholar Dr. Grant Horner continues,

> But since much of what humans produce is morally questionable, and all of it is tainted by sin, the teacher must judiciously expose students to these texts, guiding them and teaching them the process of discerning wisdom. The constant rubric will always be the Scriptures. So each day's learning was to be 'reduc't' – boiled down to its most basic elements – in comparative analysis with what God says. This is how one learns to hate vice, and love virtue. This is the ultimate purpose of reading: to set the soul aflame for God and for Good.[27]

PRAYER

Prayer comes first before planning the curriculum. In a classical Christian school, all subjects are taught from a Christian worldview. Our thoughts should be based in the Word and our actions as teachers should embrace the

---

[23] Chuck Evans, "Doing less & learning more" (Paideia, Inc., December 2010).

[24] Dr. Dale Russell Bowne, *Harbison Heritage: The Harbison Chapel Story* (Grove City, Pennsylvania: Grove City College, 1989), 13.

[25] Dr. Grant Horner, "Firing Curiosity," *The Classical Difference* 4, no. 4 (Winter 2018): 21-22.

[26] Ibid., 22.

[27] Ibid., 22.

Word as we shepherd our students through their subjects. Not just a Bible verse tacked onto a lesson, but the Bible naturally emerging in all lessons and all discussions, with the understanding that all knowledge, understanding, & wisdom comes from God, not man. Yes, we will study secular literature and events, but through the lens of Christ and Scripture. Hand & head will be joined: thought will appear in action. We shall teach after the style of Deuteronomy 6:8 (ESV), "You shall bind them [God's Word] as a sign on your hand, and they shall be as frontlets between your eyes." His Words will be in front of us.

HUMILITY
Humility should be our hallmark. Even if we create sought-after curriculum. Mark A. Noll says,

> Before the mysteries of the incarnation, intellectuals who realize how much their own work depends on Christ's work simply accept that all intellectual endeavors are limited. Only when, in the words of 1 Corinthians 13, we see Christ "face to face" and are at last "fully known," will Christian believers "know fully." If the mysteries of the incarnation lie beyond full human comprehension, and if Jesus himself confessed during his earthly ministry that there were things he did not know, then scholars following Christ should be doubly aware of how limited their own wisdom truly is. Knowing Christ, in other words, means learning humility.[28]

We need to reinforce this humility throughout the Trivium. In his *Vanishing American Adult: Our Coming-of-Age Crisis – and How to Rebuild a Culture of Self-Reliance*, Senator Ben Sasse looks ahead to the rhetoric stage saying,

> This third stage [Rhetoric] is directionally oriented, aiming to leave the child behind and find a self-possessed young man or woman at its end. As that earliest edge of adulthood arrives, there is a new – partial but real – humility, as [Dorothy Sayers notes,] "the pupils will probably be beginning to discover for themselves that their knowledge and experience are insufficient." They will begin to realize not just what they know but also – marvelously and in a humility-inducing way – all that they do not know.[29]

In the first beatitude, Jesus began His Sermon on the Mount on the foundation of humility. Before we begin to construct our curriculum, we should also begin on a solid foundation of godly humility.

BACKWARDS DESIGN FOR DEEPER UNDERSTANDING
Since we are rebuilding so many ruins, we need a template or guide before we write our own curriculum guide for our school. Craig Doerksen of Regents School of Austin, Texas, says,

> The curriculum structure we use is borrowed from Grant Wiggins and Jay McTighe's *Understanding By Design* (2nd edition). In it they outline a curriculum that encourages…"think[ing] backwards with all curriculum – from content or activities toward the purpose of the unit, from the unit toward the purpose of the course, from the course toward the cross-curriculum purpose of the school year, from that year toward the purpose of the whole school by graduation day."[30]

Two concepts have been particularly helpful – *enduring understanding* and *the essential question*.[31] Enduring understanding takes them "beyond knowledge-focused education."[32] It asks and explores, "what does it mean to understand God loves us?" yielding the kind of "understanding…that a study of history, literature, science, and

---

[28] Noll, 61-62.

[29] Sasse, 80-81.

[30] Doerksen, 26.

[31] Ibid., 26-27.

[32] Ibid., 26.

the arts can deepen."[33] An example of enduring understanding would be that "the problem of evil cannot be 'solved' by an argument."[34]

As for *the essential question*, Regents School "seek[s] to design our curriculum not around content we cover, but by *understandings about reality that we uncover or discover* [italics mine]."[35] For example, their "juniors spend a semester studying European history and literature through the essential question…: 'When is it right to rebel?' The understanding that we seek to uncover takes them through a wide range of historical people and events, but the end will not be that they've "covered" the French Revolution, but that they've discovered fundamental challenges and realities of our human experience. Imagine how their discovery is enhanced when they are reading *Paradise Lost* at the same time."[36]

Doerksen says,

> When teachers begin to evaluate the content of their courses through the lens of backward design toward understandings that move them closer to knowing, loving, and practicing that which is true, good, and beautiful, they begin to see things that aren't as important to "cover" as others. And, as a leader of teachers, it is a joyous thing to watch teachers improve their courses toward greater fulfillment of our mission, driving towards the purpose, discovering ways to get there that no one else could imagine without their experience each day with their students. They are both freer to adapt methods to reaching the goal because they have greater clarity of what we're trying to accomplish.[37]

Doerksen recounts "the moving joy of seeing students wrestling through arguments, proofs, readings, and stories until they begin to understand not as a sentence to be memorized, but as a profound truth about our condition and God's abounding sacrificial love."[38] In her lecture "God's Garden: Cultivating and Growing Schools" 2019 ACCS lecture, Dr. Pamela McKee said, "We plant what we love. We plant what we value. Begin with the harvest in mind." We write curriculum with the end, or purpose, in mind.

CURRICULUM GUIDE

Critical to developing curriculum for your school is creating an *in-house curriculum guide* with subjects and objectives, from Grammar to Logic to Rhetoric. Former director of instruction Laura Tucker says, "Your curriculum guide with the objectives is essentially a contract." A contract between the school board/administrators & the teachers. A contract between the school & the parents. A school is to teach the objectives in their curriculum guide. The resources may change, but the objectives stay the same. When considering adding or substituting a book or text, the key question is, "Is this new text or essay or experiment meeting the objectives in the curriculum guide?" The curriculum guide is the hub of the wheel. Without the hub, the spokes have no center or consistent structure, and the wheels cannot function, nor can the child truly learn. Clear objectives for students by grade level, by subject are essential. As one teacher also noted, "We need a description of what students need to be able to do at this grade level. What is normal struggle vs. what is not normal struggle?" I encourage directors of instruction/curriculum committees to provide a section in each grade's subject binders of samples of student work both as models of what this grade level is capable of producing and what the expectations are. Provide if possible a metanarrative (a lesson about the lesson) for how students did in a particular year and what were harder & easier areas for them as well as how you taught & why you taught. Attaching sticky notes with brief comments are quick & convenient aides.

If your in-house curriculum guide is already in place, your school is a seasoned school, and mastering the objectives will be normal, not mastering the objectives will be not normal. If not normal, ask two questions:

---

[33] Ibid., 27.

[34] Ibid., 27.

[35] Ibid., 26.

[36] Ibid., 27.

[37] Doerksen, 27.

[38] Ibid., 27.

1) Is there a developmental issue? or
2) Are there learning differences?

The next step would be for the teacher to talk with the parents and talk with the administrator to determine next steps.

TOO HARD

The argument can be made that CCE is too hard. Mortimer Adler's "Invitation to the Pain of Learning," presented a high bar.

> In Adler's view of education, learning is not something one acquired externally like a new suit. It is in his own words, "an interior transformation of a person's mind and character, a transformation which can be effected only through his own activity." It is as painful, but also as exhilarating, as any effort human beings make to make themselves better human beings, physically or mentally. The practices of educators, even if they are well-intentioned, who try to make learning less painful than it is, not only make it less exhilarating, but also weaken the will and minds of those on whom this fraud is perpetrated. The selling and buying of education all wrapped up in pretty packages is what is going on, but, Adler tells us, it is not the real thing.[39]

We have a standard of excellence and we are teaching our students to love the standard. It is critical that this standard joins in alliance at home & at church.

In addition to a high standard, there is also a training to attention: for obedience, for order, for productivity, indeed, for preparation for prayer. In her "Reflections on the Right Use of School Studies with a View to the Love of God," Simone Weil says, "The Key to a Christian conception of studies is the realization that prayer consists of attention. It is the orientation of all the attention of which the soul is capable towards God. The quality of attention counts for much in the quality of the prayer."[40] Hard does not mean impossible. What is hard may be what produces the exact qualities God is shaping in a child. I would, however, say that what truly seems too hard, may be too hard for a student. The parent knows the child best and that is the parents' decision.

THE TRIVIUM

We now turn to the Trivium, the place where "three roads meet." How do we teach the classical way *via* the Trivium? Head of school Leslie Collins summarizes the Trivium in the following general fashion regarding students: "They need basic information [Grammar]. Then they need to learn how to think about it [Logic]. Then they need to learn how to communicate it to others and when and where and how and the why of how to communicate [Rhetoric]. In her 1947 essay "The Lost Tools of Learning," Dorothy Sayers uses the following terms:

- *Grammar* – "Poll Parrot" stage (facts & memorization)
  - To express Truth (the door of learning)
- *Logic/Dialectic* – "Pert" stage (rules of honorable arguing & logic)
  - To teach Truth (questions & answers to arrive at Truth)
- *Rhetoric* – "Poetic" stage (winsome persuasion with reliance on both grammar (facts) & dialectic (logic))
  - To persuade of Truth (the capstone)

Avoid popularizing, mechanizing, institutionalizing, codifying the Trivium stages. Cindy Rinaman Marsch, co-founder of a CCE school and curriculum developer for several schools, now a guest lecturer at Grove City College, says, "I believe that some CCS institutions and homeschoolers lose sight of the soul of CCE and get caught up in mechanistic curricula that gets labeled classical because it includes a lot of memorization, for example. But the poll parrot stage more describes than prescribes for children of a certain age. I find they learn much more from the stories of history than from learning lists of dates. That said, learning things by rote can help us access

---

[39] Mortimer Adler, "Invitation to the Pain of Learning," *The Journal of Educational Sociology* (February 1941): monticellocollege.org., accessed Feb. 7, 2019.

[40] Simone Weil, "Reflections on the Right Use of School Studies with a View to the Love of God" (c.1942).

them."[41] The purpose of all the Trivium's roads' meeting is as Leslie Collins defines CCE: "It is an education where human beings who are made in the image of God are given the skills and training necessary to take every thought captive in a way that is in keeping with their design. It's developmental. It's Christian. The wisdom of the ages that has been working for thousands of years. It's not overly complicated. I don't have to define classical only in terms of the Trivium. It's developmental. Ideas get more complex; they get deeper."[42] We are preparing students to go out & Edenize their world.

THE SEVEN VIRTUES
In addition to the Trivium, we keep the seven virtues at center. In his 2019 ACCS conference lecture "Noble & Free: The Powerful Purpose of Classical Education," teacher Thomas Caucutt of Evangel Classical School in Birmingham, Alabama, quoted Quintilian, *The Orator's Education*, XII.1: "We are then educating that perfect orator, who must be a good man; and therefore we require in him not only exceptional talent for speaking but also all virtues of the soul." He defined the terms as follows:

- *Virtue* – excellence, worth; strength <Latin *vir*, manly
- *Perfect* – complete, lacking nothing
- *Cardinal* – hinge, turning point

The Cardinal Virtues (Four virtues)

- *Courage* – fortitude is seen in labor & danger
- *Temperance* – in forgoing pleasures (to remain free for action, to do something better)
- *Prudence* – in choosing between good & evil (looks to past & to future)
- *Justice* – in giving to each person his due

The Christian Virtues (Three virtues)

- Faith – trust in God's character
- Hope – confidence in God's promises
- Love – self-sacrifice for others

Thomas Caucutt continued to say CCE is the "Only true education [from the Latin, *educare* meaning "to lead out"] ... leads our students out of poverty & gives them riches, ... from the prison of their own time & the blindness of their own opinions in the small bubble by granting them the society of the best & greatest minds of every age. ... Education is an eternal concern. An ennobling view of studies, of students who are made in the image of God, preparing our students to praise God in heaven." With God's enabling, we seek to develop virtue.

LIBERAL ARTS & *PAIDEIA*
Before delving into a survey of the scope & sequence of your school's curriculum, it is important to acknowledge the unity of the liberal arts & *paideia*. In the current climate of utilitarianism regarding education & career planning, it is tempting to sound like our culture and emphasize one aspect of the liberal arts over another. God created each subject and in Him, all subjects are divinely integrated. Our administrators & faculty – in unity – need to respect all subjects in both their words & attitude.

- No antipathy should exist between the arts and the sciences (*ars et scientia*). God created both. There should be no superior S.T.E.M. attitude, nor haughty humanities innuendoes. We are to delight in all of God's creation! Each teacher is helping build a *paideia* tapestry for the students that is integral to the vision of training life-long learners.
- There should be no arrogance about the Rhetoric level over any other part of the Trivium. The Rhetoric level is indeed the flowering, but it could not bloom without its counterparts. *Trivium* means "where

---

[41] Cindy Rinaman Marsch, phone interview by Kathleen F. Kitchin, June 7, 2019.
[42] Leslie Collins, interview by Kathleen F. Kitchin, Cypress, Texas, November 27, 2018.

three roads meet." Let us not cut off any arteries in our professional esteem for our model or for our colleagues.

- Likewise, there should be equal regard by administrators for faculty from each of the Trivium levels. We all are in this enterprise together and love & support each other's contribution in God's plan for our school.

SCOPE & SEQUENCE

Five prerequisites in curriculum creation are as follows:

1) Prayer, asking the Lord's wisdom
2) Godly teachers who see the hand of God in life & read the Bible
3) Classical Grammar, Logic, & Rhetoric methods
4) *The Seven Laws of Teaching*
5) Scope and Sequence of each subject, grade by grade.[43]

We create scope & sequence for our curriculum through prayer. Our boards have hired godly teachers who perceive God's work and read their Bible. Through former or present training, classical pedagogy (method of teaching) is established or is in the process of being established. *The Seven Laws of Teaching* was published in 1884 and while not strictly classical *per se*, is a modern classic that is fundamental to creating lessons that promote clarity and life-long learning. Scope is the depth and breadth of *content* to be taught in a specific grade level; sequence is the *order* in which the content should be taught for best learning (building on past knowledge) within a grade (gsu.edu) & between grades. For example, an eighth-grade European I history scope could include the Roman Empire, Middle Ages, & the Protestant Reformation; the *sequence within* that grade level would reflect the time frame of the content – 27BC through 1517AD – and the *sequence between* grade levels is that European I history would come after Ancient History (Creation through the Roman Republic (27BC)) and before European II (history since the Protestant Reformation (1517AD)). As we design our curriculum, we ask the Lord to "rightly order our loves." Listed below are some *first things first* elements to consider as you build your curriculum and beware of red flags. These comments are meant to kindle reflection & discussion.

General red flag: In the current climate of majority-based non-fiction reading and document-based questions, stand firm on 1) a reading list full of fiction classics & 2) the integration of reading book lists with the history era studied at each grade level.

General definition: *Service* is required at each level of the Trivium, performed normally after lunch and before resuming academics in the afternoon. It can range from cafeteria & classroom cleaning to leading recess games for the grammar students to grading papers to helping with various duties in the office. We are teaching our students to serve humbly, to minister, to become less as they build up others & the school itself to God's glory.

Grammar Level (Delineated in each grade): *Bible, Reading (Literature), Writing, Grammar, Spelling, History, Latin, Math, Science, Art, Music, Physical Education (P.E.), Recess, & Service*

Base curriculum on facts, not Common Core higher-level objectives. Be astute in examining curriculum. Look at the objectives. Do they reveal Common Core objectives? Most of those objectives are beyond students' frame.

Refer to your school's curriculum guide for the # of minutes/week devoted to each subject, or determine those amounts of time in the curriculum guide you are creating. Times below are typical, but not prescriptive.

Bible:

- Genesis through the four Gospels (highlights, age-appropriate)
- *Suggested Text for Younger Grades*: Mary Batchelor's *The Children's Bible in 365 Stories*.
- Bible memory verses

---

[43] Laura Tucker, reading practicum, ACCS Conference, Atlanta, Georgia, June 2019.

Reading:

- A straightforward, uncomplicated *phonics* approach is best. It is not necessary to purchase expensive options. Veteran teacher, administrator, reading specialist, and educational diagnostician, Mrs. Laura Tucker says, "The instruction in phonics is very easy, very simple. It is important to teach it in a systematic & explicit fashion. You do not need to spend a lot of money, training, or thousands of dollars on a program."[44] She further added that a teacher can be trained in an afternoon how to teach phonics. For the new student or a younger student who is having difficulty, Tucker urges the teacher to teach the parent to teach phonics. She says, "If you can't do that, it's too complicated." Excellent phonics program requirements are as follows:
  - *Explicit* – clear, direct
  - *Systematic* – organized, sequential format (scope & sequence)
  - *Incremental* – one step builds upon another
  - *Simple* – without a lot of other skills presented in the same lesson.

Literature: Read classic children's literature from the beginning of school. Over the grammar years, read C.S. Lewis' *Chronicles of Narnia* aloud to "baptize children's imaginations," in Lewis's words. In Grades 1-6, read between 8-10 classic children's books per year in addition to poetry.

Writing: Establish stepping-stones oriented to the frame of the child:

- *Step by step, over the course of the grammar level, beginning in kindergarten and ending in sixth grade*: Write alphabet letters, then words, then one-sentence answers to a question, and eventually several-sentence answers to a question, then a one-paragraph essay, then a three-paragraph essay, and finally a five-paragraph essay.
- Systematic progress in developing writing building blocks
  - *Kindergarten*: correct manuscript letter formation (early in year); sentence formation through dictation (later in year)
  - *1st grade*: sentence formation through dictation; answer questions in complete sentences (referring back to source)
  - *2nd grade*: identify topic & supporting sentences w/ teacher direction; 2-point paragraph (topic & concluding sentences *provided*)
  - *3rd grade*: 3-point paragraph (topic & concluding sentences *provided*)
  - *4th grade*: 3-point paragraph (topic & concluding sentences *directed*)
  - *5th grade*: 3 & 4-point paragraphs (topic & concluding sentences *independent*); 3-paragraph essays (teacher *directed*)
  - *6th grade*: 5-paragraph essays (teacher *directed*)
- *Dictation* for Grades K & 1 – Do every day (e.g., Kindergarten – sounds – short vowels, combine consonant with the short vowel, etc.); coincides with phonics lesson; first dictation around Christmas time.
- *Progymnasmata* – These are tools for a student's writing toolbox. Beginning with *imitation* is best for modeling the great writers, e.g., Aesop's *Fables*, myths, fairy tales, legends in 3rd & 4th grade. Move to proverb/chreia in 5th/6th; imitation of famous passages & imitation of poetry in 6th.
- *Handwriting*: Grades K-1: Manuscript; Grades 2 & 3: Cursive writing

Grammar: 8 parts of speech (Shurley grammar); learning through chants & song, and application exercises

Spelling: Spelling words should correspond with the phonics lesson & dictation lesson. More advanced words, increasing in difficulty. The key to keep in mind: it needs to be very *systematic*. Avoid switching series. Dictionary skills in 2nd grade.

History: Two days per week – but again, the importance is the total amount of time/week devoted to learning history facts & stories (vs. the # of days).

---

[44] Laura Tucker, phone interview by Kathleen F. Kitchin, September 13, 2019.

Your School's Curriculum

Latin: Ideally five days per week, but the importance is the total amount of time/week devoted to learning this language, a tool for learning.

Math: Every day. Schools tend to not teach math fact mastery. Teach math facts systematically to ensure that there is mastery of these facts. Have timed tests for automaticity. If needed, sequence it more systematically than a text might offer. A text might give exercises in all addition, with +1 and +2. Adjust the pace for mastery & automaticity. If necessary, do verbal testing for those students with fine-motor challenges in a timed format.

Science: Two days per week, but the importance is the total amount of time/week devoted to learning this subject. Teach all four domains: physical science, biology, chemistry, & physics. A red flag in biology would be a tendency to focus on lots & lots of birds and not to focus on objectives that teach to the facts. Go back to your school's curriculum guide & objectives.

Art: One day per week (the importance is the total amount of time/week)

- More than ever, in an age of anxiety & uncertainty, teachers can encourage their students that there is hope through the vehicles of their subject matter. In his chapter "The Clue of Beauty" in *The Reason for God: Belief in an Age of Skepticism*, Pastor Timothy Keller writes, "Arthur C. Danto, the art critic at *The Nation*, once described a work of art that gave him a sense of 'obscure but inescapable meaning.' In other words, while great art does not 'hit you over the head' with a simple message, it always gives you a sense that life is not a 'tale told by an idiot, full of sound and fury, signifying nothing.' It fills you with hope and gives you the strength to carry on, though you cannot define what it is that moves you."[45] Communicate hope in God.

Music: One or two days per week (the importance is the total amount of time/week)

- Tim Keller says, "Leonard Bernstein once rhapsodized about the effect of Beethoven on him:

  > Beethoven ... turned out pieces of breath-taking rightness. ... When you get the feeling that whatever note succeeds the last is the only possible note that can rightly happen at that instant, in that context, then chances are you're listening to Beethoven... Our boy has the real goods, the stuff from Heaven, the power to make you feel at the finish: Something is right in the world. There is something that checks throughout, that follows its own law consistently: something we can trust, that will never let us down.[46]

  Revel with your students in God's gift of music to man.

Physical Education (P.E.): Two days per week. Emphasize the importance of loving God with all our strength. Promote skills & healthy exercise.

Recess: Match according to the frame of the child (15 minutes each):

- Half-day kindergarten – 1 recess/day
- Early grammar – 3/day including a.m., after lunch, & afternoon
- Later grammar – 2/day including a.m. & after lunch

Logic Level (Delineated in each grade): *Theology (Christ in the Old Testament, Church History, Systematic Theology), Literature, History (Ancient History, Early European, Modern European), Latin, Math, Science (Earth Science, Logic, Analytical Science), Physical Education (P.E.), Electives, & Service*

Theology:

- Encompass both special & general revelation as God is the author of both.

---

[45] Timothy Keller, *The Reason for God: Belief in an Age of Skepticism* (New York: Riverhead Books, 2008), 137.
[46] Ibid., 137-138.

- Limit your school's sphere of theology to "mere Christianity" or primary doctrine. Avoid coming down on sides for secondary doctrine topics, such as credo/paedo baptism, old earth/young earth, end times, reformed/unreformed. That type of discussion belongs in the family and the church. Each school needs to decide the degree to which they at minimum describe each belief/interpretation.
- In *Jesus Christ and the Life of the Mind*, Mark A. Noll, Christian historian at Regent College and evangelical scholar, sharpens our vision for both Bible scholars and, indirectly, CCE teachers saying, "...the great hope for Christian learning is to delve deeper into the Christian faith itself. And going deeper into the Christian faith means, in the end, learning more of Jesus Christ. ... if evangelicals are to make a genuinely Christian contribution to intellectual life, they must ground faith in the great traditions of classical Christian theology, for these are the traditions that reveal the heights and depths of Jesus Christ. ... Since the reality of Jesus Christ sustains the world and all that is in it, so too should the reality of Jesus Christ sustain the most whole-hearted, unabashed, and unembarrassed efforts to understand the world and all that is in it. ... Christ of the Academic Road."[47]
- In 1814, Goethe wrote a poem entitled "Selige Sehnsucht" or "Blessed Longing." We are born with a blessed longing. Pastor Timothy Keller says, "We not only feel the reality but also the absence of what we long for. St. Augustine in his *Confessions* reasoned that these unfulfillable desires are clues to the reality of God. ...[W]hile hunger doesn't prove that the particular meal desired will be procured, doesn't the appetite for food in us mean that food exists?" "Doesn't the unfulfillable longing evoked by beauty qualify as an innate desire? We have a longing for joy, love, and beauty that no amount or quality of food, sex, friendship or success can satisfy. We want something that nothing in this world can fulfill."[48] It is critically important that we teachers make this longing clear for our students and what its Source is. We must not supplant that longing with *knowledge*, as knowledge puffs up and can become a badge of pride and an idol for the student.

Literature:

- Regarding literature, there are four choices:
  o Only the Bible
  o Bible & best Christian writers (in this order)
  o Bible, world's greatest writers, & best Christian writers (in this order)
  o Bible, best Christian writers, & world's greatest writers (in this order) – All truth is God's truth. Studying the "best that has been thought or said."
  o Parents & students need to understand your choice.
- Include dominant themes for each grade. Teach 6-7 classics/year; hold 15-20 round table discussions/year. *Course examples*: Literature of the Antiquities, Early European Literature, Later European Literature)
- *Writing* – Instruct & write the essay at this level. Give room to express their "argumentative" stage.
- One Shakespeare play per year (e.g., *Julius Caesar*, *The Merchant of Venice*, *Macbeth*). "...[F]or instructing a child's conscience with ideas of goodness, pity, generosity, courage, and love."[49] "...[H]is plays can be understood by anyone whose eyes are focused on living the Christian life, anyone who recognizes his own propensity to sin and need for forgiveness. ...He makes us hate sin but pity the sinner. His characters were the victims of their own choices...."[50]
- Interweave both Christian biographies & autobiographies with the Great Books. Much of modern literature is justly grim & without hope. At these tender ages, as they are hurt by disloyal friends and unrequited crushes, as they try to make their way in an often pathless world, have pity & love to include

---

[47] Noll, 22.

[48] Keller, 139.

[49] Karen Andreola, *A Charlotte Mason Companion* (n.c.: Charlotte Mason Research Co., 1998), 227.

[50] Ibid., 230.

words from the life experiences of Christians, such as Augustine's *Confessions* at the Logic level, for "Augustine is not the main character in his autobiographical *Confessions*. God is."[51]

- Discuss timeless themes. *Content example:* Read J.R.R. Tolkien's and C.S. Lewis's books whose authors "believed that every human soul was caught up in a very great story: a fearsome war against a Shadow of Evil that has invaded the world to enslave the sons and daughters of Adam. Yet those who resist the Shadow are assured that they will not be left alone; they will be given the gift of friendship amid their struggle and grief. Even more, they will find the grace and strength to persevere, to play their part in the story, however long it endures and wherever it may lead them."[52]

History:

- Align your literature with your history chronologically to help students stay on track. Teach the sweep of the centuries with key people, places, & ideas. *Content example:* Ancient history through the Reformation to Modernity
- Discuss what truths & ideas are being defended in times of justly called war. For example, Joseph Loconte, associate professor of history at the King's College writes, "Perhaps the character of Faramir, the Captain of Gondor in *The Lord of the Rings*, expresses it best. He possesses humility as well as great courage – a warrior with a 'grave tenderness in his eyes' – who takes no delight in the prospect of battle. As such, he conveys a message that bears repeating at the present moment, in a world that is no stranger to the sorrows and ravages of war. 'War must be, while we defend our lives against a destroyer who would devour all,' he explains. 'But I do not love the bright sword for its sharpness, nor the arrow for its swiftness, nor the warrior for his glory. I love only that which they defend'"[53] and "'The soil of the Shire is deep,' explains Merry in *The Return of the King*. 'Still there are things deeper and higher; and not a gaffer could tend his garden in what he calls peace, but for them.'"[54]
- *Writing*: Instruct & write the essay at this level. Write first full research paper in eighth grade and another in ninth grade (5-8 pages) on a critical issue or event in history. Give explicit instructions. Give room to express their "argumentative" stage.
- Tie ancient events to current events. Don't leave history stuck in the past. Make practical application to today. "…[T]here is nothing new under the sun" (Ecclesiastes 1:9).

Latin: Overtly teach derivatives so that your students can apply Latin to English. Students do not necessarily bridge this connection on their own. To have a usable tool, you must *train* to use the tool.

Math: Teach math as a language. For Algebra, it is absolutely crucial to begin using graphs, including 3-D graphs, so the students develop a sense of how changing parameters affects the curve. Start relating curves on graphs to physical things that exhibit the same kinds of behavior or motion, i.e., a parabola is the motion of a tossed stone. *Suggestion*: Encourage teachers to read Jean Lee Latham's *Carry On, Mr. Bowditch* who taught logic-age sailors how to navigate using basic math & Algebra.

Logic:

- As we instruct our students in logic, we remind them often that arguments are to be made with grace and humility, not arrogance or exulting. Share with them Rabindranath Tagore's quote, "A mind all logic is like a knife all blade. It makes the hand bleed that uses it." Often these debates can get intense, so I urge an approach I appreciate from Alan Jacobs' *How to Think: A Survival Guide for a World at Odds*:

> Members who interviewed for some leadership position in the YPU [Yale Political Union] would usually be asked, "Did you ever break someone on the floor?" To "break on the floor," in the society's parlance, was to change your mind in the

---

[51] Stephen J. Nichols, *A Time for Confidence: Trusting God in a Post-Christian Society* (Sanford, Florida: Reformation Trust Publishing, 2016), 102.

[52] Loconte, 183.

[53] Loconte, xix.

[54] Ibid., 182.

middle of a debate, right there in front of everyone. To break someone on the floor was a signal achievement. But – and *here is the really essential thing* – the candidate would also be asked, "So, have *you* ever broken on the floor?" And to this question... "The correct answer was yes." After all, "It wasn't very likely that you'd walked into the [Yale Political Union] with the most accurate possible politics, ethics, and meta-ethics. If you hadn't had to jettison some of your ideas several years in, we had our doubts about how honestly and deeply you were engaging in debate." James Boswell, in his famous *Life of Samuel Johnson*, speaks of Johnson's habit of "talking for victory," but in the [Yale Political Union], at least at its best, this would not be a virtue [italics mine].[55]

We need to model humility ourselves and correct our students for them to grow in self-control to build, not destroy our neighbor with our new skills (making deductions on their grade in a debate or discussion, mentoring, and perhaps by showing them & their parents the taped version of the debate).

Science:

- At the outset, explain science in light of the Bible. Our understanding of science is as yet incomplete. Science today is Aristotelian. It is only "what you can sense or measure." No miracles or supernatural. God, however, is the Author of general revelation & special revelation, and therefore both are coherent. All truth is God's truth. In *That Hideous Strength*, C.S. Lewis says, "Despair of objective truth had been increasingly insinuated into the scientists; indifference to it, and concentration upon mere power, had been the result.'"[56]
- Discuss the consequence of ideas. In *A Hobbit, A Wardrobe, and a Great War*, Joseph Loconte says, "The perverse relationship between technology, science, and power became a defining reality of the postwar years. Eugenics, communism, fascism, Nazism: these were the revolutions and ideologies that arose in the exhaustion of the democracies of Europe, all in the name of advancing the human race. All began by promising liberation from oppression; all became instruments of totalitarian control... 'Dreams of the far future destiny of man,' wrote Lewis, 'were dragging up from its shallow and unquiet grave the old dream of Man as God.'"[57]
- Teach the distinctives of both creationism *and* evolution so that students know the difference and can articulate those differences. This instruction will require parental agreement. If they don't get this now, the great majority of colleges will be all about pushing one form of evolution or another.

Physical Education (P.E.) – twice/week. Apply skills learned in grammar years to mental and physical tactics & strategies.

Electives – A delightful place to see students blossom. Less structured. More character issues. More opportunities to speak truth into their lives.

Rhetoric Level (Delineated in each grade) – *Theology (Bibliology & Hermeneutics, Understanding the New Testament, Apologetics), Literature, Rhetoric, American History/Philosophy, Language, Math, Science (Biology, Chemistry, Physics), Physical Education (P.E.)/Sports teams, Electives, & Service*

Theology/Apologetics:

- *From Randy Newman, apologist with the C.S. Lewis Institute in Washington, DC*: "Our approach to apologetics, both as teacher & as students is the desire to see people rescued. Two recent books are quite helpful in refining our approach in today's world: Os Guinness's *Fool's Talk* (IVP, 2015) and Dallas Willard's *The Allure of Gentleness: Defending the Faith in the Manner of Jesus* (HarperOne, 2015). These two books reflect a shift from winning arguments to winning people. Willard says apologetics is a

---

[55] Alan Jacobs, *How to Think: A Survival Guide for a World at Odds* (New York: Currency, 2017), 52.
[56] Loconte, 158.
[57] Ibid., 158.

loving service." Randy Newman outlines three changes in our approach to apologetics: 1) a "shift emphasis from questions (theirs) to character (ours). Answers & arguments must be pursued & with the utmost rigor, but we dare not divorce apologetics and discipleship. Apologetics needs to be done in the spirit of Christ & with his kind of intelligence that is made available to us. Willard says, 'We need to ask God to reshape us so we truly love people and see them as precious, eternal, valuable souls.'" 2) "We must adjust our approaches according to dramatic changes in our culture. In the past, we assumed a readiness to hear. Now most are 'not open, interested, or needy. Many are more hostile.'" 3) "We can admit our doubts to outsiders & invite them to compare theirs with ours. We can share reasons for having confidence to believe. Doubt can stimulate you to ask questions. Challenge non-Christians to doubt their doubts." Newman suggests these applications: 1) "[D]evelop close alliances with strong believers who can tell us if we are harsh or uncaring or argumentative. Deepen our reservoirs of grace. Grow in our wonder at how much we are loved through the Cross & find ways to express kindness to outsiders." 2) Step out & begin conversations. Rely on our sovereign God. 3) Consider *how* to say things. Recover the art of Christian persuasion. Have breaks in your story/sequence. Ask, "Do you think there is such a thing as Truth?" 4) Be mindful of your "tone, volume, & facial expression" as all affect interpersonal communication. "We may not be as gracious as we think we are. Include stories of ways we've been changed by the gospel. The hope of the resurrection is just as important to express as its historicity."[58]

- *Suggested Reading*: *Questioning Evangelism* by Randy Newman

Literature:

- Include dominant themes for each grade. Teach 8-12 classics/year; have discussion around a key question or two for each text. Less is more. Add a *reading journal* requirement for each of the rhetoric years. *Course examples*: American Literature, Literature of Antiquity & Christendom, Literature of U.S. History & Modernity
- *Writing* – Even less direction on paper assignments; more freedom to express their "poetic" stage.
- One Shakespeare play per year (e.g., *The Tempest, Midsummer's Night Dream, Hamlet*). See reasons under "Logic Level, Literature."
- At these still tender ages, as they are hurt by disloyal friends & unrequited crushes, as they try to make their way in an often pathless world, have pity & love to include words from the life experiences of Christians, such as Darlene Deibler Rose's *Evidence Not Seen: A Woman's Miraculous Faith in the Jungles of World War II* for *senior* rhetoric students, as well as other classic missionary biographies.
- One teacher's caution about the rhetoric level: "beautiful articulation without smelling it or seeing it under the surface."

Rhetoric

- Thesis Process
  o The manner in which project tasks are presented is critical in producing humble students. Avoid telling the student "You are the expert." As one teacher remarked, "No 18 year old is an expert." Encourage balance & humility about claims, helping the student realize "I am a limited person."
  o The great majority of thesis topics are policy papers where a position is to be argued using persuasive writing.
- Include more teaching on expository writing, writing that informs or describes.
- In contrast to a Benedictine option, author Michael Cromartie offered an alternative, the "Augustinian Option," saying that we "live at the intersection of the ages, between the City of Man and the City of God that is to come [which] means that we develop what one great sociologist, John Murray Cuddihy, called 'an esthetic for the interim.' This is a way of looking at life with an awareness that we are living 'between the times.' Therefore we are encouraged to exercise patience and put a ban on all ostentation and

---

[58] Randy Newman, 14-minute speech, C.S. Lewis Institute, 2016.

triumphalism." Cromartie went on to urge civility in our public discourse and presentations with a "governor" on our tone and virtue as our goal, to show a fundamental respect and decency for people we are seeking to persuade. Rhetoric at its prime! "Put simply: we must speak with confidence and tranquility, with kindness and gentleness, so that people will begin to say of us that we speak with a 'Galilean' accent that sounds a lot like Jesus."[59]

- Quintilian: *Vir bonus dicendi peritus*, "the good man speaking well."

History/Philosophy:

- Cover American history & two years of philosophy (first year – Western thought from the Classical period to the Medieval; second year – Western thought from the birth of 17th century Enlightenment humanism to 21st century).
- Institutions can end up incorporating Platonic, Aristotelian, or Pythagorean paradigms, but because these paradigms are pre-Christian, we need to acknowledge their inherent flaws. We should, of course, study Socrates, Plato, Aristotle, & Pythagorus. God graced each with truth. Teachers need to lead their students to respect these men's insight and recognize their manifestations in today's culture, but also to see the limitations of their philosophy. For example, Socrates excelled at asking insightful questions, but looked only at the horizontal, or human, plane. From the Christian perspective, however, we must include the vertical plane, looking to the one True God. The problem with the Socratic method was Socrates would never say what *he* thought. Socrates was a searcher, but did not have God, Christ, or the Bible. He was searching for the principles. As teachers, we need to help our students see Socrates' limitations. Christianity transcends philosophy. Similarly, Aristotle looked to the particulars on the horizontal plane. His logic was valuable, but limited to what you can sense & measure, and his philosophically fueled aspects of science from the Enlightenment to today. As Dr. K. Scott Oliphint says, we must keep in view the fact that "Theology 'governs' philosophy."[60] *Caution*: Beware of having philosophy govern theology.

Language

- Consider offering a minimum of 3 years of a conversational language to meet some colleges' requirements. More selective colleges require 3 years. Latin does not count toward that total. From one selective college: If incoming student has 3 years of a modern, widely-spoken language in high school, there is no language requirement in college. If incoming student has 3 years of classical language, they still must take a full year of a conversational language or of international culture. *Suggestion*: Take online program to complete 3rd year of a conversational language; ensure college's reciprocity.

Math: Teach math as a language. For Geometry, it is worthwhile to invest in a colored plexiglass model of the various shapes so that students can see a plane cutting diagonally through a cone, etc. For Pre-Calculus & Calculus, pace the students through the basis for calculus (series, expansions, the concept of infinitely small/large, & infinite sums) quickly enough so that they have time to do calculus and become facile at it. Before students graduate, they should also become acquainted with matrix algebra (for efficiently solving simultaneous equations) or they will become hamstrung in college.

Science: See Logic Level, above.

Physical Education (P.E.): If in school's competitive sports program, P.E. not required. If not in sports program, P.E. twice/week: lifetime recreation/fitness.

---

[59] Michael Cromartie, *"What Now? Faithful Living in Challenging Times"* (lecture, C.S. Lewis Institute *Broadcast Talks*, Capitol Hill, October 23, 2015), 11.

[60] Dr. K. Scott Oliphint, *Christianity and the Role of Philosophy* (Philadelphia & Phillipsburg, New Jersey: Westminster Seminary Press and P & R Publishing, 2013), 16.

Electives: A delightful place to see students blossom. Less structured. More character issues. More opportunities to speak truth into their lives.

SUMMARY OF SCOPE & SEQUENCE

Once your school's curriculum guide is completed, *refer to it consistently throughout the year* for writing long-range goals & lesson plans to ensure its goals are being taught & learned. Add refinements as the Lord leads you in this vineyard work. Deliberative labors help keep your school on track.

BOOKS & RESOURCES

- Textbooks are *not* the curriculum. The objectives in your in-house curriculum guide are the curriculum. Ask, will such-and-such a text teach this objective? To reiterate, the text does not drive you. *The objectives are the driver.*
- Head of school Leslie Collins says that schools may think, "'So if I am classical, I order from *these* catalogs.' No, if you're classical, you don't even need a catalog." Yes, we need some funds, but we do not necessarily need to purchase entire curricula or boxed programs that can be quite expensive.
- Despite limited funds, provide complete textbook (not books with missing chapters).
- If you are launching a school, however, buy established curriculum guides from another CCE school to start with so that your teachers and their students have something with which to work and will not be as confused. Better books & resources may come along later, but you need to start with something concrete. Having no solid books to work with at most levels of the school can cause your school to move off track (history & philosophy being exceptions due to the difficulty of finding age-appropriate resources for non-college students). New teachers particularly need a text from which to launch. *Note*: Teach objectives, not texts.
- Logic and rhetoric colleagues add to the continuity of the curriculum by building a collection of resources together. You all are building libraries of great treasure in each school! Each of us is standing on others' shoulders in classical Christian education. In building a storeroom of texts to use in the classroom, ask, *"Does this type of literature develop the type of student you wish to 'produce' in your school's vision?"*

LESSON PLANS IN GENERAL

Lesson plans of all types are *footprints for the future*. Lesson plans, therefore, need to be addressed in a systematic approach. As you write your lesson plans, both long-range plans and weekly plans, think of your audience:

- Yourself (the teacher)
- Your director of instruction/academic dean/curriculum committee – lesson plans should be due each week at a set time & accumulated both in hard-copy form in binders by grade/subject and in digital form on computer. Make certain all administrators know where those binders & digital copies are located!
- Your colleagues – in order to synchronize and "load level" major projects, that is, balance out the tests, debates, discussions & essays/term papers, meet with the appropriate administrator prior to the beginning of each marking period, grade by grade.
- Your substitutes (they need to track you)
- Your students' parents – You may possibly need to photocopy or send electronically your lesson plans for a student with a long-term absence for parents who are helping them do make-up work at home.
- A future teacher (no need to "re-invent the wheel"; ministers to those who follow you)
- The continuity of your school's program
- *Note*: Avoid using school lingo (our MRPs and SKWs, etc.) – parents, future teachers, & substitutes will have no idea what you are referring to. The first time you use an acronym, SIOWP (Spell It Out Within Parentheses).

Your School's Curriculum

LONG-RANGE PLANS (LRPs)/YEAR-LONG OVERVIEW

- Main goals of long-range lesson plans: 1) Bring glory to God by leaving footprints of what & how to teach a topic. 2) Help teachers organize & then work this plan, continually depending on the Holy Spirit for tactical guidance. 3) Help students by teaching them a course of study in an orderly, cohesive fashion.
- *Strategic* – Big picture plan
- Long-range plan template includes the following:
  - Teacher's name
  - Subject w/ GRADE (e.g., Algebra I – 8th Grade)
  - School Year in heading (in full, e.g., 2020)
  - Long-range Plan (as the title)
  - School Name/Trivium Level OR Lower School/Upper School
  - Week #
  - Date – Month & Dates (e.g., Sep 7-10)
  - Notes column: School calendar items that might conflict with plan (e.g., assemblies, faculty meetings, field trips)
  - Topic/Lesson Description
  - Assessments (tests, papers, graded discussions, debates, speeches)

WEEKLY LESSON PLANS

- Main goals of weekly lesson plans: 1) Bring glory to God by leaving footprints of what & how to teach a topic. 2) Help teachers articulate the lesson according to *The Seven Laws of Teaching*. 3) Help students to apply & reproduce what they have learned.
- *Tactical* – Big picture brought down to daily & weekly objectives. Biblical principles & application appear throughout the plan.
- Avoid these words in objectives (vague): *study*, *learn*, & so forth.
- Lesson plans cite Grade/Subject/Unit/Lesson/Full Date including year:
  - *Objective* – The Teacher knows the truth or lesson.
  - *Introduction* – The learner attends with interest.
  - *Review* – Unknown is explained by means of the known.
  - *Supplies* – Books & items needed for this lesson.
  - *Lesson* – The language used as a medium must be common to both. Student is a discoverer.
  - *Assessment* – Require student to reproduce in own language.
  - *Review, Re-Think, Re-Know, Re-Produce*
  - *Summary* – Encapsulates lesson.
  - *Preview* – Looks toward next lesson.
  - *Reminders* – Homework/projects/items to bring to class
  - *Resources* – Other books and so forth consulted for this lesson

It is never too much to review in full & follow John Milton Gregory's unabridged *The Seven Laws of Teaching when creating lesson plans and teaching them* (1886):

- Law #1: Know thoroughly and familiarly the lesson you wish to teach; or, in other words, teach from a full mind and a clear understanding.
- Law #2: Gain and keep the attention and interest of the pupils upon the lesson. Refuse to teach without attention.
- Law #3: Use words understood by both teacher and pupil in the same sense — language clear and vivid alike to both.
- Law #4: Begin with what is already well known to the pupil in the lesson or upon the subject, and proceed to the unknown by single, easy, and natural steps, letting the known explain the unknown.

- Law #5: Use the pupil's own mind, exciting his self-activities. Keep his thoughts as much as possible ahead of your expression, making him a discoverer of truth.
- Law #6: Require the pupil to reproduce in thought the lesson he is learning — thinking it out in its parts, proofs, connections, and applications until he can express it in his own language.
- Law #7: Review, *review*, REVIEW, reproducing correctly the old, deepening its impression with new thought, correcting false views, and completing the true.

Grammar Lesson Plans & Developmental Needs

- *Key words for lesson plans:* "Poll Parrot" stage (facts & memorization)
  - Bloom's Taxonomy: Knowledge & Comprehension, largely
- *Stage*: To express truth (the door of learning)
- *Needs*:
  - Be concrete. Teach chants, songs, memorization.
  - Open Houses prior to enrollment, Back-to School-Night, & Parent-Teacher Conference

Logic/Dialectic Lesson Plans & Developmental Needs

- *Key words for lesson plans:* "Pert" stage (rules for honorable arguing/logic with reliance on Grammar (facts))
  - Bloom's Taxonomy: Application & Analysis, largely
- *Stage*: To teach truth (questions & answers to arrive at Truth)
- *Needs*:
  - Avoid treating logic students like Grammar students. The first year of the Logic level needs more explicit direction, but by eighth grade needs less direction (but not none). Their parents still need to be closely involved but need to avoid the two extremes of 1) hovering & 2) being completely hands-off. They still need to support, just less.
  - They want to argue & catch you out. Let us train them how to take every thought captive to the obedience of Christ (2 Corinthians 10:5) with grace.
  - What can be quite helpful to keep students & courses on track with Logic-level expectations is a *Logic-level Orientation* attended by *both* students & their parents. How is the Logic level different from the Grammar level? What are expectations of Logic students (vs. Grammar students)? What are the values your school wishes to develop in your Logic students? What serving tasks can they be apprenticing for for when they become Rhetoric students?

Rhetoric Lesson Plans & Developmental Needs

- *Key words for lesson plans:* "Poetic" stage (winsome persuasion with reliance on both Grammar (facts) & Logic (Dialectic))
  - Bloom's Taxonomy: Synthesis & Evaluation
- *Stage*: To persuade of Truth (the capstone)
- *Needs*:
  - Avoid treating rhetoric students like Grammar or Logic students. By this point, there is far less direction as students work independently. By senior year, teachers are increasingly viewed as friends/mentors.
  - What can be quite helpful to keep students & courses on track with Rhetoric-level expectations is a *Rhetoric-level Orientation* attended by *both* students & their parents. How is the Rhetoric level different from the Logic level? What are expectations of Rhetoric students (vs. Logic students)? What are the values your school wishes to develop in your Rhetoric students? What tasks can Rhetoric students do to serve the school community?

For Both Logic & Rhetoric Levels: HUMILITY IN LEARNING
At the beginning of the school year, read Dr. Mark Graham's "An Ancient Answer to a Timeless Question," from Augustine's *De Doctrina Christiana*. [See "Appendix."] Discuss with your class how one can "love the Lord your God with all your heart, soul, mind" and "your neighbor as yourself."

ADMINISTRATOR'S ROLE

How does an administrator ensure "stirring the appetite" and that teaching & learning is actually occurring? All too often, it is tempting for administrators, directors, or committees of instruction to become shackled to their computer, their office, & the demands that pour into their schedule daily. Director of instruction for 16 years at Rockbridge Academy and frequent speaker at ACCS conferences, Mrs. Laura Tucker is a strong advocate of administrators being *in the classroom*. Every day, an administrator needs to walk through each classroom. This brief drop-in or drop-by time helps the administrator to know her teachers. These informal evaluations also provide a broader picture of the teacher and the students beyond just the formal evaluation. Tucker *built this walk-through time into her schedule as a "meeting,"* thereby ensuring the urgent did not overwhelm the important.[61]

These walk-through appointments allowed Tucker to hear an earful of a lesson. If she had a concern of any nature (teacher-oriented or student-oriented), she would stay longer. Secondly, she looked at the students to observe and note if they were doing what they should be doing. Thirdly, she glanced at the board work. Fourthly, she referred to lesson plans to see how they were reflected "live" in the classroom – orally, visually, and overall aromatically. In secondary classrooms, she discerned whether there was interaction, and not pure lecture. As directors of instruction make observations, she says they can tell pretty quickly if the spirit of the Lord was in the lesson plan, but not in the "live" lesson and if not, she would follow up to meet with the teacher to discuss that together.

GRADING

Literature/History/Rhetoric Classes – Grading should reflect the frame of the child at each of the Trivium levels. When the child is young, we have concrete expectations & small subtraction points for errors. When the child is older, expectations increase regarding ability to form abstract ideas and self-edit errors. More is expected of the child both *as they grow throughout a year* and *as they grow throughout the Trivium*. Match expectations to the student's frame. *Goal:* to train, not exasperate the child.

- Grading
  - Grammar Level
    - Content – 80%
    - Structure – 10%
    - Spelling/Mechanics (Sp/M) – 10% (-.1/error)
      - Mechanics is capitalization & punctuation, but can also loosely include grammar & usage.
  - Logic/Dialectic Level
    - Content/Logic – 60%
    - Structure – 20%
    - Spelling/Mechanics (Sp/M) – 20% (-.25/error)
  - Rhetoric Level
    - Invention (Content & Logic) – 30%
    - Arrangement (Structure) – 30%
    - Style – 30%
    - Spelling/Mechanics (Sp/M) – 10% (-.5/error)
- Nature of & Instructions on assignments
  - Grammar Level

---

[61] Laura Tucker, interview by Kathleen F. Kitchin, Annapolis, Maryland, September 22, 2018.

- Concrete & highly specific written instruction for written assignments, including templates for outlines
  - Short assignments
  - Not graded on structure or invention & style
- Logic/Dialectic Level
  - Concrete & specific written instruction regarding structure & logic
    - 7th grade
      - 2-½ page paper
    - 8th & 9th grades
      - 5-8 page paper
    - Praised, but not graded on style

- Rhetoric Level
  - Minimal written instruction for essays
    - 10th grade 8-10 page paper
    - 11th/12th grades thesis paper (research paper/term paper with a speech and formal evening presentation, including cross examination by panel & vetted questions from the audience)
- Do not pass students who are truly failing. Seek remediation and assessment for them.

MEETINGS

- Before the school year in the summertime, the head administrators will meet to pray and set goals, essentially a "Grand Lesson Plan" for the year. All of these goals should return to the vision/mission/core values. What are the big goals? For example, on a personal level, is it restoration of fellowship after a rough year? On an academic level, is it focusing on writing as the topic for faculty meetings this year or training the faculty in *progymnasmata*? Perhaps it is prayer and discussion regarding the aroma of our school. Who are we? At this "Grand Lesson Plan" for the year planning session, determine the timeframe of meetings/goals.
- Before the school year in the summertime, the head of school & the director of school operations will meet to set the school calendar. Do this before the school year begins. Over the years, fold in when field trips typically occur (month). Make this calendar available to faculty/staff. Post general calendar online.
- The director of instruction/curriculum committee looks at the entire year and makes long-range plans for in-service times. Consider, "What are the goals we need to accomplish?" "What are the purposes of each meeting?" "What are we trying to accomplish in our meetings?" "What do our teachers need?" These questions will guide what and how many meetings need to occur. Do not waste people's time. Pray. Plan. Purpose. Then act.
- Attend ACCS, Society of Classical Learning, & other conferences.
- Utilize ClassicalU.com for meetings & administrator/faculty enrichment.
- Teacher-Training over summer
  - In-house (1 to 2 weeks before school starts)
  - Elsewhere: Logos School, Rockbridge Academy, or other site.
- Teacher Preparation Weeks before school begins (typically 1 week) *Ensure enough time for teachers to work alone in their classrooms.* It places undue stress on teachers if most of the week is claimed for meetings. They need time to "open up shop" as veteran administrator Laura Tucker says.
  - Keep new teacher training separate from (& earlier than) veteran teacher training regarding the basics. One administrator has her veteran teachers take quizzes online to refresh their knowledge of procedures & security measures. Avoid tedium for your veterans.
  - Hold grade-by-grade teacher meetings with the appropriate administrator/lead teacher to discuss particular needs of students, to help teachers plan to disciple students jointly, to synchronize overall long-range lesson plans with each other and level the quiz/test/paper load on students. These are approximations.

    ○ Perhaps later grammar teachers need to work together to ensure transition from the grammar to the logic stage, what one school called the "*grammalectic.*"

- School-wide faculty meetings – Decide frequency. [See Chapter 4, "Your School's Administrators."]
- Lower-school meetings – Decide frequency. [See Chapter 4.]
- Upper-school meetings – weekly (Monday/Tuesday) – Enter your tests, quizzes, & papers into the school's electronic grade book scheduler. Discuss this chart grade by grade to help level the student homework load and avoid having too many large demands on any one day (2 maximum; for example, 2 tests, or 1 test & 1 paper due). Identify students who need help academically & otherwise. At the end of faculty meetings, try to reserve a 15-minute timeframe to discuss *an idea about education, discipline, or a common challenge* that faculty are experiencing. Keep these meetings to no more than 1 to 1-½ hours. Teachers have already been up with the sun & need to get home.

BACK-TO-SCHOOL NIGHT

- Have a separate orientation for parents who are new to the school.
- For everyone, have a Back-to-School Night. Make sure parents have the opportunity to meet of all their children's teachers, not just some.
- Have greeters at the door & in the gathering room to welcome & direct.
- Display books & resources by Trivium level in the gathering/refreshment room.

STUDENT HANDBOOK

Have a written policy for passing (e.g., 70% mastery) and failing. See websites of schools mentioned in this book for ideas.

FILES

- *Each Teacher's Binders* – Label the spine of each binder by GRADE/SUBJECT. Every teacher should maintain their binders of long-range plans, lesson plans, quizzes, tests, & handouts throughout the year and especially at year's end *in chronological order* for each section.
  - ○ With both paper copies & digital copies: Typically build on old lesson plans, improving & modifying to align with *The Seven Laws of Teaching* and with curriculum objectives. Cull out earlier versions if no longer helpful. Remove; keep the best.
  - ○ Organize lesson plans by subject and then by week order (Week 1, Week 2, etc.). Each year, revise lessons and type in dates *including the full year* for each week.
    - ▪ Within lesson, cite *exact title* of quiz or test (i.e., "Latin IIB Quiz #1 Chapter 1" or for history "Roman Empire Test" so that substitute or subsequent teachers can easily find it in your physical & digital files. Remember to leave footprints not only for today, but also for whoever follows you.
    - ▪ Under "Supplies or Texts," provide *full title of books* AND add immediately after title the abbreviation in parentheses (e.g., Palmer & Colton's *A History of the Modern World* (P & C)).

- *Administrators' Binders of Teachers' Plans & Handouts*
  - ○ Most schools have teacher's long-term/year plans (LRPs), lessons, handouts, quizzes & tests on Google documents digitally, but *hard copy binders of same should be maintained yearly as well in chronological order by week*. Before teachers leave for the summer, have them toss old/unnecessary items from binder, and replace with current year's photocopied/hole-punched LRPs, lessons, handouts, quizzes, tests, & final exam. Handouts should have a title that is referenced in quotation marks in the lesson plan. For each quiz and test, include a blank (with a sticky note saying "Original") and an answer key. Each quiz and test should have a unique title that is repeated in quotation marks in the lesson plan.

SENIOR YEAR

At the heart of the classroom is just that – the heart. Former administrator Laura Tucker's goal was to help Rhetoric students, soon to be launched beyond high school, through getting to know them. The school also offered once-per-week classes, such as "Seminar in Ideas," that made real-world application and relatable issues their focus. As Dr. Roy Atwood, former president of New Saint Andrews College in Moscow, Idaho, says, "The cement is still wet" upon graduating high school. Helping build character through the curriculum courses helps build the heart and solidify the cement.[62]

Ora et labora. We pray & work toward a fine commencement for our alumni.

CASE STUDY

I interviewed Dr. George Grant at the 2019 ACCS conference. He reflected on the history of classical Christian education since the early 1990s, saying,

> ...we actually live in a different culture than we did when we started our schools. CCE began before the cultural earthquakes that we are now experiencing were even tremors. As a result, we're not dealing with the same kind of families that we bring into our schools, we're not dealing with children that face the same kinds of temptations. My kids growing up, the biggest temptation was too much TV. Now, we have computers in our pockets that can take us anywhere in the world and usually to the worst places in the world. That's a totally different cultural landscape and so I think one of the great dangers for a very successful institution in CCE is to think that we've got it nailed, that we've got it figured out, that we know what a student actually needs, that we know what spiritual disciplines will actually move them on in maturity. We're in a very different place. We've got to think constantly in terms – to use the business language – in an "entrepreneurial sort of way." We've got to think about the cultural challenges in a whole fresh perspective. I don't think that we face grave dangers of slipping into an unbiblical perspective of life & culture from sort of a normative basis. The norms are pretty established at most of our schools. There are always temptations to accommodate ourselves to the world. I think that the greatest danger is for us to not realize that the world we're ministering to is not the same world that we started out with. ...We live in a *very* different world. I think our schools are in the same place. I don't think the same arguments work any longer. I don't think the same methodologies work any longer. We've got to be a *lot* more intentional than ever before. I think *the personal discipleship aspects of CCE are more important than ever* [italics mine].[63]

As for the curriculum for his own course, he said that

> I have taught the same set of courses in a 4-year cycle for 27 years. At the end of every school year, I throw away all my notes. ...I have got so many of the categories in my head, the structure and the lectures will be in some semblance of the same sequential order, & the facts don't change, but I throw all of those notes away so that I'm starting fresh. I'm starting fresh even though I've got a lot of the quotes & the stories in my head and they will invariably come out because they are my favorite quotes & stories.

I remarked that "It's delighting in the glory of God in front of our students, showing them what that looks like so that theology is always being given precedence, not just 'this is knowledge that's empowering you to start becoming puffed-up' – for all knowledge puffs up – but it is that delighting, that joy that you are talking about." To which he responded, "And delight always comes from the grace of God if we model for our students our apprehension of grace, our own repentance, then we're modeling for them the gospel. We can tell them the gospel all day long, but if we're *modeling* for them the gospel, that's where the true delight comes from and it's vital that our students see & hear that."

Prayer

Dear heavenly Father, We praise You for You are the Source of all wisdom. In our studies, we return ad fontes, *back to the ancient sources of Greek & Latin, back to classics & primary sources, declaring all truth finds its*

---

[62] Dr. Roy Alden Atwood, "Higher education's golden calf," *Higher Expectations: The College Magazine of New St. Andrew* 1, no. 1 (Fall 2006): 14.

[63] Dr. George Grant, interview by Kathleen F. Kitchin, Atlanta, Georgia, June 13, 2019.

fountainhead in You. Help us prepare our lessons in the Light of Your love & Truth. Help us treat our students as we would like to be treated. Help us, Father, to remember that love is the greatest of all the gifts. Help us love our students. Help us shower grace on them when they fail or sin. We, too, fail & sin. We thank you that You sent your only Son to live a perfect life here on earth & then to be crucified to pay the penalty of our sins with His blood, to save those who have faith in Him. Thank you that through your sacrifice of self, we are forgiven & can forgive others. Lead us on the three paths of the Trivium, guiding our pilgrimage, guiding these precious souls. Help us to teach, to listen, to learn, to love. In Christ's Name, Amen.

Red Flags

- Only classical, but not overtly Christian. Not intertwined with essential Christianity. Teachers who are "clever devils" producing students who are "clever devils."
- Truly Christian, but not classical. Kind-hearted, but not necessarily robust. Need to integrate the Trivium with the frame of the child.
- Believing that education can transform society at large (only God can do that). We labor in His vineyard daily, pray for His guidance and strength, & commit our work to Him.
- "Getting lost in rigidity and short-sightedness, and losing the soul of education."
- Inevitably, "being in denial about the degree to which we are controlled by our god-substitutes."[64]
- Being child-centered. Believing that children are born good (no sin nature).
- Bending to the pressure that education must be foremost utilitarian/pragmatic and produce jobs for students.
- Emphasizing the head & cerebral capacity, and not also the heart.
- Faculty being stove-piped into just Grammar, just Logic, just Rhetoric without visiting each of the other levels to observe a class periodically.
- The director of instruction's not accumulating documentation. Lacking a curriculum binder for each subject at each level: Grammar, Logic, and Rhetoric. A school without these curriculum binders may be teaching brilliantly, but is not creating footprints for others to follow and build upon.
- Each teacher's not having an organized digital filing system. Filing by document only – a nightmare to navigate because you can't. Organize by *category* as suited to each level of the Trivium, but minimally have the following folder categories by subject: Long-Range Plan (LRP), lesson plans in number-of-week order (Week 1, etc.), handouts/worksheets, quizzes, tests, and final exams. *The name of the document should match the title on the document itself which should also match the reference to this document in the lesson plan.*
- Not being prayerful & thoughtful about selecting classic pagan writers, and not sharing the reading list with parents. Overdosing students with a yearlong series of novels of despair. Running the risk of luring children away from Christ. *Discussion Topic*: How do we balance pagan sources with Christian biography & autobiography? How do we handle modern classics which exude no hope?
- Not observing & evaluating the teachers. No positive feedback. As one young CCE teacher says, "An evaluator never appreciates growth if they assess a teacher once per year." Perhaps relying on gossip for teacher evaluations.
- Not giving teachers grace to grow over time as they develop lesson plans. Having high standards and demanding perfection can crush new teachers.

Sober Reflection

For Director of Instruction/Academic Dean/Curriculum Committee

- What is our school's vision statement? Where is it located? Our mission statement? Our core values? Our educational philosophy? Our statement of faith? Our rules? Have I/we read and become familiar with them? Have I memorized, or do I keep these foundational documents close at hand?
- *Faculty Meeting Suggestion*: Do we read *aloud* these foundational documents at the *beginning* of each school year as a faculty & staff?

---

[64] Keller, *Reason for God*, 172.

- *Faculty Meeting Suggestion*: Do we read these foundational documents at the *end* of each school year as a faculty & staff and reflect on what was done well and what needs improvement?
- Am I incorporating the school's vision, mission, values in the foundational documents into my every day, every week, every month, every year lesson plans?
- Am I reinforcing parents' knowledge of these foundational documents?
- Are teacher's lesson plans *and* teaching reflecting the vision? How so?
- My Interactions with the Board: See Sober Reflection section of Chapter 4, "Your Administrators."
- My Interactions with My Fellow Administrators: See Sober Reflection section of Chapter 4, "Your Administrators."
- My Interactions with Teachers
  - Do they see me as someone on their side? As an encourager? As someone who corrects with truth and grace? As someone with high expectations, but someone who also cheers them on to success?
  - Do I view myself as superior to them?
  - Do I see myself as an administrator that is there to set standards, to see that they are upheld, and to promote teacher & student success to that end?
  - Do they see me in their classroom several times each year, or am I absent?
  - How frequently am I providing positive feedback to my teachers?
  - Do I write a *brief* note/email of encouragement two or three times per year? My compliments should not only be heard.
  - Do I direct? (<Latin. *di* = distinctly; *regere* = put straight, control the operations of, manage, or govern)
  - Do I provide constructive feedback to my teachers when necessary?
  - Do I guide them to set one or two goals per subject per year?
  - Do I follow up their goals with discussion, feedback, & support?
  - If we make changes to the curriculum guide, are those changes communicated ahead of time with the faculty? Are these changes then transparently communicated to the parents with reasons?
- My Interactions with Students
  - Do students know that I love them?
  - Do students respect me as I train them in the nurture & admonition of the Lord?

For Teachers

- What is our vision/mission/values statement? Where is it located? Our educational philosophy? Our statement of faith? Our rules? Have I read and become familiar with them & keep them close at hand?
- Do I have a curriculum guide with the school's objectives for my subject/grade?
- Am I developing lesson plans that incorporate both my school's curriculum guide, and rely on the best aspects of prior teachers' lesson plans for this subject, as well as enhance following John Milton Gregory's *The Seven Laws of Teaching* & Bloom's Taxonomy of objectives?
- Am I compromising to making all lessons "fun" instead of making them engaging & challenging?
- Do students know that I love them?
- Do students respect me as I train them in the nurture & admonition of the Lord?

Getting Back on Track

- Pray for God's wisdom to develop your curriculum guide, acknowledging that it is going to involve much "picking up a shovel & digging a ditch."[65] Canned curriculum may work to a point, but we are still rebuilding the ruins.
- For directors of instruction/curriculum committees:
  - Because you may not have time to work from ground zero, use someone else's curriculum guide and then branch out as you grow through the years, adapt, add on & delete, and write the objectives for each grade & subject area. Start with tried & true curriculum.

---

[65] Laura Tucker, interview by Kathleen F. Kitchin, c. 2018.

- o Remember: The curriculum is *not* the textbook.
- Train teachers in pedagogy and the curriculum guide by walking around the school, having formal & informal observations, & talking with them.
- *Suggested Project*: Ask each teacher what he or she *specifically* needs to help him or her get back on track (textbooks, maps, lab equipment, etc.). Have two-way communication.

Healthy School

- "When liberal learning is offered to God, it becomes *an act of worship* [italics mine]."[66]
- A healthy school lives out the gospel. It is mindful & deliberate in how Truth & grace is transformed into shoe leather. Jesus "is the way, the truth, & the life." (John 14:6)
- A healthy school consciously remembers that all roads in the school lead to Christ. All courses have Christ at center, not only implicitly but also explicitly; and the director of instruction observes to see if the vision/mission/core values are coming out the fingertips of each teacher.
- A healthy school teaches students to honor God and to learn *how to learn,* not teach toward a job.
- A healthy school teaches to the whole person: heart, mind, & soul.
- A healthy school has a view to continuity between the three levels of the Trivium at their school. They have occasional joint meetings with & classroom observations of the Grammar, Logic, & Rhetoric level faculty who teach the same subject.
  - o *Project Suggestion*: Once per year have faculty view lesson plans/handouts of the subject they teach at other Trivium levels than the one they teach & meet with those teachers. For example, 4th-grade grammar history (Grammar), 8th-grade history (Logic), & 11th-grade history/philosophy (Rhetoric) faculty all look at a *similar lesson* on the Middle Ages that all three teach (perhaps Martin Luther & Protestantism). Have these teachers observe a class of each other's as well that covers a topic that all three teach, but at their different levels. Total time for both of these suggestions: 1.5 hours (45-minutes/meeting). Time well worth the investment.
- A healthy school holds a meeting with the teachers directly involved if a major change to curriculum is to be made. They inform the teachers of the proposed change and provide an opportunity for discussion and feedback.
- A healthy school avoids making knowledge an idol, guards itself against being puffed up, & gently corrects students who are getting puffed up.
- A healthy school enculturates. *Suggestion*: A monthly parent book meeting, using books selected from the curriculum.

Setting a Goal

- Pray for God's wisdom. The *director of instruction* can write down 2 or 3 goals for each teacher and should keep this in each teacher's file, but also in a working binder to refer to throughout the year. The director of instruction or curriculum team can also write down 2 or 3 goals for curriculum development for each Trivium level each year and one or two goals for improving as a curriculum person.
- Ask *each teacher* if they would pray and write down 2 goals for this year; at their evaluation, discuss their progress. The curriculum team or director of instruction should keep a copy of these goals in their file, but also in their working binder to refer to throughout the year.
- Refer to these goals throughout the year.
- Reflect on these goals at year's end. Rejoice in God's grace.

Expressing a Desire

- Pray for God's wisdom. Write one or two desires for getting your curriculum better on track *that depend on others' cooperation* and enter that desire in your working binder to refer to throughout the year.

---

[66] Arthur F. Holmes, *Building the Christian Academy* (Grand Rapids: William B. Eerdmans Publishing Company), 118.

- Pray about this desire throughout the year.
- Reflect on this desire at the end of each year. Rejoice in God's grace.

Encouragement

- In an article written for New Saint Andrews College, President Dr. Roy Atwood said, "From the earliest universities in Medieval Europe, Christian higher education's singular purpose was the same as education for younger children: to guide the child through the *paideia* of the Lord into Christian maturity and faithful adulthood. Educators did not *train* them to *do* something, but *educated* them to *be* someone: a man or woman of unimpeachable Christian character equipped for every good work."[67]
- Simone Weil, "Reflections on the Right Use of School Studies with a View to the Love of God":
  - "Above all it is thus that we can acquire the virtue of humility, and that is a far more precious treasure than all academic progress."
  - "The solution of a geometry problem does not in itself constitute a precious gift, but the same law applies to it because it is the image of something precious. Being a little fragment of particular truth, it is a pure image of the unique, eternal and living Truth, the very Truth which once in a human voice declared 'I am the Truth.'"
- "Our vision was to have a community in which our kids could together learn the things we valued. It is so exciting to find others who love learning." (founder of a CCE school)
- Leslie Collins regarding Rod Dreher's *The Benedict Option*: "The more we promote strength and not fear, the more likely people will follow us. In the future, the barbarians are going to take over and we are just going to have these little, sweet communities...we're going to be over here birthing the Renaissance. We are just going to love well and raise up human beings who are flourishing and then when you are finished playing your little game, you're going to say, 'Whoa, what do you have going on over there?' Rod Dreher's desire is that we would see all these little thriving cloisters of communities. I believe that's what God has called us here to do. Our families are excited...."
- "The goal is not perfection but faithfulness and trusting in the One who is perfect to bring redemption to a flawed world." (a CCE student)

---

[67] Atwood, 14.

Chapter 7
Your School's Parents

"Train up a child in the way he should go:
and when he is old, he will not depart from it."

Proverbs 22:6

"No discipline seems pleasant at the time, but painful. Later on, however, it produces
a harvest of righteousness and peace for those who have been trained by it."

Hebrews 12:11

"We are forever to embark on the task of learning."

Dr. George Grant

I remember once commenting to a parent how wonderfully behaved her 13-year-old child was. She smiled and said, "I cannot tell you how many times a day – years ago – they were disciplined over and over and over again." We smiled together, rejoicing in the harvest.

On the other hand, the line between parent & child roles has generally become muddled over the past few decades. A head of school recently said he sees parents increasingly allowing the students to choose which school they wish to attend. Elsewhere, in more startling revelation, we hear of a nine-year-old child calling 911 because her parents told her to clean her room. Even more troubling was hearing a teacher share about her classical Christian students' lack of exposure to the Bible saying, "It made me question how much their home understood the gospel." When this teacher asked the class, "What is Christianity?" they responded with works-based answers and did not have a clear picture of Jesus or the gospel.

To put the home and school in perspective, Association of Classical Christian Schools (ACCS) board member Rob Tucker, says, "We were always meant to be a blessing to the family, not a replacement. Families also need to grow in the Lord. Churches need to grow in the Lord."[1] Classical Christian Education never intended to be the parents, but to be *in loco parentis*, "in the place of a parent." This distinction is important as it brings biblical order.

ORDER & LOVE OF TRUTH IN THE HOME

Order in society begins with order in the home. In his article "Not by freedom alone," Dr. Paul Kengor, professor of political science at Grove City College, says,

> The great conservative thinker Russell Kirk, in his 1974 classic, *The Roots of American Order*, spoke of "ordered liberty." Kirk talked of the need for "inner order" by American citizens before they and their countrymen and country could successfully govern through "outer order." Ordering ourselves internally was critical to the nation's external order. The nation's first president, George

---

[1] Rob Tucker, interview by Kathleen F. Kitchin, Annapolis, Maryland, September 22, 2018.

Washington, argued the same, stressing the need for citizens to self-govern themselves before they could self-govern their nation.[2]

This order at home is based on God's Truth. CCE pioneer Douglas Wilson gave focus to parents' role in his 2019 ACCS conference speech, "Arrogance and Humility: Worlds in Collision," saying, "Your job as parents is to impart a LOVE of the Truth, not to have your children just conform to the Truth." This is a heart issue vs. a behavioral issue. Do I myself love God's Truth? Do I love and seek Jesus? Are my children observing that? Charles Spurgeon wrote, "'A jealous God will not be content with a divided heart; He must be loved first and best.'" Am I putting Jesus first and best? In his book *The Return: An End-time Epistle to the Church in America*, pastor-author Matthew Casey exhorts us to

> Return to Family. For decades the American Church has seen the family through the lens of the world. ... God is calling us to prioritize our families' spiritual health over material gain, for the one is eternal while the other will be consumed with fire. ... Return to Fellowship. The days ahead will show us that we need one another, and God is calling us to return to genuine fellowship now. For many of us, this will mean placing Biblical priority on gathering with Believers, on being an active part of a local fellowship through serving and giving, and on using the gifts God has given us to build up His Church. ... [I]t is vital that we invest our lives in a local fellowship that is 1) seeking the Lord, 2) preaching God's entire Word with power, 3) walking in the Spirit, and 4) saving lost souls. God's people are supposed to live with a joyful, quickening anticipation of Jesus' return.[3]

We need order in our homes. We need to devote time daily to read the Bible that informs us of that order. We cannot, however, go this alone. We have the Holy Spirit as our guide. Our God-honoring, Christ-following church families help us and we help them on our pilgrimage to the Celestial City as we follow Christ our Shepherd.

Suggested Reading: *God is My Delight* by W. Phillip Keller

AUTHORITY IN THE HOME

In addition to putting Jesus first and establishing God's order and love of Truth, we also need to have a biblical view of authority. Pastor Mark Dever in his *Nine Marks of a Healthy Church* reveals the source of authority in the home, another vital ingredient in bringing order to our homes: "...[E]ven the very social structures of authority that we have in our families derive from him and from his authority. So authority and leadership are not matters of indifference to us as Christians; they are matters of great concern, because they are part of the image of God that we are to reflect in our lives."[4] Our children need us not only to be their parents, but to parent. God gives us that authority. Ephesians 6: 1 & 4 tells us that children are to obey their parents in the Lord, and fathers are told to raise their children in the fear and admonition of the Lord and not to provoke or exasperate their children, meaning "irritate to anger" (from the Latin *asper*, meaning "rough"). Dever continues, "When we exercise authority in a good and proper way – through the law, around the family table, in our jobs, in the scout troop, in our homes, and especially in the church – we help to display God's image to his creation."[5] In the sphere of the family, the father is the head. Not so popular to say nowadays, but this is what the Bible says. A father's investment in his children should model God's relationship to His Son Jesus Christ, not Samuel's permissiveness with his irreverent sons or David's non-involvement with Amnon and Absalom. If there is a husband, his wife is his helper, not the head of the family. As we follow God's principles, He will faithfully lead us.

What is often so difficult for us parents, at least for my husband and me, is that 1) we were not raised in Christian homes, and 2) we needed much guidance in how to be Christian parents – to find the track and to stay on it. Both the church and the school can be powerful forces in committing to this responsibility and coming alongside

---

[2] Dr. Paul Kengor, "Not by freedom alone," *The Gedunk: Grove City College Alumni Magazine* (Summer 2015): 50-51.

[3] Matthew Casey, *The Return: An End-time Epistle to the Church in America* (Richmond, Virginia: Elijah Books, 2010), 105-106.

[4] Mark Dever, *Nine Marks of a Healthy Church* (Wheaton, Illinois: Crossway, 2013), 255.

[5] Ibid., 256.

parents, with the church taking eminence. Chapter 9 explores how the church can help their parishioners keep first things first, thus overflowing to the home and to the school.

In this chapter, we will explore how parents can help their children, how parents can help the school, and how the school can help the parents keep first things first.

HOW PARENTS CAN HELP THEIR CHILDREN

DEVOTING TIME

We all have been swept up in it. The "tyranny of the schedule" controlling the parents rather than the parents controlling the schedule. Guilt nags that you have to do everything and attend everything. You don't. That is false guilt. You are not obliged. The goal is first things first. In *The Reason for God*, Pastor Tim Keller says,

> Consider parenting. Children come into the world in a condition of complete dependence. They cannot operate as self-sufficient, independent agents unless their parents give up much of their own independence and freedom for years. If you don't allow your children to hinder your freedom in work and play at all, and if you only get to your children when it doesn't inconvenience you, your children will grow up physically only. In all sorts of other ways they will remain emotionally needy, troubled, and overdependent. The choice is clear. You can either sacrifice your freedom or theirs. It's them or you. To love your children well, you must decrease that they may increase. You must be willing to enter into the dependency they have so eventually they can experience the freedom and independence you have. All life-changing love toward people with serious needs is a substitutional sacrifice. If you become personally involved with them, in some way, their weaknesses flow toward you as your strengths flow toward them. ... substitution is at the heart of the Christian message.[6]

Christ came to this world incarnate, from the Latin *incarnare*, meaning "into flesh." He came to be *with* us. Children need to *experience* the love of Christ before they can *hear* about the love of Christ. The only way that that love gets filled up in their little beings is for us to be *with* them, to pray for them, to hold them, to snuggle together reading books to them, to hold their little hands, and take tiny steps into this big world. As we learn to parent, we are soothed to know "He tends His flock like a shepherd: He gathers the lambs in His arms and carries them close to His heart; He gently leads those that have young" (Isaiah 40:11). We are called to be shepherds to our children and that means devoting time to them and *being with* them.

BEING AN ADULT

As we shepherd, we also need to ask ourselves a blunt question: am I acting more like a child or like an adult? Senator Ben Sasse quoting Neil Postman's *Amusing Ourselves to Death: Public Discourse in the Age of Show Business* says, "'Without a clear concept of what it means to be an adult,' there can then 'be no clear concept of what it means to be a child.' As so-called adults become ever more childlike, neither child nor adult knows how to transition, not just biologically but socially and morally, from child to adult. Everyone ends up confused and dissatisfied."[7] Sasse says ironically as America became more child-centered, "childhood" itself began to disappear. Quoting Postman again, he says, "'Everywhere one looks, the behavior, language, attitudes, and desires – even the physical appearance – of adults and children are becoming increasingly indistinguishable."[8] As a result, "In the face of unprecedented prosperity and freedom from convention, the generation coming of age is stuck in a hazy, extended adolescence, never allowed simply to be children, and yet also rarely nudged to be fully adult."[9] First Corinthians 13:11 directs us: "When I was a child, I talked like a child, I thought like a child, I reasoned like a child. When I became a man, I put the ways of childhood behind me." Again, the Lord is our Shepherd, leading us into adulthood.

---

[6] Timothy Keller, *The Reason for God: Belief in an Age of Skepticism* (New York: Riverhead Books, 2008), 202.

[7] Ben Sasse, *The Vanishing American Adult: Our Coming-of-Age Crisis – and How to Rebuild a Culture of Self-Reliance* (New York: St. Martin's Press, 2017), 51.

[8] Ibid., 51.

[9] Ibid., 52.

CULTIVATING FAITH & WORSHIP

We parents help our children as we devote time to be *with* them, as we choose to be the adult, and especially as we cultivate a home culture of faith and worship. Are we cultivating a Christ-centered culture in our home?[10] Dads, are you respected at the city gate, and Moms, are you clothed with strength and dignity, speaking with wisdom and faithful instruction, watching over the affairs of your household (Proverbs 31: 23, 25-27)? Are we men & women who fear the Lord?

With God's guidance, it is crucial to create a counter-culture within our homes. In *The Reason for God*, Tim Keller says,

> This upside-down pattern [of Christ] so contradicts the thinking and practice of the world that it creates an "alternate kingdom," an alternate reality, a counter culture among those who have been transformed by it. In this peaceable kingdom there is a reversal of the values of the world with regard to power, recognition, status, and wealth. In this new counterculture, Christians look at money as something to give away. They look at power as something to use strictly for service. ... Those who are shaped by the great reversal of the Cross no longer need self-justification through money, status, career, or pride of race and class.[11]

Do our children see us as living counter culturally, or are they witnessing our idols of latest fashions, cars, entertainment, upper-echelon life, & careers? Choose this day whom you will serve...

Christian apologist Josh McDowell says, "Christian parents need to *live out their faith before their children* [italics mine]"[12] in an age-appropriate and transparent fashion because our example impacts our children profoundly. McDowell continues, "Don't go it alone. Learn from others how to be an effective parent. ...Live out your faith in a way that attracts kids to Christ." Avoid drop off-and-go at church, at school, and in life in general. Be there *with them*. Train them up in the way they should go and they will not abandon it later in life. Look at the family calendar and map out times to bike ride, have game nights, lie on sleeping bags under the stars. Several families I know opt for a *one-activity*-per-child policy to protect family time. CCE schools often do not assign homework over the weekend to preserve the sanctity of the home sphere. Finally, pray, asking the Lord to lead your family to a healthy Jesus-following, Bible-believing church. Don't sleep in on Sundays. A truly Christian fellowship will change your lives. Worship: Serve Him. Bless Him. Thank Him.

Suggested Reading: *What is the Father Like?* by W. Phillip Keller reveals what being a mature Christian looks like by looking at our heavenly Parent.

PRACTICAL IDEAS FOR LOVING & TRAINING

Author Ruth Bell Graham said, "You have your children for a few short years. Train them before the time is gone."[13] Here are some ideas for helping our children grow up. I wish I could hear your ideas, too!

- *Bible*
  - Read stories of the gentle and manly strength of Jesus.
  - Read stories of heroes in the faith, like Moses, Joshua, ...
  - Say grace and pray at mealtimes.
  - Sing together.
- *Bedtime* consistency. Children need 9-11 hours/night; teens 8-10. Their minds & bodies need sleep time to rest, and process & store all they are learning.
- *Chores*
  - Small tasks for smaller hands; large tasks for larger hands

---

[10] Leslie Collins, lecture, Pasadena Evangelical Presbyterian Church, Pasadena, Maryland, April 11, 2009.

[11] Keller, 204.

[12] Josh McDowell, interview by Davies Owens, Basecamp podcast, March 28, 2017.

[13] Billygraham.org.

- o You have a cleaning lady? Still have your children clean their own rooms (starting young with "pick up 10 things" to teens "tidying weekly; cleaning monthly").
- *Discipline* – consistent, not in anger; uncover sin and cover with grace.
- *Food* – more whole foods, less processed, less sugar.
- *Money* – Make or give your child a small bank with 3 sections, teaching them to tithe 10% to church, save toward a goal or a prized possession or cause, and so forth, in this order:
  - o Church
  - o Savings
  - o Spending
- Rites of passage have a corollary parent component with giving them more "leash" and talking to them in more adult ways.

Ideas for sparking awakenings & promoting active not passive adults:

- Short exploratory walks outside with toddlers noting the moon, the airplane, the crawling bug, or sweet flower
- Quiet times for little ones to nap or entertain themselves safely with toys & books
- Interaction in conversation with others
- Library visits hauling treasures home: non-fiction, fiction, plays, & poetry
- Art books around the house of classic art
- Music playing from fine classical, jazz, bluegrass, country, & other sources
- Museum & zoo visits
- Tending of a vegetable garden (fertile Bible object lessons)
- Short bike rides or camping, hiking, & fishing expeditions
- Aid to older members of your church or community with tasks like leaf-raking or bringing in groceries
- One extracurricular activity per child (not one every day of the week producing exhaustion)

REAL EXPERIENCES

We can also help our children by expanding their horizons in and then beyond the home with real experiences. Firstly, Senator Ben Sasse asks if parents are life-long learners themselves. He says when our children see us read and discuss and engage with them and others, that will become a part of their own culture for themselves. Regarding teenagers, Senator Sasse focuses on "five uses of a teen's time – five habits to cultivate – to transition from childhood to adulthood"[14] in his book, *The Vanishing American Adult: Our Coming-of-Age Crisis – and How to Rebuild a Culture of Self-Reliance*, ranging from fleeing age segregation, to embracing work pain, to consuming less, to travelling to see, to building a bookshelf. His book is an important and delightful read. He likens these habits to "bodybuilding for the mind and soul" and that the "scar tissue of character ... happily awaits."[15] He endorses self-denial and delayed gratification and "to cultivate the habit of gratitude at the satisfaction of real and basic needs."[16] Regarding travel, Sasse quotes historian Daniel Boorstin, "'the tourist sees less of the country than of its tourist attractions. Today what he sees is seldom the living culture, but usually specimens collected and embalmed especially for him or attractions specially staged for him: proved specimens of the artificial.'"[17] Instead, Sasse encourages historian Edward Gibbon's Grand Tour advice regarding the habits of a good explorer: "He should be endowed with an active, indefatigable vigour of mind and body, which can seize every mode of conveyance, and support with a careless smile every hardship of the road, the weather or the inn. It must stimulate him with a restless curiosity, impatient of ease, covetous of time...."[18] Seek "real experiences." *Travel* comes from the word *travail*, meaning "work," therefore, travel is "to do something laborious or troublesome, but meaningful."[19] While we usually collapse on Friday nights, we all need to resist

---

[14] Sasse, 85.

[15] Ibid., 87.

[16] Ibid., 173.

[17] Ibid., 181.

[18] Ibid., 181.

[19] Ibid., 183.

majoring in Netflix binges. Maybe rest as a family Friday night over pizza and then have a weekend goal after the chores on Saturday or on the Sabbath.

Ideas for "real experiences":

- Go crabbing on the bay
- Spend hours on a beach (with hat and water!), climbing over rocks and making "hotels" for hermit crabs
- Attend a prayer group in a church you are visiting (On Tangier Island in Maryland, we visited one and got to hear Elizabethan English and shaped-note singing!)
- Bicycle as a family
- Hike together at a regional park
- Explore a pond, a wetland, or beach & discover what lives there and its ecosystem, marveling in awe at God's creation
- Explore a woods, a meadow, or a field with a bug jar, binoculars, magnifying glass, & nature guidebook
- Spend time getting to know a veteran
- Risks & challenges for the teen years – Back when our son was 16, we sent him on a flight by himself to San Antonio, Texas, to attend a conference on film-making. We did dry-runs on navigating public transportation at our local international airport and into our local city, giving him the task to take us to one of the hotels in that city. We talked about money; how to pay, treat, & tip taxi-cab drivers and waiters; how to read paper maps of the historic Menger Hotel of Teddy Roosevelt fame and of San Antonio itself. He loved this milestone!

BOOKS & READING

Read to your children. When they are teeny. When they are teens. What joy it is to read together! Try different voices for different characters or even going to the place mentioned in the book. As a professor, Dr. Mark Graham of Grove City College says he can tell which students have been read to in childhood, as there is "an attentiveness."

You may say, but my child does not like to read. Years ago, my mother heard a lecturer say, "If your boy likes baseball, get him a book on baseball!" My mother did, and to this day, my brother reads tomes on history and other subjects. On building a bookshelf, Senator Ben Sasse says, "The truly free have always required literacy."[20] In fact, liberal arts education comes from the Latin *liber* meaning "free (man)." Sasse and his wife desire "to have [their kids] be not just functionally literate but fully habituated to reading important things by the time they depart from under [their] roof. ... They need to feel a desire in their chests to become people of the book, even amid the seductive lure of the screen."[21] With his eclectic literacy, Sasse personally promotes no one set canon, but suggests parents guide their teens and then encourage them to develop their own canon, being open to recommendations and developing a robust list. As a model, he urges that "...our kids should be able to perceive by our habits that there is one special bookshelf of more life-changing works to which we return again and again."[22] "Our lists most certainly should be debated – and humbly revised."[23] With their timeless value, Christian classics and classics are the natural first choice.

Senator Sasse's ideas for building a booklist:

- 50-60 books, ranging from child to adult, from Christianity, to Greek, to medieval to Shakespeare, to American historical classics to markets to tyrants to science to American fiction to the Great Conversation and so forth ...
- "Challenge [yourselves] to read for 60 minutes without looking at smartphones, televisions, or computers."[24]

---

[20] Sasse, 242.

[21] Ibid., 209.

[22] Ibid., 227.

[23] Ibid., 241.

[24] Ibid., 210.

If you cannot afford a home library, work with your church to establish a communal library there.

STANDING FAST

We stand fast on limits with our little ones and as we lessen our grip on our teens, we do not lessen our grip on principles. In *The Benedict Option: A Strategy for Christians in a Post-Christian Nation*, author Rod Dreher says, "The teen years are when kids become intensely aware of their parents' anxiety about making their children seem like outcasts, or themselves look weird in the eyes of their own parental peers. If Mom and Dad don't stand firm and are not willing to be thought of as peculiar by their own friends for their strictness, then the kids don't stand a chance."[25] We gave our kids a code word that they would use if away from home that was innocuous to a listener, but to us meant "Come get me right now!" We need to be there, no matter what.

ALL HOMES ARE SCHOOLS

Dr. Chris Thompson refers to "our little schools at home" and says, "Home is a school and a seminary."[26] We send our children to school, but we are the primary educators. How are we handling that? Dr. Mark Graham at Grove City College seizes the opportunity to walk with his children each morning to school and has done so for nine years. They talk, he listens, and they can talk of God (Deut. 6:7). My own son said those natural discussion times with us were the best for his faith, rather than rigid times. Each family can pray for God's guidance in family devotions. Pray at the table, share Biblical application over the day's stories told in the car on the way to soccer practice. Read Bible stories to them at the end of the day and tuck them in with your prayers. Share stories of how God has been faithful to you, stories of how you have been "redeemed from bondage to sin," and teach them "to look to the grace of the cross."[27]

In his book *The Vanishing American Adult*, Senator Ben Sasse warns against falling into the progressive educator John Dewey's snare: "To the degree that we have forgotten the fact that a school should be a tool – a means to an end, not an end in itself – Dewey is the culprit. For him, the school would become everything – the literal center of the world, he said on occasion. In Dewey's dream, the school ceased to be an instrument supporting parents and became instead a substitute for parents."[28] Sasse continues to say,

> For these deeper communities [parents – and grandparents and neighbors and local communities] are ultimately responsible for nurturing children toward the kind of living and serving that befits free and independent nearly-adults with big and complicated souls. Great teachers don't try to be the exclusive center of life, but rather instrumental servants of a larger life. Great school administrators know and honor the limits of their institutions; they don't try to displace families and the deeper and wider institutions of life that are based on love.[29]

Critically important is Dorothy Sayers' insight. "She yearned for a great education for all, but she knew that such a dream could be realized only once children were individually and personally engaged."[30] While a great supporter of education and particularly Classical Christian Education, Ben Sasse argues "*against the mindless assumption made by too many of the rest of us* that schools and their teachers can awaken all of our kids alone inside just one institutional form. Rather, all of us need to be more engaged at helping spark these awakenings."[31] Reject any pressure from a school to "leave the driving to us." You are absolutely critical to the nurture and admonition of your child. Parents, the school your children are attending and the teachers who are teaching them truly love your children and are pouring their lives out to serve you and them. Do not, however, let yourselves let them become everything and do not let them takeover becoming the center of everything. Do not let them displace you and the home.

---

[25] Rod Dreher, *The Benedict Option: A Strategy for Christians in a Post-Christian Nation* (New York: Sentinel, 2018), 127.

[26] Dr. Chris Thompson, sermon, South River Baptist Church, Statesville, North Carolina, May 13, 2018.

[27] Ibid.

[28] Sasse, 26.

[29] Ibid., 27.

[30] Ibid., 81.

[31] Ibid., 81.

HOW PARENTS CAN HELP THE SCHOOL

The ideal of how parents can help the school is partnership. Regarding teamwork and co-laboring with parents, one teacher shared, "I didn't feel like I was working as a team with parents." What does working like a team look like? Schooling our children is a shared mission. Mission comes from the Latin *mittere* meaning "send." We are sent out to do this together! Here are some ideas for us parents.

Regarding the school:

- Pray for the school and staff.
- Attend school orientation and events.
- Visit your child's classroom just to observe.
- Read information sent home to parents.
- Be engaged in your child's progress at school, asking them questions about their day at school, looking at their papers, praising them for their efforts.
- Attend back-to-school night & parent-teacher conferences.
- Help to chaperone fieldtrips.
- Volunteer one or two times per year as a helper, a special speaker, a pizza server at lunch, and so forth. Each bit of volunteering gives you a window to the school and an opportunity to help build it up.
- Attend plays & sports events.
- Be a coach.
- Host a class party over the summer.
- Go on field trips or Grand Tour with your child.
- Attend any free summer training your school may offer.
- Attend the annual meeting of the school.
- Read books about classical Christian education that you seek on your own and/or the school suggests. One teacher said that they saw their role as advocate for CCE overshadowing their being a partner with parents. That can be the natural in a young school; however, as parents read to learn more about CCE for themselves, they may become more invested because they understand more about the vision, resulting in advocating for the school and CCE.

Regarding your child and the school:

- Inform the school of your child's learning needs and challenges. Help the school help your child. So helpful for all!
- Honor the Communication Chain:
  - Write/call the appropriate person when there is a concern. To help everyone stay on track, speak with the *involved* parties, not those uninvolved.
    - If the issue regards...
      - *Another parent's child* – talk with the teacher if the problem occurred during school; talk with the other child's parent if it was an after-school problem.
      - *A parent* – talk with the parent (not the school)
      - *A teacher* – talk with the teacher (not the administrator)
      - *The head of school or a principal* – talk with them directly (not other parents)
        - Do speak with the head of school or a principal if an issue with a teacher could not be resolved directly with the particular teacher.
      - *The board of directors* – present that to the head of school (not other parents)
- Hear a teacher out and assume that most likely they have a legitimate point before responding defensively.
- Speak well of the school & staff (no bad-mouthing or gossiping).

PARENTAL PRESSURE

What winds and waves receive the most emphasis in your school? Are parents pushing sports over commitment to academics? On the other hand, we parents can be driven for academic achievement, but "How do we measure success – Harvard or heaven?"[32] Josh McDowell says it is *relationship* that must be nurtured. Academics are important. Extra-curricular activities are important. There needs to be balance. Avoid pressing for sports first, hovering over our children as they grow, insisting on all A's, stressing if a child gets a "C." I always told my kids that as long as they were living out their God-given potential, I was fine. Even if that meant a "C." I love that Josh McDowell took his kids out for ice cream after report cards to celebrate their doing the best they could.

Regarding whether CCE is right for a particular child, Mrs. Lisa Borgeson, former teacher and administrator, says to "Be in prayer."[33] She elucidates further: "Knowing your child's frame is probably the most important aspect because CCE is rigorous. It is not for everyone." Borgeson suggests the following:

1. Go observe in the classroom (not just the Open House). Do your research. It is important to be on the same page. ...Don't just look at "the pretties."
2. Be prepared to accept your child's ability. Be prepared to hear hard things; be open to criticism of your children.

THE NEGLECT OF DISCIPLINE

But you might think, "I remember how sweet my child looked in their crib!" They truly were and always will be in our hearts. God gives us a strong, protective love for our children. Regarding all children's sin nature, Lisa Borgeson says, they were the "cutest little sinners I've ever seen." We parents need to remember our children are not born good. Just as with us, there is a mutiny in their heart that says, "I want to be the captain of my ship!" Sin is a cosmic rebellion against God.[34] Our children are no exception.

We might say, "I am just so worn out after a full day at work" or "Kids will be kids; they'll grow out of this misbehavior." Yes, we all are tired if not exhausted. Yes, kids can be childish – they *are* children! Are we postponing needed discipline again and again because of our fatigue or the inconvenient timing? Are they just being childish (okay), or are they being disobedient (not okay)?

What are God's priorities? Our job as parents is to nurture and admonish. To discipline our children. To set limits & boundaries. To base those limits on biblical principles. To train them up in the way they should go. We need to depend on God to give us the energy and appropriate response. We can send up "arrow-prayers" to Him, asking for His help. Truly, we must discipline in love and not in anger. If we are angry, we can tell our child that we are leaving the room to cool down and in a few minutes will be back to discipline him or her. We are also not to provoke or exasperate our child. We need to keep in mind their frame. We are not to irritate them intensely or infuriate them.

We can search the Bible for sins that require discipline: defiance, lying, hitting, biting, kicking, disobedience, stealing, cursing, disrespect, name-calling, teasing, complaining. If misbehavior is not corrected, we are allowing it and condoning it. If we want it to cease, we need to take loving, firm, truthful, grace-filled action. Indeed, the Bible says if we love our children, we will care if they are disobedient. If we love our children, we will address the problem. Proverbs 3:12 tells us, "...[F]or the Lord reproves him whom he loves, as a father the son in whom he delights." [See "Resources" for Tedd Tripp's *Shepherding a Child's Heart* and Paul David Tripp's *Parenting: 14 Gospel Principles That Can Radically Change Your Family* and *Age of Opportunity*.] God promises us, "For the moment all discipline seems painful rather than pleasant, but later it yields the peaceful fruit of righteousness to those who have been trained by it" (Heb. 12:11).

---

[32] Dr. Chris Thompson, sermon, May 13, 2018.

[33] Lisa Borgeson, interview by Kathleen F. Kitchin, Phone Call, May 11, 2018.

[34] Pastor Charles Wall, Adult Sunday School class, Grace Alliance Fellowship Church, Statesville, North Carolina, July 14, 2019.

Again, Ruth Bell Graham, said that we parents are foremost *trainers* of our children. Training involves repetition. Again. And again. And again. We cannot expect the school to do all of our disciplining for us. Into the teen years, we see that Solomon in the Book of Proverbs reins in his son continuously with "Listen," "Attend," and "Do not neglect your father and mother's teaching." Correcting, exhorting, disciplining all are time consuming (and situations usually arise inconveniently just as you are heading out the door or preparing dinner). Take the time. Be late. Address the problem. Ask questions. Cite the sin. Be tender. Forgive. Cover it with the blood of Jesus. Assure your child they are restored to fellowship. Discipline truly produces a harvest of righteousness.

HOW THE SCHOOL CAN HELP THE PARENTS KEEP FIRST THINGS FIRST

PARENT ENCULTURATION

Both my children attended a classical Christian school, one from 1st grade-on and the other from kindergarten-on. My husband and I cannot imagine our family's life without who and what the school was for us. First and foremost, it helped focus us more on Jesus Christ and His redemptive work in all of life. Secondly, it gave us a solid school that helped us nurture & admonish our children in the Lord. Thirdly, it grew us into understanding CCE. Fourthly, it gave us opportunities to serve as volunteers and to teach. My Christian colleagues, their labors for the Lord and for our children, and the books, resources, conversations, & discussions enriched all of us beyond measure. I asked Keith Nix, head of Veritas School in Richmond, Virginia, about the family and parent enculturation & education.[35] Their school has what they call "Veritas U" two or threes times per year on a Friday night and serve coffee. About 250 parents come (1 parent/family). The school publishes a babysitter list to help aid parents' availability. The event builds community, again in a *paideia* fashion. There are several classes for 2 hours and they change each time, although some are taught annually like the class on Singapore Math. Other topics have included 1) Latin, 2) Roman history, 3) the Beauty of Math, 4) Reboot – helping your child navigate technology and social media, 5) Boy/Girl Relationships, 6) The Role of Athletics in CCE, 7) Parenting with Grace, 8) Peace-making... and many more. [See "Appendix," "Invitations to Veritas U."]

Veritas School also gives parents a suggested "summer reading list" of maybe three books. They choose one to read over the summer. In the fall, there is a discussion where about 40-50 parents come for these book meetings. In addition, once a month 15-25 parents meet for a book club, reading something from the curriculum and then discussing it. Grace Classical Christian Academy in Granbury, Texas, is a younger school and holds a Parent Academy three times per year "learning what it means to be educated classically and biblically. ...[T]hey gather...[to] share what they are learning about how to raise up children in the nurture and admonition of the Lord Jesus Christ."[36] If you are new to this, start with one book, one meeting.

Providentially, the neighborhood of Veritas School is a place where faculty and families can afford to live with a good range of housing costs. Over the years, close to 80 families have moved to this neighborhood from the suburbs, or out of town. Keith Nix believes there needs to be a proper understanding of Rod Dreher's book, *The Benedict Option*. It is "healthy, not just retreating. We need to do a lot of retreating to train. Retreat to train." Keith says "parent education & enculturation and deepening in the community" is happening. He says, "I am not the only one who has to explain why we don't have AP tests. Hopefully, I have 100 parents who could explain it." In other words, "Many parents are so well enculturated that they are doing some of the enculturation of other parents."

CONFRONTING IDOLATRY

In Orlando, I interviewed head of school Rev. Robert Ingram at the Geneva School who said, "Some of toughest conversations involve having to tell parents that the children are the new idolatry."[37] He continued saying,

> They have been guilty of putting their children on a pedestal and not having a biblical understanding of their capacity to sin, at times to be devious, to be sneaky. To the very best of my ability I have backtracked all this situation and there is a unanimity of opinion that little Billy is

---

[35] Keith Nix, interview by Kathleen F. Kitchin, Richmond, Virginia, June 5, 2019.

[36] Grace Classical Christian Academy, Granbury, Texas, website, accessed July 29, 2019.

[37] Rev. Robert Ingram, interview by Kathleen F. Kitchin, Orlando, Florida, February 21, 2019.

what his demerits say he is and you don't like those demerits and you don't like me reaffirming that Billy is this way here at school. I need to tell you that this is the case.

Every one of us parents has probably gone a bit overboard or mother-bear when our child's behavior is called out. I know I have. But I have learned we should respect the experience and expertise of the teacher and vice versa. Mutual respect. Most teachers are working sacrificially. If they are taking the time to share a problem with our child's behavior, there most definitely is a valuable – though painful – truth to be learned.

PARENT CARE

At Hope Academy in Minneapolis, Minnesota, head of school Russ Gregg says, "One of the members of the leadership team leads care for our families: Parent Support & Care. Right at the highest level of our work. Pastoring and caring for our parents. It's really needed. It is pretty unique to our model." I responded by saying, "That's needed everywhere at some level; it might look a little different from place to place. Again, it's the word *incarnate*. It's the Word. We are little Christs. And we are trying to speak that love & truth and be that as ambassadors for whom we meet."

CASE STUDY

Hope Academy – Minneapolis, Minnesota – Mr. Russ Gregg – 490 students

"Out-of-school time together builds trust. One of our biggest challenges is how to support that relationship-building, especially in a cross-cultural context. Those kinds of sacrificial acts of love are more necessary than ever. Hire those values. Not an 8-5 job. We're looking for people to be 'all in.'"[38] A call that spills beyond normal school hours. Two relationship-builders are 1) an annual home visit and 2) two Saturday events – all parents are required to attend this parenting workshop where they attend workshops on how to support their child's education and visit their child's classroom.[39]

1) *Parenting workshop*
   a. "We try to make clear up front 'We are a school for the children of parents who are willing to be deeply involved in their child's education. If that doesn't sound helpful to you or exciting, this is probably not going to be a good fit.'"
2) *Parent report card*
   a. Required meetings
   b. "We realize that all the most successful people in the world set up systems of accountability for themselves because they recognize how weak we are, how much we need that kind of thing. That's the idea. We're all weak. We all need this kind of support and help."
   c. "We try to pick the things that the parents of all successful children do."
3) How do we help each other? It's a *partnership*.
   a. "We rent table rounds and fill the gym with ~40 tables – instead of talking at the parents all that time, … it's parents talking with other parents. Building relationships amongst one another. Parents have come away saying, 'Now *that's* really helpful. Sharing struggles. Seeing other parents have struggles, too.'"

Russ Gregg says, "All over America, people are feeling isolated. How do we step in & build community?"

Red Flags

- Parents do not understand what classical Christian education is about, nor read to understand.
- Parents and school are not on the same page.
- Parents let their kids stay up too late and then have little time to themselves.
- Children are not obeying their parents.

---

[38] Russ Gregg, interview by Kathleen F. Kitchin, Minneapolis, Minnesota, May 20, 2019.

[39] Sarah Eekhoff Zylstra, "The Exponential Growth of Classical Christian Education," *The Gospel Coalition*, January 9, 2017.

- Children routinely boss their parents.
- Children are prideful or arrogant. Where is this coming from? The home? The community environment? The school's perception of itself?
- One teacher found that the "parents can be overall supportive" while "Some don't care, don't respond to emails, say, 'We'll work on it,'" but there are no changes. Some "entitled" parents were "over-directive regarding homework and what they deem allowed/not allowed." It was "A pretty gossipy community which "Makes it hard to get to know them," because they are "miners" for information.
- One teacher said that "As a whole, parents were not on board with the vision. It came down to grades (All A's.). If the child did not achieve all A's, it was the teachers' fault. There were inflated expectations."
- "Having every moment of the day institutionalized. Minus the screens, let kids be kids during downtime."

Sober Reflection

Individual (Do individually & then jointly with spouse)

- Do my kids see me reaching for my Bible or my phone?
- Am I making time to read my Bible & pray?
- Am I studying the Bible in order to grow as a parent?
- Am I observing godly parents in order to grow as a parent?
- Am I aware of the vision of the school, or have I asked the school for their vision statement?
- Am I speaking kindly of the board of directors, the head of school, my children's teachers & staff, and students?
- Am I asking God for a guard on my mouth so that I share what should be shared and do not share what should not be shared? Is there a "need to know"?
- If there is a problem, am I going to the right person? (Determine who is at the source of the problem and go to that person – my child's teacher, a fellow parent, an administrator.)
- Am I placing a halo around my child? Am I humble about my child's strengths? Am I teachable about my child's weaknesses? Fathers, are you helping "mother-bear" to hear hard but lovingly truthful criticism of her child?
- Am I reading with my child?
- Am I putting my phone away – far away – and devoting family time to dinner at home, time together to work, to play, to rest?
- Is this school and our family headed to the same destination (God-honoring or world-enticed)?

School Administrators

- Are we providing the vision statement to the parents? Mission? Core values?
- Are we providing practical examples to parents of how the teachers and school are bringing that vision statement to life?
- Are we providing a concise reading list of "Top Ten" books on CCE?
- Are we providing reading lists for students and their parents to elect to delight in?
- Do we offer lectures & book discussions for parents, once or twice per year?

Getting Back on Track

- Have set bedtimes for your children. Negotiate them more in the mid- to older teen years.
- *Family Project*: "…[F]ind a central place in the home, far from the bedrooms, and park the screens there before bedtime." This helps your child associate bedroom with sleep.[40]

---

[40] Andy Crouch, *The Tech-Wise Family: Everyday Steps for Putting Technology in Its Proper Place* (Grand Rapids, Michigan: Baker Books, 2017), 118.

- *Family Project*: Buy an inexpensive alarm clock so your device does not have to be where you are sleeping.
- Take full advantage of your children's devices' parental controls. If appropriate for your child, choose a most-basic phone instead of a smart phone.
- *Parent Project*: Make use of internet-provider filters & blocks.
- Have total access to your children's devices.
- "Dads & granddads, the greatest gift you can give to your children and grandchildren is to be a Spirit-filled man. Pray, asking God to fill you with His Holy Spirit."[41]
  - *Desire/Thirst* to be filled with the Holy Spirit.
  - *Denounce* any sin in my life.
  - *Dedicate* myself, my attitudes, my thoughts to Him. "The Holy Spirit won't fill what you haven't given to Him."
  - *Depend/Trust* Him for His control.

Healthy Home

- Jesus Christ is at the center of the home.
- God's Word is revered and read. Dad & Mom read and study the Bible.
- The family attends a Christ-following, Bible-believing church.
- Outside activities are limited. Some families choose one activity per child.
- Family invests in family time around the table, at home together.
- Parents read emails/notes home/parent-student handbook as partners in their child's education.

Staying on Track during a Crisis

From several parents...

- *For you:*
  - Ask the Lord's help to keep your eyes on Jesus. Ask for His peace, protection, & direction.
  - Dwell in the shelter of the Most High (Psalm 91: 1a).
  - Read your Bible and be in His Word.
  - Be in prayer, leaning into Him to supply your needs.
- *With your spouse:*
  - Read the Bible and be in His Word.
  - Be in prayer together as a team.
  - Pray for an educational plan for your family.
  - As former director of instruction Laura Tucker once told me regarding parenting, "Be faithful to what God is telling you to do. God blesses this."
- *As a family:*
  - Read the Bible and be in His Word (e.g., the Exodus story of deliverance).
  - Pray out loud as a family – before meals, after meals, during a special family worship time.
  - Remind your family of your mission: to glorify God and enjoy Him at all times.
  - Sing, play, walk, bike, and take breaks as a family.
  - *Suggestion*: *Mama's Refill* by Pam Forster of Doorposts – an email Bible study for mothers as well as a component for their children (e.g., Psalm 91).
- *Ahead of lesson times:*
  - Read teacher emails every night for assignments for the next day.
  - Print out handouts for younger children.
  - Make a family schedule & post it in a central place.
    - Who goes on the computer first, second, and so forth, if sharing a device.
    - Set meal times.

---

[41] Pastor Charles Wall, sermon, Grace Alliance Fellowship Church, Statesville, North Carolina, June 30, 2019.

- Maintain a routine for your children.
  - o If you have multiple children at home, think of your home as a one-room schoolhouse. Create & post a specific, written academic schedule for your young children; enlist the help of your older children to work together on theirs or they can create it on their own & get your approval.
    - State the order that subjects should be done (Math, Reading, etc.).
    - Include break times – chores, pets, exercise, play.
- *With your children:*
  - o Hear your children's fears, tears, & concerns. Listen to them. Hug them. Assure them of God's love, of your love. Post Bible verses around your home as constant reminders of God's love, protection, provision, & sovereignty (e.g., Psalm 46). "When the bottom falls out, you need to know He is in control. Worshipping God keeps you from being crushed. I have to worship God or this is going to crush me. Satan has not gotten out in front of this situation where God is trying to play 'catch-up.' God is always in control. God has His purposes. Purifying the church, not punishment."
  - o Each morning – praise the Lord; thank Him for a new, fresh day of life.
  - o Have them make their bed (discipline, accomplishment, & order all at once).
  - o Eat a healthy breakfast.
  - o Begin each day's lesson times with Bible & prayer. Lean into the Lord, asking His help; your children need to see & hear this during stressful times.
  - o Read together.
  - o Do the next thing (from an old poem, popularized by Elizabeth Elliot).
  - o Oversight
    - Oversee young children closely; half-way with logic students, and just lightly with rhetoric students.
    - Overwhelmed? Back off, pray, set a new goal, take a break from an assignment or occasionally maybe even cancel school for a day to avoid exasperation.
    - Patience
      - Often parents work *and* homeschool *and* care for their own parents at various levels. Be gentle with yourself.
      - Some grandparents are the new teachers & are learning new systems. Be gentle with them.
      - No matter who is overseeing, set the bar at a reasonable height & set manageable goals. Major in priorities.
- *As new homeschoolers:*
  - o At first, your children will need much help. As time goes on & familiarity with distance learning increases, they will become more independent. There is more work for you up front; however, over time, remove the scaffolding as they gain proficiency.
- *Dealing with a crisis together as a family:*
  - o One parent says,
    - "Homeschooling gave us time to be together, to be quiet, to feel safe, to abide together in the shadow of the Most High. To be together at this time was a blessing."
    - "When our younger daughter who was a believer passed away, we wanted to stay together & talk as much as our children were willing to talk. We parents talked with the kids. We walked individually with each child and talked. Together we read aloud *Safely Home* by Randy Alcorn, and the kids colored a poster together as they listened. This book brought thoughts about heaven to their mind, but they didn't know how to put words to them, and brought God's Word to those places in their heart where they had questions they might not have been able to verbalize. This was a comforting, healing thing. The loss was the same, but there was the truth of the future with that loved one with the Lord in heaven."
    - "You turn to other things for lessons in daily life, weaving them into the fabric of the day."
- *At all times*: God is with you & will never leave or forsake you.

Setting a Goal

- Pray for God's wisdom. Set one or two goals for getting the vision for *your family* better on track. Enter that goal in your phone or planner.
- Refer to this goal throughout the year.
- Reflect on this goal at year's end. Rejoice in God's grace.

Expressing a Desire

- Pray for God's wisdom. Write one or two desires for getting the vision for your family better on track *that depend on others' cooperation*. Enter that desire in your phone or planner.
- Pray about this desire throughout the year.
- Reflect on this desire at the end of each year. Rejoice in God's grace.

Encouragement

- Senator Ben Sasse calls parenting "...this most fundamental calling of nurturing little workers, little citizens, and eternal souls."[42]
- "While Sundays might feel more like a wrestling match, a battle of wills, or a circus, your time, efforts, and distracted worship are worth it. It is not wasted. Thank God for [His] grace – and keep it up."[43]
- One teacher says, "As a weary parent myself, homeschooling multiple children while one was in a local school, I know exactly how easy it is to think, 'I've paid my tuition (at sacrifice) and have so much else I must do – I'm glad to drop him/her off at school and know that's taken care of.' Few have time to do what a visionary school would most want – cultivate their own knowledge, enjoy their children's growing understanding, etc. I love it when a school offers lectures and discussion groups to cultivate an atmosphere of learning among the whole community – that's the magic of education – a shared experience."
- One teacher says, "I can say that it is breathtaking what a tidal wave our culture is. We had not realized to what extent that was so, and parents who wish to 'protect' or 'equip' their children for faithful living in the culture must realize that education is vitally important but may not deliver what we hope or engineer, however exhaustive our efforts. That's when we must trust the Lord for His care of each precious soul, and keep doing our best, but not be surprised if we are for a time, even a long time, disappointed. 'When he is *old* he will not depart from it' is the promise – not 'never depart from the way he should go.'"
- "[B]eing confident of this, that He who began a good work in you will perfect it until the day of Jesus Christ" (Philippians 1:6, ASV).

---

[42] Sasse, 275.
[43] Emily Carrington, Park Hill United Methodist Church, Facebook, February 5, 2019.

Chapter 8
Your School's Students

"Then our sons in their youth
will be like well-nurtured plants
and our daughters will be like pillars
carved to adorn a palace."

Psalm 144:12

When interviewing head of school Leslie Collins at Covenant Academy in Cypress, Texas, a pivotal word recurs in conversation – *communication*. [1] We had already discussed how important two-way communication was between administration and faculty/staff. Likewise, Collins seeks to build relationships in her school with students. She says, "Talk about a sticky school – how do you keep the people that you have? How do you *build trust* with your students?"

She says the following pattern in building relationships is "successful because this is an incarnation of what God does for us":

1) Enter into their world. Know where they are.
2) Make eye contact with them.
3) Give them a voice. Reciprocity. Do you listen to them?
4) Give age & gender-appropriate physical contact (knuckle-bumps, pat on the back)
5) Give them healthy & safe boundaries.

Leslie says the Lord's Prayer has those same five desires. She says, "You have to get beyond behavior. People focus too much on the behavior." We can focus on these five core elements as we build relationships with our students:

1) Acceptance
2) Affirmation
3) Respect
4) Comfort
5) Success

This chapter is the most tender of all as it is about the boys & girls we teach, the young men & women we care for as their *alma mater*, or "nurturing mother." We care for their spiritual, academic, social, & physical well-being. We are not their parents, but after teaching hundreds of students, I still refer to them as "my kids."

I started teaching in a public high school right out of college at age 22, and my oldest student was two years younger than I. My battle scars were earned those first few years, and it was a tough tutelage with great challenges and great wells of joy as students talked with me after class or after school, sharing their journeys with me. I was young, and I guess they felt they could relate to me. I heard all kinds of stories. Five years later, I invited all my 10th & 11th grade classes to my wedding. I remember having told my husband on our first date when he asked about my teaching, that I felt that when you teach, you are holding a tender soul in your hands. Even today,

---

[1] Leslie Collins, interview by Kathleen F. Kitchin, Cypress, Texas, November 27, 2018.

when the Lord brings a student to my mind, I pray for them right away, not knowing what their challenge might be, but knowing the all-seeing Father does.

Education does not involve *just a mind to be filled*. We care for the whole person: *spiritual, academic, social, & physical*. We run off the tracks if we forget one of these aspects or do not tend to it enough. For example, if our school overemphasizes sports, the attention to academics is affected. If our school does not provide several recess times for our youngest members, the attention to their physical needs is not addressed. If our focus is on academic success to such a degree, implicitly or explicitly, that expectation can discourage, if not crush, their spiritual development & discipleship. Each one of our students is a unique human being made in the image of God. Most importantly, we seek to disciple. Veteran teacher and administrator Laura Tucker says, "Discipleship is taking a personal interest in your students. That's what they need. Helping them academically. You are standing in the place of parents, and parents want their children to grow spiritually and in their character. Taking them from point A to Point B and having a vision for who they are and who they can become."[2]

SPIRITUAL

We love our students and our heart's desire is for these young men & women to grow *spiritually*, to know Jesus Christ and to hunger for God's Word and His wisdom. In 3 John 1:4, our hearts sing with John's who said, "I have no greater joy than to hear that my children are walking in the truth." This is an active process.

> My son, if you receive my words and treasure up my commandments with you, making your ear attentive to wisdom and inclining your heart to understanding; yes, if you call out for insight and raise your voice for understanding, if you seek it like silver and search for it as for hidden treasures, then you will understand the fear of the Lord and find the knowledge of God. (Proverbs 2:1-5)

This passage from Proverbs 2 describes a young man in the active, not passive frame of mind. *Receive, treasure, making, inclining, call, raise, seek, search, understand,* & *find* are all active verbs. We guide more heavily in the grammar years, but on all the Trivium paths, we should not do for our students what they can do for themselves. Help them actively seek and actively receive His treasures so that over time they may grow in spiritual formation & discernment.

To cultivate spiritual development and discipleship, we need to *get to know* the students. To shepherd effectively, we have said *parents* need time with their children. To shepherd effectively, *teachers* need time with their students. As former administrator and educator Steve Sheets says, "You cannot get to know your students without spending time with them." Before homeroom, between classes, over lunch, after school, at sports & drama events. We love them by showing interest in investing in them and getting to know them.

Part of this love is *discipline*. If we love our students, we will train them to obedience. Matt Whitling says, there are "three kinds of students in every classroom: the wise, the fool, and the naïve."[3]

- Correct a fool and the wise breathe a sigh of relief.
- Correct a fool and the naïve learn.

Students should be nurtured and admonished in the Lord. We set the rules, and we must enforce the rules. Avoid rewarding students for good behavior. Good behavior is expected of all. If students are required to "Obey right away," make sure they do. Do not allow children to disobey. The first few weeks of school will be exhausting but fruitful as limits will be tested, tried, and consistently enforced. Whatever you let slide, they will let slide. Hold a high, but reasonable standard. They will rise to that standard as you consistently enforce the rules. For example, if students are to line up quickly, correct the stragglers. If students are not to speak with disrespect, do not let disrespect go unaddressed. Refuse to be spoken to with disdain or have eyes rolled at your requests. Train the heart; do not just correct behavior. Leslie Collins says, "We get beyond behavior. People focus too much on the behavior. No shaming – no names on the board. In my school you won't do that." Indeed, one of the sweetest spots on the Covenant Academy campus is a bench on one side of the courtyard. I saw a teacher

---

[2] Laura Tucker, phone interview by Kathleen F. Kitchin, February 21, 2020.

[3] Matt Whitling, quoted by Leslie Collins, Rockbridge Academy Substitute Teacher Training, 2003.

sitting next to a small child on that bench during the school day. It was a discipline time. How quiet and peaceful it was to witness the teacher come alongside the child, by posture saying, "I am with you; I struggle, too" as she helped the child see their sin, repent of their sin, ask forgiveness, be granted forgiveness – a gospel-soaked culture.

As parents and teachers, we model Christian *standards of behavior and conversation* for these young minds. If we are sarcastic, they will soak that up. If we are thoughtful in our presentations, stories, and answers, they will soak that up. Luke 6:40 says, "The student is not above the teacher, but everyone who is fully trained will be like their teacher." This is a sobering consideration. In fact, James 3:1 says, "Not many of you should become teachers, my fellow believers, because you know that we who teach will be judged more strictly." Our audience is God. Does our speech shame Him, make Him wince, bring Him dishonor? Virtue is our goal and our prayer.

As part of spiritual development of our students, we model the virtue of *respect* and expect them to do likewise. We show respect for God, people, & property. No swearing or casual references to God, but reverence and honor. They are to show respect to parents, administrators, teachers, & fellow students. They are to demonstrate good stewardship of materials and the school facility.

We show our students *consideration* and expect them to show consideration to us & to their peers. As Philippians 2:4 directs us to think of others: "Let each of you look not only to his own interests, but also to the interests of others."

We expect our students to be *diligent*. Students must do their work "heartily as unto the Lord" as Colossians 3:23 instructs. We also need to check in with our students about the amount of homework. At Mars Hill Academy in Mason, Ohio, they do a homework survey twice/year to determine anonymously from the students if the homework load is dialed in.[4] They also say, "We call study halls 'work periods,' and the students are expected to work." School uniforms serve their place in this purposefulness. Mars Hill Academy tells students, "This is a workplace; therefore, we wear workplace clothing in a workplace." As for students' attitude, former administrator Steve Sheets delineates between "can't" and "won't." If the attitude toward the work assigned is "I can't," we come alongside to help.[5] If it is "I won't," we come alongside to correct and discipline.

Another virtue expected is *honesty*. It is refreshing if students can share what they really think about the literature they read for homework and what they did or did not do regarding their math homework.

Another way to encourage first things first is to have students *serve* at their school. At Hope Academy in inner-city Minneapolis, they have peer counseling. They have found sometimes a peer's calling out a trouble area in another peer has even more impact than a teacher's. Beautiful results have blossomed out of their peer counseling program, bringing honor to the gospel – exposing the sin, covering it with grace. Jesus died for our sins; we are saved and forgiven through faith in Him and His finished work. Another way students can serve is being a teacher's aide. At Bayshore Christian School in Fairhope, Alabama, the teacher's student aide goes to the classroom where the teacher has jobs for them. They grade spelling tests, create bulletin boards, & make copies for the teacher. A breathing hole for teachers and a marvelous opportunity for future teachers.

Our cultivating an environment of love and truth and grace and discipline is an ongoing daily cultivation. We may also have Chapel at our schools, another opportunity to speak God's love & truth into their lives & souls.

---

[4] Mark Cotterman, head of school, interview by Kathleen F. Kitchin, Mason, Ohio, May 3, 2018.

[5] Steven Sheets, interview by Kathleen F. Kitchin, Greenville, North Carolina, September 5, 2018.

Thoughts on Chapel

When I interviewed Dr. George Grant at the 2019 ACCS conference, I asked, "What are several practical ways for schools to *keep our focus on Christ*?"[6]

Dr. George Grant said chapel time "needs to be fresh and substantive and needs to look like classical Christian education. It often looks like grammar level only with recitations, memorized stuff, school song, & verse – that's great. You want the grammar stage. But that's it? It needs to be logic and rhetoric as well, to the wisdom stage. Kids ought to *want* to go to chapel. ... If we are declaring we are going to walk in Christ, that we are going to love Christ, that we are going to obey Christ, and it's the time that we least like? There's something wrong with this. The danger is to try to make chapel a church service. It's not a church service. It's chapel. You've got to really think through what is chapel, what is it supposed to accomplish, and it needs to look like CCE. It's not just grammar."

I interviewed a teacher who has devotedly served in chapel for a number of years and who described different approaches to chapel, beginning with questions.

- What is the purpose of chapel? A vague sense of worshipping together and that's good, or a Sabbath rest in the midst of the school week?
- Is chapel going to be chapel, or is it going to be chapel with announcements/birthdays/an assembly tagged on afterwards?
- Is chapel going to be one large gathering, or is it going to be divided into sections by age?
- Is chapel going to be the part-time job for one teacher, who may be known as the chaplain, or will it be the on-the-fly job of a few teachers who are not given prep time or homeroom coverage so they can select and practice music and so forth for the chapel time?
- Will teachers bring the chapel's sermon back to their classroom for a couple of minutes through questions, such as "What was the sermon about?" and "What did you think about it?"

One school divides chapel into three separate chapels (3 versions of homily):

1) Kindergarten & 1st grade (20 minutes total)
2) 2nd grade - 6th grade (30 minutes total)
3) 7th grade – 12th grade (30 minutes total)

The order of chapel was as follows with a liturgical emphasis on the different seasons of the church calendar:

1) Students & faculty enter silently while a prelude hymn plays.
2) Chiming of the hour, 9 times at 9AM
3) Lighting the 3 candles, representing the Trinity
4) Welcome/Call to Worship
5) Song (stand)/Scripture (sit)/Song (stand)/Scripture (sit)
6) 10-minute homily follows the upcoming weekend's lectionary reading
7) Pray.
8) Sing one more song.
9) Benediction
10) Exit in silence.

This school has a different, *separate* assembly that brings everyone together. Chapel is chapel. It is about worship. Tacking on other agendas changes the *tone* of chapel.

Drawbacks to having separate chapels according to age:

- Everyone is not together.
- More planning time devoted to chapel.

---

[6] Dr. George Grant, interview by Kathleen F. Kitchin, Atlanta, Georgia, June 13, 2019.

Benefits to having separate chapels according to age:

- Each chapel is framed to the child's frame, both in time & in content.
- Children are not being exasperated: the young do not endure a too-long sermon, and the older do not feel chapel is not for them and become jaded.
- Chapel can meet in a smaller area, perhaps enhancing reverence for God.

Reasons for chapel:

- So much of school is self-oriented and focused on what they are doing in their classes.
- Teachers are teaching faithfully, yet some students get through not caring about the Christian part; but Chapel is a wonderful time to say that it is good to set aside everything else – all the work, all the study – to say we need God. We cannot do it without Him. It is good to worship Him.
- It is multi-sensory – chimes, candles, marking special time that is different.
- The chaplain incorporates James K. A. Smith's *You Are What You Love*, in finding practices & habits that form our lives and looking to ancient practices of the church. As Chapel starts and ends the same way and proceeds in its practices & habits, it can become spiritually formative for students.

ACADEMIC

As we help cultivate spiritual development, we also help cultivate *academic* development. The goal in academics, whether it is class instruction, lesson planning, quizzes & tests, discussion, labs, or written assignments, is *to set the student up for success*. With the student's permission, I was allowed to listen in on a thesis conversation between head of school Leslie Collins and a student about special education inclusion. Setting up a student for success involves modeling how the spiritual & academic are inseparable. Leslie asked the student what her focus was for special education inclusion – as an ideal or here's how or do you want to go with the benefits of learning as a whole? Leslie explained to the student that she was doing all three in her thesis statement. Leslie counseled the student that "because of *imago Dei* (the beginning point), because we are made in the image of God, we have abilities and talents, we live in community because the Trinity is a community, we are made to be in fellowship, we have a purpose. All of this is the answer and mindset of education. Education is about helping them become a flourishing human being. If a person with a disability is pulled away into a special education school with other people like them, they lose the community and a sense of purpose and then their education does not help them to flourish." Leslie drew in Genesis 1:26 as the key text. Here, the teacher, in this case, the head of school, comes alongside the student and listens, advises, guides, & directs the thesis project. A red flag is if the teachers are doing the work for the students. *Do not do for a student what they can do for themselves*. They are young, but potentially capable.

Another important red flag to be cautious of is *perfectionism* in academics. Former administrator and second-grade teacher Lisa Borgeson says, "Problems students and alumni have had in CCE is that there is a perception that one 'needs to be perfect.' This methodology was hard on the little ones. Some students can become physically ill and put so much stress on self."[7] In some instances this led to cheating. Parents and teachers need to set reasonable academic expectations. Parents and teachers need to partner in helping the student not exalt grades or accomplishment.

Chapter 2 addressed the tarnishing red flag of *pride*. The virtue we seek is humility for ourselves and for our students through submission to God and dependence on Him.

Probably the most monumental and menacing red flag is the one that comes *after* classical Christian school – college & university. Many colleges and graduate schools are systematically dismantling exactly what a biblically based CCE school is establishing as its foundations. Before starting a college search, consider your child's heart and ascertain their readiness for college. Ask your child what he or she is looking for in a school. If you have children who are naïve or foolish, you might seriously consider *not* sending them to college directly after graduating high school. Perhaps they need a gap year or work

---

[7] Lisa Borgeson, phone interview by Kathleen F. Kitchin, June 11, 2018.

year or a year or two in community college. Four-year colleges are in the business of selling themselves, and the sales pitch can be far different from the reality. Examine course titles & descriptions, textbooks at the school your child is applying to, observe classes, interview professors, talk with students on campus, listen to your tour guide, have your child do an overnight stay on their own. Choose a college that has a strong church & community. Once enrolled, encourage your student to avail themselves of a church, community, & friend group that will build them up and not tear them down, that will disciple them as they navigate new territory in becoming an adult. Ultimately and most importantly, parents should focus on loving their child, not loving their child's future career, their education, their sports potential. Show them the love of Christ. Once they do attend college, don't just leave the driving to the college. Monitor the college. Keep in touch with your child. Peruse their textbooks when they come home on break. Just as your child is in a new phase of life, you are in a new phase of being a parent. As one friend said recently, when your child becomes a young adult and leaves home, you really become a prayer warrior.

SOCIAL/SCHOOL COMMUNITY

We cannot overlook the social aspect of education. *Social* comes from the Latin *socialis*, meaning "allied," and from *socius*, meaning "friend." Friends are delightful fruit of our schoolhouse experience. Former administrator and educator Steve Sheets says, "Show me your friends and I'll show you your future." As parents, we are careful who our children's allies are. We share with them Proverbs 13:20, "He who walks with the wise grows wise, but a companion of fools suffers harm." We train them in discernment by being discerning for them and gradually aid them in processing their experiences with friends and what true godly friendship is as they grow to be discerning for themselves. "As iron sharpens iron, so one man sharpens another" (Proverbs 27:17) and "A friend loves at all times, and a brother is born for adversity" (Proverbs 17:17). *Community* comes from the Latin *communis* meaning "common." We strive to encourage uplifting friendships and a community that holds certain values in common. Parents & faculty alike can pray for healthy, solid friendships.

Suggested Reading: *The Four Loves* by C.S. Lewis.

 One value is not having romantic relationships between students displayed in the school. There is no PDA (public displays of affection), no encouragement of relationships at this young age in the school. "Are you ready to support a wife now?" is one approach to discourage romantic connections. A feature that reinforces this concept at classical Christian schools is the absence of "Prom," instead opting for an elegant evening out at a restaurant and then the symphony or play in a nearby city, preceded by weeks of training in manners & modesty, etiquette & grace. These boundaries in relationships during school time help keep classical Christian schools on track.

On the sports field, another social opportunity emerges. You have the incredible camaraderie of fellow overcomers in endurance, victory, & defeat. ACCS board member Rob Tucker says, "If you want to get a view into virtues, look what's happening on the sports field. Character can be controlled. True character shows itself outside of the classroom."[8] Tucker adds, "You want the children to be in places they'll get bumped." What comes out – vinegar or honey? Then we can draw alongside the child and bring the gospel to bear on the situation and help them grow. Tucker actually said his son one time lost his temper on the field after a bad call, and while the coach told Tucker the lad just "lost his cool," Tucker would have nothing of it. He told the coach to bench his son as there is a difference between righteous and unrighteous anger. The cultivation of virtues.

The logic-stage years, however, can challenge friendships. Students have unrequited crushes, disloyal friends, loneliness, indeed, a longing can arise for a friend who would always be loyal, like a Samwise Gamgee in *Lord of the Rings*. Is loyalty being modeled and encouraged in the family? Is loyalty being modeled and encouraged at school? Classic novels like Charles Dickens' *Great Expectations* can give voice to the pain in discovering who your true friends are and who are not. Sometimes there is reconciliation amongst seniors as they look to Jesus, look back to their logic years, see the incongruity, and together, repent, ask forgiveness, & restore relationships. In other situations, the pain lingers. Are we as parents and teachers listening to students' pain, praying, & helping foster an uplifting atmosphere in the classroom? Are we pointing our dear children & students to the love of

---

[8] Rob Tucker, interview by Kathleen F. Kitchin, Annapolis, Maryland, September 22, 2018.

Christ that never fails? Are we correcting students who form cliques, who reject their peers, who leave others out? Is our school prayer team praying for brothers to dwell together in unity?

Communication is a large part of being social. Head of school Leslie Collins tells students, "It's okay for you to tell your teachers that something bothered you." She says, "Any relationship is reciprocal. If it is only top down, it is not a relationship." Likewise, teachers & administrators can bring together children who are in conflict with each other to learn how to work it through...a crucial life skill.

PHYSICAL

Another aspect of healthy balance in education is the *physical* well-being of children. Children need to be mobile. One recess per day is simply not enough for young children. One extra-long recess is not the solution, either. Former administrator and second-grade teacher Lisa Borgeson said Rockbridge Academy in Millersville, Maryland, had the following schedule:

- *Kindergarten* (1/2 day) had one 15-minute recess
- *Grades 1-3* had three 15-minute recesses – 10am, 12pm, and 1:30pm. (Morning K went out with Grades 1-3 during 10:00am recess, afternoon K went out with 1:30 pm recess.)
- *Grades 4-6* had two 15-minute recesses – 10am and 12pm.
- *Grades 1-6* also had two 30 min P.E. classes each week while *Grades 7 and up* had P.E./afterschool sports only.

Mrs. Borgeson was also famous for her Friday hugs! Kids need appropriate touch, and we need to be sensitive to those who would not appreciate that. I liked to give the older kids a quick pat on the back.

Another helpful physical task is school service. Does your classroom have chore time? It is a character-building time, a friendship-building time, a service-to-others time. In grade-wide gatherings & events, the older serve the younger. For example, your older students may gather and stack the grammar students' chairs. For post-lunch service time, the rhetoric students are leaders and train logic level leaders-in-training for the next year. Always assign a teacher advisor for each chore area for safety, guidance, & accountability.

Finally, having explicit directions in your parent-student handbook regarding fever, illness, childhood diseases, & common parasites, as well as assigning in-school chores to disinfect doorknobs and handrails everywhere & promoting reminders of soap-&-water hand washing are essential for school health.

STUDENT SURVEY

Head of school Leslie Collins believes in student surveys for evaluation. She says, "Give people a voice. Then act on it. It is a relationship, not just a service. Grades 7-12 fill out a survey of their teachers. We give them access to the laptops and set up the feedback on Survey Monkey." Their process is as follows for the student survey:

- The students are given between 4-6 questions.
- The feedback is given in an appropriate way, being taken seriously and holding others accountable. Students are holding themselves accountable; students are holding teachers accountable, too, because this is about relationship.
- Sample questions include the following:
  - Do I know what I am supposed to do in order to be successful in this class?
  - Is my teacher invested in me, do they care about me, do I feel that I am heard? Do I have a relationship with them?
  - Is discipline fair? Is it carried out fairly?
  - The principal also asks them: Is there anything else you want me to know?
- For follow-up, Leslie Collins asks the students:
  - Are you okay with sharing your anonymous feedback from Survey Monkey with your teachers? Your feedback matters.

- ○ The students said, "Yes."
- ○ Collins says the older the students, the better their feedback.
  - ▪ They care when discipline is not carried out consistently, e.g., teachers letting students chat and getting off on rabbit trails.
- Collins lets teachers see the surveys.
- There is rarely anything Collins did not already know prior to the survey.

Collins agrees with the model of a *walking* manager (administrators, including the head of school, who walk around the school and do their own eyes-&-ears surveys), as well as administering surveys. The teachers are holding the kids accountable. The students are to some level holding themselves accountable. And the students are to some level holding their teachers accountable. This is a community. Collins says, "Any relationship has to have *reciprocity*. If it is only top down, it is not a relationship. It's just authority."

Jesus is the epitome of relational authority. My husband David Kitchin says, "As God, He has ultimate authority; however, by becoming man for the rest of eternity so that we might become His brothers & sisters through faith, He demonstrates the importance of relationship. So the God-man Himself has a relationship with those over whom He has authority and views us not just as functional entities or just as a 'cog' in His plan."

Just as Jesus grew in wisdom and in stature and in favor with God and man (Luke 2:52), classical Christian schools partner with parents to help nurture & admonish their students spiritually, academically, socially, & physically, knowing that the greatest gift is loving their students. We, too, like 2 Timothy 3:17 can help them flourish "...so that the man of God may be complete and proficient, outfitted and thoroughly equipped for every good work."

CASE STUDY

A teacher classically educated as a student who later taught in a CCE school

One teacher I interviewed had two perspectives: as a CCE student and as a CCE teacher. The experiences were vastly different.

As a CCE student

This teacher began CCE schooling in the 7th grade. She had sweet, wonderful teachers. It was hard, however, to transition to logic without having had the Grammar level, and she had poor study habits. She worked super hard and was "filled to the brim." She "mourned a little bit" not having had the Grammar stage. Her overall comment about the Logic years was that they were "FULL years and it was so hard to catch up." With this experience, she recommends starting CCE at the beginning in grammar.

She proceeded to the Rhetoric stage. It was a rich experience, and she thrived at this level. There was much theology, and she greatly respected one of her teachers. "He took us seriously so we took him seriously. He helped me navigate my questions. Because I knew I could trust him with my questions, I looked up to him as a mentor." What she loved about CCE is that "My parents whetted my appetite for deep things. Grammar & Logic trained my appetite – I was going to want to desire the deep things, and then you let it go wild at the Rhetoric stage in pursuit of these deep things."

There was such "beauty, richness, and thriving – all true – but the culture of my CCE school by my senior year changed dramatically. The school's reputation was strict and rigorous. You need structure to be able to dig into all this. The demerit system was effective. The student handbook had rules for homework, uniform, etc. From 7th-11th, there were rigorous academics, but the handbook was not enforced, e.g., hair ribbon and nail polish colors. Heretofore, there was a healthy and respectful teacher/student relationship from 7th-11th grades; then a new student mentioned to a new teacher that dress codes were not applied. The result: teachers started cracking down on these details, to the point of this interviewed student feeling paranoia and not sure of what to do." This former student said,

- Correction was rampant and nit-picky.
- Demerits were constant.
- This created a gap between teachers & students.
- Students started to question. They were accused of bad attitudes.
- The headmaster became distant. This student felt no one is "for" us.

Her overall comment about this stage was "A sweet aroma at the school turned into legalism with accompanying tension and anger."

The faculty had initiated this move. The headmaster was informed in writing & orally, but there was no meeting of the headmaster with the faculty to craft a plan of action. Things came to a head in spring of senior year in a combined junior/senior class: senior girls were targeted and demerited while junior girls were not.

- This student was accused of wearing make-up, but she actually was not. She was told she had a bad attitude.
- The teacher had them read a story as a metaphor for how the class had been behaving. It was so painful, three girls left the room, crying. This student, now teacher, was so broken, completely and felt utterly humiliated.
- Students were exasperated.
- Parents tried to initiate meetings with the teachers, but they were available only during work hours and the parents also worked.
- Correspondence with the headmaster was not effective.

This student-now-teacher says, "True discipline yields fruit."

She graduated. Consequently, there were some student withdrawals from the school. The affected students got out of touch, but this student, now teacher, found healing in college.

Meantime, the school began to struggle financially along with other schools, was taken over by a large church, and became a "consumer-oriented" school (where students could choose more of an academics course or a sports course, and so forth).

A couple years later, one teacher apologized and emailed this student, now teacher, and her parents and the other girls involved. The teacher had written self-reflective journals, praying, and became convicted of how they wronged these students. It was painful, but there was reconciliation in Christ. The former student was surprised, not expecting it. She had focused on healing in her own life, but this reconciliation experience "only has grown more meaningful to her over time." She "never thought this would happen. The reconciliation became increasingly meaningful and part of the healing which has taken a lot of time. It was so redemptive."

In retrospect, her senior year was painful; she questioned hearing about "grace" but it was not exhibited. Her school had become "A culture of legalism with the language of the gospel, but not the reality of it."

It took one year of healing. As a college freshman, she was "waking up to what the gospel is." "I had known a midnight, but I had seen the morning." Time passed. She was healed enough and was able to articulate it, but did not understand why it happened. Then a significant gathering occurred where a man who writes CCE curriculum in Africa said, "I know this story. The culture of the school gets built in around itself. As Dietrich Bonhoeffer said in *Life Together*, 'When you love your vision for community more than you love your community, you destroy your community.'" That encapsulated everything for this student. It was a huge moment in her healing process.

As a CCE teacher

Years after the bad experience, her teaching at a different CCE school has redeemed all that happened. Her interview with the board was extraordinary. There was "something different in the board members that captured her – they expressed a vision for students and a portrait of a graduate in language that was so beautiful– this is the deep, rich image ...this can cultivate." She felt jaded and thought "they probably don't want me." She figured they would call only if they were desperate. She shared the name of her school. The board had heard of it and its

[handwritten margin note:] Any driver going the speed limit when you want to speed is "legalistic"

reputation. She shared her story. She felt scared, but God was telling her to step by faith back into this story. She told them that God was leading her to work there to help them not experience her story.

She was hired. At her training in another state, the first day was about "The Heart of Discipline" which was so healing she wept, absolutely amazed at the specificity of what God was doing. To think that God was creating a way for her to be able to speak into the starting of a school was so powerful to her. This new school accepted brown, black, or blue shoes. One day a student's school shoes had been muddied the day before, and she had to wear suede boots to school instead. One board member saw that and said, "Aren't their shoes so cute? We should revise the handbook."

I asked this person if the years the locusts had eaten had been restored, and she replied, "Yes. Ten-fold." She said, "A sign of when God is in something is when God uses pain for good. My high school had become elitist, had become 'the best,' and demonized the rest." In contrast, she heard the board who hired her using humble language. Her overall comment about this stage was "Teaching at a CCE school has been wildly redemptive."

She continues to teach at this tutorial-model school. "It's really scary not to have a head of school," she says, but it is a growing school. In the absence of a head of school, "The board is stretched thin to simply keep things going – they are in 'survival mode.' They support and breathe life into the teachers," but they also have the daily management of the school with two board members on site every day and are "losing margin for the bigger picture." Every board family has too much responsibility. It is not sustainable. Since this interview, an individual was hired to manage the daily operations, thus freeing the board members to return to their role as vision-maintainers & policy makers and allowing for a smoother, more peaceful school year.

We then talked about her marriage of 3 years. She said her husband & she have chosen to honor the Sabbath and "that has sustained our souls. It is vital to our spiritual life and our marriage."

Regarding her teaching, she said, "The beauty of the collaborative model is you get to support families in their primary roles and get to walk beside them and support them." She says, "The students' parents say, 'We are so busy. Life is a blur.' She is amazed at all the things her students are involved in: piano, tae kwando, intramural basketball, wrestling class, …. Her viewpoint is that they need "structure at school and they need structure in the home, too." She feels a head of school can help discuss with parents their children's being overloaded. The word *paideia* is used all the time: raise your children in the *paideia* of the Lord "family/homes/campus rhythm."

Faculty distinctives/metrics are given to teachers at the beginning of the school year. Her annual review included a self-survey based on these faculty distinctives. Teachers fill it out before their end-of-year de-briefing. At the end-of-year debrief, two board members meet with each teacher and in a very specific & intentional manner, to

1) discuss the teacher's strengths & weaknesses;
2) discuss how the teacher has grown;
3) outline hopes for next year.

It was a blessing to interview this teacher, once student, who shared her painful experience and the redemption Christ wrought through it. We may have had a smooth-sailing journey through our education. We may have had rough sailing. As schools keep their eyes on Jesus, as we admit our faults to the Lord and others, God will honor that. Again, in Joel 2:25, the Lord says, "So I will restore to you the years that the locusts have eaten." If, however, our eyes have slipped away from Jesus, if we are suppressing the truth and insist there are no problems in our character, in our behavior, in our hearts, we can be assured that God will not be mocked. Galatians 6:7-9 says, "Be not deceived; God is not mocked: for whatsoever a man soweth, that shall he also reap." Lord, help us sow and reap unto You.

Red Flags

- Seeing parents and teachers on different spiritual pages. Students need godly, consistent messages. "Can two walk together, except they be agreed?" (Amos 3:3, KJV)
- Seeing young children making the decisions instead of their parents.
- Seeing parents overburden their children with too many outside activities.

- Seeing children avoid examining each task in which they have struggled or failed. "Above all it is thus that we can acquire the virtue of humility, and that is a far more precious treasure than all academic progress."[9]
- Seeing only one-way communication – only from teachers to students.
- Seeing in students both arrogance & flaunting of the school's talents.
- Seeing students shamed by their teachers with students' names on the board and other visible techniques that publicly indicate the child's misbehavior. *a red flag- really?*
- Seeing students think they are equals of their parents or their teachers. This is difficult for younger teachers.
- Diluting or compromising Chapel time by tacking on announcements & other miscellany.
- Exuding legalism, not grace and the gospel.

Sober Reflection

- Are we loving our students?
- Are we nurturing & admonishing them in the Lord?
- Are we protecting them without stifling them?
- When they are overwhelmed, are we together looking toward the Lord, asking Him for strength?
- Are we treating them not as children, but as young men & young women?

Getting Back on Track

- *Project*: Read *Shepherding a Child's Heart* by Tedd Tripp.
- *Project*: Read *Parenting: 14 Gospel Principles that can Radically Change Your Family* by Paul David Tripp.
- Come alongside and help students learn to depend on God as they seek to love Him with all their heart, soul, mind, & strength. (Mark 12:30)

Healthy School

- A healthy school tenderly realizes that some students may not look like "a success," but actually may be more like Christ than their high-achieving peers.
- A healthy school acknowledges achievement.
- "A healthy school realizes a student should not be in the mold of the school, but should be poured into as an individual. This is personal discipleship." (from a CCE student) *Realistic? Relationship? What does that mean?*
- A healthy school has a high standard of excellence, but does not pressure toward success, knowing the Bible is about dependence on the Lord.
- A healthy school focuses on humility and honesty vs. a "success ideal." It acknowledges it does not have everything figured out and does not act like it is perfect.
- Head of School Keith Nix: "Every year each family has to re-enroll and sign again. Gatekeeping things. Every year. Church involvement evident. …They have committed."
- A healthy school pairs each new student with a student mentor, a returning student in the same homeroom. The administration gives a set of written guidelines 1) to the student mentor who is responsible to convey them to the new student, and another set 2) to homeroom teachers, both designed to help the new student acclimate to their new school.
- Children are an inheritance from the Lord (Psalm 127:3) and are to be a blessing to their parents.
- A healthy school views children as future adults. As ACCS board member Rob Tucker says, "We need to think generationally … and look at a third grader as one day a future parent. We look forward toward the next generation of educators, parents."

---

[9] Simone Weil, "Reflections on the Right Use of School Studies with a View to the Love of God."

Setting a Goal

- Pray for God's wisdom. Then set one or two goals for getting *your vision* for students better on track. Enter goals in your phone or binder that goes with you everywhere.
- Refer to this goal throughout the year.
- Reflect on this goal at year's end. Rejoice in God's grace.

Expressing a Desire

- Pray for God's wisdom. Write one or two desires for getting your vision for students better on track *that depend on others' cooperation*. Enter that desire in your phone or binder that goes with you everywhere.
- Pray about this desire throughout the year.
- Reflect on this desire at the end of each year. Rejoice in God's grace.

Encouragement

- "... [B]eing confident of this, that He who began a good work in you will perfect it until the day of Jesus Christ" (Philippians 1:6, ASV)
- *From a parent*: "My own experience of CCS and classical homeschooling graduates generally gives me a sense of wonderfully well-rounded young people who have in their hearts a foundation to lead to a lifetime of learning. And that's what we're really about – connecting new knowledge to old knowledge to move forward in our lives."
- *From a CCE student*: "The two most important things in learning are 1) to know that Jesus loves us & 2) To love Jesus and to love others. ... What really mattered to me was the faithful witness of parents, teachers, & students."

Chapter 9
Your School's
Feeder Churches

"How then will they call on Him in whom they have not believed? And how are they to believe in Him of whom they have never heard? And how are they to hear without someone preaching?"

Romans 10:14

"Grace...the merciful kindness by which God, exerting his holy influence upon souls, turns them to Christ, keeps, strengthens, increases them in Christian faith, knowledge, affection, and kindles them to the exercise of the Christian virtues."

from Strong's Concordance,

quoted in Matthew Casey's The Return[1]

"We must know again that awe-inspiring mystery which comes upon men and churches when they are full of the power of God."

A.W. Tozer

Paths to Power: Living in the Spirit's Fullness *(1940)*

In his preface to Mark Dever's *Nine Marks of a Healthy Church*, Pastor David Platt says, "...we desperately need to hear what God says about his church in our day...we need to recover a cherishing of the church...we need to ask God, 'What do *you* value in *your* church?'"[2]

In *The Reason for God: Belief in an Age of Skepticism*, Pastor Tim Keller notes, "In ancient times it was understood that there was a transcendent moral order outside the self, built in to the fabric of the universe" and that there were severe consequences of violating that. "The path of wisdom was to learn to live in conformity with this unyielding reality."[3]

In contrast, stands our culture. Quote after quote about our post-Christian culture reflects its humanist opinions. Stephen J. Nichols' *A Time for Confidence: Trusting God in a Post-Christian Society* says, "A culture that thinks

---

[1] Matthew Casey, *The Return: An End-time Epistle to the Church in America* (Richmond, Virginia: Elijah Books, 2010), 56.

[2] Mark Dever, *Nine Marks of a Healthy Church* (Wheaton, Illinois: Crossway, 2013), 10.

[3] Timothy Keller, *The Reason for God: Belief in an Age of Skepticism* (New York: Riverhead Books, 2008), 73.

it knows better than the Bible surrounds us."[4] In *The Reason for God*, Keller quotes Robert Bellah's *Habits of the Heart*, saying "expressive individualism" prevails in our American culture and that as far as back as 1985, "80 percent of Americans agree[d] with the statement 'an individual should arrive at his or her own religious beliefs independent of any church or synagogue.'"[5] Robert Bellah concluded, "'the most fundamental belief in American culture is that moral truth is relative to individual consciousness.'"[6] Keller says, "The spirit of modernity, then, gave *us* the responsibility to determine right and wrong [italics mine]."[7] Like the Greek Protagoras, our culture says, "Man is the measure of all things."

In *A Time for Confidence*, in his chapter on confidence in the Bible, Nichols says, "The Greco-Roman world was rife with philosophers who peddled their philosophies. They would hustle into town with their oratorical skill and would set up on the porch in the public square, and they would wow the crowd with a new idea or some new application of an idea. There were plenty of 'words of men' in Paul's day. ...They reveled in the words of men. ...Contrary to the words of men, Peter says this Word, the Bible, came from above."[8] In contrast to reveling in the words and works of man, Keller says, J.R.R. Tolkien "wrote *The Lord of the Rings* about the consequences of seeking power and control rather than wisdom and glad enjoyment of the 'givenness' of God's creation."[9] Standing separate from our culture, in but not of the world, we "set [our] minds on things that are above, not on things that are on earth" (Colossians 3:2). We gladly enjoy God and His creation and choose His wisdom. In the midst of enjoying Him, in between the promise and the fulfillment, between the now and the not yet (1 John 3: 2), we have confidence in Christ: "[The Bible says to stand firm] ... the opposition is great, because there are challenges, and because the Christian life is difficult. We have challenges from without, from culture. We have challenges from within the church, from false teachers. We also have challenges from within ourselves, from our sin nature."[10] But "We stand firm," and as R.C. Sproul said, "we stand firm not just for today, and not just for tomorrow, but for the sake of generations, even centuries, to come."[11] We cannot stand using our own strength for "Admitting our weakness is *key* to putting our confidence in Christ [italics mine]."[12] We seek to become like Him, for "God is the measure of all things."

COMPROMISE

The church today has compromised. In Matthew Casey's *The Return: An End-time Epistle to the Church in America*, he says,

> In just one generation, evangelical pastors and ministry leaders have sabotaged the Church's future by abandoning the faith of our past. In our lust for acceptance and validation by the culture, we have traded timeless, eternal truth for humanistic and relativistic ideals. Consider the Biblical pillars we have downplayed, minimized, or even omitted in our frantic attempts to make Christianity more palatable or "culturally relevant"....[13]

In a later chapter, "Cheap Grace, Easy Believism, and Self-love," Casey says, "Jesus set the bar very high for those who would follow Him, while the American Church constantly looks for ways to lower it. ... never once did Jesus lower the standard of discipleship nor 'soft sell' the cost to those who would come after Him. *The cost was the cross*. 'If anyone desires to come after Me, let him deny himself, and take up his cross daily, and follow Me. For

---

[4] Stephen J. Nichols, *A Time for Confidence: Trusting God in a Post-Christian Society* (Sanford, Florida: Reformation Trust Publishing, 2016), 44.

[5] Keller, 72.

[6] Keller, 72.

[7] Keller, 74.

[8] Nichols, 52.

[9] Keller, 73-74.

[10] Nichols, 74.

[11] Ibid., 75.

[12] Ibid., 85.

[13] Casey, 33.

whoever desires to save his life will lose it, but whoever loses his life for My sake will save it' (Luke 9:23-24)."[14] The church's charge is clear:

> Christ commissioned us to make disciples that obey His commands (*see Matthew 28: 19-20*). Today, we make converts who are unaware that such commands exist. Real evangelism requires making real disciples who are devoted to Jesus, not converts to our way of thinking or brand of religion. However, we tend to reproduce ourselves. If we would make disciples, we must first be disciples.[15]

Is our church compromising, or are we cultivating real disciples? Casey says the "...awareness of sin leads to awareness of need, leading to salvation."[16] Are we preaching about sin?

SIN
In *The Reason for God*, Pastor Tim Keller says, "In *The Nature of True Virtue*, one of the most profound treatises on social ethics ever written, Jonathan Edwards lays out how sin destroys the social fabric. He argues that human society is deeply fragmented when anything but God is our highest love."[17] As we schedule our weeks, is reading the Bible given precedence each day? Is church on Sunday top priority? Are the "big rocks" placed on the schedule first, or is a substitute or other activities allowed to squeeze Bible and church out?

EFFECT ON SCHOOLING
In looking at culture, heads of school have challenges as they ascertain families' church experience and the effect it has or is not having on their children's schooling. Leslie Collins, head of Covenant Academy, says,

> Families think that this system of education is fabulous, but more and more families today are less deeply connected to a church and they seem to take it very casually. That is going to be to the detriment of our success. We are just trying to continue to strengthen the families' understanding that we the school can't put in what they are leaving out. What we are doing is *discipleship*. We are partnering with parents to disciple children to follow Christ, and we believe that the liberal arts is a way of helping them follow Christ and obviously that is heavy in humanities, heavy in S.T.E.M. – it's connected. But if the parents aren't discipling them, they can't pay us to put in what they are leaving out and if parents think that just sending their kid to a Christian school is going to disciple them in following Christ, they are completely missing the point. We exist as a school *for* the church. That doesn't mean that we are an affiliate with the church, but that we exist to strengthen the church on the planet. That is why we exist.[18]

If some families are not attending church or they attend a watered-down church, many families and their children are not hearing the gospel.

THE GOSPEL
In *A Time for Confidence: Trusting God in a Post-Christian Society,* author Stephen J. Nichols in his chapter "Confidence in the Gospel" says, "As R.C. Sproul...often said, 'The human dilemma is this: God is holy, and we are not. God is righteous, and we are not.' Our problem is the wrath of holy God. No amount of righteousness can solve that dilemma. Paul testifies to only one solution: the righteousness that comes through faith in Christ."[19] This is the Good News! "He who knew no sin became sin for us that we might become the righteousness of God" (2 Corinthians 5:21).

---

[14] Ibid., 60.

[15] Casey, 60.

[16] Ibid., 41.

[17] Keller, 174.

[18] Leslie Collins, interview by Kathleen F. Kitchin, Cypress, Texas, November 27, 2018.

[19] Nichols, 102.

In Ephesians 3:1-14, Paul lays out the gospel in "one long and glorious sentence in the Greek."[20] Nichols expounds on this passage:

> First, the gospel and God's plan of redemption unite all things and restore all things. All the broken pieces, all the disjointed fragments are restored and united. The gospel brings restoration and wholeness to the fractured heap. Second, the gospel is our inheritance. We enjoy so many things now – forgiveness of sins; freedom in Christ; fellowship with the triune God; fellowship with one another; purpose, meaning, and direction in life; the assurance of the Holy Spirit. We enjoy so many things now, but these are but a down payment of the life to come and of the full inheritance that awaits God's children. Not only is the gospel our inheritance, but we are sealed. There is absolute certainty here. We are guaranteed delivery. The Holy Spirit is our seal. Third, Ephesians 1:3-14 teaches us that the gospel is to the praise of the glory of God's grace. ... The gospel leads us to worship. It has been said that theology leads to doxology.[21]

THE GOSPEL FRONT & CENTER

Is the *gospel* in every sermon, every meeting, every class, and every life group? My son who is in seminary says that his college years' minister and mentor, Ethan Magness, told their group of pre-seminarians the test of a sermon: "Did Jesus have to die for this sermon to be written?"[22] Is the focus on what *man* can do to please God? Or is the focus on what *Jesus* died for so that we do not have to earn God's pleasure in us? Religion says, "I obey – therefore I am accepted by God" vs. "I am accepted by God through what Christ has done – therefore I obey."[23] Pastor Timothy Keller recalls his faith during his college days:

> When my own personal grasp of the gospel was very weak, my self-view swung wildly between two poles. When I was performing up to standards – in academic work, professional achievement, or relationships – I felt confident but not humble. I was likely to be proud and unsympathetic to failing people. When I was not living up to standards, I felt humble but not confident, a failure. I discovered, however, that the gospel contained the resources to build a unique identity. In Christ I could know I was accepted by grace not only despite my flaws, but because I was willing to admit them. The Christian gospel is that I am so flawed that Jesus had to die for me, yet I am so loved and valued and that Jesus was glad to die for me. This leads to deep humility and deep confidence at the same time. It undermines both swaggering and sniveling. I cannot feel superior to anyone, and yet I have nothing to prove to anyone. I do not think more of myself nor less of myself. Instead, I think of myself less. I don't need to notice myself – how I'm doing, how I'm being regarded – so often.[24]

Chapter 12 of Tim Keller's *The Reason for God*, "The (True) Story of the Cross," is an outstanding resource to help your congregation see how Jesus' sacrifice changes lives (He changed places with us) and how they can be released from fear and pride through the power of the Holy Spirit.

FULL COUNSEL OF SCRIPTURE

Are you indeed preaching the Bible? Are you teaching the hard parts of the Bible? Are you teaching "between the Bible stories"? How are you allowing for questions and doubts to be expressed and discussed in your middle school and high school Sunday school classes so that they may have a closer intimacy with God, their great Good Shepherd? So that they may have a deeper understanding of His word, His steadfast love, His never abandoning them? Are adults allowed to safely share their lingering, nagging doubts without judgment, but in Christian community, with iron sharpening iron as the priesthood of believers ministers to them (Proverbs 27:17; 1 Peter 2:5-9)? Is church membership catechism class taught in such a way it does not overlook the gospel?

---

[20] Ibid., 116.

[21] Nichols, 116-117.

[22] Ethan Magness, Grace Anglican Church, Grove City, Pennsylvania, 2017.

[23] Keller, 186.

[24] Ibid., 187.

CHURCH AT HOME

If we have gone off the rails of Bible reading and church going, how do we reorient as a family? In *The Tech-Wise Family: Everyday Steps for Putting Technology in Its Proper Place*, author Andy Crouch says, "The first family for everyone who wants wisdom and courage in the way of Jesus is the church – the community of disciples who are *looking to Jesus to reshape their understanding and their character.*"[25] He elaborates,

> But if the church is to be our first family, it cannot just be a friendly, weekly gathering. The first Christians met in homes, and those homes were not single-family dwellings but Greco-Roman "households" that often included *several generations* as well as uncles and aunts, clients, and indentured servants of the "paterfamilias." The church too was a household – a gathering of related and unrelated persons all bound together by grace and the pursuit of holiness.[26]

Crouch continues,

> So here's the complicated, wonderful truth. If our families are to be all that they are meant to be – schools of wisdom and courage – they will have to become more like the church, households where we are actively formed into something more than our culture would ask us to be. And if our churches are meant to be all they are meant to be, they will have to become more like a family – household-like contexts of daily life where we are all nurtured and developed into the persons we are meant to be and can become.[27]

The way of Jesus is *paideia,* or complete enculturation.

An objection arises: But aren't schools overstepping their bounds into the sphere of the church?

SPHERE AUTHORITY

When interviewing Keith Nix, head of Veritas School in Richmond, Virginia, we discussed Abraham Kuyper's spheres of authority regarding the home, the school, and the church.[28] I asked Keith, "How do you balance it so that you as a school don't become the 'one-stop shop'?" He replied,

> You're balancing and holding in tension an ideal and practical kind of necessity. You've just got to know we're in tension, and you have to be thinking about them and talking about them all the time. When I was first head of school, I took this ideal, this purist kind of mentality. I would say over and over, 'We're not the church...We're not the church. We're not doing that or that.... We're never going on a mission trip (still don't). ... The church does missions trips. I would really resist this getting in front of the church and saying, "We are not the church." Every year that's gone by I probably hold less to the ideal and make peace with more practices and us taking a lead, or at least a lead voice in their lives in areas *because I am making promises to deliver a type of education.* Those promises actually require some things out of the parents. I'm frequently saying, "You need to do this at home for me to meet my promises to you." Currently, we are the institution who is speaking the most profoundly and loudly about issues regarding sexuality, technology – 'cause the church isn't. The ideal would be I am not the one delivering the seminar. I try to do it a lot where we host seminars here, and we get churches involved and coordinate with them to host certain events on certain topics. James K.A. Smith – have him come in with a voice and saying things that we know are supporting and undergirding what we are doing as a school. School initiates it. I am not in a position to wait on the church – sexuality and boy/girl relationships, for example. We have good churches that are hosting and addressing some of these issues. We try to inform families. We work hard not to get in the way of anything the churches are doing, like no Sunday things, Wednesday very minimal here, athletics and co-curricular things right after school between 3:30-5.

---

25 Andy Crouch, *The Tech-Wise Family: Everyday Steps for Putting Technology in Its Proper Place.* (Grand Rapids, Michigan: Baker Books, 2017), 60.

26 Crouch, 61.

27 Ibid., 62.

28 Keith Nix, interview by Kathleen F. Kitchin, Richmond, Virginia, June 5, 2019.

No 7:00 or 9:00PM practice. We try to protect the family and the church so they can have time. I want those pastors around town to know I am working hard not to interfere in their schedule. We speak out against the risks and challenges with youth travel sports. If you have all your kids doing that, then what I'm trying to do with them at school isn't going to take. So we are saying things and being a voice in areas I would rather not be.

I replied, "So are the spheres of church, home, & school actually overlapping in a cooperative fashion?" and Keith responded, "Trying to. I would hope that the pastors who are connected with our school would speak up if they feel like Veritas is overstepping."

I also asked Mr. Russ Gregg of Hope Academy in Minneapolis what their sphere authorities of church, home, and school looked like.[29] Regarding church, he said, "Our hope is the best thing that we can do for our students is to help their parents be involved in a healthy local church." For the past 18 months-2 years, that has been one of their "big rocks," or goals. When I asked Mr. Gregg for a definition of a healthy church, he said they were "still working on it. One where our parents would really feel connected, one that is going to come around those parents and really support them with the Word of God, with prayer, with love, and loving support." Mr. Gregg elaborated further, "One of our challenges is so many of our students have experienced so much higher levels of trauma than what most schools are dealing with. The term for this category of trauma is ACE (Adverse Childhood Experience). We would love to be able to hire counselors for one-on-one support. We would like for families that are going through those experiences to have...support from their church, have community around them. But so many of our churches are compromising on so many issues, are struggling themselves, have lost the focus on Christ themselves."

Then I asked, "Where then are the lines for Kuyper's spheres of authority for your school?" and Russ Gregg took a pen and redrew the separate spheres diagram and he, too, said, "I would prefer to see more overlap." In his end-of-year talk to seniors at their Senior Dinner, Russ Gregg planned to tell them: "A spiritual coldness is coming. Jesus said, 'Because of the increase of wickedness, the love of many will grow cold, but those who persevere to the end will be saved.' There's a growing spiritual coldness. My encouragement is how to keep the fire of love for Christ alive in that. If I'm a church, to have a partner like a school encouraging those things for 45 mins/week vs. 30 hrs/wk., I can't imagine that a church that had an interest in the spiritual health of their teenagers to not want that kind of thing, and the home wants that kind of thing, too. Historically, people have talked about the three-legged stool, how the three legs give stability and strength, and how to have everybody aligned in a similar vision." This is the call to churches. Classical Christian schools yearn for partnership with the church in ascendance.

In *The Benedict Option: A Strategy for Christians in a Post-Christian Nation*, Rod Dreher says,

> A good classical Christian school not only teaches students the Bible and Western civilization but also integrates students into the life of the church...[Saint Constantine School in Houston's] president John Mark Reynolds's model integrates the school as much as possible with families and churches. He calls it a kind of "new monasticism" that seeks to harmonize church, school, and family life for its students. "In the past, schools have functioned fairly independent of the family and the church. That was defensible when our culture was more Christian, but it's not really true anymore," he says. Believing that the school must reinforce the life of the church if parishioners and students are to grow in their faith, the school works around the church schedule, making sure that students have time and space on the calendar for their spiritual lives. The spiritual results of this kind of integration are tangible. A classical Christian school headmaster in the Southwest told [Rod Dreher] that these schools are often surprised to discover themselves leading Christian families and churches back to tradition. "Though we are the only one of those three not ordained by the Bible to form our children, this is how it's turning out in lots of places," he said.[30]

---

[29] Russ Gregg, interview by Kathleen F. Kitchin, Minneapolis, Minnesota, May 20, 2019.

[30] Rod Dreher. *The Benedict Option: A Strategy for Christians in a Post-Christian Nation* (New York: Sentinel, 2018), 161-162.

Your School's Feeder Churches

To keep our schools on track, boards and heads of school need to persevere in reaching out to the churches in their communities, to build relationships in order to support & encourage each other, and ultimately to help flourish the students & families involved in both.

CATECHESIS

In light of how churches and schools can build relationships and work in concert, Keith Nix continued our discussion and talked about Veritas's work to build...

> this thick Christian community of Christian formation and catechesis. This subject came up and pastors spoke up honestly and said, "This is so important for you to be doing this because we don't get that much time with them, no more than a few hours per week." They are glad, not frustrated. I think the churches are having a hard time doing Sunday School well and doing real Christian education.

I commented that much of the modern diet of Sunday School can be meager, shallow, & unsatisfying; and Keith agreed saying,

> There's not a lot of catechesis going on. They're biblically illiterate, yet have been in church their whole lives. In our classical Christian community of faith and learning with parents, with students, with grandparents, Veritas is inviting them into the conversation. We don't have all the answers. These are issues we haven't faced. What is the impact of screens on our lives? How to address issues of sexuality in your family? This is a new world. You've got to be talking about it. [Regent University professor] Steve Garber once said to me, "Make sure your classical school is a place where people are asking honest questions and getting honest answers." That continues to shape how I think about it. Probably not in a public classroom, but, do they have the relationships with their parents, administrators, or teachers? If they are really struggling with some issue, can they ask the question and feel like they're not going to get a cliché or just memorized answer but someone is going to listen and kind of say, "That is tough." I am not saying we perfectly come alongside churches and families, but what happens when you state that that's your goal is, you put yourself out there. We are not going to do this perfectly.

For Keith Nix, it's all about being *covenantal*, making agreements and standing by them.

> We are not going to execute on any of these standards perfectly. We are not going to support every teacher perfectly. But if a teacher were to hear me talk about our commitment to support and invest in their professional development and recognize them, what ought to be on the table is they ought to be able to say, "I didn't feel that way." So, state and lay out your commitments. So if we're saying we're trying to partner and a parent says, "I don't feel like this is partnership." That is when it is working – not when you're executing partnership perfectly, but when you're so clear about what you mean by it that when you don't do it, they get to call "foul." A teacher can call "foul," a pastor could call "foul." I just love that principle of setting the highest standards for your commitments (to parents, to churches, to faculty) so that if you are not doing it, it is a good meeting when people can come and say, "That's not how it feels to me."

This refreshing approach to sphere authority and commitments takes clarity & courage. It involves standing on the Rock (Jesus Christ), on the Word (the Bible), and on fellowship (the unity we have with our brothers & sisters in Christ). It is utterly dependent on God's grace and the Holy Spirit.

In the chapter, "God's Plan for a Glorious Church" in Matthew Casey's *The Return*, he says,

> Countless churchgoers who have believed that Christ's call was to "self-discovery" instead of self-sacrifice will find themselves adrift on stormy seas of adversity, lacking the anchor of a vital knowledge and experience of God's Word. Our shallow, me-centered theology will wear thin in the reality of lack, persecution, and suffering. In such a day, people will start to seek a real faith in a real Savior who can provide real hope and help. And those who really know God – who have proved His promises and tasted His goodness, who have been through battles and seen His

faithfulness – such people will be magnets for the hurting and questioning ones. Then the Word of God in our hearts and on our lips will be a healing balm to wounded souls, a beacon of salvation pointing the lost to the Savior.[31]

Dear Lord, please help us to seek You first in our life, to find a church that does likewise and will help us through the power of the Holy Spirit to grow into maturity in Christ so that we, too, may be magnets for "the hurting and questioning ones" and can point them to Jesus.

CASE STUDY

I interviewed my pastor and his wife, Pastor Charles & Mrs. Denise Wall, in North Carolina, asking them about engagement in the local church.[32]

The church body feels the vacancy when attenders no longer attend. Mrs. Denise Wall, my pastor's wife, says,

> When we gather as the church, it's like a family gathering around the supper table. As kids grow up and they have to start working, the rest of the family is keenly aware when they sit down for supper when one of those people is missing. And it affects the family dynamics. Those absent are not so aware because they are at work and they're involved in something, but the ones who are there at that shrinking table are very aware.

Pastor Charles Wall asks, "How do you build body life? If the kids are here only an hour a week, how do they really begin to develop the relationship that's going to hold them here as they hit late teens & early twenties?"

Denise extends the around-the-table metaphor.

> As a family, we always had breakfast & dinner together. It enriched us. When our teens got a job, they were only allowed to miss 1 meal a day. They had to be here for at least 2 meals a day with the family. If you think of a family and you only ate together on Sunday lunch and you never ate together the rest of the week, what kind of bond would your family have with each other? That's what is happening in the church. That picture of the shrinking family. We see it especially affecting the young people.

Pastor Wall says, "There is an enrichment when you come together as the Body, and yet many people can't see that exactly and so they don't realize what they're missing and also what they're depriving their children of and other people's children of."

If you are a sports-oriented family, are you prioritizing sports over church? Some parents "bust their gut all week to get their kids to sports but stay home Sunday morning because they're exhausted, but we don't hear 'We are exhausted, and you aren't going to practice tonight.' This trend has been really growing over the last number of years. You have a good desire for your children's lives, but in the long haul is that going to help be positive in the child's life in terms of their commitment to Christ & the church, or is it going to be detrimental? I think that part – the long term – is not something they think about too much."

Denise says, "We grew up going to prayer meeting with our parents, and we learned to pray by hearing the saints pray. It wasn't entertaining and we weren't always engaged, but we were there and we heard it and we saw it. Some parents say, "Our kids aren't really into that so when they're older and can understand it, then we'll bring them. But they hear and learn it and gradually it becomes their culture." I mentioned that as parents, we are training the affections and you do that before they can talk. Pastor Chuck then said, "By the time the youngest child came to the age the parents thought they should start coming, they've already developed a habit of not

---

[31] Casey, 87.

[32] Pastor Charles Wall and Mrs. Denise Wall, interview by Kathleen F. Kitchin, Statesville, North Carolina, August 28, 2019.

coming to church Sunday night and already developed other things they did on Sunday and so it didn't happen and so the kids have drifted away." Denise added, "And the older they get, the more it shrinks. It doesn't grow."

Pastor Chuck says they recommend Robbie Castleman's *Parenting in the Pew* as it has good suggestions on how to teach your children. They say, "Parents don't realize how they can parent the child while in church."[33] Denise said that Noel & John Piper's article "The Family: Together in God's Presence" shows

> how Mrs. Piper nurtured her children into the culture of the church, how she helped them engage. Children learn to worship by watching their parents worship. Seeing parents engaged with the God of the universe in genuine, humble admiration and appreciation and worship of Him and seeing that in their faces as they sing from their hearts. Pastor John Piper talks about their church on Sunday morning being like the Mount of Transfiguration in awe, in the presence of Holy God. Other services were like more of a fellowship time and laid back.

I said that by training over and over, little by little it accrues. Pastor Chuck noted that "What parents do in moderation, their kids will tend to do in excess (which can be a positive or a negative). For example, if a parent attends church one hour per week, their kids will likely do less."

Red Flags

- *Reading Suggestion*: I cannot recommend highly enough Mark Dever's *Nine Marks of a Healthy Church* to help identify red flags.[34]
- *A wrong view of Scripture* – A church's believing that Scripture has errors.
- *Compromise* – Pastor David Platt says, "We're fixated on what works... Almost unknowingly, however, we subtly compromise God's Word in our efforts to supposedly reach the world. As we draw people into the church, we end up polluting the very church we are drawing them into." (*Nine Marks*, 9)
- *Church search based on our requirements, not God's requirements* – David Platt warns of self-pleasing vs. faithfulness to God: "A church is a good church if it makes us feel good, so we hop and shop from one church to the next, looking for the place and programs that most cater to our needs." (*Nine Marks*, 9)
- *Secularization* – Mark Dever quotes Os Guinness in Guinness's *Dining with the Devil*, "the two most easily recognizable hallmarks of secularization in America are the exaltation of numbers and of technique." (*Nine Marks*, 29)
- *Untrustworthy shepherd* – "To appoint a person as a leader who doubts God's sovereignty or who seriously misunderstands the Bible's teaching on it is to set up as an example a person who in his own heart may be unwilling to trust God. Such leadership is bound to hinder the church as it tries to trust the Lord together." (*Nine Marks*, 80)
- *The Gospel* – "Too often [the gospel] becomes a thin veneer spread lightly over our culture's values, being shaped and formed to the contours of our culture rather than to the truth about God." (*Nine Marks*, 87)
- *Self-contradiction or hypocrisy* – "Or, have you claimed that you know a love from God in Christ and yet live in a way that contradicts that claim? Do you claim that you know this kind of love that knows no bounds, and yet in loving others you set bounds saying in effect, 'I'll go this far but no farther'?" (*Nine Marks*, 164)
- *Who converts?* – "Who can deny that much modern evangelism has become emotionally manipulative, seeking only a momentary decision of the sinner's will yet neglecting the biblical idea that conversion is the result of the supernatural, gracious act of God toward the sinner?" (*Nine Marks*, 136)
- *Sin not confronted* – "And yet, the church, in trying to look like the world in order to win the world, has done a better job than it may have intended. It does not display the distinctively holy characteristics taught in the New Testament. Such an apparently vigorous church is truly spiritually sick, with no remaining immune system to check and guard against wrong teaching or wrong living. Imagine

---

[33] Robbie Castleman, *Parenting in the Pew: Guiding Your Children into the Joy of Worship* (Downers Grove, Illinois: InterVarsity Press, 2013). An excellent resource.

[34] Mark Dever, *Nine Marks of a Healthy Church* (Wheaton, Illinois: Crossway, 2013). Citations for Dever's book shall be noted as follows for the remainder of this chapter: (*Nine Marks*, page number).

Christians, knee-deep in recovery groups and sermons on brokenness and grace, being comforted in their sin but never confronted. Imagine those people, made in the image of God, being lost to sin because no one corrects them." (*Nine Marks*, 198)

- *Self-discovery instead of self-sacrifice*
- *Sweet aroma of Christ is lacking* – Feels more like a funeral than worship. One of my fellow church members said it all about churches like that: "God wadn't there."
- *Manners without commitment* – Polite, but not invested in the church Body of believers. Attending church as if it were an "event" and then leaving.
- *No mention of sin* (The Cross & the Blood)
  - "The new gospel gives no mention of sin (which would necessitate talking about the Cross and the Blood). 'Sin' has been replaced with the terms "mistakes" or "poor decisions," both of which sound harmless enough, and certainly less indicting. While it is true that we all make both mistakes and poor decisions, neither of those will send us to hell – but sin will."[35]
- *"Twin Tragedies"*
  - First tragedy: "...we have made idols with our own set of celebrities and heroes, especially preachers, authors, televangelists, Christian entertainers, and (perhaps worst of all) worship leaders."[36]
  - Second tragedy: "...we have lost the manifest presence of God by creating worship in our own image, making it whatever and however we want it to be. Modern worship is more influenced by trends of secular society than by God's Word, more informed by the opinions and whims of man than by the wisdom and desires of the Creator. I have known pastors with more fear of appearing '*irrelevant*' and out of touch with pop culture than *irreverent* to the Lord before whom they will stand on Judgment Day...Weekend worship comes and goes and no one is changed: for we have been merely in the presence of man, heard only the words of man, sung songs written with the goal of moving only men's emotions. God is not truly sought, not welcomed, and not likely to show up because our 'golden calf' is in the way. We do not see His glory anymore, and we do not seem to know what we are missing. Perhaps this explains why over seventy percent of churchgoers claim they have never experienced the presence of God in a worship service."[37]

Sober Reflection

For Churches

- What is our vision? Who is our vision?
- "Will our authority be the Word of God? Or will it be the sensibilities of our age? Is it the Bible? Or is it us? ... Have we moved the line [personally] because culture is trying to erase the line?"[38]
- Is our pastor's mind increasingly shaped by Scripture? (*Nine Marks*, 45)
- In our sermons, are we directly seeking to address cultural challenges in order to strengthen our people? Are we avoiding hot topics to avoid being judged? Do we fear man more than we fear God?
- What 3-5 topics do we need to revisit every few years in helping our church members grow (parenting class, marriage seminar, etc.)?
- Are we seeking to come alongside area Christian schools to partner together to host conferences and lectures to help the Body of Christ grow?

For Parents Seeking a Bible-believing Church

- Does the church you are visiting believe in the inerrancy of Scripture?
- What spirit do you sense when you walk into a particular church? Is it the Holy Spirit?

---

[35] Casey, 41.

[36] Ibid., 24.

[37] Ibid., 27-28.

[38] Nichols, 48.

- Do you see people connect with you? Do they reach out? Do they reach out to others in the church as well?
- Are youth & adults intermingling, or do you observe separate age cliques? Is there "grown-upping" occurring, where older believers are inviting youth to help in "adult" activities, such as cleaning up after a church supper or helping on church cleanup day?
- Are parents setting priorities? Are we "busting a gut" to get to sports, but not to church?

For Regular Attenders

- Am I so busy during the week that I am too exhausted to go to church on Sunday?
- Am I thinking about the long-term effect on my children's not being at church each week in terms of "their commitment to Christ and the church"? (Pastor Charles Wall)
- Am I praying for my pastor & his family?
- Am I praying for the elders, deacons, & trustees?
- Am I thankful for my church and expressing that appreciation?

Getting Back on Track

- Rod Dreher, *The Benedict Option*: "...the church can't just be the place you go on Sundays – it must become the center of your life. That is, you may visit your house of worship only once a week, but what happens there in worship, and the community and the culture it creates, must be the things around which you order the rest of the week....we should strive to be like [Benedictines] in erasing as much as possible the false distinction between church and life."[39]
- Pastor David Platt, Foreward to *Nine Marks*: "A watching world will know that Jesus has been sent from God when they see his glory on display in his people (John 17: 20-23). ... Jesus is the one who established the church, and the church is his to grow, not ours to manipulate. Jesus is the one who purchased the church... 'with his own blood (Acts 20:28)'." (*Nine Marks*, 10-11)
- Pastor Matthew Casey, *The Return*:
  o "Ask God to guide you to a fellowship that is healthy (not perfect). ... While there are no perfect churches, there are yet healthy fellowships where God's Word is spoken in love and power (Ephesians 4:15), where Believers are knit together in loving relationships (Acts 2:46), where God is worshiped in Spirit and truth (John 4:23-24), and where the Christian learns to be a disciple, growing in the likeness of Christ (Romans 12:2).[40]
  o Genuine revival will (must) include:
    ▪ "Conviction of sin, leading to the cleansing of our lives and a heart's desire to please God;
    ▪ A rekindling of love for Christ; lukewarmth destroyed, passion restored;
    ▪ A burden for souls, leading to salvation. A true revival not only revives the saved, but saves the lost."[41]
  o Biblical pillars[42]
    ▪ "The anointed teaching of God's Word. We have gone from meat to milk... to formula;
    ▪ Preaching the reality and consequences of sin. The mere mention of sin is [not] deemed insensitive or distasteful;
    ▪ Preaching true repentance as a prerequisite for salvation;
    ▪ The unapologetic proclamation of the Blood of Christ as the only means of atonement and redemption;
    ▪ Discipleship as the normal Christian life, not just for missionaries and the super-spiritual;
    ▪ Taking up our cross (a life of self-denial) as the expectation of all Believers;
    ▪ Suffering as a prerequisite for glory;

---

[39] Dreher, 131.
[40] Casey, 113.
[41] Ibid., 10.
[42] Ibid., 33-34.

- The power of the Holy Spirit as a normative and indispensable part of every Christian's life, and the only source of true power for victorious living;
  - Real fellowship (think "friendship") with other Believers as a necessity for a healthy church and healthy Christians;
  - Our calling to live a sanctified life, one that is set apart for God's will and ways;
  - Growing in God's holiness."

- "...One school has local pastors (among others) lead Friday chapel meetings and then takes a photo with the speakers and the schoolchildren to post on social media. I love that way of connecting in the community." (a founder of a CCE school)

Healthy Church

- Believes in the *inerrancy of Scripture.*
- *Has a congregation that is committed to the Word.* "...[T]he congregation's commitment to the centrality of the Word coming from the front, from the preacher, the one specially gifted by God and called to that ministry, is the most important thing you can look for in a church." (*Nine Marks*, p. 58)
- *Is distinct from culture.* "...[W]e need churches that are self-consciously distinct from the culture. We need churches in which the key indicator of success is not evident results but persevering biblical faithfulness. We need churches that help us to recover those aspects of Christianity that are distinct from the world, and that unite us." (*Nine Marks*, 32)
- *Has expositional preaching.*
  - "...[E]xpositional preaching is preaching that takes for the point of a sermon the point of a particular passage of Scripture." (*Nine Marks*, 44)
  - "'We can create a people' around a number of things such as choir, building project, denominational identity, care groups, community service project, social opportunities, men's or women's groups. We can even create a people around the personality of a preacher. And God can surely use all of these things. But in the final analysis the people of God, the church of God, can only be created around the Word of God. Reformer Martin Luther said, 'I simply taught, preached, wrote God's Word: otherwise I did nothing ... The Word did it all.' The Word of God brings life." (*Nine Marks*, 54)
- *Is "trusting in the power of the Holy Spirit."* (Pastor Chuck Wall)
- *Embraces Biblical theology.*
  - "We need to understand the truth that the Bible presents about God and about us. Sound teaching in our churches must include a clear commitment to the teachings of the Bible, even if those teachings are neglected by many churches. If we are to learn the sound doctrine of the Bible, we must study even the doctrines that may be difficult or potentially divisive, but that are foundational for our understanding of God." (*Nine Marks*, 69)
- *Preaches the Gospel.*
  - "...[I]t will begin to dawn on me that I am myself rightly the object of God's wrath, of his judgment – that I deserve death, hell, separation from God, spiritual alienation from him, and even his active punishment now and forever. This is what the theologians call *depravity*, or spiritual death. It is the death which deserves death." (*Nine Marks*, 91)
    - "True Christianity is realistic about the dark side of our world, our life, our nature, our hearts. But true Christianity is not ultimately pessimistic or morally indifferent, encouraging us to settle in and accept the truth about our fallen state. No, the news that Christians have to bring is not just that our depravity is so pervasive but that God's plans for us are so wonderful – because he knows what he made us for." (*Nine Marks*, 91)
    - "The message of Jesus Christ is about teaching us to live with a transforming longing, with a growing faith, with a sure and certain hope of what's to come." (*Nine Marks*, 91)
    - "It is only as we thus contemplate the greatness of God that we begin to realize that his love has a depth, a texture, a fullness, and a beauty that we in our present state can only wonder at." (*Nine Marks*, 93)
  - THE GOSPEL – "The good news is that the one and only God, who is holy, made us in his image to know him. But we sinned and cut ourselves off from him. In his great love, God became a man in Jesus, lived a perfect life, and died on the cross, thus fulfilling the law himself, and taking on himself

the punishment for the sins of all those who would ever turn and trust in him. He rose again from the dead, showing that God accepted Christ's sacrifice and that God's wrath against us had been exhausted. He ascended and presented his completed work to his heavenly Father. He now sends out his Spirit to call us through this message to repent of our sins and to trust in Christ alone for our forgiveness. If we repent of our sins and trust in Christ we are born again into a new life, an eternal life with God. At the very center of the gospel stands the great exchange of Christ's righteousness and our sin. His substitutionary, in-our-place death on the cross is the heart of the message." (*Nine Marks*, 98)

- *Has a Biblical understanding of conversion.*
  - "I fear that one of the results of misunderstanding the Bible's teaching on conversion may be that evangelical churches are full of people who have made sincere commitments at some point in their lives but who have not experienced the radical change that the Bible calls conversion." (*Nine Marks*, 121)
    - *God, not man, does the convicting in evangelism.*
      - "If, in our evangelism, we imply that becoming a Christian is something we do ourselves, we disastrously pass on our misunderstanding of the gospel and of conversion. ...we must be partners with the Holy Spirit, presenting the gospel but relying on the Holy Spirit of God to do the true convicting and convincing and converting." (*Nine Marks*, 34)
    - "Conversion includes both the change of the heart toward God that is repentance, and the belief and trust in Christ and his Word that is faith" (*Nine Marks*, 111). "Repent and believe the good news." (*Nine Marks*, 124)
    - *Repentance* – "...[T]he change we need is not merely to 'discover' ourselves, but to *turn*. One word for *repent* in the Old and New Testaments literally means 'to turn.' It means to turn from our sin and *to* the one true God [and His Way]. We need to resign our claim to be the final judges and governors of our own lives, and acknowledge that that role belongs to God alone. Our past sins need to be forgiven. Our present lives need to be reoriented. Our future destiny needs to be changed from the hell of God's righteous judgment to the heaven of God's gracious forgiveness in Christ. ...It is in this great change that we are saved. We understand our state apart from this change to be dire, and so we call this change *conversion*, or salvation. We call it being born again. The real change that we need is this conversion from worshipping ourselves to worshiping God, from being guilty in ourselves before God to being forgiven in Christ." (*Nine Marks*, 110-111)
- *Has a Biblical understanding of evangelism.*
  - "Evangelism...is following Christ's agenda. It is the positive act of telling the good news about Jesus Christ and the way of salvation through him." (*Nine Marks*, 133)
  - "When you understand that evangelism isn't converting people, but that it is telling them the wonderful truth about God, the great news about Jesus Christ, then obedience to the call to evangelize can become certain and joyful." (*Nine Marks*, 136)
  - John 14:6; Acts 4:12; Romans 10 – "Jesus is the only way to God. The only way that sinners and the holy God can be reconciled."
- *Has a Biblical understanding of church membership.*
  - "Do you have a vital relationship with Christ that changes your life and the lives of those around you? ...Do I understand that following Christ fundamentally involves how I treat other people, especially other people who are members of my church? Have I covenanted together to love them, and do I give myself to that?" (*Nine Marks*, 163)
- *Undergoes Biblical church discipline rarely, but when warranted.*
  - "We need to be able to show that there is a distinction between the church and the world – that it means something to be a Christian. If someone who claims to be a Christian refuses to live as a Christian should live, we need to follow what Paul said and, for the glory of God and for that person's own good, we need to exclude him or her from membership in the church." (*Nine Marks*, 184)
- *Has a passion for discipleship and spiritual maturity.*
  - "In a healthy church, people want to get better at following Jesus Christ." (*Nine Marks*, p. 210)
  - Not simply numerical growth. "The New Testament idea of growth involves not just more people, but people who are growing up, maturing, and deepening in the faith. We read in Ephesians 4:15: 'Instead, speaking the truth in love, we will in all things grow up into him who is the Head, that is,

Christ. From him the whole body, joined and held together by every supporting ligament, grows and builds itself up in love, as each part does its work.'" (*Nine Marks*, 213)

- o "We grow as the body of Christ as God causes growth." (*Nine Marks*, 214)
- o In the final analysis, "...growth of the kingdom of God does not finally depend on us." (*Nine Marks*, 214)
- o Paul, writing to the Thessalonians about their growth, "thanks God for it. Growth doesn't have to produce pride. Growth can cause humility and recognition that it is *God who gives growth* [italics mine]: "We ought always to thank God for you, brothers, and rightly so, because your faith is growing more and more, and the love every one of you has for each other is increasing' (2 Thess. 1:3)." (*Nine Marks*, 214)
- o "God's Word is what we need if we are to grow... To learn what we most need in our lives, we need to turn to God himself. We need to hear his Word – all of it – preached expositionally, so that we don't just hear selective themes....We love our ministers, but more than that we love the Word of God. That's what we want to hear. That's what the church is built on: hearing God's Word speak to us as his Holy Spirit uses it in our hearts." (*Nine Marks*, 216-217)
- o "According to [Jonathan] Edwards, ... the only certain observable sign of such growth is a life of increasing holiness, rooted in Christian self-denial. The church should be marked by a vital concern for this kind of increasing godliness in the lives of its members." (*Nine Marks*, 226)
- o "If we are to grow as individual believers and as churches, we must sit under the Word. We must pray for the Holy Spirit to plant and to weed the gardens of our hearts. This spiritual growth is not optional; it is vital, because spiritual growth indicates life. Things that are truly alive, grow."(*Nine Marks*, 227)

- *Has Biblical church leadership.*
  - o "...we must realize how important a part of our Christian life the upbuilding of the church is to be – not merely organizationally, but building up one another in our love and concern and prayers. We are all called to initiate involvement in each other's lives." (*Nine Marks*, 249)
  - o Christ is the model for church leadership universally. Leaders in each local church are to reflect Christ. Mark Dever uses the mnemonic device "BOSS" with four distinct triangles respectively pointing up, right, left, & down, reflecting four aspects of Christ's leadership – Boss, Out Front, Supply, Serve (*Nine Marks*, 250-254). The *Boss* is careful "to teach, to give instructions, to be willing to exercise authority when [H]e calls us to do so." The *Out Front* aspect of leadership is "being out front, taking the initiative and setting the example." The *Supply* attribute "strategically works to give shape and focus and freedom to the work that others are called to do. Leaders direct the traffic of the church, cutting up ministry into bite-sized bits that others will be able to do" and "give people the tools they need to go out themselves," "supplying and equipping others." Finally, the *Serve* role is "perhaps the most distinctly Christian kind of leadership." This requires self-sacrificial devotion as leaders shepherd God's flock with eager willingness. All four aspects form biblical church leadership.
  - o "...[T]he capacity to trust is a crucial component of reflecting the image of God and of operating within the relationships of life in which that image is played out and expressed." (*Nine Marks*, 255)
  - o "This is a tremendous call that God gives us, to recognize and respect godly authority in the church. This is a sign of a healthy church and of healthy Christians." (*Nine Marks*, 257)

- *Agrees with 19ᵗʰ century Scottish minister Robert Murray M'Cheyne who said*: "I see a man cannot be a faithful minister until he preaches Christ for Christ's sake, until he gives up striving to attract people to himself, and seeks only to attract them to Christ." He could boldly say, "I am better acquainted with Jesus Christ than I am with any man in the world." Robert Murray M'Cheyne then continued to say: "Study holiness of life. Your whole usefulness depends on this, for your sermons last but an hour or two; your life preaches all the week. If Satan can only make a covetous minister, a lover of praise, and pleasure, he has ruined your ministry. A holy minister is an awful [mighty] weapon in the hand of God. A word spoken by you when your conscience is clear, and your heart is full of God's Spirit is worth ten thousand words spoken in unbelief and sin." Lying upon his deathbed with a raging fever, M'Cheyne lifted his hands in prayer, he exclaimed, "This parish Lord, this people, this whole place."[43]

---

[43] Robert Murray M'Cheyne, quoted by David Smithers at oChristian.com.

- *Stands for purity.* "A transformed life stands for purity in a world of cultural decadence."[44]
  - "It would be a potent testimony to the power of the gospel simply to be a people of purity in this world"[45] through the power of the Holy Spirit. (Pastor Chuck Wall)
- *Has confidence in God, not the flesh.*
  - Stephen J. Nichols, *A Time for Confidence*
    - Confidence in God
      - Aware of enemies. "From the beginning, they have been three: the world, the flesh, and the devil. … They stand in opposition to God, His people, and His kingdom."[46]
    - Confidence in the Bible
      - "Martin Luther once said that the Word of God assaults us. It takes off the rough edges, cuts away, and hones us to God's desired shape....Luther quickly added, however, that the Word of God comforts us. Whether assaulting or comforting, the Word of God is at work in shaping and forming us."[47]
      - "Scripture cannot be partially inspired; neither can it be partially authoritative. The moment we speak of 'partly,' we are the ones who decide which parts. We are setting ourselves over Scripture as the authority."[48]
    - Confidence in Christ
    - Confidence in the Gospel
    - Confidence in Hope
- *Connects with the youth*, not necessarily through a youth group, and calls them "to join with us in the Body as we follow Jesus." (Mrs. Denise Wall)
- *"We are trusting in the Lord* not only to lead, but to gift people in what we need to do." (Pastor Chuck Wall)

Setting a Goal

- Pray for God's wisdom. Set one or two goals for getting *your church* or *your church search* better on track. Enter that goal in your phone or personal planner.
- Refer to this goal throughout the year.
- Reflect on this goal at year's end. Rejoice in God's grace.

Expressing a Desire

- Pray for God's wisdom. Write one or two desires for getting your church or church search better on track *that depend on others' cooperation*. Enter that desire in your phone or personal planner.
- Pray about this desire throughout the year.
- Reflect on this desire at the end of each year. Rejoice in God's grace.

Encouragement

- "… [B]eing confident of this, that He who began a good work in you will perfect it until the day of Jesus Christ" (Philippians 1:6, ASV)
- From *The Reason for God*: "That is why God is infinitely happy, because there is an 'other-orientation' at the heart of his being, because he does not seek his own glory but the glory of others."[49] "We were made to join in the dance. If we will center our lives on him [not ourselves], serving him not out of self-interest,

---

44 Nichols, 141.

45 Ibid., 137.

46 Ibid., 24.

47 Ibid., 54.

48 Ibid., 62.

49 Jonathan Edwards, quoted by Timothy Keller, *The Reason for God*, 227.

but just for the sake of who he is, for the sake of his beauty and glory, we will enter the dance and share in the joy and love he lives in ... We were made to center our lives upon him, to make the purpose and passion of our lives knowing, serving, delighting, and resembling him. This growth in happiness will go on eternally, increasing unimaginably (1 Corinthians 2:7-10)."[50]

- Denise Wall (pastor's wife): "We have had to encourage ourselves with 'Don't look at the numbers, just continue on faithfully to preach the Word rightly. Rightly divide the Word of Truth and trust God for the movement in people's hearts and live out the Truth.' You live it out faithfully and then you've got to let it go and let Him do it.'"

- Pastor Chuck Wall (for fellow pastors): "The program's not the answer. It is life in the Spirit and being faithful in the primary ways that God's called you and that is through the preaching accurately of His Word and loving the people."

---

[50] Keller, 228.

Chapter 10
Your School's Community

"But seek the welfare of the city where I have sent you into exile, and pray to the Lord on its behalf, for in its welfare you will find your welfare."

Jeremiah 29:7

Just as we pray for and desire to have the sweet aroma of Christ in our schools, we strive to carry that same fragrance with us in our dealing with the community, town, or city in which our school is located. *Community,* coming from the Latin root *communitas* meaning "common," is a society of people living under the same (or common) rules and regulations. We are fellow countrymen, we are under the same law of the land, and most importantly, we are to love our neighbor who is made in the image of God.

If you are building a new school or renovating a building for your school, bridge across to neighbors before the actual building or renovating begins. Inform them of the type of school you have. Invite them for an evening social event to meet & greet each other. Give your neighbors a flavor of your school, to prove that it is different from a school they may be fearing will upset the peace of the neighborhood. With all neighbor relationships, we seek their welfare and not just our own.

As for sportsmanship out on community athletic fields and in area gymnasiums, we wish again to be above reproach. It is such a joy to see the glory given to God when a sports team exemplifies self-control, fair play, & consideration. Praise the Lord when a head of school receives an email praising the behavior of the school's team on the field, taking a knee when the opposing team's member was injured, praying before the game began, being good sports when they lost, and in general leaving the sweet aroma of Christ long after the game was over.

Regarding interactions with local businesses whether going to them or them coming to us at the school, Rockbridge Academy's policy in their vision statement states that "we aim to be above reproach in our business dealings and supportive of the local business community. We further seek to exemplify the unity of the body of Christ, to develop greater fellowship and understanding with the churches, and to bring honor to our Lord in all our endeavors."

Romans 12:18 says, "If possible, so far as it depends on you, live peaceably with all." Lord, please help us to reflect You in our community.

Red Flags

- Building buildings without building relationships first in the community.
- Bringing undue traffic into the community.
- Being rude on the athletic fields. Not representing Christ on the field. Another school observes that and associates Christianity with poor sportsmanship.
- Promoting the reputation of constant door-to-door selling in order to make the school budget, leaving a bad taste in the community's mouths. Tuition must cover operating costs.
- Developing a reputation of being remiss in paying bills promptly to local businesses.

Sober Reflection

- In what ways are we striving to be a good neighbor?
- How does the community perceive our school?
- How do we determine what community perceptions of us are?
- Do they see Christ?

Healthy School

- A healthy school seeks to bless its community and bring glory to God by its interactions with the community, such as local businesses, churches, & civic organizations.
- A healthy school seeks to be above reproach in its business dealings.
- A healthy school trains its students in the script and manner in which to communicate with area businesses both orally & in written form (e.g., in yearbook & journalism classes).

Setting a Goal

- Pray for God's wisdom. Set one or two goals for getting *your relationship* with your surrounding community better on track. Enter goals in the binder or document that goes with you everywhere.
- Refer to this goal throughout the year. Reflect on this goal at year's end. Rejoice in God's grace.

Expressing a Desire

- Pray for God's wisdom. Write one or two desires for getting your relationship with your surrounding community better on track *that depend on others' cooperation*. Enter that desire in the binder or document that goes with you everywhere.
- Pray about this desire throughout the year. Reflect on this desire at the end of each year. Rejoice in God's grace.

Encouragement

- Michael Cromartie, former author and vice president of the Ethics & Public Policy Center:

  > Until we reach that final destination, we must learn how to sing the songs of Zion in this our foreign land. [We are to] "seek the welfare of the city where I [God] have sent you into exile, and pray to the LORD on its behalf, for in its welfare you will find your welfare" (Jeremiah 29: 7, ESV). We are to do what we have always been commanded to do: build houses, raise families, plant gardens, and produce good art, good music, and good culture. We are to seek justice, love mercy, care for the least of these, and love our neighbors. ...to treat everyone...with respect and dignity as we go about our daily lives and vocations. The late Richard John Neuhaus said it well: it is our duty to strive to build a world in which the strong are just, and power is tempered by mercy, in which the weak are nurtured and the marginal embraced, and to see to it that those at the entrance gates and those at the exit gates of life are protected both by law and by love. ... [We are] to "not be conformed to this world, but be transformed by the renewal of your mind, that by testing you may discern what is the will of God, what is good and acceptable and perfect" (Romans 12:2, ESV). ...[S]how forth the beauty of the good news of the gospel in an age that so desperately needs to hear Good News. ...Our task is to bless our neighbors, cultivate Shalom, and continue to remind people of the wonderful news of the gospel....[1]

---

[1] Michael Cromartie, "*What Now? Faithful Living in Challenging Times*" (lecture, C.S. Lewis Institute *Broadcast Talks*, Capitol Hill, October 23, 2015), 15, 12, 13, 16.

Chapter 11
Your School's Volunteers

"And let us not grow weary of doing good,
for in due season we will reap, if we do not give up."
Galatians 6:9

It is always a blessing to observe a dad operate the sound board for the school play or to see a grandmother serve pizza in the cafeteria or to watch a mom speak about Joan of Arc and even dress up as her for a fourth-grade class! God has gifted each of us with specialties that are a joy for us to share. We are the richer as we work shoulder to shoulder, as a group called together for this time and place, cultivating God's garden through volunteer work.

The word *volunteer* derives from Latin, meaning "a person who freely offers to take part in an enterprise or undertake a task" from the Latin *vuluntas*, meaning "will." It is something done out of choice and willingness. Each of us can perhaps do something – at home, before school starts, after school during sports or play practice. Each effort builds our community as we serve God together.

Our classical Christian schools cannot operate without our volunteer corps. Whether it's painting walls or sewing curtains or creating flashcards or listening to Bible memory verse recitation, each devoted service builds our schools.

As a note to parents, our hearts' desires do not always match our season of life. I think of Nancy Wilson's injunction to "import before you export."[1] Make sure the home front is taken care of first before volunteering your time. I was eager to volunteer in my daughter's class when my son was two. He went to a babysitter's and I found out the whole time I was gone volunteering, he had his diaper bag looped over his arm and was standing at the door crying. I was needed at home and that came first. That was my joy! A few years later, I volunteered, then a couple years after that began substituting, and eventually taught at my children's school. Timing is important, and God promises that there is a time for every season under heaven.

Perhaps your school has several volunteers at the younger grades, but it slopes off quickly beyond that. It can be difficult to find folks to help out during the day, but how about the grandparents in your community? Many seniors would love to serve a hot lunch, listen to a child recite their memory verse, help with gardening, assist with mailings, do handyman projects, sort used uniforms, inventory the library, and help out in the classroom or even substitute. It would be wonderful to see grandparents in all our schools as generations gather in serving Christ by helping enact our schools' vision. A potential name for this grassroots effort: The Grandparents' Guild! These same grandparents might serve in conjunction with the local churches as well as the school – a triumvirate of sorts – and the overlapping vision that heads of school Mr. Keith Nix and Mr. Russ Gregg mentioned in Chapter 9.

Covenant Academy near Houston, Texas, devotes a section of their website to "Patriot Projects" that lists "volunteer opportunities to grow our school." They have an icon for each project, a label naming the project, a brief description, as well as an estimated time commitment and what age level may volunteer (e.g., upper school students, adults only, upper school students/adults). Projects include helping with landscaping, gardening, events, office work, classroom volunteering, driving for sports, handyman work, window washing, restocking

---

[1] Nancy Wilson, source unknown.

supplies, organizing uniforms, library help, field trip helper, and photo sorting & selection for website/promotional materials. Delightfully, they add "Create your own Patriot Project" with the question, "How would you like to help?" The volunteer can sign up on the website with a preference ranking of two or three tasks. They also have space on the website to arrange a project meeting to receive your assignment and discuss a deadline and arrange a project completion meeting to finalize the project.

It is essential to train your substitute teachers as they are *in loco magister*, "in place of a teacher." As head of school Dr. Pamela McKee says, "They need support, clear direction, and goals. Have them observe your strongest teachers." Substitutes probably are paid in most schools, but they may not be if a school is just beginning. The training is certainly as a volunteer. Payment begins once the substituting begins. Ideally, develop a Substitute Training booklet. Have a training video and/or verbal training session where you share the school's philosophy, the meaning of the Trivium, the routine, how to handle transitions, recess, lunch, duties, & end-of-day routine. Go over your school's discipline process and whom they should contact if necessary. One example of a school's five-step process of discipline is as follows:

1) *Question: "Why did you do this?"* (Question first and then hear child's answer.)
2) *Presentation of God's Word.* This part is the Law. God does the convicting.
3) *Presentation of the Gospel* – that all sin can be forgiven because of Jesus' blood.
4) *Extension of forgiveness.*
5) *Restoration of student.* If a public sin, the student asks for the class's forgiveness. If a private sin, private forgiveness is sought.

On the day of substituting, have a printed schedule of the day for the substitute teacher including the class period & room(s) where they will be teaching, a map of where each classroom is in your building, the lesson plans, & the location of all the necessary textbooks. Identify the location of the teacher's office & the teachers' bathrooms.

Train your other volunteers as well if only in a document that they sign, for example, the "Principles of Partnership" document that head of school Mr. Keith Nix uses. [See "Appendix."] In particular, the phrase *in loco parentis* may be unfamiliar to volunteers. Explain it to them. For example, if you bring on a volunteer to coach or to direct the school play, absolutely ensure that they understand this phrase and go over your school mission, vision, & values with them. If necessary, have them sign paperwork attesting to these agreements. If a volunteer is new to CCE, administrators need to keep an eye & an ear to the rail to ascertain if the volunteer is truly following *in loco parentis* and your agreements or setting up their own rules.

CASE STUDY

Covenant Academy website – Cypress, Texas

> "Covenant Community Life (CCL) is the parent partnership arm of Covenant Academy. CCL is a volunteer-led parent/teacher fellowship (or PTF) organization that exists to facilitate community among families, friends, staff and faculty through service to Covenant. You are invited to utilize your gifts and talents to serve in the classroom and in the entire school community. One of the many ways CCL is dedicated to serving the school is through our family events. Family events take place throughout the school year and include: Thanksgiving Feast in November, Christmas Concert in December, Chili Cook Off in February, and Fine Arts Night in spring. As part of our parent partnership, we ask that each House [in our House System] help by hosting one event throughout the school year. Our family events are crucial to building and maintaining our close-knit community...."

Red Flags

- There is no vision or outreach to bring appropriately vetted volunteers into the school.
- There is no training of volunteers.
- There is no verbal & written appreciation of volunteers.

- Students are not trained to express their respect & oral and written thanks to volunteers.
- A small pool of volunteers is overburdened and presumed upon to carry the full weight of the school's needs.

Sober Reflection

For Coordinator of Volunteers

- What is our vision/mission/core values statement? Where is it located? Our educational philosophy? Our statement of faith? Our rules?
- Are we seeking capable volunteers from our parents, grandparents, & Christian community?
- Have we printed a "Substitute Training" booklet?
- How do we discover "latent" talents & skills of potential volunteers?

For Volunteers

- Are you seeking to serve Christ by serving the school?
- Are you leaning into Him and praying for the teacher, the class, & yourself?

Healthy School

- A healthy school provides volunteer opportunities.
- A healthy school trains its volunteers.
- *Curriculum Project*: A healthy school stores lesson plans BOTH in 1) hard-copy binders by grade & by subject with all lesson plans organized by week, in the event that lesson plans cannot quickly be accessed for the substitute teacher, & 2) electronic form, easily provided by an administrator. If the electronic form is not easily accessed, the paper copy is.

Setting a Goal

- Pray for God's wisdom. Set one or two goals for getting *your vision for volunteers* better on track. Enter goals in the binder or document that goes with you everywhere.
- Refer to this goal throughout the year.
- Reflect on this goal at year's end. Rejoice in God's grace.

Expressing a Desire

- Pray for God's wisdom. Write one or two desires for getting your vision for volunteers better on track *that depend on others' cooperation*. Enter that desire in the binder or document that goes with you everywhere.
- Pray about this desire throughout the year.
- Reflect on this desire at the end of each year.

Encouragement

- Thank you for all you are doing! You are providing a valuable service to the school.
- Ephesians 3:20-21 (NKJV): "Now to Him who is able to do exceedingly abundantly above all that we ask or think, according to the power that works in us, to Him *be* glory in the church by Christ Jesus to all generations, forever and ever. Amen."

Chapter 12
Your School's
Alumni & Donors

"...the one who receives instruction in the word should share
all good things with their instructor."
Galatians 6:6 (NIV)

My great aunt is 97, and every five years she attends her "50th-plus" high school reunion. That is a marvel to me. To have such loyalty, such fond remembrance, such sense of place in one's life.

My mother, who also attended her 50th high school reunion, fondly recalled Miss Helen Fitting who taught her four years of English, two years of Latin, two years of French, and sponsored the Future Teachers of America. I myself remember visiting one of the last classes Miss Fitting taught, admiring her poise, her classic dress, her knowledge, and wisdom. I wanted to be like her!

I have been to only one reunion of my high school class because there was only one reunion. There were no teachers there, but I remember Miss Barbaralee Berté, my French teacher whom I admired for her poise; her simple, neat dresses; her knowledge; and *joie de vivre*. I wanted to be like her, too!

The vision of a school sets the plan for the foundation. The day-to-day work of a school pours the foundation. As we age, we can appreciate more significantly how those beginnings shaped us, and we can return to our *alma mater*, our nurturing mother, to acknowledge that impact.

While at the 2019 ACCS conference in Atlanta, I asked Dr. George Grant what areas he saw maturing in classical Christian education.

> I think one of the greatest areas of maturity that I see is our students' returning to teach in the classroom. The students who have had this richness change their lives and stir their hunger. They are thinking outside the box. They realize there is a better way to do this and they have a fresh enthusiasm that we want to make sure that we don't stifle. When we have the children of children who have graduated from our school enrolled in our school, those parents are the ones who are most on fire. One of our alumni came back two years ago and served as our admissions director and she was able to enhance school visits, improve introductions. She knew exactly what to say to stir the hunger in prospective families. She has now gone on to get her Master's while she was our admissions director. Now this coming year she is going to be in the classroom because she realized this has been great, but it's just stirred in her a hunger to be in the classroom.[1]

As G.K. Chesterton said, "Education is simply the soul of a society as it passes from one generation to another." How blessed it is when our students return to substitute, to teach, to volunteer, to be heads of school themselves one day. As the vision captures their hearts, they, too, can pass on the soul of classical Christian education to the generations following them, as they continue to sharpen first things first, and help to keep their schools on track.

---

[1] Dr. George Grant, interview by Kathleen F. Kitchin, Atlanta, Georgia, June 13, 2019.

Another area Dr. Grant saw growing was alumni's ideas for enhancement of existing arrangements. "At our school we had a house system for years, but it wasn't until one of our alumni came back and caused that house system to now just be fully alive that we really started to see the house system work the way we'd always envisioned." He said that "setting it up just as a system, there is not as much 'buy-in.'" The alumnus "changed the house's names from virtues to names of our heroes of the faith. Much more personal." The school had symbols. The alumnus created crests. Medieval heraldry revived! In addition, "Each house has its own sword, so that when students come in at the beginning of the year when they come in for the swording of the houses, we have this ceremony and it's like a knighting. What was this sort of dry idea, but really a wonderful idea, good idea, necessary idea, is now…this living thing because he's brought it to life."

Some students return to work at their schools, but how can we stay in touch with all of our students after they graduate? Below is an example of communicating connection:

Alumni page on Veritas School website, Richmond, Virginia:

> Even though you have graduated from Veritas, please know you are still an important part of our community. We value the friendships made over the years, and we welcome you back to visit whenever you can. Come see what's new, visit with your favorite teachers, root for your alma mater at an athletic event, attend Commencement, and reminisce about your days here. Please make sure you keep us up to date! We want to hear from you when you have a major accomplishment, win an award, get married, travel to an exciting place, or start a new job—the Veritas community welcomes the opportunity to celebrate these milestones with you! You may submit a class note or update your contact information by emailing our Director of Development, --- at ---.

As for donors, one school has donor retreats to help raise funds for the school. Other schools have a donation section on their website.

The first-things-first priority with your school's alumni and donors is *relationship*. God has brought you together for a season of life, and may there be wonderful times in the future to refresh that connection. May they be filled with His joy!

Red Flags

- The school has no communication with alumni.
- Alumni avoid the school because of school hurt.
- People no longer donate because they are grieved that the vision has changed or been jettisoned.
- People donate to see their name, not Christ's, uplifted.
- The school asks for money while the alumni are in college or post-college and have not yet gotten their feet on the ground. They are not yet established, and they do not feel valued by their *alma mater*, their "nurturing mother."

Sober Reflection

For Board/Alumni Relations Coordinator/Development Officer

- What is the school's vision for alumni?
- What is the school's vision for donors?

For Alumni

- Am I proud of my *alma mater* in a fond, yet humble fashion?
- Do I seek to return or to write, sharing "all good things" with my instructors (Galatians 6:6)?

For Donors

- As able, am I joyously giving to my *alma mater*, rejoicing in helping to support its vision?
- Am I giving in order to seek influence and control in a school, or am I simply giving in the service of Christ?

Getting Back on Track

- *Suggested Project*: Reach out to alumni through cards their first year in college (& maybe student care packages!).
- *Suggested Project*: Send them your annual/biannual newsletter.
- In the newsletter, make it clear you welcome their updates & stories (that could appear in future newsletters).
- Most importantly, cultivate friendships with former students.
- Donors, cheerfully give without seeking to be given to in return.

Healthy School

- The school waits until the alumni are more established before sending requests for money. Perhaps 10 years after graduation?
- The school has an annual event – a homecoming or reunion – for alumni to gather.
- The school sends its biannual newsletter to alumni, not under or over-communicating with them, but staying in touch.
- A college student who graduated from a classical Christian school in Michigan recounted with thankfulness and fondness his returns to his *alma mater*, a place where relationships were built intentionally across grades and what most impressed me about his stories was – love.

Setting a Goal

- Pray for God's wisdom. Set a goal for getting *your school's plan* for alumni and its plan for donors better on track. Enter that goal in the binder or document that goes with you everywhere.
- Refer to this goal periodically throughout the year.
- Reflect on this goal at year's end. Rejoice in God's grace.

Expressing a Desire

- Pray for God's wisdom. Write one or two desires for better reaching out to alumni and to donors that *depend on others' cooperation*. Enter that desire in the binder or document that goes with you everywhere.
- Pray about this desire throughout the year.
- Reflect on this desire at the end of each year. Rejoice in God's grace.

Encouragement

- "For God is not unjust so as to overlook your work and the love that you have shown for his name in serving the saints, as you still do" (Heb. 6:10, ESV).

Epilogue

We have identified foundational fundamentals in Classical Christian Education. We have also identified red flags. Let us now return to the four types of schools presented at the beginning:

- If you have run off the rails and were not aware of it due to inexperience or blind spots, thank God that if He is the author of your school, He will guide, teach, and encourage you. Be encouraged that "...[He] who began a good work in you will bring it to completion at the day of Jesus Christ" (Philippians 1:6).

- If you have run off the rails due to pride, thank God for His shepherding rod & staff. Confess this sin to Him and to others whom you may have hurt. "Humble yourselves before the Lord, and He will exalt you" (James 4:10). Go forward in the grace of God.

- If you have run off the rails and suppressed the truth, thank God for exposing your unfruitful deeds of darkness. Confess sin to God and to others whom you have hurt. Jesus died for our sins. "If we confess our sins, He is faithful and just to forgive us our sins and to cleanse us from all unrighteousness" (1 John 1:9). Pray to re-establish trust, seek a godly accountability partner or board, and trust in God.

- If you have run off the rails and know it, thank God that He shows favor to the humble (1 Peter 5:5). Confess to Him and to others. "If you continue in My word, you are truly My disciples. Then you will know the and the truth will set you free" (John 8:32).

Please, dear Lord Jesus,

Help us to keep You first. Help us keep our schools on track.

Help us love and educate these precious young lives to Your glory;

Guide us to educate as Christ would, the best Teacher & Shepherd.

Guide us to educate classically, but not at the expense of biblical truth, love, & humility.

Help us recognize, identify, and act upon red flags in our schools.

Help us repent and ask forgiveness of You & others when we have sinned.

Help us be in Your Word and open our eyes to it and to You, that we may be like You,

our Master, Lord & Savior.

Soli Deo Gloria.

Appendix

An Ancient Answer to a Timeless Question*

How can one "love the Lord your God with all your heart, soul, mind" and "your neighbor as yourself" via teaching and/or studying?

The following answers are given in St. Augustine's *De Doctrina Christiana*

1. **All enjoyment, ultimately, should be focused on the Triune God. (l.5)**
   - The world is divided into that which can be **used** and that which can be **enjoyed** (Rom. 11:36). All study is to be used to the end of enjoying God. (l. 3)
   - Even the study of mathematics should "turn all this to the praise and love of the one God from whom he knows it all proceeds" (ll.57).

2. **Recognizing the source of Truth.**
   - "None of us, though, should claim our understanding of anything as our very own, except possibly of falsehood. Because everything that is true comes from the one who said, "I am the truth" (Jn 14:6). What do we have, after all, that we have not received?" (Prologue)
   - "All (truth among the heathen) is like their gold and silver, and not something they instituted themselves, but something which they mined, so to say, from the ore of divine providence, veins of which are everywhere to be found."

3. **Pursuing Truth relentlessly.**
   - "all good and true Christians should understand that truth, wherever they may find it, belongs to their Lord." (ll. 28)
   - "If those, however, who are called philosophers happen to have said anything that is true, and agreeable to our faith, the Platonists above all, not only should we not be afraid of them, but we should even claim back for our own use what they have said, as from unjust possessors." (ll.60)

4. **Refuting the errors of the day.**
   - "Repudiate all superstitious fictions, and grieve over and beware of people 'who while knowing God, have not glorified him as God...'" (Rom. 1:21-23) (ll. 28)

5. **Resisting Pride**
   - "Let us be on our guard against all such dangerous temptations to pride..." (Prologue 6)
   - With regards to rational discourse and mathematics, "all that one has to be on guard against here is a passion from wrangling and a kind of childish parade of getting the better of one's opponents."
   - "never stop reflecting on that maxim of the apostle's, 'Knowledge puffs up, love builds up'" (1 Cor. 8:1) (ll. 62)

6. **Pursuing all worthwhile human 'institutions.'**
   - "But all such human institutions which contribute to the necessary ordering of life are certainly not to be shunned by Christians; on the contrary indeed, as far as is required they are to be studied and committed to memory." (ll. 40)
   - Logic and rhetoric give us "more pleasure at the spectacle of truth at work ... sharpen our wits" so long as we do not let them make us "more spiteful or more conceited." (ll. 55)
   - "for the needs of this life, ['eager and bright young people'] should not neglect those humanly instituted arts and sciences which are of value" (ll. 58)

* Courtesy of Dr. Mark Graham, Grove City College, 2018

Appendix B
A Curriculum Issue to Consider

Literature: Christian and Pagan Classics

A prominent consideration in selecting curriculum is deciding the mix of the Christian and the pagan classics. My suggestion would be to prayerfully select pagan literary classics. Before diving into the pagan classics, consider beginning the logic level with Christian literary classics, such as Augustine's *Confessions* and St. Patrick's biography. Pagan classic literature effectively focuses on godlessness and its consequences. Our students' minds are new to so much, however, and we wish to encourage them, not depress them by giving them too steady a diet of life without God. By beginning with Christian biography, our students can "crawl into" these Christians' skin and see how they sorted out joys, challenges, questions, and life in general – from a Christian perspective. A vicarious experience. The concern is that if we teach too much pagan literature or pagan literature alone, we run the risk of limiting our children's scope and hope. Alternatively, parents may question your teaching the pagan classics. Cheryl Lowe has a fine article, "The Top Ten Reasons: Why Christians Should Read the Pagan Classics," in a Memoria Press online article (2012), encompassing topics on architecture, virtue, science, education, natural law, government, religion, philosophy, human condition, & literature, including accompanying classic titles for each of these subjects. We study the classical writers for they possessed general revelation. We can compare and contrast them to the Bible to show the great Light of the Gospel. We can also encourage students to see connections from the present back to these classic roots. In our passionate interaction with our subject matter in CCE, *we must not leave our students with the impression that we are worshipping at the Greek or Roman altar*. All of our work points to the ultimate Author, Christ, for, yes, we are teaching, but we are also contributing to students' spiritual formation.

An Example of Approaching Classic Pagan Literature with a Christian Worldview: With regard to virtue, we can have students read and contrast the *Apology of Socrates* with the Good News. As for *Aristotle*, students may study "*Nichomachean Ethics* – one of the most influential works of all time – teaching his son Nichomachus principles of virtue in the individual and in the state – politics based on ethics, but the Greeks had no solution for the Gordian knot of human virtue and our failure to achieve it." As for Plato, students can read selected excerpts of *The Republic* where one of society's chief problems was deemed Ignorance and, therefore, Education was deemed the key. "And so Plato constructed his ideal Republic, where philosopher kings would receive the ideal education that would lead to true wisdom and virtue and thus guide the rest of us into doing what we ought to do." Lowe says, "And here we see another value of Greek wisdom: It leads us to Christ. It is just where human reason has reached its limit that revelation gives us an answer that satisfies the mind and the heart. We fail to achieve virtue because we are fallen.... Greek reason failed to see the nature of sin and man's need of salvation. The whole salvation story of Scripture explains how and why we are not what we are supposed to be, and what we can do about it." The Gospel of John was written to the Greeks and makes multiple references to the Cave & the Light analogy found in Plato's *Republic* (John 1 & 1 John 1). Students can read Cicero's *De Officiis* (On Obligations, or On Duties), written to his son, and compare that to proverbs and other biblical passages. As for

Christian writers, students can read Peter Kreeft: *Back to Virtue* "written from a Christian perspective and will inspire you to value virtue!"

Educator Cheryl Lowe says,

> A serious objection to classical literature is one echoed by Plato: the necessity of learning about the pagan gods." Two points about this objection are made by Chesterton who says there were 1) Good pagans – Greeks & Romans who had "beautiful, benevolent gods that did not require human sacrifice or temple prostitution" and 2) Bad pagans – Baal, Tyre, Carthage, & Canaan. The Punic Wars were the battle between these two religions/between Rome and Carthage. The Romans won. "Rome destroyed Carthage and the religion of Baal once and for all. The Romans, then, actually accomplished what the Hebrews were unable to do in the Old Testament. God works in mysterious ways."

May we be faithful to bring our subject matter always back to Scripture.

Source: Cheryl Lowe, "The Top Ten Reasons: Why Christians Should Read the Pagan Classics," *Memoria Press* online article (2012), accessed May 22-23, 2018.

Appendix C
How Parents can Help Their Family with Technology

The Tech-Wise Family: Everyday Steps for Putting Technology in Its Proper Place by Andy Crouch (2017) does a beautiful job sharing principles & practical application of how to change the culture of your home, to shape it around something other than technology. Here is a handful of their suggestions:

- **Choosing Character:** "We develop wisdom and courage together as a family." (p. 47)
- **Shaping Space:** "We want to create more than we consume. So we fill the center of our home with things that reward skill and active engagement. ...Fill the center of your life together – the literal center, the heart of your home, the place where you spend the most time together – with the things that reward creativity, relationship, and engagement. Push technology and cheap thrills to the edges; move deeper and more lasting things to the core." (an invitation to creating culture) (p. 71). Hearth (<L. *focus*) reminds us that fire was once the center of our homes. Fire as mesmerizing and beautiful. Fire "generates its own light, and our eyes are drawn to it, watching it play and dance." (p. 72) What could you place in the center of your home?
    - Books, paper, paint, clay, simple musical instruments, boxes to create homes or forts in, colored pencils, markers, crayons, obstacle courses, legos that come in basic not preselected sets, wooden blocks, little ships & dolls to create worlds of stories in.
- **Structuring Time:** "We are designed for a rhythm of work and rest. So one hour a day, one day a week, and one week a year, we turn off our devices and worship, feast, play, and rest together." (p. 83)
    - "... The beautiful, indeed amazing, thing about all disciplines is that they serve as both diagnosis and cure for what is missing in our lives. They both help us recognize the exact nature of our disease and, at the very same time, begin to heal us from our disease." Our devices have "Off" switches. (p. 102)
- **Waking and Sleeping**: "We wake up before our devices do, and they 'go to bed' before we do." (p. 111)
    - "Sleep seems, in a strange way, to be where the learning required to be accomplished human beings actually happens. It is the way our bodies deal with the immense complexity and demands of growth of all kinds – intellectual, physical, emotional, and even spiritual. Heart, mind, soul, and strength all are nurtured while we sleep." (p. 112)
- **Learning and Working:** "We aim for 'no screens before double digits' at school and at home." No screens before age 10. (p. 123)
- **The Good News about Boredom:** "We use screens for a purpose, and we use them together, rather than using them aimlessly and alone." (p. 139)
    - "The technology that promises to release us from boredom is actually making it worse – making us more prone to seek empty distractions than we have ever been. In fact, I've come to the conclusion that *the more you entertain children, the more bored they will get*." (p. 140)
- **The Deep End of the (Car) Pool:** "Car time is conversation time." Sing songs, identify alphabet letters, read aloud, listen to & discuss audiobooks, and talk about & process the kids' day. (p. 155)

- **Naked and Unashamed:** "Spouses have one another's [non-work] passwords, and parents have total access to children's devices." (p. 165)
  - "All sin begins with separation – hiding from our fellow human beings and our Creator, even if, at first, we simply hide in the 'privacy' of our own thoughts, fears, and fantasies. Anything that short-circuits our separation, that reinforces our connection to one another and our need for one another, also cuts off the energy supply for cherishing and cultivating patterns of sin." (p. 178)
  - Install filters on Internet access & also use the parental controls provided on your children's devices.
- **Why Singing Matters:** "We learn to sing together, rather than letting recorded and amplified music take over our lives and worship." (p. 183)
  - "... [Singing is the] most immediately accessible and engaging to children (listening to sermons takes a while longer!)."
  - Helps reinforce memorization. (p. 192)
  - "Simply, singing may be the one human activity that most perfectly combines heart, mind, soul, and strength. Almost everything else we do requires at least one of these fundamental human faculties: the heart, the seat of the emotion and the will; the mind, with which we explore and explain the world; the soul, the heart of human dignity and personhood; and strength, our bodies' ability to bring about change in the world. But singing (and maybe only singing) combines them all. When we sing in worship, our minds are engaged with the text and what it says about us and God, our hearts are moved and express a range of emotions, our bodily strength is required, and – if we sing with 'soul' – we reach down into the depths of our beings to do justice to the joy and heartbreak of human life." (p. 191)
  - "[Family] singing...[is] the sort...where you are fully known and fully able to be yourself. And it will be a rehearsal for the end of the whole story, when all speech will be song and the whole cosmos will be filled with worship." (p. 193)

An Email Invitation to Pastors

Dear [Pastor's first name],

We look forward to you joining us
on the campus of Veritas School
for one of our Community Leader Lunches!

———————————————

Thursday, October 3, 20--
12:00 Noon
3400 Brook Road, Richmond, Virginia 23227

———————————————

Come hear about great books, great conversations,
and how a classical, Christian education
can shape the lives of young people
in important and long-lasting ways.

We'll also share the exciting story behind Veritas School
and the impact it is having in Richmond,
particularly the Northside.

After lunch, we hope that you can join us
for a brief tour of our historic campus.

———————————————

Please park in the Westwood Avenue visitor lot
near corner of Brook Road and Westwood Avenue.

When you arrive, we will meet you at the
Main Office in Graves Hall – first building on the left.

We look forward to seeing you soon!

Questions? Contact [Full name of contact person]

804-***-****

VERITAS
FRIDAY, APRIL 5

The 'Art of Orchestral Strings'
for the Non-String Player

Lilli Benko

Cultivating the Virtue of Hope
when Hopelessness is in Vogue

Robyn Burlew

Charlotte Mason and Classical Education

Katie Earman & Jim Reynolds

Intro to Theological Aesthetics:
The Common, the Uncommon, and the Mediocre

Joshua Gibbs

Friendship, Dating, Sex, and Adolescence

Keith Nix

'No Permanent Place in the World
for Ugly Mathematics'

Josh Betts

Parents and grandparents are invited to join us on
Friday, April 5, from 6:45 - 9:00 PM in North Hall.
To register, please use the link in the Lion's Roar or email Sara Kennedy
at skennedy@veritasschool.com.

VERITAS
FRIDAY, NOVEMBER 9

A Primer on Classical Education

Andrew Smith

Book Study:
The Consolation of Philosophy by Boethius

Josh Gibbs

**Parenting as Ambassadors, Not Owners
and Other Gospel Principles for Parenting**

Jim Reynolds & Robyn Burlew

**Lower School Math:
Principles and Practices using Singapore Curriculum**

Beverly Schuping & Annie Thurston

**Lingua Latina:
A Fun, Welcoming Introduction to Latin Study**

Will Killmer

Parents and grandparents are invited to join us on
Friday, November 9, from 6:45 - 9:00 PM in Lingle Hall.
To register, please use the link in the Lion's Roar or email Sara Kennedy
at skennedy@veritasschool.com.

Job Description
Director of Instruction

I. Instructional Program
   A. Monitors all instructional aspects of the school
   B. Communicates the status and evaluation of school program to Headmaster and Secondary Principal weekly
   C. Assists Headmaster in implementing school instructional goals

II. Staff Instruction
   A. Observes teachers formally as requested by the Headmaster and informally regularly
   B. Implements instructional training of teachers as directed by Headmaster
   C. Reads weekly and long-range teacher plans, evaluates plans, writes comments (improvements and encouragement)
   D. Provides resources and revises current materials to meet teacher/student needs
   E. Meets with teachers to assist them in improving student learning
   F. Encourages teachers to teach curriculum objectives and maintain appropriate pacing and standards according to short and long-term plans
   G. Assists Headmaster in building CCE vision in staff
   H. Assists teachers in completing and monitoring report cards
   I. Observes and evaluates teacher interviewees
   J. Provides training and academic recommendations for teachers during parent/teacher conferences
   K. Assists in planning faculty teaching assignments

III. Student Instruction
   A. Observes and monitors academic progress of students in accordance with curriculum objectives
   B. Assists in the evaluation of students who are having difficulty
   C. Recommends and assists in the implementation of academic plans for struggling students
   D. Assists in evaluating academic readiness of entering students and in developing appropriate academic plans for them

IV. Curriculum
   A. Evaluates current curriculum and makes recommendations of resource and objective revisions
   B. Establishes yearly curriculum goals and vision in conjunction with Headmaster
   C. Establishes an excellent quality standard in the publication and sale of school's material
   D. Assists in the planning of parent meetings

  E. Communicates regularly with other CCE schools regarding their instructional resources and courses

 V. Parent Constituency
  A. Provides resources and recommendations to parents as they assist their children
  B. Assists teachers in parent meetings when there are academic concerns

 VI. CCE Vision
  A. Assists other classical Christian schools (phone calls, visits, teacher training) in developing curriculum, objectives, and school teacher training

 VII. Standardized Testing
  A. Assists Headmaster in training teachers to administer tests
  B. Assists Headmaster in accomplishing directed tasks

VIII. "Honest Broker"
  A. Acts as bridge of communication between teachers/students/ parents and the administration

Source: Mrs. Laura Tucker, M.Ed., NCED
Nationally Certified Educational Diagnostician

Lesson Plans – European I   Week 9
8th Grade 20-- - 20--   11/2 – 11/6
Teacher's First & Last Name

Overview:

Monday & Tuesday – The Five Good Emperors (96-180AD)
Wednesday – Commodus & the Dawn of Disorder: The Roman Empire in Decline
Thursday – **Short Paper due.** Review for test; update timelines.
Friday – The Roman Empire: Early Persecution of the Church

Homework:

> ➢ Teacher: Gather & check two students' notebooks per day between Monday, 11/2, and next Friday, 11/13, with four on Tuesdays and Thursdays.
> ➢ Monday, Tuesday, & Wednesday evenings – 30 minutes/evening for journal entries on Greco-Roman philosophy today
> ➢ **Short Paper on Greco-Roman philosophy due Thursday, 11/5**

Monday
Objective: The students will examine the second golden age of the Roman Empire, "The Five Good Emperors," and determine what was good and not good about these leaders.

Principles:
> ➢ 1 Thessalonians 5: 21 "Test everything and hold onto the good."
> ➢ Do not accept terms in history books at face value.

On board: The Five Good Emperors (96-180AD)
Review:
1) What is significant about 180AD? (end of *Pax Romana*)
2) What questions naturally come to mind about this fact? (Why did the *Pax Romana* end? How did it end? What changed exactly? Was there war?)
New questions/caveat:
1) What other question do you have about these facts on the board? (What is good about the emperors? What wasn't good about the emperors?)
2) *Caution*: It is quite easy to accept historical labels at face value without questioning them. The Bible says to test everything and hold onto the good.
3) It is important to ask questions in our research and writing as well.
4) We will ask these questions about the good and the bad again at the end of our discussion.

Lesson: **The Roman Empire: The Second Golden Age, 2nd Century: The Five Good Emperors (96-180AD)**
1) Study Nerva. Why didn't the senate abolish emperorships since the Flavian Dynasty ended with no heir? (See Durant, "Nerva." Praetorian Guard's aggression; Nerva's concession. The Senate wanted the power back to elect the leader, but could not under hereditary succession. *Principate* – constitutional monarchy as co-ruler with Senate. *Paterfamilias* – Especially with immense size of the empire. Augustus had established order and peace. Symbolic power of one person over entire Roman Empire.)
2) How did succession work with the five good emperors? (adoption)
3) How did this eliminate trouble? (no feuding/bloodshed over successors)
4) We now have senators adopting other senators who will become the next emperor.
   a) Nerva, Trajan, Hadrian, Pius Antoninus, & Marcus Aurelius
5) Quote from the great historian Edward Gibbon (18th C. English historian) regarding this period:

a) *"If a man were called upon to fix a period in the history of the world during which the condition of the human race was most happy and prosperous, he would without hesitation name that which elapsed from the succession of Nerva to the death of Aurelius. Their united reigns are possibly the only period of history in which the happiness of a great people was the sole object of government."* Durant, *Caesar and Christ*, 425

6) Discuss Trajan.
   a) Expanded empire to it greatest extent (parts of or all of 40 modern-day countries)
   b) Trajan's Column
7) Discuss Hadrian.
   a) Most brilliant emperor
      i) *Supposedly* wrote, dictated, listened, and conversed with his friends all at the same time – the "frequency of this tale invites suspicion" (Durant, *Caesar and Christ*, p. 416). Hadrian would have been an IM-ing, cell-phoning, iPod-ing, twittering kind of guy today!!
   b) Cultured emperor
   c) Hadrian's Villa
   d) Hadrian's Wall
   e) Pantheon

Assess: How would you describe the years 96-180AD in the Roman Empire? (military emphasis, emperors' power increased, Senate's power decreased)

Sources: Durant, *Caesar and Christ; Western Civilization;* our text

Tuesday

Objectives: The students will study Antoninus Pius, as well as Marcus Aurelius and his son Commodus. They will examine biblical truth regarding the parent-child relationship and contrast Aurelius' standard with that of the Bible.

Review:
   o What group of emperors did we study last week? (*The Five Good Emperors*)
      o This era is also called the second golden age of the Roman Empire.
   o What principle did we apply from the Bible to this label?
      o 1 Thessalonians 5: 21 "Test everything and hold onto the good."
      o Do not accept terms in history books at face value.
   o Today we will study Pius Antoninus, Marcus Aurelius, and his son Commodus.
   o What was the moral equivalent of the pool hall in the Roman Empire? (gladiatorial schools)

Lesson: **The Five Good Emperors**

1) Discuss Antoninus Pius.
   a) Quiet and mild (Foxe's *Book of Martyrs*).
   b) Antoninus Pius desired peace to such a degree that he created what burden for Marcus Aurelius? (barbarians' spilling over the borders)
   c) Remember, *ideas have consequences.*
2) Discuss Marcus Aurelius.
   a) A Stoic, at age 12 he took on the cloak of philosopher; slept on a bit of straw on the floor, not on the couch his aristocratic mother urged him to.
   b) Philosopher-King
      i) Disciple of Plato
         (1) Plato's *Republic*
            (a) Three classes of people – What are the three classes he identified?
               (i) Philosopher-kings – upper class, ruling class
               (ii) Warriors
               (iii) Masses – concerned with material goods - merchants, farmers, artisans
   c) Read excerpts from his *Meditations*.
      i) How can you tell Marcus Aurelius is a Stoic from his famous writing, *Meditations*?
   d) What kind of a father will he be do you think?
3) Commodus, his son, spent his time at the gladiatorial schools. Result? > crude

    a) "Marcus was too good to be great enough to discipline or to renounce him; he kept on hoping that education and responsibility would sober him and make him grow into a king" (Durant, *Caesar and Christ*, p. 430).

    b) Of whom does this remind us? (Tiberius and Caligula)

4) *Principles*:

    a) Proverbs 22: 6 "Train a child in the way he should go, and when he is old he will not turn from it."

    b) Proverbs 13:20 "He who walks with the wise grows wise, but a companion of fools suffers harm."

    c) Can you think of other Bible verses that apply to Commodus/childrearing?

        i) Proverbs 30: 17 "The eye that mocks a father, that scorns obedience to a mother, will be pecked out by the ravens of the valley, will be eaten by the vultures."

5) What does the Bible say about national security and childrearing?

    a) Read Psalm 127.

    b) Who wrote this psalm? (Solomon)

    c) Who was his famous brother? (Absalom)

    d) What had Absalom done to their father David? (Absalom dishonored his father David – 2 Samuel 15: Absalom "would get up early and stand by the side of the road leading to the city gate. Whenever anyone came with a complaint to be placed before the king for a decision A. would call out to him, 'What town are you from?' He would answer, 'Your servant is from one of the tribes of Israel.' Then Absalom would say to him, 'Look, your claims are valid and proper, but there is no representative of the kings to hear you.' And A. would add, 'If only I were appointed judge in the land! Then everyone who has a complaint or case could come to me and I would see that he gets justice.'" . . . A. would kiss strangers, he "stole the hearts of the men of Israel," eventually declared himself king in Hebron, turned against his father, battled him, yet David instructs his men to be gentle with Absalom.)

    e) Where does national security lie, according to Solomon and the Bible? (the Lord's care (vv. 1-2); not in humanistic solutions (v.1), superior technology, or materialism (v.2); in the manner of childrearing (vv. 3-5))

6) What do you see in today's culture that encourages you about our future national security? That alarms you about our future national security?

7) Why is Rockbridge teaching you to *think* in the dialectic stage?

Assess:

1) Do you agree with the following quote from the famous historian Edward Gibbon regarding this period:

    a) *"If a man were called upon to fix a period in the history of the world during which the condition of the human race was most happy and prosperous, he would without hesitation name that which elapsed from the succession of Nerva to the death of Aurelius. Their united reigns are possibly the only period of history in which the happiness of a great people was the sole object of government."* Durant, *Caesar and Christ*, 425

2) What is significant about 180AD? (end of *Pax Romana*) Who came to power? (Commodus) What questions naturally came to mind about this fact? (Why did the *Pax Romana* end? How did it end? What changed exactly? Was there war?) (*Answer*: Commodus began the "Period of Decline.")

3) How would you describe the years 96-180AD in the Roman Empire? (military emphasis, emperors' power increased, Senate's power decreased)

4) *What was good about the good emperors?*

    a) treated ruling classes with respect

    b) cooperated with senate

    c) ended arbitrary executions

    d) maintained peace in the empire

    e) supported domestic policies that were beneficial to the empire

5) *What was bad about the good emperors?*

    a) Trajan and Marcus Aurelius persecuted Christians or allowed the persecution of Christians.

    b) Marcus Aurelius' beliefs about childrearing

Essay Question in December: When did the Roman Empire begin to fall?

Wednesday

Objective: The students will determine multiple trends as they hear the "roll call" of the emperors from 180-305AD in the Roman Empire.

Principles:
- o Proverbs 3: 5 "Trust in the Lord with all you heart and lean not on your own understanding; in all your ways acknowledge him and he will make your paths straight."
- o Proverbs 22: 6 "Train a child in the way he should go, and when he is old he will not turn from it."
- o Proverbs 13:20 "He who walks with the wise grows wise, but a companion of fools suffers harm."
- o Mark 3:25 "If a house is divided against itself, that house cannot stand."

Review:
- o What method of childrearing did Marcus Aurelius employ? (*laissez-faire*)

Questions:
- ▪ What do you forecast will be the result for Commodus? (dissipation; assassination)
- ▪ For the Empire? (decline)

Lesson: **Commodus and the Dawn of Disorder: The Roman Empire in Decline (180-305AD)**

Students' Task: Listen to brief biographies of many of the emperors, make observations, and then identify several general trends in the decline of the Roman Empire on an outline, provided by the teacher.
- a) Military-selected emperors
- b) Emperors are military men themselves.
- c) Often the emperor was assassinated by his successor.
- d) Family assassinations reappear.
- e) Short reigns
- f) Various backgrounds of emperors
    - i) Septimius Severus – lst African
    - ii) Macrinus – a Moor
    - iii) Maximinus the Thracian – Thracian peasant
- g) By the mid-3rd century AD, the Roman Empire was entirely on the *defensive* in a desperate fight for its existence.
- h) Blame is increasingly placed on whom for the barbarian invasions? Remember one of the arguments pagan critics had. (Christians. In the 5th century, Augustine will pen an immense rebuttal of this charge in his *City of God*.)

Assess:
- ✓ What are the trends marking the decline of the Roman Empire? (decline; increasing emphasis on military and defense as the barbarians make greater inroads)
- ✓ What do you think will happen next? (fall of Empire? Not yet. Diocletian/Constantine; the rise of Christendom)

Thursday

Objectives: The students will update their timelines, review for their test, and continue their analysis of Commodus' reign.

Collect short Greco-Roman Philosophy paper.

Lesson: **Timelines; Review for Test**
- *1)* *Timelines* – Review the timeline of Ancient Rome from 753BC to 180AD.
- *2)* *Summation/Review:*
    - a. Review study guide for test.
    - b. The Jewish Revolt (66-73AD)

      i. What occurred in 70AD? (burning of the Temple; destruction of Jerusalem)

     ii. *Why was the Temple destroyed?* (Jesus prophesied it; the Jews rejected Jesus; they knew not the time of His visitation; animal sacrifice no longer required.)

    iii. *Why hasn't the Temple been rebuilt?* (Jesus' prophecy of destruction; John 2:9 *Jesus* is the temple; 1 Cor.:19 "*Your body* is the temple of the Holy Spirit who is in you"; Eph 2:19-22 *God's people* are the temple; Rev 11:19 *God's temple in heaven,* ark of the covenant)

    iv. What was left of worship for the Jews from 70AD to this day?
  1. synagogue, but no temple
  2. rabbis, but no priests
  3. prayers, but no sacrifice

     v. *Contrast* the religion of Judaism to the relationship Christians have with Christ.

  c. Greco-Roman Philosophy (c. 300BC)
      i. Review charts.

  d. The Five Good Emperors (96-180AD)
      i. Review salient points about each emperor's reign and character.

Friday

Objective: The students will read a brief history as well as accounts of the persecution of Christians, thus building their understanding of God's purposes in the persecution of Christians during the first four centuries AD.

Review: What multiple trends in the Roman Empire's "Period of Decline" (180-305AD) do you recall?
  a) Military-selected emperors
  b) Military emperors
  c) Assassinations by successors
  d) Family assassinations
  e) Short reigns
  f) Various backgrounds of emperors – African, Moor, Thracian
  g) By the mid-3rd century AD, the Roman Empire entirely on the *defensive*
  h) Blame for the barbarian invasions increasingly placed on Christians *and atheists.* (In the 5th century, Augustine will pen an immense rebuttal of this charge in his *City of God*.)
  i) *New*: Increased taxes to fund defense
  j) *New*: Increased Germanic leadership in military and government (over time)

Principles:
  ➢ God's purposes were to purify and increase the church.
    o There is a time for every purpose under heaven. Ecclesiastes 3:3b "a time to tear down and a time to build
    o Ecclesiastes 3:11 "He has made everything beautiful in its time."
    o Matthew 5:10 "Blessed are those who are persecuted because of righteousness, for theirs is the kingdom of heaven"
    o Matthew 10: 18, 28 "On my account you will be brought before governors and kings as witnesses to them and to the Gentiles. But when they arrest you, do not worry about what to say or how to say it. At that time you will be given what to say, for it will not be you speaking, but the Spirit of your Father speaking through you."
    o Tertullian: The blood of the Christians is the seed of the church." (written in Commodus' time)
  ➢ True Christianity brings civil and religious freedom.
  ➢ The best way to study history is to read the Bible.
    o Make time for God and His Word.
      ▪ Immerse yourself in it that your mind may be renewed for "Then you will be able to test and approve what God's will is – His good, pleasing and perfect will" (Romans 12: 2)

Lesson: **The Roman Empire: Early Persecution of the Church**

1) Traditional Roman religion was inextricably intertwined with social and political purposes. (Demonstrate braiding of three ribbons: red-Roman religion; blue-Roman society; white – Roman politics.)

2) What is piety (*pietas*) to the Romans? (honoring of family => honoring of ROME; remember *paterfamilias*)

3) How did the Romans categorize the early church?
   a) The Romans interpreted the early church through their understanding of associations/societies and clubs. Words used to describe Christian gatherings, but were not a "fit" for this religion:
      i) occupational society
      ii) burial society
      iii) religious society
      iv) political club *(hetaeria)*

4) Pliny, Tacitus, and Suetonius defined Christianity as a superstition ("impiety").
   a) *superstitio*- < Latin. "to stand beyond"
   b) superstition = belief/practices that were strange and foreign to the Romans (i.e., the Eastern cults that had penetrated the Roman Empire)

5) Why were Christians a threat to Rome? (Why would this separation, this "in this world but not of it" stance, threaten Roman emperors?)
      i) Social and political - Christianity was separate from traditional Roman religion, Roman society, and Roman politics and thus threatened the very fabric of society and government control.
      ii) Political - Halted emperor worship from this sector.
      iii) Economic - Decreased the sales of victims for sacrifice.
      iv) CHRISTIANITY IS NOT A NATIONAL RELIGION.

6) *Note*: Not worshiping other gods or not worshipping the imperial cult was treason punishable by death.

7) What was the test that Christians were forced to take?
   a) Bring in statues of Trajan and Capitoline gods (Jupiter, Juno, Minerva)
   b) Answer, "Are you a Christian?"
      (1) If "yes," they were executed. What is a *martyr*?
         (a) **martyr** – < Gk. a witness; one who is killed for his faith
            (i) Are suicide bombers martyrs?
               ▪ Dying to save self?
               ▪ Dying for one's beliefs?
      ii) If "no," they were tested.
         (1) forced to call upon the gods,
         (2) make an offering of wine and incense to the emperor's statue,
         (3) curse Christ, and thus become apostate. What is an *apostate*?
            (a) **apostate** - < L. "stand away" a person who under pressure gives up his religion/beliefs (n., adj.)

8) What was the pagans' goal? (*to exterminate Christians and Christianity*)

9) What were God's purposes? (*to purify and increase the church*)

10) Definition of *persecution*
   a) <L. *secut* – to follow. "close pursuit to oppress with injury or punishment for adhering to principles or religious faith"

11) View map of "Expansion of Christianity in the 2nd Century."

12) Treatment of the individual - Greeks and Romans trampled the individual, whereas Christianity taught and acknowledged him. Worship was voluntary, not compulsory.

13) *Key People*
   i) Martyrs
      (1) Who was **Ignatius**, to what did he compare himself before he was martyred, and why is this profound? (Bishop of Antioch, during Trajan's reign, first Christian martyred in the Colosseum. He heard the lions roaring and said, "I am the wheat of Christ: I am going to

be ground with the teeth of wild beasts, that I may be found pure bread." (Foxe) To what is he comparing himself? (communion/Christ)

(a) Another version: compared himself to wheat (*"I am the grain of the field and must needs be ground by the teeth of lions to become as bread fit for the Master's table"*)

(2) Who was **Polycarp** and what were the circumstances of his martyrdom? (Pius Antoninus' reign (had nothing to do with martyring Christians) - *bishop of Smyrna, burned at stake; couldn't be burned initially/similar to fiery furnace; sweet fragrance!*)

ii) **Tertullian** (*c. 160-225, Christian Latin writer*): "The blood of the Christians is the seed of the church." What time do you think this was written? (*during Commodus' reign*)

iii) **Perpetua** – Famous female martyr of the early church in Carthage during Septimius Severus' reign

iv) **St. Alban** – first martyr in England (200s AD)

14) Handout: "How Did the Early Christians Describe Themselves?"
   a) Epistle to Diognetes, c. 130AD
   b) From the Apology of Tertullian, 197AD

15) Handout on "The Era of Persecution"

16) There were 10 waves of persecution, beginning with Emperor Nero and ending with Diocletian.
   a) Nero
   b) Domitian
   c) Trajan
   d) Marcus Aurelius
   e) Septimius Severus (African emperor - Perpetua was martyred during his reign.)
   f) Maximinus
   g) Decius – entire empire
   h) Valerian
   i) Aurelian
   j) Diocletian – entire empire

17) What does Matthew in the Bible say will happen when/if we are arrested/presented before governors to testify to our faith? (*the Holy Spirit will provide us the words*)

18) Read accounts of the persecution of Christians.
   a) Perpetua
      i) Ignatius & Polycarp (Bible class)

19) View photographs of the catacombs.

Assess:
   ✓ Why were Christians persecuted from the pagans' point of view?
   ✓ From God's point of view?

Quote: John Foxe's *Book of Martyrs,* referring to Christ's building "His church so strong that the gates of hell should not prevail against it." In which words three things are to be noted:

o First, that Christ will have a Church in this world.
o Secondly, that the same Church should mightily be impugned, not only by the world, but also by the uttermost strength and powers of all hell.
o And, thirdly, that the same church, notwithstanding the uttermost of the devil and all his malice, should continue."

Sources: Wilken, *The Christians as the Romans Saw Them,* C.S. Lewis Institute's *Knowing & Doing* newsletter, Foxe's *Book of Martyrs*

Review:
   o Review the timeline of Ancient Rome from 753BC to 180AD.
   o What method of childrearing did Marcus Aurelius employ? (*laissez-faire*)
   o Identify several general trends in the decline of the Roman Empire.
      (a) Military-selected emperors
      (b) Emperors are military men themselves.
      (c) Often the emperor was assassinated by his successor.

      (d) Family assassinations reappear.
      (e) Short reigns
      (f) Various backgrounds of emperors
          (i) Septimius Severus – 1st African
          (ii) Macrinus – a Moor
          (iii) Maximinus the Thracian – Thracian peasant

- By the mid-3rd century AD, the Roman Empire was entirely on the *defensive* in a desperate fight for its existence.
- Blame is increasingly placed on whom for the barbarian invasions? Remember one of the arguments pagan critics had. (Christians. In the 5th century, Augustine will pen an immense rebuttal of this charge in his *City of God*.)

Assess:

- What are the trends marking the decline of the Roman Empire? (decline; increasing emphasis on military and defense as the barbarians make greater inroads)
- What do you think will happen next? (fall of Empire? Not yet. Diocletian/Constantine; the rise of Christendom)

Next week:

- ❖ Early Persecution of the Church/Mutations in the Visible Church: Hierarchalism
  - Sacerdotalism & Clerical Celibacy (Church History class to cover)
- ❖ **Jewish Revolt/Greco-Roman Philosophy/Five Good Emperors Test**
- ❖ Deterioration of the Roman Empire & Its Reorganization under Diocletian
- ❖ Overview of Debating; Debate Videotape
- ❖ Debate Preparation: *Resolved: That there should be one official language in America*

Appendix H
Vision Statement Model

We aim to graduate young men and women who think clearly and listen carefully with discernment and understanding; who reason persuasively and articulate precisely; who are capable of evaluating their entire range of experience in the light of the Scriptures; and who do so with eagerness in joyful submission to God. We desire them to recognize cultural influences as distinct from biblical, and to be unswayed towards evil by the former. We aim to find them well prepared in all situations, possessing both information and the knowledge of how to use it. We desire they be socially graceful and spiritually gracious; equipped with and understanding the tools of learning; desiring to grow in understanding, yet fully realizing the limitations and foolishness of the wisdom of this world. We desire they have a heart for the lost and they distinguish real religion from religion in form only; and that they possess the former knowing and loving the Lord Jesus Christ. We desire them to possess all of these with humility and gratitude to God.

We likewise aim to cultivate these same qualities in our staff and to see them well paid so that they may make a career at [school]. We desire them to be professional and diligent in their work, gifted in teaching, loving their students and their subjects. We desire they clearly understand classical education, how it works in their classroom, and how their work fits into the whole; that they possess a lifelong hunger to learn and grow; and that they have opportunity to be refreshed and renewed. We desire to see them coach and nurture new staff and to serve as academic mentors to students. We look to see them mature in Christ, grow in the knowledge of God, training their own children to walk with the Lord.

We aim to cultivate in our parents a sense of responsibility for the school; to see them well informed about the goals of our classical and Christ-centered approach. We desire them to grow with the school, involved in and excited about the journey. We aim to help them follow biblical principles in addressing concerns, to be inclined to hear both sides of a story before rendering a verdict, and to embrace the Scripture's injunctions to encourage and stir up one another to love and good works.

Finally, in our relationship with our community, we aim to be above reproach in our business dealing and supportive of the local business community. We further seek to exemplify the unity of the body of Christ, to develop greater fellowship and understanding with the churches, and to bring honor to our Lord in all our endeavors.

April 28, 2008

To: ECCS Teachers

Re: Summative Classroom Observations

I will be visiting in your classroom soon to conduct summative teacher evaluations.

The purpose of this summative evaluation is to report on how the teacher has improved his/her skills and effectiveness on the job over the course of the school year. Constructive summations, accolades, and commendations will be made following the classroom observation to encourage the teacher's growth and mastery of subject matter and skills. The goal is to motivate teachers to continue their successes in teaching classically and leading spiritually.

Please fill out the attached Pre-Observation Data Sheet and place in my box at least the day prior to your observation. Please contact me as soon as possible if there is a scheduling conflict.

You may schedule a time after school or during your break to meet with me the following week in order to go over your observation evaluation together. Otherwise, a copy will be placed in your mailbox for your records.

This has been an outstanding year!

Thank you for a job well done,

Pamela E. McKee

Principal, ECCS

Pre-Observation Data Sheet

Teacher: _____ Date: _____

I would like to visit your class on, _____ during the hours of

_____ (approximately ½ hour total). Subject:_____

***Please complete the following questions and return this form to my mailbox at
least one day prior to your observation:***

Where are you in this course or unit (unit, lesson, card number, etc.)? _____

_____

_____

(You may copy this form to complete the following questions for each subject being covered.)

What is the <u>topic or concept</u> to be presented today? _____

_____

_____

Is this a new, review, or extension lesson? _____

List at least three <u>objectives</u> of today's lesson: _____

_____

_____

How will you determine if the objectives were achieved? _____

_____

_____

What <u>classical methodologies</u> will you use to achieve the objectives? _____

_____

_____

_____

What <u>materials</u> will you use to reinforce the lesson and teach to each learning style?

_____

_____

What will you do to provide <u>biblical integration</u> during the lesson? _____

_____

_____

Are there any special problems/students that I should be aware of in observing this class?

_____

_____

_____

Observation Report List

Items   Comments/Recommendations

Instruction:

☐ Evidence of in-depth knowledge of subject
☐ Teaching to objectives
☐ Relating activities to objectives
☐ Biblical integration of lesson
☐ Observance of individual differences in students
☐ Keeping students on task
☐ Evidence that students understand what is being taught
☐ Using the Socratic method of teaching
☐ Integration of classical methodology
☐ Prior research of subject matter
☐ Outside resources collected and used
☐ Other (specify)

Environment:

☐ Appearance of room
☐ Cleanliness of room
☐ Physical arrangement of furniture
☐ Creativeness and appropriate use of bulletin boards/wall space
☐ Climate for learning
☐ Organization of teacher desk/papers/trays
☐ Other (specify)

Management/logistics:

☐ Class management
☐ Handling behavior problems
☐ Rapport with students
☐ Coping with unforeseen events
☐ Opening of lesson
☐ Closing of lesson
☐ Transition between lessons
☐ Making assignments
☐ Use of multi-media/kinesthetic materials
☐ Use of outside resources (special guests)

ECCS Classroom Observations

Date: **March 10, 2009**

Teacher: -----

Subject: Spelling/Math   GRAMMAR LEVEL

1. Was the classroom setting appropriate to the age and development of the student? *Yes*
2. Was the classroom decorated seasonally and according to prescribed instructions? *Yes—Happy Easter bulletin board*
3. Were lesson plans/assignments followed as stated on Renweb?
4. Did the lesson follow the ECCS Scope & Sequence?
5. Were all students engaged? *Yes*
6. Were all students called upon for verbal communication? *No, please draw names to call on all students*
7. Were all students attending and on task? *Yes, see note below* *
8. Were there any discipline issues and how were they addressed? *None observed*
9. What visuals were used to teach the visual learner? *Teacher drawing on board; Tangram card*
10. Was appropriate information given to teach to the verbal learner? *Work on clarity. Good definitions from books.*
11. What aids were used for the kinesthetic learner? *Bags of letters and Cheese-it letters; Play-doh*
12. Was appropriate "movement" interjected within the lesson? *Yes—good.*
13. Did the teacher challenge the cognitive learner? *This could have been stronger—just add more questions—require them to think. (Example: "Who can put this into their own words?" "Where else do we see symmetry in nature?" "Let's look at some examples of what isn't symmetrical."*
14. What resources were utilized throughout the lesson to encourage cognition, curiosity or research? *Math book. Could have used a mirror, other animal photos, and/or other examples of symmetry.*
15. Was higher-level thinking skills sought, encouraged, and expressed? *?*
16. What worldview was presented? *?*
17. What scripture was used to connect truth to the lesson? *Ps. 19 and Bible trivia*
18. How will this information be used in their daily lives? What is the connection to their personal lives and was this discussed? *Teacher connected spelling words to literature book—good!*
19. What was the "main point" of the lesson taught? *Constellations and symmetry*
20. Was the lesson presented on grade level? *Yes*
21. Did the assignments represent quality of thought and good use of time? *Yes*
22. How was the information introduced into memory?
Student recitation of Phonogram sound-off—very good.

23. What other classical methodologies were employed? *?*
24. Did the structure of this lesson facilitate student learning/ownership of the information? *I hope so, except for mental math.*

25. What was the standard of collaboration among students? *Groups of four students created spelling words with paper letters*
26. How might the students describe this lesson? *fun*
27. What point of integration was made? *Connected spelling words to literature and science.*

* Notes: *Please keep a close watch on Student X's progress. She seemed to consistently look on her neighbor's paper and did not sing along on any of the songs or read the science paragraphs. She also copied Student Y's mental math answers. She is so quiet; these issues could be easily overlooked.*

- <u>Strengths</u> recognized during this observation:
1. *Good elements chosen to strengthen spelling skills*
2. *Very strong kinesthetic elements in the lessons—loved the cheese-its!*
3. *Good use of time and white boards*
   - <u>Improvements</u> to be made for future lessons:
1. *In spelling game, do not give students the words, but rather have a spelling list available to them and perhaps give the first letter of their words or the number of letters within their words.*

2. *Please work on improved communication/clarity—teacher's instructions were slow, extended, and unclear. Be very deliberate and specific with wording and instructions. (Example: "Students today our helpers are passing out play-doh to each of you and I'd like for you to mold your play-doh into a star shape. Here is an example.")*

3. *Speak louder and with authority. (Teacher said, "As you are cleaning up Nicolas and Grant will take up the science binders as we say our math facts." No one moved. Teacher had to ask them again to stand and recite the math facts.)*

4. *Please plan a peer-observation to Mrs. Murdaugh and Mrs. Wade's classroom.*

5. *Mental math must all be "mental"—no pencils and no problems written on the board*

6. *Are you using the "Word of the Day"?*

Thank you for the good teaching you are doing. Your choice of elements and activities was excellent. Please work on the points mentioned above and you will achieve the very effective lesson for which you are aiming.

Appendix K

The Geneva School Leadership Team
2017-2018 Playbook

Six Critical Questions:

1) *Why do we exist?*
   a. We exist because students need an education that orders their loves and renews their minds in preparation for service in the Kingdom of God.

2) *How do we behave?* (Core Values)
   a. We cultivate an educational community of faith and learning within the Christian, liberal arts tradition.

3) *What do we do?*
   a. As a community of learners, we study, re-imagine, and teach within the Christian, liberal arts tradition.

4) *How will we succeed?* (Strategic Anchors)
   a. We re-imagine and embody the richest practices of Christian, liberal arts culture, curricula, and pedagogy.
   b. We educate each constituency of the school community (board, administration, faculty, staff, parents, students, prospective families, friends of Geneva) regarding our purpose and core values.
   c. We leverage the student experience for the purpose of dignifying each student, fostering educational growth, spurring retention, and boosting recruitment.

5) *What is most important right now?* Study and Celebrate the renewal of the Christian, liberal arts model
   a. Defining Objectives (DOs)
      i. Develop consensus as an administrative team about the meaning of the model
      ii. Develop tracks for new students so they can take courses that align with the model, including a process for admissions and student services to work together to place new students in the right courses
      iii. Review our course/school schedule, starting with math, writing and Latin, in light of the model to increase flexibility so new students do not miss classes that are foundational to the model and current students are fit well to classes
      iv. Effectively communicate the decisions we make related to the model as well as the meaning of the model to faculty, parents, and students
      v. Celebrate our 25th anniversary well
   b. Standard Operating Objectives (SOOs)
      i. Building plans and ground-breaking/athletic fields (*Name of person/people responsible, and so forth throughout the SOO section*)
      ii. Director level leadership development
      iii. Parent education and communication
      iv. Parent community and trust building
      v. Staff and faculty morale
      vi. Long-term subs for faculty leaving during school year
      vii. Student experience
      viii. Retention and recruitment

  ix. Annual fund

  x. Technology practices and upper school curricula mapping

  xi. Pedagogy, curricula, and scheduling – implementing the model

  xii. Revise the professional development and evaluation model to better align with our playbook and our mission statements

  xiii. Begin implementation of the Mastery Transcript model

  xiv. Launch the campaign to raise $$$ for the upper school building

  xv. Revise and fully implement the discipline code across K4-12th

  xvi. Develop trust and partnerships with faculty and staff to increase support for the admissions process

  xvii. Provide support for new teachers so they flourish as they learn our culture and practices

  xviii. Develop and implement strategic faculty and staff hiring plans

  xix. Other topics: international students, college credit courses

6) *Who must do what?*

Headmaster	
Dean of Students	
Academic Dean	
Dean of Faculty	
Director of Advancement	
Director of Early Childhood	
Director of Admission	
Director of Student Services	
Athletic Director	
Director of IT	
Controller	

Leadership Team Meetings

1. *Daily Check-in*: 5-10 minute standing meeting
2. *Tactical Staff Meeting*: weekly; quick reports, review DOs and SOOs, end with action items and communication plan
3. *Ad-hoc Topical/Strategic Meeting*: as-needed meetings to address one or two critical issues, end with action items and communication plan
4. *Quarterly Off-Site Reviews*: one or two days, review 4 disciplines and the "6 Critical Questions"*

*Six Critical Questions: Patrick Lencioni's *The Advantage* (2012).

Questions for Post-Observation Conference

Teacher's Name: _____ Date: _____

How do you think the lesson went during the observation?

What were you especially pleased about during the observation?

What happened during the lesson that you would have liked to change?

If you were doing this lesson again, would you do it the same way?

What measures would you take to change the above situation?

Please make any comments that you would like regarding any circumstances or situations that occurred during the observation visit.

Please make the following improvements/changes for the next observation:

_____
_____
_____
_____
_____
_____

BCS Pre-Observation Data Sheet

Dear BCS Teacher,

The following questions will inform me during your upcoming classroom observation. This observation will be based on the principles presented in John Milton Gregory's book, <u>The Seven Laws of Teaching</u>. Please be as specific as possible as you complete this form. <u>Please email or place a copy of the completed form in my mailbox prior to your scheduled observation.</u>

<u>Thank you!</u>

Teacher's Name:

1. What is the topic/subject?

2. What main concept/s will be presented?

3. Is this a new, review, or extension lesson?

4. Where are you in this course/Sc. & Seq. (unit, week, lesson, page numbers in text, etc.)?

5. Are you on schedule with the Scope & Sequence?
    a. Yes ☐ No ☐ If not, please explain:

6. What are the main objectives for this lesson?
    a.
    b.
    c.

7. How will you prepare to teach this lesson? (Law #1)

8. What elements/resources will you include in this lesson to ensure that you are teaching to the four learning styles?

    a. Verbal:
    b. Auditory:
    c. Visual:
    d. Kinesthetic:
9. How will you gain the students attention? (Law #2)
    Give details of an effective anticipatory set:

10. What prior knowledge will be included? (Law #3)

11. What vocabulary or other medium will be introduced or reviewed to ensure a common understanding to both teacher and learner? (Law #4)

12. What means will be used to inspire the learners? (spiritually and/or intellectually) (Law #5)

13. How will the students be required to apply the knowledge learned? (Law #6)

14. What questions will you ask to promote higher-level thinking skills?

15. How will you determine if the objectives were achieved? When? (Law #7)

16. What resources or other materials will you use?

17. What biblical integration will be included in the lesson?

18. What classical methodologies will you use during this lesson?

19. Are there any special problems or needs that I should be aware of in observing this class?

20. How can I help to make this observation more comfortable or beneficial to you?

Thank you! I look forward to visiting your class!

Pre-Observation Data Sheet

(6th Grade Math)   **GRAMMAR LEVEL**

Please be very specific as you complete this form, and please place it in my mailbox at least one day prior to your scheduled observation.

1. What is the topic/subject? *Math- Mixed Numbers and Improper Fractions*
2. What main concept will be presented? *How to convert mixed numbers to improper fractions and vice versa*
3. Is this a new, review, or extension lesson? *New for this chapter, however students should recall this topic from previous years of math.*
4. Where are you in this course/Sc. & Seq. (unit, week, lesson, page numbers in text, etc.)? *Chapter 4, Sec. 4.6, pgs. 194-198 – Week 8-9*
5. Are you on schedule with the Scope & Sequence?
   a. Yes ☐ No *X* If not, please explain:
      I am behind by one week due to a half day missed for my class and two days of re-teaching different topics so far this quarter.
6. What are the main objectives for this lesson?
   a. *Students will be able to change fractions from improper to mixed numbers and vice versa.*
   b. *Students will be able to explain how an improper fraction is made into a mixed number through use of manipulatives.*
   c. *Students will be able to understand the importance of changing fractions into improper from a mixed number for ordering of fractions.*
7. How will you prepare to teach this lesson? (Law #1) *Review of material is essential for any lesson, but for this topic I chose a new activity so practicing and playing out in my head and physically the activity is key to make sure that it will convey what I want it to for the students.*
8. What elements/resources will you include in this lesson to ensure that you are teaching to the four learning styles?
   a. *Verbal: asking questions for them to answer about how mixed numbers are different from improper and why it is needed to change them.*
   b. *Kinesthetic: having the students move into groups and then place objects in a particular order*
   c. *Auditory: give the students explanations about what we will be doing and learning in the class for the day at the beginning and then confirm again at the end what we have learned.*
   d. *Visual: Showing procedure on the whiteboard in colors of how the process works to convert the fractions.*
9. How will you gain the students attention? (Law #2)
   Give details of anticipatory set: After our regular procedures of beginning class with review of homework and quiz review then I will bring up a brown paper bag with our supplies for the activity in it. Questions for students will include, "How can you make a fraction into a whole something?" "Why do we need to make a fraction into a whole something?"

10. What prior knowledge will be included? (Law #3) *Prior knowledge of what a fraction looks like, numerator and denominator, and how to find common factors for making equivalent fractions, and also comparing and ordering fractions.*

11. What vocabulary or other medium will be introduced or reviewed to ensure a common understanding to both teacher and learner? (Law #4) *Reviewing the ordering of fractions will be important for this lesson to be thoroughly completed for assessment. Introduction of most terms, like proper and improper fractions and mixed numbers, will be review form previous years of math. Process for changing a mixed number into an improper fraction will be different from the text book demonstration due to a method I have taught in previous years.*

12. What means will be used to inspire the learners? (spiritually or intellectually) (Law #5) *Use of our scripture, Phil. 4:13, will be applied as many of the students are very hesitant when it comes to having to work fractions. Also the enthusiasm of an edible manipulative (marshmallows) will probably inspire them quite a lot!*

13. How will the students be required to apply the knowledge learned? (Law #6) *Students will be assessed through a take home worksheet for the actual processes. However in class students will demonstrate their knowledge through a group/partner explanation of their improper fractions found.*

14. What questions will you ask to promote higher-level thinking skills? *1. "How will changing fractions be important to things in real life?" 2. "How do you know through the use of the manipulatives that you have changed the fraction over correctly?"*

15. How will you determine if the objectives were achieved? When? (Law #7) *During class the students will be demonstrating with their manipulatives how they achieved a change of fractions, and through an assessment in the form of a worksheet for a homework assignment*

16. What resources or other materials will you use? *Marshmallows as the manipulatives, along with toothpicks and number cards. Homework Worksheet that is not from the textbook.*

17. What biblical integration will be included in the lesson? (Plan at least two.)
    a. *I will discuss the ways of fractions from Biblical times and how precise we have come to measure things and break them down to specific numbers or parts which leads into our topic for the next lesson, fractions into decimals.*
    b. *With math it is not a natural conversation of a Biblical sense of every topic covered however the overall theme and desire of my classroom is that all students know that even on the hard material "their strength is in Christ."*

18. What classical methodologies will you use during this lesson? (Plan at least two.)
    a. *Collaborative work in group*
    b. *Presentation of findings from group work*

19. Are there any special problems or needs that I should be aware of in observing this class? *There is a student who has auditory processing problems so to make sure that he is comprehending things I tend to be more by his side to help him out.*

Thank you! I look forward to visiting your class!

Pre-Observation Data Sheet

(completed by teacher)

Teacher's Name: -----   *Grade/Subject: Logic 7th Grade*   **LOGIC LEVEL**

Date of Observation: *3/16/16 Time of Observation: 10:36-11:23*

Please complete this form and place it in Mrs. McKee's mailbox at least one day prior to your scheduled observation.

What is the topic/subject to be taught? What main concept will be presented? Is this a new, review, or extension lesson?
The topic will be on immediate inferences. The main concept that is being taught is the three types of immediate inferences. This lesson is introducing new material.

Where are you in this course/Sc. & Seq. (unit, week, lesson, page numbers in text, etc.)? *I am on Unit 4: Week 24, Lesson 27, and page 195.*

What are the main objectives for this lesson?
 1.To understand the three types of immediate inferences 2. To understand how to correctly put a syllogism in standard categorical form from everyday language.
*3.*_____

What visuals, resources, or other materials will you use?
I plan to use the white board often and will implement syllogisms from everyday life.

What biblical integration will be included in the lesson?
I will allow them to practice immediate inferences on certain Bible passages.

What classical methodologies will you use during this lesson?
I will use the Socratic method throughout the lesson. Also I plan to continually call on and interact with their answers to Lesson 26. I also plan to integrate from Biblical passages into the mix as well.

How will you prepare to teach this lesson? (Law #1) *I will read over the lesson and will come up with extra syllogisms that will further incite their curiousity. I will also review previous concepts to make sure that I have a mastery to be able to explain them well.*

How will you gain the students attention? (Law #2)
I will gain their attention by writing a syllogism that they will not recognize at first. There will be issues in this syllogism that they will not be able to solve. This should gain their attention to see how to solve this.

What prior knowledge will be included? (Law #3)
The Students will have a prior knowledge of implication and inference. There will also be an assumed knowledge of syllogisms, categorical form, and the concept of distribution.

What vocabulary or other medium will be common to both teacher and learner? (Law #4)
The Letters of the Square of Opposition, the Square of Opposition, Distribution, Rules of Validity, and Standard Categorical Form.

What means will be used to inspire the learners? (Law #5)
I will seek to show everyday arguments that have immediate inferences. I hope to inspire the students to further see how the English language works and how two statements can be equivalent to one another.

How will the students be required to apply the knowledge learned? (Law #6)
They will complete Exercise 26 and to see their comprehension of the Lesson.

How will you determine if the objectives were achieved? (Law #7)
We will complete Exercise 26 as a class and will ask them questions to make sure that they have mastered the lesson. Also, as the lesson is going along, I will test the student's knowledge by calling them up to the whiteboard. We will complete additional problems at a later date as well. There will also be testing over the material at a later date.

Are there any special problems of which I should be aware?

Is there anything that I can do during this observation to make you feel more comfortable? *No.*

What was the class average (GPA) for this subject during the previous quarter? *88.7*

Please have an extra copy of all class work sheets and texts for my perusal.

Thank you!

BCS Pre-Observation Data Sheet

___

Dear BCS Teacher,
The following questions will inform me during your upcoming classroom observation. This observation will be based on the principles presented in John Milton Gregory's book, <u>The Seven Laws of Teaching</u>. Please be as specific as possible as you complete this form. <u>Please email or place a copy of the completed form in my mailbox prior to your scheduled observation.</u>

<u>Thank you!</u>

Teacher's Name: ----- **RHETORIC LEVEL**

1. What is the topic/subject?
    The nature of the "after life" and how it should impact our lives on earth.
2. What main concept will be presented?
    The soul does not cease to exist in death, and the afterlife is not a state of unreality, but is in fact more real than this life; Christians believe that the soul (spirit) will one day be reunited with the body in resurrection, and there will be a new heaven and earth.
3. Is this a new, review, or extension lesson?
    In a way, this is new material for the students to be discussing from their previous night's reading, but the dialogue they have been reading has been building up to these ideas.
4. Where are you in this course/Sc. & Seq. (unit, week, lesson, page numbers in text, etc.)?
    I am in week 26 of my scope and sequence in the Plato unit.
5. Are you on schedule with the Scope & Sequence?
    a. Yes ☐ No *X* If not, please explain:
    Truly, my planning for this year was a bit ambitious, and I didn't have much to go on from previous years. I saw that we wouldn't have time to read all of the Republic (and that my students needed a break), so I rearranged my scope and sequence. They still needed to read some Plato and become acquainted with his philosophy, so I exchanged reading the whole Republic for selections from the Republic and some dialogues from The Last Days of Socrates. I plan to make these adjustments official for next year's revised Scope and Sequence.
6. What are the main objectives for this lesson?
    a. *Students will understand Socrates' view of life and the afterlife.*
    b. *Students will evaluate Socrates' view of the afterlife and contrast it with the Christian view.*
    c. *Students will be able to articulate the purpose of death and resurrection in the Christian worldview.*
7. How will you prepare to teach this lesson? (Law #1)
    I will review the reading that they have done for homework and look to other source's interpretation of the work. I will review, study, and pray over the passages in scripture that discuss death and the afterlife.
8. What elements/resources will you include in this lesson to ensure that you are teaching to the four learning styles?
    a. Verbal: *Much of the lesson will be a question and answer type of discussion.*
    b. Kinesthetic: *I will ask students to take personal notes, write on the board for me, and draw important concepts on the board as we discuss.*
    c. Auditory: *We will read aloud important passages for students to listen to, and students will listen to discussion.*

    d. Visual: *Aside from just writing on the board, we will draw pictures to illustrate passages from the reading.*

9. How will you gain the students attention? (Law #2)
Give details of an effective anticipatory set:
I will ask students to illustrate part (if not all) of how Socrates describes the structure of earth or something that happens in the afterlife. Students will have 3 minutes to work on these cartoons.

10. What prior knowledge will be included? (Law #3)
We will review what Socrates has said about the nature of the soul and the role of philosophy in preparing mankind for the afterlife. We will also refer back to Plato's allegory of the cave.

11. What vocabulary or other medium will be introduced or reviewed to ensure a common understanding to both teacher and learner? (Law #4)
We will discuss the term "myth" and what it means in the context of Socrates' "myth of the afterlife." I will explain that all of the literal details in a myth don't have to be true, but rather that myths strengthen and illustrate beliefs and doctrines.

We will also discuss the term "metanarrative," which is the over-arching story. The story that is above and at work in all of scripture is creation, fall, redemption, and consummation. We will discuss what all of these terms mean, especially consummation: the point at which something is made complete or finalized. (Latin: con= altogether + summa=sum total → consummatio=brought to completion) We will discuss how the resurrection of the body is the consummation of the gospel: through the resurrection our bodies are made perfect to dwell with God.

12. What means will be used to inspire the learners? (spiritually and/or intellectually) (Law #5)
Intellectually, I will (attempt) to urge the students to make sense of the reading with a question and answer time concerning their comprehension of the reading.

I will then ask them: must this myth be interpreted literally? (No... see definition of myth)

After having an intellectual understanding of the text, I will then ask students several questions in attempt to inspire them spiritually:

- *From a Christian perspective, why is there a need for judgement after death? Does punishment make God mean? Do you have a hard time understanding the need for justice and punishing sin?*
- *Has Socrates' description of the place of the afterlife helped you understand the Christian idea of death? How? Why is it that a pagan could help us understand Christian truths?*
- *What is wrong with Socrates view of what happens to souls after death? (Souls go on to no longer be associated with the body.) Why is our view of the resurrection so important? Consider the metanarrative of scripture*

We will then read 1 Corinthians 15:12-58 aloud and discuss.

13. How will the students be required to apply the knowledge learned? (Law #6)
They will have an oral interview assessment on Thursday in which they will be expected to be able to articulate answers concerning Socrates view of certain subjects and how they follow or depart from Christian thinking.

14. What questions will you ask to promote higher-level thinking skills?
I will ask them evaluative questions, as seen above. I will also ask them if they know what scripture says about death, the resurrection, and the new heavens and the earth. If they don't, they should go research it for their oral assessment tomorrow. I will also remind them of the follow questions again:
   - *How should our view of death impact our view of this life?*
   - *What is the metanarrative of scripture? How does death fit in with this concept (what role does it play)? [Answer: Creation, fall, redemption, consummation. Through death and resurrection, God will achieve consummation by uniting our souls with our new bodies and we will be reunited in a new heaven and earth.]*

15. How will you determine if the objectives were achieved? When? (Law #7)
I will see if their objectives are achieved based on their participation in discussion, the recap at the end of the class, and in the oral interview on Thursday.

16. What resources or other materials will you use?
The Internet Encyclopedia of Philosophy, the translation and notes from The Last Days of Socrates, the Bible (1 Corinthians 15, etc), and People of Mars Hill sermon notes.

17. What biblical integration will be included in the lesson?
The entire lesson will compare and contrast the Biblical views of life and death with the Platonic understanding of it.

18. What classical methodologies will you use during this lesson?
I will be using the dialectic method for the entirety of the lesson.

19. Are there any special problems or needs that I should be aware of in observing this class?
No, but I would remind you that I am meeting in Mr.Howard's classroom because of the 7th grade taking the SAT tests in my classroom.

Thank you! I look forward to visiting your class!

PRINCIPLES OF PARTNERSHIP

At Veritas, we believe learning can truly be a 'garden of delight', a place where young plants are given excellent nourishment, rich 'soil', and joyful encouragement. **Partnering with Christian parents who are growing in their faith, in the care of a church community, means that the minds and hearts of students are cultivated not only at school, but also at home and church.** We pray that in each setting, our students are being established and equipped to bear much fruit – for the glory of God and the good of others.

This partnership is at the very core of who we are as a community of faith and learning. By partnership, we mean we are in covenant with one another, and with God, in this shared vision and mission. The relationship between parent and school must be a cooperative and collaborative one for us to be successful.

As such, the Veritas partnership philosophy is based on three main ideas:

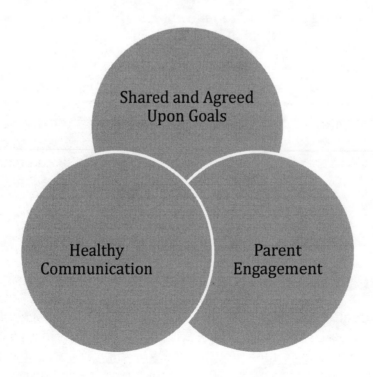

Appendix Q – Principles of Partnership – Veritas School

1. **Shared and Agreed Upon Goals**

   One of the beautiful things about a Veritas education is clearly established "telos" – meaning the purpose or end goal. We have a clear picture of what we want to be the outcome of a Veritas education. Therefore, we think in terms of working backwards from graduation all the way down to our youngest students. Everything we do flows out of what we call the "**Portrait of the Graduate**." In joining the Veritas community, families are agreeing on the primary objectives captured in that portrait.

   Besides the Portrait of the Graduate, we work hard to clearly communicate other priorities, goals, and objectives that are core to who we are. We are calling these our "**Core Commitments**". They include things like instruction in Latin and logic, the pursuit of the heart rather than just behavior, the value of great literature, art and music, the integration of disciplines, the cultivation of the affections, and so on.

   Together, these make up the "90%" that define us as a school and drive the curricular and co-curricular activities and programs. We will never all agree on the remaining "10%" and therefore we all have to compromise to some degree. Certainly, families will have a different preference as to the next language they want for their child, the sports they want offered, a uniform preference, or whether or not a snow day is called. When we use the term, the "**90% Rule**", we are saying that if you are aligned and in agreement with the 90%, we ask you to be understanding and gracious about the 10% that might not be your particular preference.

   If we are truly aligned on the major objectives, walking shoulder to shoulder in the same direction, we avoid much of the distraction and division that so often characterizes school communities.

2. **Healthy Communication**

   Partnering well requires healthy, biblical communication from everyone in our community. The school has to communicate clearly the goals and priorities mentioned above, teachers must communicate how a student is fairing - academically and otherwise, parents must communicate if they have questions or concerns. The Veritas Standard outlines principles and practices that we are all committed to in being a part of this community. We ask that parents and teachers pay particular attention to this section of the Standard both on an annual basis, and when a challenging situation arises.

   Normalizing Conflict

   The Gospel is clear: we are all sinners, fallen short of God's glory. We experience destructive conflict because we want what we do not have. As we seek to satisfy our desires, we may find others do not always cooperate with our plans. In the Veritas School environment, almost 500 men, women and students are brought together five days a week, seven hours a day. While not the defining experience of our life in community, conflict is neither abnormal nor to be avoided, but rather a welcome opportunity to examine our hearts, our desires, and how we seek their fulfillment. Because we believe the Gospel's indictment of our own hearts, we are neither shocked nor disheartened when conflict arises at school, but ready to open a conversation that moves beyond symptoms to the root cause. What a privilege to move together from conflict to peace-making, through the revealing, healing work of the Gospel!

In the Midst of Conflict

While understanding that conflict is a normal, and even helpful part of growing together, working through our disagreements can still be very difficult. With this in mind, we believe the following principles provide a helpful foundation as we seek mutual understanding and biblical reconciliation:

> *We will believe the best of one another, giving the benefit of the doubt when misunderstandings or miscommunications arise.*
>
> *Our goals are truth, restoration and partnership; these goals trump seeking vindication or one of us needing to be right. Conflict resolution is not a zero-sum game.*
>
> *We will remember that most conflicts are brought about by a confluence of peoples' sin rather than one sole contributor - a sinful act eliciting a sinful response. We will acknowledge that we all sin and that we don't know everything about any given situation.*
>
> *We will remember that both parental and school authority are not based on moral superiority but on position; before God we are all equally destitute and in need of a Savior. The Gospel helps us to be humble and vulnerable with one another, and points the way to reconciliation.*
>
> *When we feel the swell of self-defense, we will listen longer and/or ask a question rather than begin talking.*
>
> *We will apologize for the small issues that may have contributed to the conflict along the way to resolution of the bigger issue.*
>
> *When appropriate, we will give one another space and time to prayerfully consider the issue before us, without demanding immediate answers and resolution.*

3. **Parent Engagement**

Parent "engagement" might be a better term than parent "involvement" when describing the role parents play at Veritas. While involvement is important, the bigger issue is engagement. More than anything we want parents to be engaged – both in what your child is learning but also in the lives of those we are in community with. To be a part of Veritas is to not only partner with the school but to partner with the other families God has brought together in this important work.

Modeling

By God's design, parents are, by far, the most significant influence in a child's life. While Veritas School will consistently put before students that which is true, beautiful and good, will provide tools for a life of learning, will fill classrooms with faculty who love God and others, the daily witnessed practices of parents are far more important.

For the partnership between parents, church and school to be of greatest effect, the experience of each must be consistent, winsome, authentic and compelling. Children are keen observers. Hypocrisy, double-standards and inconsistency are deeply felt.

What do our children witness as we navigate conflicts with our spouse, neighbor, boss, pastor? How are we most entertained and who do we invite to dinner? Which books are dusty on the shelf and which do we read over and over? How do we speak of those in authority? Do we remain faithful to our commitments and how do we handle disappointment? How and how often do we seek forgiveness? Are we kind?

The truth is that we all – without exception – regularly fail our better selves, and those in our lives. In these moments, what do our watching children learn about God? About His grace and about making things right? Do they witness lives humbly submitted to the sanctifying work of Christ?

Veritas is not a perfect school seeking to partner with perfect parents who attend perfect churches. We do, however, desire to humbly seek to honor God and His good and perfect gifts by together giving attention to that which is praise-worthy.

Spreading Hope Network

Dan Olson, Executive Director, Hope Academy, Minneapolis, Minnesota

1) Making it transferrable.

2) Each school is independent...they are NOT Hope Academy.

3) *How can we come alongside & share what God has given to us?*

4) God has given much to us, & we have a responsibility to share that with others.

5) Fellows Program – invited to come learn, to self-implement.

6) Founders Group – Select 2 or 3 cities from the Fellows group.

    a. Work more intensively with them on a 3-year path

        i. Year before launch

        ii. Launch year

        iii. Year after launch

"Intentionality and the Legacy of Truth: Succession Planning Among ACCS Schools," Amy Shore, ACCS Conference 2019

"How can we ensure the survival of the classical Christian education movement for the coming generations?"

"Who will take these teachers' place when they are gone?"

"Covenantal succession is blending business forethought with gospel growth."

137 CCE schools were polled.

18.8% were involved in succession planning

62.3% had discussed it

7% already have a committee in place

3.5% already have a written succession plan

50 people in the survey have been a part of formal succession planning at their own school or at another school and could be a good base for networking to gain from their experience & wisdom.

For succession planning:

- Have a vision statement.
- Write down the "culture attributes you want to pass on."

Highlights of our School

Fourth Grade

BCS Fourth Graders study:

- Middle Ages, Renaissance, and Reformation
- Land Animals and Habitats
- Biblical Timeline of Chronicles through Malachi
- Language Arts subjects of Spelling, English Grammar, Writing, Poetry, and Cursive
- Literature books including: *The Twenty-One Balloons, Adam of the Road, Thunderstorm in the Church, Door in the Wall, The Best Christmas Pageant Ever, Prince Caspian, Crispin: The Cross of Lead, The Saturdays,* and *100 Cupboards*
- General mathematics using BJU Press Math 4
- Latin vocabulary, grammar, and translation passages

Field Trips

- Monastery Field Trip
- Humming Star Alpaca Farm Field Trip
- Jousting Tournament Field Trip
- Bay Minette Veteran's Home visit
- Monk Day Service Project

BCS Fourth Graders participate in:

- Weekly Chapel Services
- Latin Classes 4x per week furthering knowledge of verb tenses, adjectives, 2nd and 3rd noun declensions, pronouns, and adverbs
- PE Class 1x per week learning more about Archery, Basketball, Fitness Circuits, Soccer, Football, Volleyball, Running, and Softball
- Music class 1x per week learning music history, vocal technique, and music theory using recorders.
- Art Class 1x per week creating art in various mediums while studying Da Vinci, Illuminated Manuscripts, Weaving, Medieval Painting techniques, and Medieval architecture.
- Medieval Faire Day with costumes, student presentations, time period games, and a themed feast
- Spelling Bee & Geography Bee
- Owl Pellet dissection

Memory Work

- Scripture passages from Ephesians, Lamentations, 2 Chronicles, Isaiah, and James
- New City Catechism questions and answers
- Latin vocabulary, declensions, conjugations, etc.
- 30 History Songs summarizing dates, locations, and facts
- Math Facts
- Shurley Grammar Jingles
- Poetry selections such as
  - "Non Nobis Domine"
  - "The Destruction of Sennacharib"
  - "A Christmas Carol"
  - "The Vision of Belshazzar"
  - "The Reeds of Runnymede"

Revised 4/16/2018

CORE BELIEFS

Mission
Veritas exists to glorify God by cultivating students of wisdom and virtue through a Christ-centered, academically rigorous classical education.

Statement of Faith
Veritas is a non-denominational Christian school. We embrace the historic tenets of Christianity as presented in this Statement of Faith. Beyond these primary doctrines, we respect and acknowledge the primacy of the family and refer any secondary doctrinal questions to parents for clarification.

1. We believe there is one eternal God existing in three persons: Father, Son and Holy Spirit.
2. We believe the Bible is the Word of God, verbally inspired and inerrant, and is the supreme and final authority in faith and life.
3. We believe God created the Heavens and the Earth, and created man in His image.
4. We believe that God wonderfully and immutably creates each person as male or female. These two distinct, complementary genders together reflect the image and nature of God.
5. We believe that humankind, by disobedience, fell from a sinless state at the suggestion of Satan. This fall plunged humankind into a state of sin and spiritual death, and brought upon all humanity the sentence of eternal death. From this condition, regeneration by the Holy Spirit is absolutely necessary for salvation. By God's grace only, through faith alone, are we saved from our sin.
6. We believe Jesus Christ is God manifested in the flesh, born of a virgin; He lived a sinless life, suffered and died on our behalf, and He arose bodily from the grave, ascended to the right hand of the Father and is coming again in power and glory.
7. We believe faith without works is dead. The present ministry of the Holy Spirit is to indwell (live within) the Christian, enabling him to live a godly life.
8. We believe that God's design for marriage is the uniting of one man and one woman in a single, exclusive union, as delineated in Scripture. We believe that God intends sexual intimacy to occur only between a man and a woman who are married to each other.
9. We believe there will be a bodily resurrection of the saved to life and of the lost to damnation.
10. We believe that God offers redemption and restoration to all who confess and forsake their sin, seeking His mercy and forgiveness through Jesus Christ.

Educational Philosophy
At Veritas, we believe entwining a high standard of academic scholarship with authentic, grace-infused discipleship in a nurturing and joy-filled environment beautifully prepares students to discover their purpose and potential. Three concurrent commitments undergird and illumine our philosophy: 1) education via the **classical** method, 2) intentionally **Christ-centered** in curriculum and culture, 3) and in **covenant** with God, and in partnership with the school and one another.

By Classical we mean:

Appendix U - Veritas Academy Core Beliefs

The uniqueness of classical education primarily lies neither with the particular subjects pursued nor with the specific curriculum employed but with the method by which knowledge is acquired. The classical method seeks to develop in the student:

1. A body of knowledge essential to educated men and women
2. Sound thinking and reasoning skills
3. The capacity for beauty and clarity of expression

At Veritas, we base our educational approach on the classical teaching model known as the Trivium, which divides the educational life of the child into three stages (grammar, logic, and rhetoric) and takes advantage of the student's natural capacity for certain types of learning at each of these stages. This method develops logical thinking, reasoning, and communication skills that equip students for a lifetime of learning.

By teaching students how to learn, we provide a solid foundation for mastering the specific subjects encountered throughout their formal education. The subject material and curricula at Veritas are carefully chosen to prepare students for a variety of post-secondary educational experiences, but our primary objective is that students gain the skills of learning for themselves. In the end, our teachers strive to instill in students a genuine love and enthusiasm for learning that will remain with them throughout their lives.

By Christ-centered we mean:

Instruction at Veritas acknowledges that all life, knowledge, and meaning extend from our Creator. Our Christ-centered curriculum means we do more than simply provide a religion class among many other classes; rather, by integrating the Scriptures throughout the curriculum, we present the Lord as the One in whom all knowledge is united. This approach requires that all subjects, whether history, art, music, literature, mathematics, or science, be taught in the light of God's existence and His revelation to humanity through His Son, Jesus Christ. We lead students in a pursuit of truth knowing that all truth points to God, and we encourage every student to develop a deep, genuine relationship with God through Jesus Christ.

By Covenantal we mean:

As a covenantal Christian school, Veritas serves children of believing parents. We require that parents be professing Christians and be committed to a Christ-centered "paideia" (full instruction and upbringing of a child). At Veritas, parents can have confidence they are in a partnership with other Christian parents that share similar commitments.

As believers, we are brothers and sisters in Christ, joint-heirs in the gospel and, therefore, have a great privilege and responsibility in our relationship with one another and with the mission of the school. While we are not the local church, we are a community often engaging in prayer, service, fellowship, and Biblical instruction.

Therefore, as a covenant community of parents, staff, faculty, and students, we abide by Biblical principles of Christian conduct. Words and actions which are expressly forbidden in Scripture, including but not limited to blasphemy, profanity, dishonesty, theft, drunkenness, sexual intimacy outside marriage, and homosexual practice, are not acceptable.

We expect all members of the Veritas community to be growing in their faith, pursuing godliness, and repenting of the "sins of the spirit", notably pride, covetousness, jealousy, lust, immodesty, as all are destructive to the unity of the Body of Christ. Furthermore, we will seek to nurture the fruit of the Spirit – love, joy, peace, patience, kindness, goodness, faithfulness, gentleness, and self-control.

Covenant partnership at Veritas means much more than involvement. It means that we share core and agreed upon principles and objectives (see *Principles of Partnership* document), that we commit together to do the hard work of honest, timely, and biblically-guided communication and that we will strive to model for the children entrusted to our care those things that are true, good and beautiful. We are convinced that if we are truly aligned on the major objectives, walking shoulder to shoulder in the same direction, we will not only avoid much of the distraction and division that can characterize school communities, but will give our children a profoundly formative academic, social and spiritual education.

Veritas School maintains a commitment to the principle of "in loco parentis." This simply means we recognize that we operate as an extension of the family, the responsible unit in God's plan for the education of children. Accordingly, we see our teachers as functioning with delegated authority from parents who are accountable to God for the education of their children. As a result, we strongly encourage parental involvement at Veritas, and we enthusiastically invite parents to participate actively in the school. We also expect parents to submit to the policies and decisions of the school.

Board members, administration, faculty, coaches, and staff of Veritas School, whether full time, part-time, or volunteer, and both parents of each student must agree with and abide by the above Mission, Statement of Faith, and Educational Philosophy evidenced by their signing a statement of agreement annually. Limited exceptions are addressed on a case-by-case basis.

Resources

*"Teach us to number our days
that we may gain a heart of wisdom."*

Psalm 90:12

Online Articles

Doerksen, Craig. "Deeper Understanding by Design." *CLASSIS* 25, no. 1 (March 2018): 26-27.

Douglas, Brian. "Five Temptations for Classical Christian Education." *First Things* (November 8, 2012).

Goodwin, David. "Classical Christian Education is more possible than ever." *Circe Institute* (December 13, 2016).

Horner, Dr. Grant. "Firing Curiosity." *The Classical Difference* 4, no. 4 (Winter 2018): 21-22.

McDowell, Josh. "The 7 A's of Parenting." Josh.org website. Accessed August 17, 2018. https://s3.amazonaws.com/jmm.us/JoshTalks/7As/7+A%27s+-+Steps+to+a+Loving+Family+Relationships+Handout.pdf

Perrin, Christopher. "The Kitchen Table." *Inside Classical Education* (February 19, 2013).

———. https://www.thegospelcoalition.org/article/the-exponential-growth-of-classical-christian-education

———. https://scholegroups.com/wp-content/uploads/2016/10/A-Small-Glossary-of-Educational-Vocabulary.pdf

Podcast

McDowell, Josh. Podcast interview by W. Davies Owens. *BaseCamp Live*. March 28, 2017.

Books

Adler, Mortimer J. *The Paideia Program: An Educational Syllabus*. Lexington, Kentucky: Institute for Philosophical Research, 2011 [Orig. 1984].

Andreola, Karen. *A Charlotte Mason Companion: Personal Reflections on the Gentle Art of Learning*. Lake Oswego, Oregon: Charlotte Mason Research Company, 1998.

Augustine. *On Christian Doctrine: De Doctrina Christiana*. Limovia, 2013 [Orig. 397/426AD].

Blanchard, Kenneth. *Leadership & the One-Minute Manager: Increasing Effectiveness Through Situational Leadership II*, New York: William Morrow, 2013 [Orig. 1985].

Bowne, Dale Russell. *Harbison Heritage: The Harbison Chapel Story*. Grove City, Pennsylvania: Grove City College, 1989.

Resources

Bridges, William, with Susan Bridges. *Managing Transitions: Making the Most of Change*. Boston: Da Capo Press, 2016.

Casey, Matthew. *The Return: An End-time Epistle to the Church in America*. Richmond, Virginia: Elijah Books, 2010.

Clark, Kevin, and Ravi Scott Jain. *The Liberal Arts Tradition: A Philosophy of Christian Classical Education*. Camp Hill, Pennsylvania: Classical Academic Press, 2013.

Cloud, Dr. Henry, and Dr. John Townsend. *Boundaries: Revised*. Grand Rapids, Michigan: Zondervan, 2007.

Cromartie, Michael. *What Now? Faithful Living in Challenging Times*. Springfield, Virginia: C.S. Lewis Institute, 2015.

Crouch, Andy. *The Tech-Wise Family: Everyday Steps for Putting Technology in Its Proper Place*. Grand Rapids, Michigan: Baker Books, 2017.

C.S. Lewis Institute. *Aslan Academy Parents Guidebook: Helping Parents Disciple their Children Pre-K through Teen Years*. Charleston, South Carolina: n.p., 2014.

Dever, Mark. *Nine Marks of a Healthy Church*. Wheaton, Illinois: Crossway, 2013.

Dreher, Rod. *The Benedict Option: A Strategy for Christians in a Post-Christian Nation*. New York: Sentinel, 2018.

Edwards, Jonathan. *Religious Affections: A Christian's Character Before God*. abridged and edited by James M. Houston. Vancouver, British Columbia: Regent College Publishing, 1984 [Orig. 1746].

Gamble, Richard M., ed. *The Great Tradition: Classic Readings on What It Means to be an Educated Human Being*. Wilmington, Delaware: Intercollegiate Studies Institute, 2010.

Garber, Steven. *Visions of Vocation: Common Grace for the Common Good*. Downers Grove, Illinois: InterVarsity Press, 2014.

Graff, Gerald. *Professing Literature: An Institutional History*. Chicago: The University of Chicago Press, 1987.

Gregory, John Milton. *The Seven Laws of Teaching: Unabridged Edition*. Moscow, Idaho: Charles Nolan Publishers, 2003 [Orig. 1886].

Holmes, Arthur F. *Building the Christian Academy*. Grand Rapids, Michigan: William B. Eerdmans Publishing Company, 2001.

The Holy Bible.

Jacobs, Alan. *How to Think: A Survival Guide for a World at Odds*. New York: Currency, 2017.

Jenkins, Jerry. *12 Things I Want My Kids to Remember Forever*. New York: Vigliano Books, 2012.

Joseph, Sister Miriam. *The Trivium: The Liberal Arts of Logic, Grammar, and Rhetoric: Understanding the Nature and Function of Language*. Philadelphia: Paul Dry Books, Inc., 2002 [Orig. 1937].

Resources

Keller, W. Phillip. *God is My Delight*. Grand Rapids, Michigan: Kregel Publications, 2010 [Orig. 1991].

———. *A Shepherd Looks at Psalm 23*. Grand Rapids, Michigan: Daybreak Books, 1970.

Keller, Timothy. *The Reason for God: Belief in an Age of Skepticism*. New York: Riverhead Books, 2008.

Lencioni, Patrick. *The Advantage: Why Organizational Health Trumps Everything Else in Business*. San Francisco: Jossey-Bass, 2012.

———. *The Five Dysfunctions of a Team: A Leadership Fable*. San Francisco: Jossey-Bass, 2002.

Lewis, C.S. *Mere Christianity*. New York: Macmillan Publishing Company, 1979 [Orig. 1943].

———. *The Abolition of Man or Reflections on education with special reference to the teaching of English in the upper forms of schools*. San Francisco: HarperCollins, 1974 [Orig. 1943].

Loconte, Joseph. *A Hobbit, a Wardrobe, and a Great War: How J.R.R. Tolkien and C.S. Lewis Rediscovered Faith, Friendship, and Heroism in the Cataclysm of 1914-1918*. Nashville: Nelson Books, 2015.

Machiavelli, Niccolo. *The Prince*. New York: Dover Publications, Inc., 1992 [Orig. 1513].

MacDonald, Gordon. *Ordering Your Private World*. Nashville: Thomas Nelson, 2003.

Nichols, Stephen J. *A Time for Confidence: Trusting God in a Post-Christian Society*. Sanford, Florida: Reformation Trust Publishing, 2016.

Noll, Mark A. *Jesus Christ and the Life of the Mind*. Grand Rapids, Michigan: William B. Eerdmans Publishing Company, 2011.

Oliphint, K. Scott. *Christianity and the Role of Philosophy*. Philadelphia and Phillipsburg, New Jersey: Westminster Seminary Press and P & R Publishing, 2013.

Peterson, Eugene. *Under the Unpredictable Plant: An Exploration in Vocational Holiness*. Grand Rapids, Michigan: William B. Eerdmans Publishing Company, 1992.

Peterson, Michael L. *With All Your Mind: A Christian Philosophy of Education*. Notre Dame, Indiana: University of Notre Dame Press, 2001.

Sande, Corlette. *The Young Peacemaker: Teaching Students to Respond to Conflict God's Way: Intermediate & Middle School Level*. Wapwallopen, Pennsylvania: Shepherd Press, 1997.

Sande, Ken. *The Peacemaker: A Biblical Guide to Resolving Personal Conflict*. Grand Rapids, Michigan: Baker Books, 2006 [Orig. 1991].

Sasse, Ben. *The Vanishing American Adult: Our Coming-of-Age Crisis —and How to Rebuild a Culture of Self-Reliance*. New York: St. Martin's Press, 2017.

Sayers, Dorothy. "The Lost Tools of Learning." Lecture at Oxford University, 1947.

Scazzero, Peter, with Warren Bird. *The Emotionally Healthy Church: A Strategy for Discipleship that Actually Changes Lives (Updated and Expanded)*. Grand Rapids, Michigan: Zondervan, 2010.

Resources

Schaefer, Francis A. *Escape from Reason*, 1968. Downers Grove, Illinois: InterVarsity Press, 2006.

——. *How Should We Then Live? The Rise and Decline of Western Thought and Culture*. Wheaton, Illinois: Crossway Books, 1976.

Shirer, Priscilla. *Breathe: Making Room for Sabbath*. Nashville: LifeWay Press, 2018.

Smith, James K. A. *Desiring the Kingdom: Worship, Worldview, and Cultural Formation*. Ada, Michigan: Baker Academic, 2009.

——. *You Are What You Love: The Spiritual Power of Habit*. Ada, Michigan: Brazos Press, 2016.

Swanson, Kevin. *Passing on the Faith through Literature: 9 Video Series & Curriculum*. Elizabeth, Colorado: Generations, 2018.

Tobias, Cynthia Ulrich. *Every Child Can Succeed: Making the Most of Your Child's Learning Style*. Colorado Springs: Focus on the Family Publishing, 1996.

Tozer, A.W. *Paths to Power: Living in the Spirit's Fullness*. Chicago: The Moody Bible Institute, 1940.

Tripp, Paul David. *Age of Opportunity: A Biblical Guide to Parenting Teens*. Phillipsburg, New Jersey: P & R Publishing, 2001.

——. *Parenting: 14 Gospel Principles that can Radically Change Your Family*. Wheaton, Illinois: Crossway, 2016.

Tripp, Tedd. *Shepherding a Child's Heart*. Wapwallopen, Pennsylvania: Shepherd Press, 1995.

Tulgan, Bruce. *It's Okay to Be the Boss: The Step-by-Step Guide to Becoming the Manager Your Employees Need*. New York: HarperCollins, 2007.

Webster, Noah. *American Dictionary of the English Language*. San Francisco: Foundation for American Christian Education, 2012 [Orig. 1828].

Weil, Simone. "Reflections on the Right Use of School Studies with a View to the Love of God." https://archive.org/stream/Weil1951ReflectionsOnTheRightUseOfSchoolStudiesWithAViewToTheLoveOfGod/Weil - 1951 - Reflections on the Right Use of School Studies With a View To the Love of God_djvu.txt [accessed 12/30/19].

Wickman, Gino, and Mark C. Winters. *Rocket Fuel: The One Essential Combination that will Get You More of What You Want from Your Business*. Dallas: BenBella Books, Inc., 2016.

Wilson, Doug. *The Paideia of God and Other Essays on Education*. Moscow, Idaho: Canon Press, 1999.

——. *Recovering the Lost Tools of Learning: An Approach to Distinctively Christian Education*. Wheaton, Illinois: Crossway, 1991.

Woerner, Dr. Ralph. "Overcoming Hurt." Birmingham: Gospel Publishing Association, 1992.

For Administrators

Keller, W. Phillip. *A Shepherd Looks at Psalm 23*. Grand Rapids, Michigan: Daybreak Books, 1970.

Robbins, Pamela M. *The Principal's Companion: Strategies for Making the Job Easier*. Thousand Oaks, California: Corwin, 2009.

Websites for administrators

http://www.accsedu.org

> Classical U – Essential School Leadership Course with Keith Nix

> First two are free. 1) Overview of Six Essentials of Effective School Leadership, 2) Vision, 3) Strategy, 4) Talent, 5) Culture (Part 1), 6) Culture (Part 2), 7) Working with Your Board (Part 1), 8: Working with Your Board (Part 2), 9) Finances, 10) Keith's Favorite Books on Leadership

http://www.eosworldwide.com

> *Traction* by Gino Wickman; *Get A Grip*, by Gino Wickman and Mike Paton; & a variety of other helpful resources

http://www.isminc.com –Independent School Management (ISM)

> For outstanding help with feedback systems & surveys for boards of directors (Strategic Board Assessment II), administrators (Executive Leadership Survey), faculty culture, student Experience Profile (Grades 5-12).

> Also includes an outstanding list of 20 statements regarding Head of School rating. Helpful for job description.

http://www.rocketfuel.com

For Boards

Association for Christian Schools International. REACH: Rubrics Manual for Accreditation. Colorado Springs: ACSI, 2018.

> REACH (Reaching for Excellence Through Accreditation and Continuous Improvement for Higher Achievement).

Bridges, William, Ph.D., with Susan Bridges. *Managing Transitions: Making the Most of Change*. Boston: Da Capo Press, 2016.

> A good resource to determine your school's level of development.

Websites for boards

http://www.accs.org

> Rich resources for classical Christian schools.

> The Ambrose School's *Articles of Incorporation & Bylaws* (available on the ACCS website to members), Meridian, Idaho. It also includes questions for board of director candidates.

Resources

https://www.acsi.org/resources/cse/cse-magazine/how-does-a-board-enable-effectiveness-102

>   For Christian boards of directors from ACSI.

http://www.ADFMinistryAlliance.org

>   For Alliance Defending Freedom's invaluable "11 Ways to Prepare Your Ministry for Religious Freedom Threats."

http://www.eosworldwide.com

>   *Traction* by Gino Wickman; *Get A Grip*, by Gino Wickman and Mike Paton; and a variety of other helpful resources available at this website

http://www.rocketfuelnow.com

For Faculty

Batchelor, Mary. *The Children's Bible in 365 Stories*. Colorado Springs: David C. Cook, 2010 [Orig. 1985].

Keller, W. Phillip. *A Shepherd Looks at Psalm 23*. Grand Rapids, Michigan: Daybreak Books, 1970.

For Parents

The Holy Bible.

Castleman, Robbie. *Parenting in the Pew: Guiding Your Children into the Joy of Worship*. Downers Grove, Illinois: InterVarsity Press, 2013.

Crouch, Andy. *The Tech-Wise Family: Everyday Steps for Putting Technology in Its Proper Place*. Grand Rapids, Michigan: Baker Books, 2017.

C.S. Lewis Institute. *Aslan Academy Parents Guidebook: Helping Parents Disciple their Children Pre-K through Teen Years*. Charleston, South Carolina: n.p., 2014.

>   Chapters range from a review of fundamentals, understanding and encouraging heart change, developing character and faith that lasts, teaching the Bible to your children, introducing spiritual disciplines to your children, helping children understand and explain their faith, family read-alouds. Suggestions for starting an Aslan Academy gathering.

Keller, W. Phillip. *God is My Delight*. Grand Rapids, Michigan: Kregel Publications, 2010 [Orig. 1991].

——. *A Shepherd Looks at Psalm 23*. Grand Rapids, Michigan: Daybreak Books, 1970.

Knott, Kerry A., Aimee Riegert, and Joel S. Woodruff, Ph.D. *Keeping the Faith: Equipping Families for Effective Discipleship* Program and Guidebook, C.S. Lewis Institute, 2019.

Lockman, Vic. *The Catechism for Young Children with Cartoons*, Books I and II. Grants Pass, Oregon: n.p., 1984.

Piper, Noel and John. "The Family: Together in God's Presence." Desiringgod.org. 2013.

>   Marvelous principles & practice for parents to bring their children to worship during the church service.

Plowman, Ginger. "Wise Words for Moms." Wapwallopen, Pennsylvania: Shepherd Press, 2001.

Pratt, Richard L., Jr., *Designed for Dignity*. Phillipsburg, New Jersey: P & R Publishing, 2000.

Prentice, Pastor Brent. "A Means to an End" blog. bprentice.wordpress.com, July 12, 2012.

Sande, Ken. *The Peacemaker*: *A Biblical Guide to Resolving Personal Conflict*. Grand Rapids, Michigan: Baker Books, 2004.

Sasse, Ben. *The Vanishing American Adult: Our Coming-of-Age Crisis –and How to Rebuild a Culture of Self-Reliance*. New York: St. Martin's Press, 2017.

Tripp, Paul David. *Parenting: 14 Gospel Principles that can Radically Change Your Family*. Wheaton, Illinois: Crossway, 2016.

Newsletter for parents

> *Dawn Treader* monthly e-newsletter from the C.S. Lewis Institute in Washington, DC – provides readings & questions for your family devotion & discussion times.

Websites for parents

http://www.cslewisinstitute.org (C.S. Lewis Institute, discipleship of heart & mind)

http://www.ligonier.org (Ligonier Ministries, the teaching fellowship of R.C. Sproul)

http://newcitycatechism.com (the New City Catechism, a modern-day resource aimed at helping children and adults learn the core doctrines of the Christian faith via 52 questions and answers)

Devotionals

Chambers, Oswald. *My Utmost for His Highest*. edited by James Reimann. Grand Rapids, Michigan: Discovery House Publishers, 1992 [Orig. 1935].

———.*Still Higher for His Highest*. edited by D.W. Lambert. Grand Rapids, Michigan: Zondervan Publishing House, 1971.

Cowman, Mrs. Charles E. *Streams in the Desert*, Grand Rapids, Michigan: Zondervan Publishing House, 1925.

School Websites

Bayshore Christian School, Fairhope, Alabama – https://www.bayshorechristian.org

Covenant Academy, Cypress, Texas – https://www.covenantcypress.org

Geneva School, Winter Park, Florida – https://genevaschool.org

Hope Academy, Minneapolis, Minnesota – http://hopeschool.org

Mars Hill Academy, Mason, Ohio – https://marshill.edu

Veritas School, Richmond, Virginia – http://veritasschool.com

Credits